6/03

BLOOD OF NOBLE MEN

THE ALAMO

SIEGE & BATTLE

BLOOD OF NOBLE MEN

THE ALAMO
SIEGE & BATTLE

An Illustrated Chronology

Written by

Alan C. Huffines

Illustrated by

Gary S. Zaboly

Foreword by

Stephen L. Hardin, Ph.D.

EAKIN PRESS   ★   Austin, Texas

Published in the United States of America
By Eakin Press
An Imprint of Sunbelt Media, Inc.
P.O. Drawer 90159 ★ Austin, TX 78709-0159
email:eakinpub@sig.net
website:www.eakinpress.com

ISBN 1-57168-194-9

Library of Congress Cataloging-in-Publication Data

Huffines, Alan C.
    The blood of noble men : an illustrated chronology of the Alamo siege and battle / by Alan C. Huffines
and illustrated by Gary S. Zaboly ; foreword by Stephen L. Hardin.
        p.   cm.
    Includes bibliographical references (p.   ) and index.
    ISBN 1-57168-194-9
    1. Alamo (San Antonio, Tex.)—Siege, 1836—Chronology. 2. Alamo (San Antonio, Tex.)—Siege, 1836—
Pictorial works. I. Zaboly, Gary S. II. Title.
F390.H924   1999
976.4'03--dc21
                                                                                                                    98-48359
                                                                                                                    CIP

To the glory of God

and

for the ladies in my life—

Caroline, Morgan, and Madison.

"History is a cruel trick played on the dead by the living."

—Mexican proverb

Contents

Illustrations

Foreword

In Texas, the Alamo constitutes a kind of religion. Ponder the rhetoric Texans employ. They celebrate Travis, Bowie, and Crockett as the *trinity* of heroes. They eulogize the *sacrifice* of the defenders and commemorate the *redemption* of San Jacinto. The *martyrs* even offered their lives in an abandoned mission, on *consecrated* ground as it were. Indeed, as if by some empyrean design, the fort fell on a Sunday.

Consider for a moment the tag line for John Wayne's epic film: "The Mission that became a Fortress . . . The Fortress that became a Shrine." This was not merely the catch phrase of some Hollywood press agent. Today, as they have since 1905, the Daughters of the Republic of Texas maintain the Alamo not as a historic site, but as a *shrine*. Words evoke specific meanings, and a shrine is "a container for sacred relics; the tomb of a saint; a site or object revered for its associations." That Texans choose religious vernacular to discuss an episode of bloody slaughter may not be as improper as it seems at first glimpse. For in a culture whose values are largely Protestant, anti-clerical, and wholly practical, the story of the Alamo is our hagiography. Its heroes *are* our saints.

This is not a new trend. Hardly had the smoke cleared over the old mission before Texans began to describe the event in grandiloquent terms. Less than three weeks after the battle, a Texas newspaperman employed lavish diction to pay homage to the fallen defenders:

> Spirits of the mighty, though fallen! Honors and rest are with ye: the spark of immortality which animated your forms, shall brighten into a flame, and Texas, the whole world, shall hail ye like the demi-Gods of old, as founders of new actions and as patterns of imitation!

In 1874 Thomas Parmer penned a letter to his old friend Moses Austin Bryant. By then, both ancient warriors were long past their prime and proud members of the Texas Veteran's Association. Parmer took the occasion to recall old battles and wax hyperbolic. In his view the Alamo was a public trust, and he offered advice on the conduct of future generations:

> Hark young man when you approach that Holy Place. Take the shoes from your feet for it is Holy Ground. Ye lovers of liberty, you tread upon Holy Ground. The life blood of a Travis, a Bowie, a Crockett and Dickson *[sic]* and many others was sown there to yeald *[sic]* up a mighty nation.

His spelling may have been a tad unorthodox, but his sentiments regarding the Alamo and its significance reflected the prevailing opinion.

The Alamo and its defenders quickly transcended mere history; both entered the realm of myth. The parable became the central scene of a Texas morality play, a melodrama in which slain champions served as primordial types. To Texans and all Americans, the Alamo became a powerful symbol of heroic sacrifice, surrounded by an aura of mystery and reverence. Such perceptions survived the romantic nineteenth century and thrive even in our alienated times. In message and tone, screen star John Wayne echoed Thomas Parmer. In 1960 he described his film *The Alamo* as "the story of 185 men joined together in an immortal pact to give their lives that the spark of freedom might blaze into a roaring flame. It is the story of how they died to the last man, putting up an unbelievably gallant fight against an overwhelming army; and of the priceless legacy they left us."

The Duke unintentionally identified the problem with the mythic Alamo. It is indeed *"unbeliev-*

ably gallant." Those of us who grew up with the Walt Disney version—who wore coonskin caps, who sang "Da-vy, Da-vy Crockett," until it drove our parents to distraction—are aggrieved when we hear that our childhood hero may not have gone down swinging ol' Betsy *a la* Fess Parker.

Over the years I have had occasion to speak to numerous groups, both avocational and professional. No matter the character of the assembly, one question is inevitable: "Did Travis really draw the line?" I then have to play the tiresome professor and inform the inquirer, "Probably not." The Alamo defenders made no "pact to give their lives." Historians now know that until almost the last moment they were expecting help to arrive. Toward the end of the siege, William Barret Travis expressed bitterness that the rest of Texas had not rallied to his continual calls for assistance. On March 3, he penned a pointed letter to the Convention at Washington-on-the-Brazos:

> Col. Fannin is said to be on the march to this place with reinforcements, but I fear it is not true, as I have repeatedly sent to him for aid without receiving any. . . . I look to the colonies alone for aid; unless it arrives soon, I shall have to fight the enemy on his own terms. I will, however, do the best I can under the circumstances[.]

Later that same day, Travis revealed even more rancor in a letter to his friend Jesse Grimes: "I am determined to perish in the defense of this place, and my bones shall reproach my country for her neglect." Alamo defenders were not the Jewish *Secarii* of Masada, nor were they Japanese *kamikazes* bent on ritual suicide. Such fanaticism was no part of their cultural tradition. They were soldiers, men who willingly placed themselves in harm's way for kith and kin. They may have been willing to die for their country, but that was never their object. They fervently hoped such a sacrifice would prove unnecessary.

I hope, having written that, folks will not dismiss me as a cynical iconoclast out to discredit all American heroes. It is important that Texans understand the Alamo myth; that we come to terms with what it means to those who concocted it and those who continue to embrace it. As with George Washington and the cherry tree, Travis and the line is a homily that conveys a vital lesson. It is a lasting part of a shared national experience and constitutes a valuable cultural touchstone. It will certainly do no harm to hear it, and it may do them some good.

But, friends, it is *not* history. As important as it is for us to understand the myth, it is even more critical that we know the historical reality of that event. Yet myth has so shrouded every aspect of the Alamo story that it becomes hard to separate the factual from the fanciful. Understand and appreciate the myth. Understand and appreciate the historical reality. But, please, graze them in different pastures. For when the mythic bull jumps the fence to service the heifer of history, the calf produced by their union is, well, befuddled.

Alan Huffines understands that. His approach to the topic is clear-eyed and hard-nosed. He tells a gripping story, one unembellished by myth, fable, or cant. To do that he proceeded as trained historians have always done and returned to the sources. Then he went a step further. He arranged the participants' accounts in a day-by-day chronology. With clear insight into the sources, he then annotated the accounts to answer lingering questions. Readers who normally shun footnotes need to curb that tendency—at least for the duration of this book. With the experience and perception of a scholar and soldier, Mr. Huffines' critical analysis is fascinating and makes a significant contribution to our collective knowledge of those thirteen days.

Still, can unvarnished fact ever be as compelling as conceived myth? You bet it can. If you doubt the validity of that statement, accept my challenge and finish reading this book. Herein readers will find no "demi-Gods," no "Holy Ground." They *will* find a "gallant fight," but, unlike the Hollywood treatments, this one is believable. What emerges from these pages are the words and deeds of flesh-and-blood human beings. For that, they are even more heroic. One comes to comprehend that the soldiers on both sides of the walls were individuals far from home, stuck with an unpleasant job, and fervently wishing they were somewhere else. Even so, when one strips away the layers of myth and mawkish chauvinism, what is left is still grandly heroic. The Alamo remains a shining moment in Texas history; those Texians and what they accomplished do not require fabrication to remind us of their legacy. For ultimately, the heroism endures. No, it does more than endure. It prevails.

STEPHEN L. HARDIN, PH.D.
The Victoria College / March 6, 1998

Acknowledgments

If one sees a turtle atop a fencepost, it is obvious the turtle did not get there by itself. The same is true with this work. Begun as an independent research project to determine siege chronology and mechanics, it grew into a master's thesis and finally evolved into this tome. Many people assisted and provided along the way.

Elohim Adonai receives all glory and credit. He has led me down this road for a reason known only to Him. Edgar Bottome, Ph.D., and George F. Hofman, Ph.D., both of my graduate program at Norwich, were invaluable in their counsel and perspectives. John T. Broom, Ph.D., also served as a graduate advisor, friend, mentor, reader and is one of the finest military historians I know. Lt. Col. (Retired) Martin L. Robbins, U.S. Army, allowed me the time to finish the initial draft and thoroughly supported the project. Sir, you were the finest battalion commander I ever served with.

I convey my appreciation to the ever helpful staff of the DRT Library at the Alamo—most especially the late Bernice Strong, who took pity on me as a child and let me annoy her with endless questions about the subject. I miss you, Bernice.

Dan Lawrence and Steve Abolt both provided valuable information into the period artillery and infantry drill manuals as well as their encouragement and friendship.

Numerous people read my various drafts and attempts at scholarship during the process; each provided guidance and direction. James Crisp, Ph.D., of NCSU, provided a page-by-page editorial of the work that must have taken weeks, something he did not have to do. I am grateful. Film producer Ray Herbeck, Jr., gave well thought out advice as well. Two-time Pulitzer nominee William C. Davis not only gave valued insight but shared some of his Mexican sources, for which I am obliged. Richard B. Winders, Ph.D., not only provided his thoughts but served as a constant sounding board on the project. Writer Steve Harrigan shared his thoughts and interpretations of the participants' intent as well as general counsel on writing style. Artists and historians George Nelson and Craig Covener were absolutely invaluable during the preparation of the many Alamo and Béxar illustrations. Texian Army Investigation's Tom Lindley proved a great source of information, having the finest understanding of Texas Revolution sources I know of. Texas Parks and Wildlife's David McDonald gave great service on translating two heretofore unpublished Mexican military documents. Maj. Russell O. McGee, USMC, has not only provided me with an "Alamo buddy" and best friend since 1978, but also gave constant thoughts and assistance toward the project. My cousin Virginia Thomas, Ph.D., has been a constant cheerleader for me in my pursuit of the past.

Technical matters are not my strong suit, and without the computer literacy of Capt. John Keeter, SFC Perry Davis Jefferies, both of the U.S. Army, and my clerical service, Ms. Gaynelle Deese and her son R. Lewis Deese, this work would never have been finished. Melissa Roberts served as the copy editor, and I am grateful for her input.

Finally, the big three. New York's Gary Zaboly is perhaps the finest military artist since H. Charles McBarron. My guidance to him was that no illustration could be a repeat of past illustrations, i.e., no Crockett last stands, no line drawings, etc., and at least 50% must be from the Hispanic perspective. Gary has added a third dimension to the accounts that will be remembered as long as the vignettes. I have never met him and to my understanding he has only visited the Alamo twice. Gary, "Ya done good." Steve Hardin, Ph.D., of Victoria College, has not only provided friendship but wise counsel and mentorship far past anything I have ever earned from him. Steve, thank you. Kevin R. Young of Forrest View Historical Services for the past eighteen years has been a generous source of accounts, information, and friendship. Kevin sits at the barometric center of the Texas Revolution and is a top scholar on Texas' military past.

Thanks to all for their assistance, encouragement, and wisdom. Regardless of help from the above, any mistakes in interpretation are solely my responsibility.

Introduction

The Alamo battle stirs the soul. It is the epic creation myth of the Texas Republic, and arguably the American West. This siege and battle, fought February 23-March 6, 1836, between the Centralist Republic of Mexico and the Federalist-minded colonists of Texas, is still part of the American character today.

But between the first day of the siege and the final battle, *what happened?* The framework has always been loose and no detailed chronology exists. It seems the events of the siege between the second and twelfth day are ignored—that they have no impact. This work is about the Alamo siege and battle, *all* of it, with an attempt to discover what other extraordinary events took place. Another emphasis is placing the Alamo into the proper context of military history. It was, after all, a battle. This time we will read from the participants primarily. They have never told their story in just this way; this tome gives them their chance.

The focus of this book is the *what*, instead of the *why*. Each day of the thirteen-day siege has its own chapter. If not much happened on that day, well, then it is a short chapter. Editorial commentary examines the siege in the footnotes and in chapter prologues. The reader may now read the participants' remembrances undisturbed by narrative commentary in the main body. This is not an attempt to analyze sources, but rather the military framework.

The accounts are arranged by date and time of day. This was done by matching up cross occurrences or harmonizing, when two or more participants witnessed the same event. The Mexican accounts are far more exacting as to date and time, and the Texians experienced the same events on their side of the wall. Combine this with Travis'

reports, and the mechanics of the siege are determinable.

There are also several different versions here of the same account, and several different versions of a participant's recollections. There are contradictory statements made by the same individual. Probably age, or the journalist weighed in more than the participant, intentionally stretching the truth. It is up to the reader to judge the accuracy of any given account, based on the participant's perspective, position, reliability, consistency, and age.

Artist Gary Zaboly has captured the events detailed in these accounts. More than forty illustrations of incredible detail are included.

The Alamo battle is a symbol of political extremes. Opposing arguments use primary accounts, with varying degrees, to assist their agendas. This book will not do that. There are precious few moments in a battle where right can be distinguished from wrong. A clash occurred between two strong, diverse cultures and ethnic groups. Their primary socio-political issues in common were that each believed the other morally inferior and both believed their system of government to be the best. Both were also extremely violent. The Mexican execution of prisoners both at the Alamo and Goliad, and the Texians essentially doing the same deed to hundreds of Mexicans at San Jacinto, prove that both armies were capable of murder.

Some of the accounts are understandably controversial. The Rose account comes to mind first. William P. Zuber received the account secondhand from his mother after alleged Alamo defender Louis "Moses" Rose came crawling up to their East Texas cabin following his suspect escape from the Alamo. Zuber, for whatever reason, waited until 1871 to share this incredible story with the rest of the world. This account is included, controversy notwithstanding. There are others.

History was a vocation to very few during this period, especially on the frontier. Journalists or archivists recorded several accounts through interviews. The journalists, rather than quoting directly, often used the words "witness then stated . . ." or such phrasing as "Mrs. Dickenson then went . . ." These passages are included as primary accounts even though they may be secondary or tertiary to the purist. If the defender's perspective is recounted, then it must be used.

Gen. Vicente Filisola, second in command of the Mexican Army, did not arrive until the day after the final battle. A good officer and deputy, he documented the events as they were undoubtedly reported to him after his arrival. Too often today there is a rush to censure certain accounts if the same participant in other recollections seemingly contradicts himself. Time, immaturity, age and "good ol' stretching" certainly happened as with all primary sources.

The accounts are not divine and sometimes are confusing, but certainly because of minor inconsistencies they should not be considered wholly suspect. This work will neither confirm nor deny the factuality of any account. Additionally, all spelling that is obviously in error within quoted material has been corrected for ease of reading, and the term "Texian" is used throughout. By the time most of these accounts were recorded, "Texan" was vogue; however, during the revolution "Texian" was the title, so the earlier sobriquet is used herein. Brief biographical sketches are included for those participants who recorded accounts. The sketches are provided to serve the reader with a humble background on individuals and to define somewhat their role in the circumstances.

Nationalities tend to be confusing during a revolution. In the United States today we have African-Americans, Chinese-Americans, Anglo-Americans, and Mexican-Americans. Texas was then a province of the Mexican state of Coahuila and was populated primarily with Plains Indians and Southern Anglo-Celtic colonists from the U.S. These people were Mexicans, or in late twentieth-century terms "American-Mexicans." Travis and Bowie were as Mexican under the law as any member of Santa Anna's army. For ease of reading, in this book's commentary the term Texian will incorporate defenders of the Alamo, and Mexican Army will be used for the Centralist forces under Santa Anna.

My goal is to relate the events of the siege and battle, blow by blow. I have merely taken participants' words and arranged them by date, time, and cross-occurrence, perhaps coming as close to the memory of that moment as words on a page can. I hope that they are now vignettes instead of accounts. The twist is to allow the people who experienced the sights, smells, sounds, and emotions of that two-week period to speak finally for themselves. If the sad stones of the Alamo could have kept a journal, maybe this is how it would read.

ALAN C. HUFFINES
New Braunfels, Texas
June 29, 1998

Artist's Introduction

It is a curious fact that the Texas Revolution produced virtually no on-the-spot artwork. A number of maps and plans of forts were made by both Texian and Mexican participants, and an inexact sketch of the exterior of the Alamo, as seen from San Antonio, was drawn by an officer in Santa Anna's army; but that nearly covers everything. Aside from a pencil portrait of William Barret Travis, purportedly made by Wiley Martin in December 1835, there is no truly contemporary imagery of the people and events in Texas—at least none that has thus far come to light.

In the decades that followed, artists such as Theodore Gentilz, Henry McArdle, and Robert Onderdonk, while planning grand-style Alamo battle paintings, extracted brief memoirs from veterans of Houston's army; and from these accounts a trickle of fresh information on Texian and Mexican uniforms was obtained and interpreted visually.

Still, the earlier deficiency of pictorial evidence continued to hobble artists who followed. Only in recent decades have there been greatly accelerated researches into determining the look of the time, place, and people involved, culled from documents and published matter scattered from Mexican archives to Manhattan libraries. Then, too, there are the museum artifacts, family souvenirs, and newly found relics to fill in many gaps. There can be little doubt that the current scholarship will greatly benefit historical artists of the twenty-first century, though the complete picture might never be painted.

Historical art is a risky business. The artist realizes that his rendering of events is clearly limited by a number of factors: by the orbit of his own experiences; by the extent of actual research he has made or has been provided with by others; by his level of skill with pen and brush; and, not unimportantly, by an inherent personal vision that springs from sources unknown.

In illustrating an episode of the Texas Revolution, the artist must become reasonably versed in a host of related areas: in the prevailing fashions of the day; in the culture of the frontier; in the military disciplines of the opposing forces; in the uniforms they wore (if any existed); in the weapons, accoutrements, equipment, provisions, and the manner of utilizing them; in the modes of transportation; in the geography, fauna, and flora; in early Spanish and Tejano architecture, both clerical and secular; in all legends, mythology, and oral traditions rising out of the time and place; and in the swirl of strong opinions and controversies that continue to reshape or muddle the history.

After all this, the artist can only hope to produce a credible reconstruction. Because Alan Huffines has made a conscious effort to present and explain these eyewitness accounts as objectively as possible, in like manner have I approached the illustrating of them, and the descriptive captioning of each. No attempt has been made to coat these depictions with a veneer of idealism or romantic symbolism. All participants receive their share of heroic honors or of shame. None are beatified.

No Alamo historian or historical artist can function in a vacuum. Any possible merits in my artwork would not have been achieved without my acquaintanceship with a number of people, most of them Texans. In order of my acquaintance with them, the first is Kevin R. Young, of San Antonio, founder of the Alamo Battlefield Association and editor-in-chief of the ABA *Journal*, as well as consultant to many a motion picture and television production. Kevin has no peer as a fountain of knowledge where all things Alamo are concerned: he is forever current with developments and research in the field, and the people working within it. He has been a boon in my own several attempts to get at the documented truths and for that I will be forever in his debt. He is also extremely versed in the oft-neglected subject of the Mexican Army, its history, various reorganizations, uniforms, and weapons.

Stephen L. Hardin, Ph.D., a prominent historian with a fine sense of prose, now residing in Victoria, possesses an innate understanding of Texas' pre-statehood condition, of its military development, of the life of the settlers, and of the singular civilization they founded west of the Sabine and north of the Río Grande. I had the pleasure of illustrating his award-winning book, *Texian Iliad: A Military History of the Texas Revolution,* and the process of doing so, thanks to Steve, was a great education for me.

Thomas Ricks Lindley of Austin is a ferocious digger into the documented past, and he has managed to uncover many a heretofore unknown gem. His opinions are always valued because they force one to think about immediately accepting oft-quoted pieces of "evidence."

Craig R. Covner of Encinitas, California, has the most meticulous mind of all in regards to the Alamo's construction as a mission; and George Nel-son of Uvalde, Texas, is unsurpassed in his knowledge of early San Antonio's physical development. Both men were gold mines of information.

William R. Chemerka of East Hanover, New Jersey, deserves long overdue credit as publisher and editor of *The Alamo Journal,* a depository of Alamo lore, significant and otherwise, and of the latest news in the field.

Also of paramount importance are the contributions made by archaeologists such as Greg Dimmick, M.D., Bobby McKinney, and Don Jank, discoverers of immense quantities of military relics, many of which, like so much else about the Alamo story, both perplex and inform.

Last but not least is Alan C. Huffines of New Braunfels, who gave me this illustration assignment. Alan is a professional military officer and a veteran of the Persian Gulf War. Combined with his thorough knowledge of early Texas, he possesses a pragmatic attitude toward military history; his ideas and concerns were of immense value in completing the drawings.

To one and all I say, again, thank you.

GARY S. ZABOLY
Riverdale, New York
June 29, 1998

THE PARTICIPANTS

The Texians

Antonio Cruz y Arocha
Tejano, Béxareño, and friend to Juan Seguín. He helped Seguín with his courier mission.

James Bowie
1795–March 6, 1836
In 1828 Bowie arrived in Texas, and by 1831 he had married into lower Mexican gentry, Ursula Vera- mendi, daughter of the vice-governor of Coahuila- Texas. His fortune was made in land, horses, and slaves. He was as notorious as famous in the old southwest, both for his shady business dealings as well as his skill with the knife his brother Rezin in- vented. In 1833 his wife, in-laws, and possibly two sons died in a cholera epidemic. He held the rank of colonel from a colonial appointment in a ranging company, and was co-commander of the Alamo gar- rison; however, on the second day of the siege he succumbed to an illness that has been described as typhoid, tuberculosis, or "peculiar." He never re- covered and was bedridden for the remainder of the siege.

Trinidad Coy
Ordered by Travis to conduct reconnaissance be- fore the arrival of the Mexican Army, he was cap- tured and spent the remainder of the siege under arrest. He escaped during the final Mexican assault.

Philip Dimitt
1801-August 8, 1841
He arrived as a colonist to Texas in 1822 and was a merchant and former commander of the Texian gar- rison at La Bahia. He designed the legendary "1824" tri-color flag of the revolution and was a signer of the premature Texas Declaration of Independence.

Upon arrival of Mexican forces, Travis sent him to "scout" the enemy. Dimitt did not scout or return to the mission, promising instead to bring rein- forcements that never came.

Brigido Guerrero
Possible *soldado* deserter from Siege of Béxar. Es- caped death at the Alamo by claiming to be a pris- oner of the Texians.

Albert Martin
January 6, 1808–March 6, 1836
Originally from Rhode Island, then Gonzales. As a captain he carried Travis' letter of the 24th and re- turned to the garrison with the "Gonzales 32."

Isaac Milsaps
1795–March 6, 1836
Arrived at Alamo with the "Gonzales 32." He was the father of seven children; his wife was blind.

Louis "Moses" Rose
May 11, 1785–1850
Born in Laferee, Ardennes, he allegedly served as a noncommissioned officer in the French 101 Infan- try Regiment during the Napoleonic wars, and was awarded the Legion of Merit. If his past was correct, he was easily the most experienced soldier in the Alamo. When offered the opportunity of flight, Rose accepted, being the only participant known to do so. He would finish his life in Louisiana.

Juan Nepomuceno Seguín
October 27, 1806–1890
Son of Don Erasmo Seguín, one of the most influ- ential Texas-born Mexicans, or *Tejanos,* in Texas.

He was a native of San Antonio de Béxar—a *Béxareño*. His father was instrumental in assisting Texas *empresario* Stephen Austin with his colony. He commanded a company of rebel *Tejano* cavalry at the Alamo and at San Jacinto. A Texian council of war sent him as a courier during the siege because of his local terrain and ethnic advantage. He organized a second command to reinforce the Alamo, but was too late.

John Sutherland
May 11, 1792–April 11, 1867

A colonist and a doctor. He had been living in Texas since 1830. He treated Bowie's illness in the days before the siege. He and John Smith discovered the Mexican advance guard on the first day of the siege. Ordered by Travis to become a courier, he did not return to the Alamo after the first day.

William Barret Travis
August 8, 1809–March 6, 1836

A lawyer and a schoolteacher. He married one of his former students, Rosanna Cato, in 1828. In April 1831 he arrived in Texas, leaving his son and pregnant wife in Alabama. He eventually gained custody of the son, but never seemed to want the daughter. He became active in the Texian War Party. He was commissioned into the Regular Texas Army as a cavalry officer on Christmas Eve 1835, and co-commanded the garrison with James Bowie. He read Sir Walter Scott, Byron, and Napoleon.

Candelario Villanueva
A trooper in Juan Seguín's company, but trapped behind Mexican lines on the first day of the siege.

Robert Williamson
1806(?)–1859

A Georgian and friend to Travis. During the revolution he was in either cavalry or ranging units. Fought at San Jacinto and wrote the only known correspondence to enter the Alamo from the colonies.

The Mexicans

Juan Nepomuceno Almonte
An illegitimate son of José María Morelos, a leader of the revolution against Spain. He was educated in the U.S. and was Santa Anna's chief of staff. In 1834 he spied on the Texian colonists. He believed the Anglo colonists of Texas to be selfish and rebellious.

Don José Batres
A colonel and aide-de-camp to Santa Anna. He carried Santa Anna's demand of unconditional surrender to the Texians, on the opening day of the siege.

Francisco Becerra
September 7, 1810–?

A first sergeant in the Active Battalion of San Luis Potosi. He marched with the advance guard of the Army of the North and was one of the first *soldados* into San Antonio. In the final assault, his column, under General Castrillon, took devastating casualties.

Ben
Almonte's cook and servant. He learned his trade as a steward on riverboats. He waited on Santa Anna and always feared for his life. The night of the final battle he kept the coffee hot for him, or else "be run through." After the Alamo fell he escorted Susannah Dickenson to Houston.

Ramón Martínez Caro
Secretary to Santa Anna.

Francisco Esparza
Brother of Gregorio and uncle of Enrique. A presidial *soldado* who did not take an active part in the siege. He buried his brother in the Campo Santo after the battle.

Don Vicente Filisola
March 17, 1789–July 23, 1850

An Italian, educated in Spain, and bloodied in the Mexican Army during the Mexican Revolution against Spain. He was second in command of the Army of the North. Although not present during the siege and battle, his reports were the most detailed of all the Mexican officers.

Manuel Loranca
A second sergeant in the Dolores Cavalry Regiment.

José Juan Sánchez Navarro
?–June 2, 1849
A lieutenant colonel on General Cós' staff. He was a patriot, and was bitter about the Mexican defeat by the Texians the previous December. In his spare time he composed poetry.

Félix Nuñez
1804–?
A sergeant in either the Permanent Battalion of Aldama or the Active Battalion of Toluca. His brigade arrived on March 3, three days before the final battle.

Juan Ortega
?–June 1862
A sergeant in the Dolores Cavalry Regiment. He accepted the surrender of several defenders early in the siege.

José Enrique de la Peña
1807–1842
A lieutenant in the Zapadores Battalion. He published several articles and had literary skill. De la Peña kept a journal during the entire campaign. In 1838 he supported an armed opposition to the Mexican government and died in prison.

Don Rafael Saldana
A cavalry company commander on detached duty from the Tampico Regiment.

San Luis Potosi
A journal kept during the siege by an officer of the Active Battalion of San Luis Potosi.

Antonio López de Santa Anna Perez de Lebron
February 21, 1794–June 21, 1876
Commander of the Army of the North, and president of Mexico. He would avenge his shame for the Mexican defeat by the Texians in Bèxar the previous December. Santa Anna believed the best way to deal with insurrection was to destroy it. His countrymen dubbed him *Don Demonio,* or Sir Devil.

Joaquín Ramírez y Sesma
Commander of the Vanguard Brigade, 1st Division, Army of the North. During the final battle he commanded the cavalry.

Fernando Urissa
An aide-de-camp to Santa Anna.

Noncombatants

Juana Navarro de Alsbury
?—July 25, 1898
In January of 1836 she married a soldier in the Texian Army, Dr. Horace Alsbury. Her husband was away from the garrison when the Mexican forces arrived and she sought shelter in the Alamo with her sister and infant son. She was a cousin of Jim Bowie, who may have assisted her arrival and shelter in the fort. Years later some survivors accused her of spying for the Mexicans; she never publicly responded. Her son Alizo, an infant during the battle, would be the last Alamo defender survivor.

Doña María Jesus Peña Arocha
Wife of Antonio Cruz y Arocha.

María de Jesus Delgado Buquor
June 10, 1826—?
A child, she lived in San Antonio and witnessed the events of the Alamo siege and battle from La Villita. She claimed to have warned the Texians of the arrival of Santa Anna.

Juan Antonio Chávez
A young *Bexareño* during the battle.

Juan Díaz
A child during the battle. He watched the battle from a rooftop.

Pablo Díaz
1816—?
A teenage carpenter and recent immigrant from Monclova, Mexico. He refused service with Segúin and the "Constitutionalists," believing right or wrong Mexico was home and he would not fight against his nation. He regretted this decision the rest of his life. He watched the events of the Alamo siege from a rooftop in the Mission Concepción.

Susannah Arabella Dickenson
1814/15–October 7, 1883
Wife of Alamo defender Capt. Almeron Dickenson, an artillery officer. They had a daughter, Angelina Elizabeth (fifteen months), who was in the Alamo as well. Before the revolution Susannah's husband was a blacksmith in Gonzales. She would spend most of the siege in the Alamo church sacristy. Texas called her the "Messenger from the Alamo" for carrying the news of the defeat to Sam Houston. She and her daughter were the sole known Anglo survivors of the battle.

Enrique Esparza
September 1828–December 20, 1917
Only a boy during the siege, he was the son of *Tejano* Alamo defender Gregorio Esparza. His mother, brother, and sister were in the mission as well. His uncle, Francisco, was a presidial in the Bexar Company and fought against the Texians in the Battle of Bexar the previous December. Enrique spent the majority of the siege with his mother in the church, in the same building his father died defending. His mother became the matriarch of the fourteen or so non-combatant women and children in the sacristy. *Soldados* killed the Anglo children that shared the room.

Joe
1813/15 —?
The slave of Travis purchased two years earlier. He stood by Travis during the battle, until his master's death. Joe took cover in a room and continued to fight until the end of the battle. The *soldados* captured him and then released him to carry the news of the Texian defeat. After the war he escaped his new owner and possibly carried the news of Travis' death to his family in Alabama. He was last seen in Austin in 1875. He may be buried in an unmarked grave in Brewton, Alabama.

José Francisco Ruiz
Alcalde (mayor) of San Antonio de Bèxar. His father, Don Francisco Ruiz, signed the Texas Declaration of Independence. He was a *Tejano*-Federalist, yet did not fight in the Alamo. He was Bowie's uncle by marriage. After the battle, the *soldados* forced him to gather wood for the Texian funeral pyres.

S. Rodríguez
A young *Bexareño* during the battle.

Juan Vargas
January 1, 1796—?
A veteran of the Hidalgo Revolution against Spain, he was in his forties during this most recent battle in the San Antonio area. The Mexican Army impressed him and forced him to do menial tasks about the *soldados* camp because of his refusal to fight against the Alamo defenders.

**Andrea Castanón de Villaneuva
   (Madama Candelaria)**
December 1, 1785–February 10, 1899
The most controversial survivor. She attended Bowie during his illness. She was possibly a *curandera*, a folk healer. Susannah Dickenson disputed her claim of having been in the garrison. None of the other Alamo survivors challenged her, however. The State of Texas eventually granted her a pension.

Eulalia Yorba
A young girl who witnessed the battle from Béxar.

DAY ONE

Tuesday
February 23, 1836

Prologue

IT WAS A LATE morning following the *fandango* on February 22 in honor of Señor Jorge Washington's birthday. Most of the Texians lived in Béxar proper as opposed to the Alamo. The Texians awoke that morning to the sound of cart wheels squeaking and oxen lowing as the majority of San Antonio's citizens left as quickly as possible. The rumor had spread the previous evening that the army of Santa Anna was bivouacked on the León River, only eight miles away, and would attack the town at any time.

Travis started detaining citizens, demanding their destination and reason for departure. Their destination was simple—out of Béxar—and the reason was just as simple. No doubt the citizens remembered the last insurrection in San Antonio in 1813. The Spanish Army executed *Béxareños* alongside the revolutionaries, and those who slipped by the executioner often had their property confiscated.

Travis posted a lookout in the tower of the San Fernando Church on Main Plaza. Just after noon the bell rang, and the sentry alarmed, "The enemy are in view." Travis sent John Sutherland and John Smith to reconnoiter. A short distance out of town, they came upon the Dolores Cavalry Regiment preparing to attack the town. Upon the return of the couriers, Travis ordered a full retreat into the Alamo.

During the withdrawal several head of cattle and bushels of corn were purchased from the residents of La Villita on the Alamo side of the San Antonio River. As the gates closed behind the Texians, the lead elements of the Mexican Army's Vanguard Brigade entered the west side of San Antonio. Some of the brigade units pushed down the river to clear the Mission Concepción in case more Texians were located there.

The Mexicans raised a blood-red banner over the San Fernando Church, as an indicator that no quarter—no mercy—would be offered. Immediately Texians, possibly ordered by Travis, fired a cannon toward the city as a response to the Mexicans' banner. Jim Bowie, perhaps more sensitive to the Mexican character, dispatched a messenger asking for a parley and apologizing for the cannon shot. Travis, upon learning this, sent his messenger to the Mexicans. Both couriers received the same answer: surrender at discretion or be put to the sword. The cannon fired again in final response to the Mexicans' demand.

In analysis of the above events, luck was definitely with the Texians on the first day. This was no sneak attack by the Centralists. The terrain and climate were harsh but hardly insurmountable. The Texians knew almost from the moment Santa Anna crossed the Río Grande and did little to prepare.

After the message from Blas Herrera, a rebel *Tejano* scout, on February 11, little active reconnaissance occurred until Sutherland and Smith's patrol on the 23d. The eighteen to twenty-one cannon of the Alamo more than likely had not been ranged and target reference points noted, and the Centralists found a large cache of weapons in Bèxar that was left behind in the rush. The suburbs or *barrios* of La Villita extended all the way up to the south wall of the Alamo, and the Federalists had not

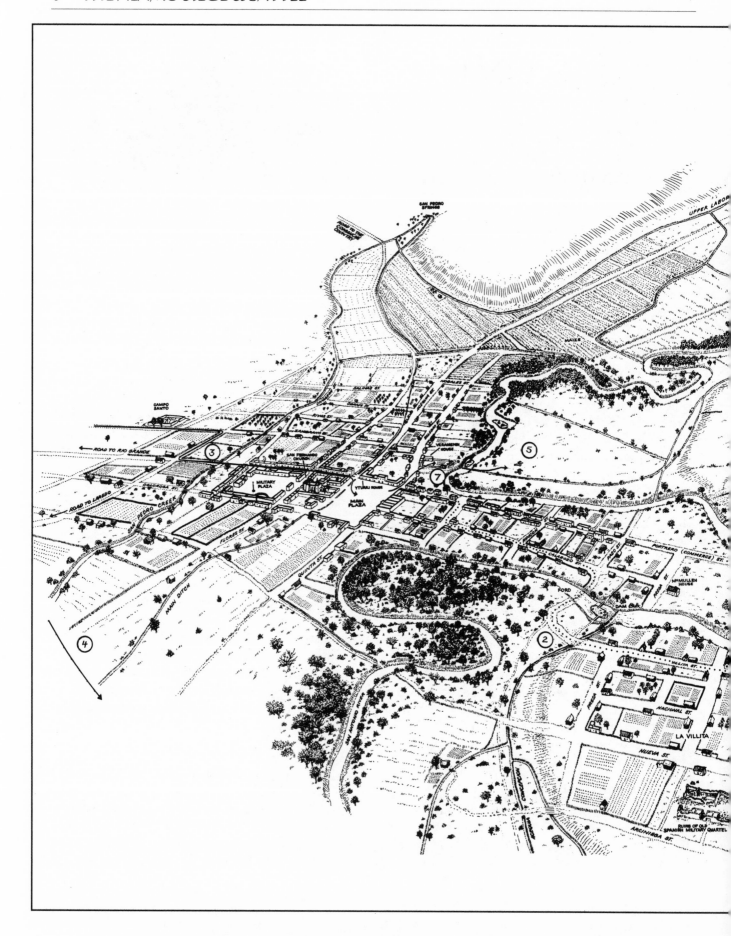

1. Texians abandon San Antonio, retreat into the Alamo, carrying along twenty or thirty cattle and a large quantity of corn.
2. Route of the Dickensons.
3. Santa Anna arrives with vanguard.
4. Second half of Mexican division marches to Mission Concepción under General Mora.
5. Two howitzers—first Mexican guns to bombard Alamo (position recalled by Juan Díaz).
6. Site of parleys.
7. Small battery erected during night of the 23d.
8. General Mora leads cavalry to positions north and east of the Alamo.

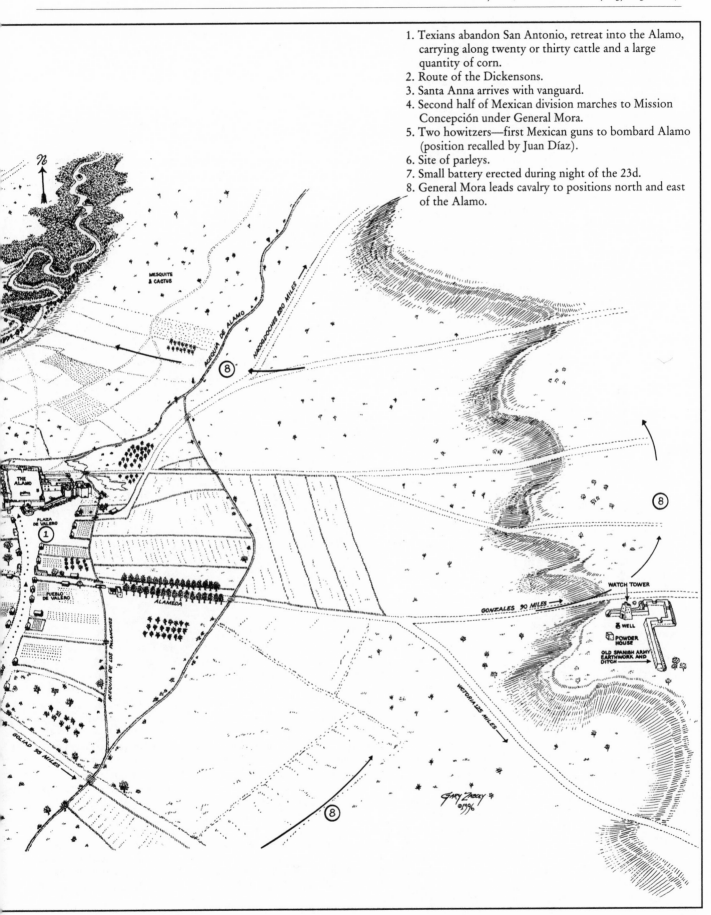

cleared the fields of fire. There was no food available, but fortunately there were beeves belonging to the Esparzas and other locals that the Texians were able to acquire. The *jacales* were scavenged for corn, a staple in the local diet.

The Texians disregarded what intelligence they received and had little respect for *soldado* (Mexican soldier) ability.

S. Rodríguez

One morning early a man named Rivas called at our house and told us that he had seen Santa Anna in disguise the night before looking in on a *fandango* on Soledad Street. My father being away with Houston's army, my mother undertook to act for us and decided it was best for us to go into the country to avoid being here when General Santa Anna's army should come in. We left in oxcarts, the wheels of which were made of solid wood. We buried our money in the house. . . . (Matovina: 114-115)

Almonte

. . . General [Ramírez y] Sesma arrived at [the Alazón Creek, by] 7:00 A.M., and did not advance to reconnoiter [San Antonio] because he expected an advance of the enemy which was about to be made

according to accounts given by a spy of the enemy who was caught. There was water, though little, in the stream of *las lomas del Alazón*. (*SHQ* 48:16-17)

San Luis Potosi

Location, Béxar. General Ramírez [y Sesma] having advanced with sixteen cavalrymen came into view of [San Antonio] at seven in the morning, at which hour none of the enemy knew of our arrival. . . . (McDonald and Young: 1)

de la Peña

On the 23rd General Ramírez y Sesma advanced at dawn toward Béxar with one hundred horsemen; although he had approached them [Texians] at three o'clock in the morning the enemy was unaware of our arrival.[1] (Perry:38)

Almonte

Tuesday at 7:30 A.M. the [main] army was put in march [from the Medina]—To the Potranca [Creek] 1½ leagues, to the creek of León or Del Wedio, 3½ leagues—To Béxar 3 leagues, in all 8 leagues.[2] (*SHQ* 48:16-17)

---

1. The day before, on the 22d, Santa Anna ordered the cavalry horses replaced by the fresher horses of the staff and infantry officers. They were to ride in during the night and surprise the Texians still in their beds. Heavy rains the night of 21/22 made road movement slow. The main force spent the day of the 22d on the west bank of the Medina River drying out and preparing for the final movement into San Antonio. To have arrived by this time Sesma must have left the Medina at around midnight. Sesma was apparently concerned over a Texian attack and chose to wait in the Alazón Creek area until the main body arrived. This area was a good place to wait; the Apache/Alazón Creek is in a valley, and from the ridge line above, the entire San Antonio River valley could be viewed.

2. The army traveled on the Upper Presidial Road, a part of the El Camino Real road network that went from the Presidio de Río Grande into Louisiana. The Medina Crossing used was four or five miles west of the Sauz Creek and Medina confluence, downstream from present-day La Coste. Almonte seems to have missed a few crossings on the march. They forded, in order, at the Medina River, Sauz or Sous, Lucas, Potranco, Medio, Leon, and Apache (the Alazón was a branch) creeks before they arrived at the Campo Santo in San Antonio. A league in the English system is approximately three miles. The exact distance in miles from the Medina crossing to the Campo Santo in San Antonio is 21.9 miles. To have left the Medina at 7:30 A.M. and arrived at the Apache/Alazón by 12:30 (all times Almonte's) was a pretty good pace. Marching 20.5 miles in five hours averages out to more than four miles per hour. The present-day United States Army, with forty to sixty pounds of equipment, foot marches at four miles an hour. It is possible the *soldados'* packs and other equipment were carried in the supply trains (carts, wagons, etc.) that followed each unit. This is more than likely due to their proximity to their destination. For more on the El Camino Real and the Upper Presidial Road see: A. Joachim McGraw, John W. Clark, Jr., and Elizabeth A. Robbins, editors, *A Texas Legacy: The Old San Antonio Road and the Caminos Reales—A Tricentennial History, 1691-1991.*

Sutherland

On the morning of the twenty-third the inhabitants [of San Antonio de Béxar] were observed to be in quite an unusual stir. The citizens of every class were hurrying to and fro through the streets with obvious signs of excitement. Houses were being emptied, and their contents put into carts and hauled off.

Much of the poorer class, who had no better mode of conveyance, were shouldering their effects and leaving on foot.

These movements solicited investigation. Orders were issued [by Travis] that no others be allowed to leave the city, which had the effect of increasing their commotion. Several [citizens] were arrested and interrogated as to the cause of the movement, but no satisfactory answer could be obtained. The most general reply was that they were going out to the country to prepare for the coming crop. This excuse, however, availed nothing, for it was not to be supposed that every person in the city was a farmer. Colonel Travis persisted in carrying out his order and continued the investigation. Nine o'clock came and no discoveries were made. Ten o'clock in like manner passed and finally the eleventh hour was drawing near and the matter was yet a mystery. It was hoped by Colonel Travis that his diligent investigation and strict enforcement of the order prohibiting the inhabitants from leaving the city would have the effect of frightening them into a belief that their course was not the wisest for them to pursue; that he, provoked by their obstinacy in refusing to reveal the true cause of the uneasiness, would resort to measures which might be more distasteful than any which would probably

follow an open confession. But in that he was disappointed. The treacherous wretches persisted in their course, greatly to his discomfiture all the while.[3] (Sutherland: 15-17)

Ruiz

. . . at eight o'clock in the morning, [the Texians] learned that the Mexican army was on the banks of the Medina River, they [the Texians] concentrated in the fortress of the Alamo. (*Texas Almanac*, 1860:56)

Loranca

About nine in the morning, President Santa Anna arrived and joined with his staff the column [under Ramírez y Sesma] which was now in the vicinity of San Antonio.[4] (*San Antonio Express*, June 23, 1878)

Santa Anna

Béxar was held by the enemy and it was necessary to open the door to our future operations by taking it. It would have been easy enough to have surprised it, because those occupying it did not have the faintest news of the march of our army.[5] I entrusted, therefore, the operation to one of our generals, who with a detachment of cavalry, part of the dragoons mounted on infantry officers' horses, should have fallen on Béxar in the early morning of

---

3. According to *Tejano* rebel Antonio Menchaca and John Sutherland, Blas Herrera, a courier from Placido Benavides, arrived on the 11th of February during a *fandango* at about 1:00 A.M. Benavides commanded about thirty rebel *Tejano* cavalry and appears to have been conducting some kind of reconnaissance operation near the Río Grande. Who he was working for or what his exact mission was remains unclear. The message stated: "*At this moment I have received a very certain notice, that the commander-in-chief, Antonio López de Santa Anna, marches for the city of San Antonio to take possession therefore, with 13,000 men.*" Bowie read the letter and called Travis over to consult. Travis answered that he "*could not stay to read letters, for he was dancing with the most beautiful lady in San Antonio.*" (Menchaca: 22-23) Travis was quite a rounder, but this behavior was hardly appropriate considering the gravity of the situation. For more on this event and the events in Béxar prior to the siege see: The Yanaguana Society publication, *Antonio Menchaca's Memories of the Alamo and its Defenders.*

4. The general, with staff and probably an escort company of lancers, must have left the Medina ahead of the main body.

5. A primary reason for the conquest of San Antonio may have been to save face. Santa Anna's brother-in-law, General of Brigade Cós, surrendered the town along with his forces to the Texians the previous December. Not only was this a blight on his family and office, but on Mexico as well. San Antonio was also symbolic. Arredondo defeated the Anglo populated Army of the Republic there in 1813. For more information on the Battle and Siege of Béxar, look at Alwyn Barr's *Texans in Revolt: The Battle for San Antonio, 1835.* For more information on the Battle of the Medina see Ted Schwarz, *Forgotten Battlefield of the First Texas Revolution: The Battle of the Medina, August 18, 1813.*

FIG. 1   MEXICAN VANGUARD AT THE MEDINA

FIG. 1   MEXICAN VANGUARD AT THE MEDINA

A little after 5:00 P.M. on February 21, 1836, Brig. Gen. Joaquin Ramírez y Sesma decides that the Medina River is too swollen with rain to ford with his detachment of sixty to one hundred dragoons of the Permanent Regiment of Dolores Cavalry. They have been ordered by General Santa Anna to surprise the unprepared Texian garrison at San Antonio. Many of the dragoons, their own mounts poor, are riding horses borrowed from Mexican infantry officers.[1] They are equipped against inclement weather with helmet covers and buff-colored, caped overcoats with green standing collars.[2] Most have the pennants of their lances protected with waterproof covers in the manner of Napoleonic cavalry. The subaltern at lower left has removed the plumes from his bicorne.

Sesma wears a dark blue cloak with cord.[3] A green sash envelops his waist, and his bicorne sports a white feathered crest and a tricolor cockade with three loose plumes in the national colors: red, white, and green.

The sergeant to the right of Sesma holds a lantern on a halberd-tipped lance. Such lances are known to have been carried in Mexico as early as 1811[4] and at least into the mid-century.[5]

In upper middleground is one of the presidial troopers accompanying Santa Anna's advance units. These were frontier garrison soldiers, some of them Texas-based and many of them experienced Indian fighters. They were of particular use to the main army by acting as scouts and foragers. This one does not wear the low-crowned *poblano* seen in Linati prints of presidials of the mid-1820s, but a black top hat derived from a painting by Lino Sanchez y Tapia made in Texas in 1828.[6] His jacket also differs from the earlier depictions by sporting three rows of white metal buttons on the chest rather than one. A *serape* covers most of his uniform. His horse's headstall and bit are also based on the Tapia painting.—GZ

February 23, 1836. My orders were concise and definite. I was most surprised, therefore, to find the said general [Ramírez y Sesma] a quarter of a league from Béxar at ten o'clock of that day, awaiting new orders. This, perhaps, was the result of inevitable circumstances; and, although the city was captured, the surprise that I had ordered to be carried out would have saved the time consumed and the blood shed later in the taking of the Alamo. (Castañeda: 12-13)

Sutherland

Finally he [Travis] was informed secretly by a friendly Mexican, that the enemy's cavalry had reached the León [Creek], eight miles from the city, on the previous night, and had sent a messenger to the inhabitants, informing them of that fact, and warning them to evacuate the city at early dawn, as it would be attacked the next day. He [the friendly Mexican] stated further that a messenger had arrived a day or two before and that it had been the purpose of the enemy to take the Texians by surprise, but in consequence of a heavy rain having fallen on the road, their march was impeded, and they were unable to reach the place in time. This statement seemed to substantiate the statement in the report given by [Blas] Herrera three days before, yet it wore the countenance of so many of their false rumors that it was a matter of doubt that there was any truth in it.

Colonel Travis came to me forthwith, however, and informed me of what he had learned, and wished to borrow a horse of me to send out to the Salado [Creek][6] for his *caballo*[7] that he might start a scout through the country. As I had two [horses], of course he obtained one, when a runner was started forthwith [for the horses?]. In company with Colonel Travis and at his request, I proceeded to post a reliable man on the roof of the old church as a sentinel. We all three went up but were unable to make any discoveries. The colonel and myself returned. The sentinel remained at his post with orders to ring the bell if he should discover any sign

---

6. The Salado Creek, a branch of the San Antonio River, was a few miles east of San Antonio. The implication here is that the Texians kept their horses grazing somewhere along the creek, most likely on Rancho de las Hermanas or Rodriguez. Whether this was just Travis, the cavalry, or all the Texians is unknown. For more on *rancho* locations see Jack Jackson's *Los Tejanos*.

7. *Caballo* is the Spanish term for "horse."

[of the Mexican Army] which he might deem ominous.[8] (Sutherland: 17-18)

Seguín

Colonel Travis had no idea that Santa Anna with his army would venture to approach the city of Béxar and for this reason, only a watch was kept on the church tower that existed where today stands the [San Fernando] cathedral of San Antonio; This watchman was an American whose name I do not now remember. (de la Teja: 194)

Almonte

At half a league, from Béxar the [1st] division [vanguard brigade of 1st division] halted on the hills [east] of [the] Alazón at 12:30. (*SHQ* 48:17)

San Luis Potosi

. . . the rest of the [1st] division arrived between twelve and one o'clock. (McDonald and Young: 1)

Sutherland

Colonel Travis went to his room, and I to the store at Capt. Nat Lewis,[9] who requested me to as-

sist in taking an inventory of his goods, saying that he had some suspicion that they would soon be taken from him. We proceeded to the task but had not been long engaged when the sentinel rang the bell and cried out, "the enemy are in view."

Immediately I went out and ran across the plaza toward the church, when a considerable crowd soon gathered around. Colonel Travis was also there. Several persons ran up to the sentinel's post and, not being able to see anything justifying the cry, halloed that it was a "false alarm" and that they "believed the whole tale was a lie" and "our fears useless." The sentinel exclaimed with an oath that "he had seen them" and that "they had hid behind a row of brushwood." The crowd disbanded; the greater part of them discrediting the report altogether.

I then proposed to Colonel Travis that if any one who knew the country would accompany me, I would go out and ascertain to a certainty the truth or falsity of the whole. John W. Smith was soon at hand. When we started taking the Laredo Road, I remarked to Travis just as I mounted my horse, that "if he saw us returning in any other gait than a slow pace, he might be sure that we had seen the enemy." This arrangement proved of some benefit. A moderate gait soon brought us to the top of the slope, about a mile and a half west of town,[10] where we were not surprised to find ourselves within one hundred and fifty yards of fifteen hundred men,[11] well mounted and equipped; their polished armor glis-

---

8. Lon Tinkle in *Thirteen Days to Glory* arbitrarily gave this sentinel the name of Alamo defender Daniel William Cloud, a lawyer from Lexington, Kentucky. In fact, the name of the lookout in the San Fernando Bell Tower remains unknown.

9. Nat Lewis owned a general store in San Antonio. When the vanguard of Mexican troops entered the west end of Bèxar, Nat Lewis left in the other direction, on foot and carrying as much of his inventory as he could. The next day Antonio Menchaca met him on the Cibolo Creek, east of town.

"Nat lewis, passed with a wallet on his back, a-foot from San Antonio, and A[ntonio] asked why he went a-foot and he answered that he could not find a horse; that Santa Anna had arrived at San Antonio with 13,000 men. A[ntonio] asked what the Americans had done. He [Lewis] said they were in the Alamo inside the fortifications. A[ntonio] asked why N[at] did not remain there and he answered that he was not a fighting man, that he was a business man." (Menchaca: 23).
Lewis returned to San Antonio after the revolution and again set up shop on the town's main plaza.

10. The Laredo Road was not the same as the Upper Presidial Road that the Mexican Army was on. The Laredo Road went due south. It is possible that Sutherland is mistaken about his route or that they took the southern route in order to avoid a collision with the Mexican Army. The "slope" is probably the rise discussed earlier, on the east side of the Alazón/Apache Creek area.

11. This was the Vanguard Brigade, 1st Division of Santa Anna's Army of Operations. The organization of the brigade was:

Commander: Gen. of Brigade Joaquín Ramírez y Sesma
Deputy Commander: Col. Eulogio González

Col. Mariano de Salas Jiménez Permanent Battalion	300 *soldados*
Col. José María Romera, Matamoros Permanent Battalion	350 *soldados*
Col. Juan Morales, San Luis Potosi Active Battalion	460 *soldados*
Gen. of Brigade Ventura Mora, Dolores Permanent Regiment (Reinforced)	369 *soldados*
Capt. Mariano Salva, Artillery; two each 8, 6, and 4 pound cannon, with two 7-inch howitzers	62 *soldados*

A total of 1,541 *soldados*.
The organization of the Mexican Army was simple. Infantry organizations were called battalions and named after heroes of the

tening in the rays of the sun,[12] as they were formed in a line between the *chaparral*[13] and mesquite bushes mentioned by the sentinel. The commander riding along the line, waving his sword, as though he might be giving directions as to the mode of the attack. We did not remain long watching their movements, but wheeled around and started full speed back to town. In consequence of a heavy rain through the previous night, the road was quite muddy and my horse being rather smoothly shod, began to slip and scramble and stopped at the end of fifty yards where with a tumbling somersault, he pitched my gun out of my hand, throwing me some distance ahead of him, and followed himself, rolling directly across my knees. Smith dismounted and pulled him off me. Having been slightly stunned, he had made no effort to rise but lay perfectly still holding me fast beneath him. After some moments he managed to get up, when by the assistance of Smith, I did likewise. Picking up the pieces of my gun I found it broken off at the breach. Being again mounted, we resumed our gait and were not long in getting to town. (Sutherland: 18-19)

Seguín

About three o'clock in the afternoon he [tower lookout] sent a messenger stating that on the road to [the] León [Creek], he saw a moving body which appeared like a line of troops raising the dust of the road. Upon the receipt of this notice John W. Smith, a carpenter, alias *"el Colorado,"* was sent to reconnoiter, and returned in the evening, about five o'clock saying "there comes the Mexican army composed of cavalry, infantry and artillery!" In the act of the moment Colonel Travis resolved to concentrate all his forces within the Alamo, which was immediately done.[14] As we marched "Potero Street," now called "Commerce," the ladies [of San Antonio]

Mexican Revolution against Spain. All cavalry organizations were called regiments and named for battles of the Mexican Revolution. There were also presidial companies of light cavalry, organized for frontier defense against the Indians and light police work along the northern Mexico frontier. Two companies of *presidials* served with Santa Anna's forces at the Alamo. The term *permanente* meant regular or permanent. *Activo*, or active, was a federally funded territorial militia and named after their home station. The active units were organized identically to their permanent counterparts. The infantry battalions were commanded by either lieutenant colonels or colonels and organized with eight companies, six of *fusileros*, or line infantrymen commanded by captains. The remaining two were preferred companies: the *grenaderos* and *cazadores*. The *"cazadore,"* literally "hunter," were actually light infantry and possibly armed with rifles. Grenadiers were selected from the tallest and most experienced soldiers in a battalion. Originally grenadiers were trained to use grenades in close combat, but the practice had generally passed by the early nineteenth century. Often task organization would bring all of a particular branch of infantry under one commander for a specific mission. Artillery companies were authorized ninety-one *soldados* and officers. Each company was divided into six squads and could crew six pieces of artillery. Artillery could have been either horse or foot; it is unknown which specific type was at the Alamo. For more information on the numbers of the Mexican Army see: Wallace Woolsey's *The History of the War in Texas Vol II*, pp. 149-156; Richard G. Santos' *Santa Anna's Campaign Against Texas, 1835-1836*; Miguel A. Sanchez Lamego's *Sitio Y Toma del Alamo*; and John B. Lundstom's article "Assault at Dawn: The Mexican Army at the Alamo" in *The Magazine of Military History*, No. 1, Summer 1973. For more information on the organization of the Mexican Army see: Rene Chartrand's "Organization and Uniforms of the Mexican Army, 1810-1838" in *Military Collector & Historian*, Vol. XLVlll, No. 1. By far the most exhaustive work on early nineteenth-century tactics is Brent Nosworthy's *With Musket, Cannon and Sword: Battle Tactics of Napoleon and His Enemies* and *Manual of Instructions for the Organization and Operations of the Army in War and Peace* copied by the Fort Sam Houston Museum.

12. Not likely. There were no *Cuirassiers*, heavy assault cavalry with armored breastplates called *cuirass*, in Mexican service in 1836, though they did serve in the Mexican-U.S. War, 1846-1848. Probably Sutherland saw lance tips or polished helmet, shako or baldric plates.

13. Scrub oak.

14. This reads as if the Texians were unsure of what to do next. Travis mentioned he decided to abandon the town, but it seems almost an afterthought. Once again the Texians were lacking any real military experience. Texian forces on the first day of the siege were approximately 150 or so able-bodied men. Lt. Col. William Barret Travis shared command with Col. James Bowie. The garrison was basically a collection of companies. Soldiers were either Regular Army, Permanent Volunteers, or Volunteer Auxiliary Corps. The companies were:

Capt. William Blazeby	56	Infantry Company
Capt. William C.M. Baker	32	Infantry Company
Capt. William Carey	29	Artillery Company with 18-21 cannon
Capt. John H. Forsyth	21	Cavalry Troop
Capt. Juan Seguín	10	Cavalry Troop
Capt. William Harrison	16	Tennessee Mounted Volunteers

More Texians joined the garrison as the siege progressed. For more on the organization of the Texian Revolutionary Army or the organization of the Alamo garrison see: Eugene C. Barker's article "The Texas Revolutionary Army" in the *Quarterly of the Texas State Historical Association* 9 (April 1906): 227-261, and Bill Groneman's and Phil Rosenthal's *Roll Call at the Alamo*.

exclaimed "poor fellows, you will all be killed, what shall we do?" (de la Teja: 194)

Sutherland

On reaching the civil plaza[15] we [Sutherland and Smith] met Colonel Crockett, who informed us that Colonel Travis had removed his headquarters, together with the entire [Texian] force, from the city to the Alamo. Smith here left me and went to his house. (Sutherland: 19)

E. Esparza

On the morning of February 22, John W. Smith, one of the scouts, galloped up to the Esparza's house bearing the news that Santa Anna was near—would be upon them by night.

What should they do? was the question. Fly they could not! Should they try and hide or go into the fortress of the Alamo. (*San Antonio Light*, November 10, 1901)

*   *   *   *

My father decided to move the family to San Felipe. Everything was ready, when one morning Mr. John W. Smith, who was godfather to my youngest brother [Francisco], came to our house on North Flores Street, just above where the Presbyterian church now is, and told my mother to tell my father when he came in that Santa Anna had come. (*San Antonio Express*, March 7, 1905)

*   *   *   *

I was then a boy of twelve years of age: was then quite small and delicate and could have passed for a child of eight. My father was a friend and comrade of [John] William Smith.[16] Smith had expected to send my father and our family away with his own family in a wagon to Nacogdoches. We were waiting for the wagon to be brought to town. My father and Smith had heard of the approach of Santa Anna, but did not expect him and his forces to arrive as early as they did. Santa Anna and his men got here before the wagon we waited for could come.

My father was told by Smith that all who were friends to the Americans had better join the Americans who had taken refuge in the Alamo. (*San Antonio Express*, May 12, 1907)

Coy

One day they [the Mexican Army] appeared before the city. Coy afterwards learned that their appearance was entirely unexpected. The [Texian] defenders [of San Antonio] were taken by surprise. (*San Antonio Light*, November 26, 1911)

Sutherland

On learning that the Mexicans had arrived Colonel Crockett returned with me. We crossed the river at the ford below [the bridge][17] and on our way up to the ford we met Captain Dimitt and Lieutenant [Benjamin F.] Nobles. The former inquired where we were going. I told him, when he remarked that "there was not enough men at Béxar to defend the place, that it was bound to fall [to the Mexican Army]" and insisted that I should go with him saying he "would see me safely out [of San Antonio]," when we would go and bring reinforcements to the garrison. I replied that "I should go and report to Colonel Travis, and could not say that I could accompany him even then." As we rode on he remarked that he would wait for me down the street at his house. It was not until attempting to dismount in front of Travis's room that I was sensible of the extent of the injury caused by the fall of my horse. On alighting from the saddle, my knee gave way and I

---

15. There were two plazas in Béxar: Military Plaza and the Main, or Civil, Plaza. The Military Plaza was the former *presidio* of San Antonio; the other was simply a town square.

16. This Smith was the same man who rode out with Sutherland. Although there were two William Smiths in the garrison, only John William was a resident of San Antonio.

17. The ford was downstream from the footbridge across the San Antonio River. Why use the ford in February? The bridge was intact; there would be a parley upon it that very night. The only explanation may be that the bridge was cluttered with people leaving San Antonio for the Alamo, or for safer environs.

fell to the ground. By the assistance of Colonel Crockett I got up and went to Colonel Travis' room, where we found him writing a dispatch. He had watched our movements and by this time no longer doubted that the enemy were upon him. I informed him of our discoveries, and of the accident which happened to me and added that "if I could be of any benefit to him I was at his service." He replied that he wished me to go forthwith to Gonzáles, and rally the settlers, if possible, to his relief. Colonel Crockett yet standing by, remarked to him, "Colonel, here am I. Assign me to a position, and I and my twelve boys will try to defend it." Travis replied that he wanted him to defend the picket wall extending from the end of the barracks, on the south side, to the corner of the church.[18] (Sutherland: 19-20)

P. Díaz

As soon as the coming of Santa Anna, which had been heralded, was known the [Texian] Constitutionalists retired to the Alamo and commenced to fortify it. Up to this time it had not been used as a military fortification, but was a church and convent. (*San Antonio Express,* July 1, 1906)

Caro

. . . His excellency [Santa Anna] took over the command [of the advance guard from Ramírez y Sesma] in order to enter the city, which he did on the 26th [*sic*, 23rd of February][19] without encountering any resistance on the part of the Americans. According to the citizens of that place, the enemy, which numbered 156, took refuge in the so-called fortress of the Alamo (a mere canal and nothing

more, built about 500 paces from the town, on the opposite side of the San Antonio River. The town is named for the river. Many of the walls of the fort are of adobe) the moment they saw our troops approaching. (Castañeda: 103)

San Luis Potosi

By that time the enemy had sounded the general alarm and had retreated in their fortification of the Alamo. They have more than fifteen pieces of artillery, but not all are mounted [on carriages] nor serviceable because they lack sufficient cannon balls. They have positioned, in direction of this town [San Antonio], one sixteen [pounder] and one eight [pounder]. (McDonald and Young: 1)

de la Peña

The rest of the [Vanguard Brigade of the 1st] division came within sight [of Béxar] between twelve and one, but by then the enemy had sounded the call to arms and had withdrawn to his fortification at the Alamo. There they had fifteen pieces of artillery, but not all were mounted and ready to use because of a shortage of cannon balls. They had an eighteen-pounder[20] and an eight-pounder pointing toward town. (Perry:38)

Villanueva

I remained at Béxar and when Santa Anna's troops were entering the town I started with Colonel Seguín for the Alamo. When we were on the way Colonel Seguín sent me back to lock his house

---

18. The picket wall, or palisade, was a single row of wood posts extending from the gate to the southwest corner of the church. It was reinforced with a trench, earthworks, abatis, and a single cannon. For a closer look at the palisade defense see Anne A. Fox's *The Archaeology and History of Alamo Plaza.* This area was manned by Harrison's company of Tennessee Mounted Volunteers. Contrary to popular belief Crockett did not command, stating he only desired to be a "high private" instead. For more on this and the organization of the Alamo garrison see Bill Groneman and Phil Rosenthal's *Roll Call at the Alamo.*

19. He undoubtedly meant February 23.

20. There were four Alamo cannon oriented toward Bèxar, though only two were immediately seen by the Mexican Army. The eighteen-pounder was mounted on a platform at the southwest corner of the Alamo. About midway on the west wall were two cannon, the southernmost a twelve-pound gunade, on separate, low platforms sighted through openings in the wall; in the northwest corner, two iron eight-pounders, one pointing toward San Antonio and the other aimed north. For more on Alamo artillery see: Thomas Ricks Lindley's "Alamo Artillery: Number, Type, Caliber and Concussion" in *The Alamo Journal,* Issue 82, July 1992, and Stephen L. Hardin's *Texian Iliad: A Military History of the Texas Revolution,* pp. 112-116.

up. Whilst performing that duty Santa Anna's soldiers got between me and the Alamo and I had to remain in town during the siege and assault of the Alamo. (Matovina: 35)

San Luis Potosi

After having rested the mission for a half-hour from behind a hill about one-half league the President-General mounted his horse and he led the way to the town with his *E.[jercito] M.[ilitar ?]* three companies of *cazadores* commanded by Colonel Morales; three [companies] of *granaderos* commanded by Colonel Romero; two howitzers and the cavalry of General [Ramírez y] Sesma. He left the rest of the [1st] division to march at the orders of General Ventura Mora to the Concepción Ranch. (McDonald and Young: 1)

de la Peña

After the division had rested for about half an hour at the foot of the Alazón Hill, two miles from Béxar, the President-General mounted his horse and started toward this city with his general staff, three companies of light infantry under command of Colonel Morales, three of grenadiers under command of Colonel Romero, two mortar pieces, and General Ramírez y Sesma's cavalry; he ordered the rest of the division to march with General Ventura Mora to Mission Concepción.[21] (Perry:38)

Almonte

At 2 [P.M.] the army took up their march [toward San Antonio], the president and his staff in the van[guard]. (*SHQ* 48:16-17)

Becerra

Colonel [Ventura] Mora was ordered [by Santa Anna] to take up the advance [guard], and when near San Antonio to move to the right, cross the river, and take possession of the Mission of [Nuestra Senora de la Purisma] Concepción [de Acuña]. Santa Anna feared the Texians might abandon the Alamo and occupy Concepción. He considered the latter place more defendable by a small force than the Alamo. (Becerra: 18)

Alsbury

. . . and his wife went into the Alamo where her protector [Jim Bowie] was, when the Mexican troops were nearby. She [Mrs. Alsbury] was accompanied by her younger sister, Gertrudis . . . . Mrs. Alsbury and her sister were in a building not far from where the residence of Colonel Sam Maverick was afterwards erected. It was considered quite a safe locality.[22] (Ford: 122a)

Dimitt

. . . On the 23rd, I was requested by Colonel Travis to take Lieutenant [Benjamin F.] Nobles and reconnoiter the enemy. . . . (Archives, TSL)

---

21. It appears that not all of the Mexican forces in the Vanguard Brigade of the 1st Division entered Béxar proper that afternoon; six preferred companies, two howitzers, and the Dolores Regiment (reinforced) moved into town. The remaining eighteen companies of line infantry and six tubes of artillery bypassed San Antonio and marched downstream to Mission Concepción. It appears that the preferred companies have already been organized into provisional battalions of *granaderos* and *cazadores*. There were no mortars with the army. "Mortar" may be a translator's error of *"obuse,"* which is a howitzer. This was possibly because Concepción was a smaller, more easily defended mission and Santa Anna was not sure which one of the missions the Texians would be defending.

22. A logbook maintained by Capt. Jefferson Peak of the Kentucky Volunteer Cavalry during the Mexican War recorded a meeting with a lady while passing through San Antonio:

> . . . Here I staid all night at the house of a Dr. from Lexington [Kentucky], his wife was Spanish woman [who] could speak English. Her husband was gone to the Río Grande.
> This lady gave me a full detail of the massacre of Colonels Crockett and Bowie. She was in the prison [of the Alamo] with them during the siege and Colonel Bowie married this ladies' cousin whilst in the Alamo.(Roberts, 1996:10)

Was this woman Alsbury's cousin or perhaps an unknown relative of Madama Candelaria? At any rate the "prison" was the gate building where Bowie stayed. It was possible he brought in his relatives as well. The building she describes in her account would have put her in the vicinity of the north wall, hardly a safe locality.

Dickenson

On February 23rd, 1836, Santa Anna, having captured the pickets[23] sent out by Col. Travis to guard the post from surprise, charged into San Antonio with his troops, variously estimated at from six to ten thousand, only a few minutes after the bells of the city rang the alarm.

Capt. Dickenson galloped up to our dwelling and hurriedly exclaimed: "The Mexicans are upon us, give me the babe, and jump up behind me." I did so, and as the Mexicans already occupied Commerce Street, we galloped across the river at the ford south of it, and entered the fort at the southern gate. . . . (Morphis: 174)

* * * *

Just before the Mexicans arrived, headed by Santa Anna, she [Mrs. Dickenson] was, together with her child, at the [Ramon] Músquiz house, near Main Plaza. The enemy appeared first in swarms early in the morning in the southeastern suburbs of the city. Their forces were from ten to thirteen thousand strong. As soon as they were announced to be coming, her husband [Almeron] rode up to the door of her *adobe* [house] and called to her to seize her child and take refuge in the Alamo. She mounted the bare back of the horse he rode, behind his saddle, and holding her child between her left arm and breast, soon reached the old church. An apartment [in the sacristy] was assigned her, while her husband turned away, after an embrace and a kiss, and an eternal adieu, to meet his obligation to his fellowmen and his country. By this time the Mexican bugles were sounding the charge of battle, and the cannon's roar was to reverberate throughout the valley of [the] San Antonio [River]. (*San Antonio Express*, April 28, 1881)

* * * *

After a last kiss and embrace my husband turned away. It was an eternal *adieu*. The bugles were sounding the charge of battle. The cannon's

roar was reverberating throughout the Valley of the San Antonio [River]. (Brogan: 37)

* * * *

The first attack of the Mexicans was over [the siege of the previous December], and all seemed peaceful, when one day [Almeron] Dickenson came hurriedly up to their home on main plaza, saying: "Give me the baby; jump on behind me and ask me no questions."

They galloped down to the crossing, at the point where the "Mill Bridge" now is,[24] but not in time to escape being fired at by the incoming Mexicans: however, they succeeded in crossing and hastened over to the Alamo. (Maverick: 135)

* * * *

The Mexicans came unexpectedly into San Antonio and the witness, [Mrs. Dickenson] and her husband and child retreated into the fort. . . . Dr. Horace Alsbury retreated into the fort for protection with his Mexican wife, Juana, and Gertrudis Navarro, his sister-in-law. (Adjutant General Papers, TSL)

Buquor

María de Jesus steps out into the yard and beholding many men approaching, calls to her mother to question her concerning them. It is the Mexican Army and Travis and Crockett hastily bid their friends farewell and hastened to the fortress and a glorious death . . . of course, rumors of this enemy's coming had been heard for days. (*San Antonio Express*, July 19, 1907)

Seguín

On the 22nd [23d] of February,[25] at 2:00 P.M., General Santa Anna took possession of the city, with over four thousand men, and, in the meantime, we fell back on the Alamo. (de la Teja: 107)

---

23. A reference to Trinidad Coy? It is possible, but no other source mentions it.

24. The future Mill Bridge location was at the intersection of Navarro Street and the river. This was also the location of the ford. See San Antonio Historic Sites clipping file, DRT Library at the Alamo.

25. Seguín must mean February 23. The subject of time at the Alamo is interesting. The hours are somewhat confusing. Today we are on what is called Standard Time. The American Railway Association developed regional time zones in 1883. In 1836 local time was used; that is, each town based its clocks on solar noon. Noon in Bèxar was about forty-five minutes earlier than today's Central Time Zone. Quite probably the Mexican forces were operating off geographic noon in Mexico City or some other Mexican city. This allows for some of the time inconsistencies. The other would be memory, the recollection being placed by the participants whenever they had last looked at their watch before or after an event recounted. Most probably had no watch but took a "swag" based on position of the sun, their most recent meal, what time they got out of bed, and the like.

FIG. 2   RAISING OF THE TWO-STAR TRICOLOR IN MILITARY PLAZA

FIG. 2   RAISING OF THE TWO-STAR TRICOLOR IN MILITARY PLAZA

"Hurry and Excitement," John Sutherland later recalled, filled San Antonio once it was confirmed that the Mexican Army had arrived. Accompanying the latter as it began entering the suburbs of the town, Colonel Almonte noticed a flag being hoisted in Military Plaza—"a tricolor with two stars, designed to represent Coahuila and Texas."[1] Evidently this was the nearest thing the Texian garrison had to a flag signifying their opposition to Santa Anna: it bespoke of his usurpation of the Mexican Constitution, and of the recently crushed uprising in neighboring Coahuila; and, too, it might have been meant to explain why a number of native *Tejanos* had joined the armed Anglos.

The scene depicts early afternoon in the Plaza. A soldier of the New Orleans Greys has just raised the flag, with an officer presenting his sword. (A flagpole at this location can be seen in a ca. 1857 print; and other artistic renditions of the 1840s suggest a flagpole somewhere in Military Plaza.)

In left foreground a volunteer from the States raises a cheer; he wears a tailored hunting coat, its upper pockets stuffed with spare cartridges and loose ball, and his shotgun slung over his shoulder.

In right foreground rides a *Tejano* landowner, wearing a reddish hat, poncho, wide slit trousers with silver buttons, and waist sash. Another *Tejano* approaches to his right, carrying a lance confiscated three months earlier from the equipment of General Cos' surrendered army, and wearing a *ranchero*'s leather hunting shirt.

In the center a Texian in a blanket coat and fur cap offers a lone salute, while others hasten to join the impromptu ceremony, or endeavor to leave. If the flag-raising was meant to delay Santa Anna's advance units, it did not succeed; nor did the Texians offer any resistance from the town itself. They lowered the flag and retired into the Alamo.

San Fernando Church sits in center background. It was considerably renovated and expanded to cathedral status more than thirty years later, although most of the original rear portion, as depicted here, is recognizable even today.—GZ

Ruiz

On the 23rd day of February, 1836, (2 o'clock P.M.) Gen. Santa Anna entered the city of San Antonio with a part of his army. This he effected without any resistance. . . . (*Texas Almanac,* 1860:56)

Yorba

I well remember when Santa Anna and his two thousand soldiers on horses and with shining muskets and bayonets marched into the little pueblo of San Antonio. The news ran from mouth to mouth that Colonel Travis, Davy Crockett and Colonel Bowie and the 160 or so other Texians who had held that locality against the Mexicans for several weeks had taken refuge in and had barricaded themselves in that old stone mission, which had been used as a crude fort or garrison long before I came to the country. It belonged to Mexico and a few stands of muskets and three or four cannon were kept there. (*San Antonio Express,* April 12, 1896)

Travis

Letter from William B. Travis and James Bowie to James Fannin:

COMMANDANCY OF Béxar: We have removed all the men to the Alamo where we make such resistance as is due our honor, and that of the country, until we can get assistance from you, which we expect you to forward immediately. In this extremity, we hope you will send us all the men you can spare promptly. We have one hundred and forty six men, who are determined never to retreat. We have but little provisions, but enough to serve us till you and your men arrive. We deem it unnecessary to repeat to a brave officer, who knows his duty, that we call on him for assistance. (Foote, 2:224)

Sutherland

So soon as Travis ascertained that the enemy were upon him he sent dispatches to Colonel [James Walker] Fannin, then [commanding Texian forces] at Goliad, representing to him his position, and requesting assistance as speedily as it could be sent to him. This dispatch was borne by a young man by the name of Johnson, and not by J[ames]. B[utler]. Bonham, as stated in some accounts. On the twenty-third, when Almonte [and the Mexican Army] arrived at Béxar, Bonham was absent from the city. He had visited Texas with a view of purchasing land and had not attached himself to the army, though he held himself in readiness to serve the country whenever an emergency occurred. (Sutherland: 22-23)

Almonte

The enemy, as soon as the march of the division was seen, hoisted the tri-colored flag with two stars, designed to represent Coahuila and Texas.[26] The president with his staff advanced to Campo Santo. The enemy lowered the flag and fled and possession was taken of Béxar without firing a shot. At 3 P.M. the enemy filed off to the fort of Alamo, where there were ——— pieces of artillery; among them one 18 pounder; it appeared they had 130 men;. . . . (SHQ 48:16-17)

P. Díaz

From the mission [Concepción] I could see also the flag of the Constitutionalists floating from the Alamo. The later flag was not the flag that was afterward adopted by the Texas Republic, but was the flag of Mexico under the constitution and prior to the usurpation and assumption of the [Mexican] dictatorship by Santa Anna. (San Antonio Express, July 1, 1906)

J. Díaz

I will never forget how that army looked as it swept into town. At the head of the soldiers came the regimental band, playing the liveliest airs, and with the band came a squad of men bearing the flags and banners of Mexico and an immense image that looked like an alligator's head.[27] The band stopped on Main Plaza. . . .

The artillery was planted where the French building now stands, and the cannoneers had a clean sweep to the Alamo,[28] for at that time there were no buildings between it and the San Fernando Cathedral. (San Antonio Light, September 1, 1907)

San Luis Potosi

As the President's column entered the plaza, they [Texians] fired a shot from the sixteen pounder. The order was immediately issued for the artillery commander, Ampudia, to position the howitzers, and four grenades were fired at them. (McDonald and Young: 1)

Becerra

When the head of the column reached the cemetery a cannon shot was fired. Skirmishers were de-

---

26. This flag was one of two that has been documented to have been at the Alamo with the Texians. The flag flown over Béxar was lowered and then raised from the church building in the Alamo. Mexican Army officer José Sanchez Navarro sketched the Alamo from a San Antonio rooftop and showed the twin star tricolor flying over the Alamo. See George T. Nelson's The Alamo: An Illustrated History.

27. This could have been the musical instrument called a "serpent." The serpent was about four feet long and resembled its namesake. In Harold L. Peterson's tome The Book of the Continental Soldier, page 197, he describes the instrument:

> Even in its day, the serpent was somewhat of a hybrid. It had a typical brass instrument mouthpiece, but it was made of wood covered with leather, and the different notes were obtained by covering and uncovering a series of holes. It was thus part brass, part woodwind, and its tone was shallow, lacking in resonance. Still it functioned as the principal bass instrument in a military band of the period.

Another instrument was a "jingling johnny," also called a "Chinese pavilion," which was basically a brass pole topped with a brass crescent moon and multi-tiered with bells. During the U.S. war with Mexico, soldier-artist Sam Chamberlain painted a watercolor, "Grand Mass Before Buena Vista." The centerpiece is a group of clerics blessing the Mexican Army before the battle, and one of the priests is holding a golden staff with a peculiar headpiece that could be mistaken for the reptile. Other possibilities are an eagle staff similar to the Napoleonic French Eagle, or perhaps some symbol of Aztec heritage.

28. The French building was in the southeast corner of Main Plaza. This location was probably a then vacant lot at the intersection of Quinta and Dolorosa streets. This was as good a place as any for the Mexican Army to establish an artillery park, as they were out of direct view of the Texians and were close to the river for swabbing the tubes and obtaining water for the oxen.

ployed, and pushed into town. They reported having encountered no resistance. (Beccera: 18)

Santa Anna

Letter from Antonio López de Santa Anna to D. Vicente Filisola:

GENERAL HEADQUARTERS OF Béxar: On the 23rd of this month at 3:00 in the afternoon. I occupied this city after forced marches from Río Grande, together with the division of *Don* General Joaquín [Ramírez] y Sesma's composed of the permanent battalions of Matamoros and Jiménez, the active one of San Luis Potosi, the Dolores regiment, and eight artillery pieces.

With the speed with which this meritorious division executed the marches over eighty leagues of road it was believed that the rebel colonists would not have known of our approach until we were within rifle range of them; because of which they had to take refuge hurriedly in the Fort of the Alamo, which they had fortified well, and stocked sufficient supplies. My objective had been to surprise them at dawn of the day before but a hard rain prevented me from doing so. (Woolsey, 2:168)

* * * *

. . . The enemy fortified itself in the Alamo, overlooking the city. A siege of a few days would have caused its surrender, but it was not fit that the entire army should be detained before an irregular fortification hardly worthy of the name. Neither could its capture be dispensed with, for bad as it was, it was well equipped with artillery, had a double wall, and defenders who it must be admitted, were very courageous and caused much damage to Béxar. Lastly, to leave a part of the army to lay siege to it, the rest continuing on its march, was to leave our retreat, in case of a reverse, if not entirely cut off, at least exposed, and to be unable to help those who were besieging it, who could be reinforced only from the main body of the advancing army. This

would leave to the enemy a rallying point, although it might be only for a few days. (Castañeda, 13)

* * * *

Our army's crossing into Texas was the cause of great surprise on the part of the filibusters, for they believed that Mexican soldiers would not cross again into Texas. Frightened by our invasion they ran to a fortress called the Alamo, a solid fortress erected by the Spaniards.[29] A garrison of six hundred men[30] under the command of Travis, a leader of some renown among the filibusters, mounted eighteen cannon of various caliber. (Crawford: 50-51)

Travis

Letter from William B. Travis to Andrew Ponton, Judge and Citizens of Gonzáles:

COMMANDANCY OF BÈXAR, 3 o'clock P.M. The enemy in large force are in sight. We want men and provisions. Send them to us. We have 150 men and are determined to defend the Alamo to the last. Give us assistance.
P.S. Send an express to San Felipe with news night and day.[31] (*SHQ* 37:13-14)

Sutherland

At this time the Texians had well nigh consumed everything they had on hand in the way of provisions. [James] Grant and [Frank] Johnson[32] had left them but a small supply of coffee, sugar, and salt which had long since disappeared, and none of these necessaries were to be found though they might have had ever so much money with which to buy them.

Their meats they obtained by driving beef from the prairie just as they needed it, and as they never had more at one time than would serve them more than twenty-four hours; it so happened they were in need just at that time.

---

29. In the preceding paragraph Santa Anna states the mission was hardly worthy of the name "fort"; later in life he called it a "hardy fortress."
30. At this point the Texians numbered around 150 men. Santa Anna consistently proves his memory poor.
31. This second appeal for assistance was dispatched with John Smith.
32. Dr. James Grant and Frank Johnson were two Texian leaders of the Matamoros Expedition, an attempt by the Texian government to capture the Mexican port at Matamoros, following the Texian success at the Battle of Béxar in December. Prior to leaving San Antonio they managed to take a large portion of Texian volunteers and materiel with them.

They were out of corn of which they made their bread and had no money to purchase more. . . . while they were retiring from the city to the Alamo they met twenty or thirty beeves coming down Alamo street, now Commerce street, and gathered around them, and drove them into the Alamo. They also got their bread by chance. During the hurry and excitement of the day, a number of Mexican *"jacales"*[33] near the Alamo had been vacated. In them they found some eighty or ninety bushels of corn. These were their supplies during the siege.[34] (Sutherland: 21)

E. Esparza

This good friend [Bowie] did not forget us. When the [wives] mothers and children [of the defenders] fled to the Alamo, *Señor* Bowie had driven in some beeves and found some corn. He gave part of his food to us. (Driggs and King: 221-222)

* * * *

A number of cattle had also been driven into the court of the convent. These later furnished food for all the besieged up to the day of the fall of the Alamo. I do not recollect the inmates having suffered for either food or water during the entire period of the siege. The only article that was scarce was ammunition.[35] This got scarcer and scarcer each day, with no chance or hope of replenishing. (*San Antonio Express*, May 18, 1907)

* * * *

Mama was worried about leaving her home, but determined to go with Papa wherever he went. He sent word that a wagon would come for us. He was busy taking our cattle to the Alamo for food for the barracks. (DRT Library, Alamo)

Travis

Letter from the 24th [excerpt]:

P.S. The Lord is on our side—When the enemy appeared in sight we had not three bushels of corn- We have since found in deserted houses 80 or 90 bushels and got into our walls 20 or 30 head of beeves. (*SHQ* 37:16)

Candelaria

A small herd of cattle had been driven inside of the walls, and we found a small quantity of corn that had been stored by priests. (*San Antonio Light*, February 19, 1899)

Dickenson

Had provisions enough to last the besieged 30 days. (Adjutant General Papers, TSL)

Sutherland

As soon as the Texians entered the Alamo they set about preparing for its defense. The beeves were secured in a pen on the north east side of the fortress. The corn was stored away in some of the small rooms of the barracks. They did not obtain water from the small canal which runs near but dug a well within the walls.[36] There being no portholes in the wall, it was necessary for them to make an arrangement by which they could shoot over it. This was done by throwing up an embankment against it on the inside. This being done they proceeded to make other arrangements that were necessary. Their

---

33. A *jacal* ranged in description from a small mud and wood thatched hut to a sturdy wooden structure. *Jacales* were numerous on the Alamo side of the river, extending from La Villita all the way to the southern wall of the Alamo. This area was Pueblo de Valero, a small suburb of the Alamo that sprang up from the Spanish cavalry garrison. The mud and thatch design starkly contrasted with the city's stone and plaster homes.

34. This hardly suggests people prepared for a battle. As the enemy is approaching, all the supplies are gathered? Granted, the Matamoros Expedition drained their resources, but that had been weeks prior. As of the first of February the Texians had confirmation of Santa Anna's movement north, yet apparently did nothing to prepare. The Texians were accountable, receipts were issued, and by September all residents had been paid for their goods.

35. According to John Smith's February 3 inventory of the Alamo's materiel, currently in the Texas State Archives, there were 19,300 cartridges.

36. This well would not be complete for several days. The Texians were forced to draw from the *acequia*, or creek, east of the mission.

guns were placed upon the wall, as soon as possible. Of these they had some thirty or forty pieces of various calibers, amongst them an eighteen pounder. Most of them they had taken from the enemy in the previous December, when Cós had surrendered. Though they had so many they were not all mounted, I think not more than about twenty were put to use during the siege. They had also obtained from the same source a considerable number of muskets, swords, and bayonets, together with any amount of ammunition, which came in play, for of their own they had but a small supply. All were armed with good rifles, single barrel pistols, and good knives. Their powder they kept in a small room in the southwest [and northwest] corners of the church which was covered over with an arched roof of stone and plastered perfectly tight so as to make it proof against sparks of fire from the enemy's shells.[37] (Sutherland: 21-22)

Dickenson

Among the besieged were 50 or 60 wounded ones from Cós's fight.[38] About 18 cannon . . . were mounted on parapet and in service all the time. (Adjutant General Papers, TSL)

* * * *

There were about 160 sound persons in the Alamo when the enemy appeared in overwhelming numbers upon the environs of the city to the west. The others were sick or wounded, among them being Colonel James Bowie who was in the last stages of consumption. (Brogan: 37)

E. Esparza

The roof of the Alamo church had been taken off and the south [east] side [of the church] filled up with dirt almost to the roof on that side so there was a slanting embankment up which the Americans could run and take positions. During the fight I saw numbers who were shot in the head as soon as they exposed themselves from the roof. There were holes made in the walls of the fort and the Americans continually shot from these also. We also had two cannon, one at the main entrance and one at the northwest corner of the fort near the [new] post office. The [Texians'] cannon were seldom fired. (*San Antonio Express*, November 22, 1902)

Candelaria

The great front door [of the compound] had been full of sand bags,[39] and there was a bare hope that we might hold out until General Houston would send a reinforcement. (*San Antonio Light*, February 19, 1899)

Sutherland

Between three and four o'clock P.M. I started, as requested by Colonel Travis, for Gonzáles. I first rode down the river, a short distance, thinking to meet Dimitt, but he had gone, taking the main Goliad road. On coming near the ford[40] I fell in with J[ohn].W[illiam]. Smith, also on his way to Gonzáles. We halted and were paralyzed for a moment when we saw the enemy march into Military Plaza in regular order. While we sat on our horses for a moment watching their movements, Captain Nat Lewis came up to us on foot. He, too, was bound for Gonzáles with as much of his valuables as he could carry in his saddle bag thrown across his shoulder—leaving the remainder in his storehouse, a contribution to the enemy. (Sutherland: 23)

37. See Alamo map on page 122.

38. According to the report of December 17 by Chief Surgeon Amos Pollard, only about seven wounded men from the Béxar fight were part of the Alamo garrison. For the complete letter see William C. Binkley's *Official Correspondence of the Texas Revolution, 1835-1836*. There is the possibility that more men were down due to illness or safety related accidents.

39. The great front door was obviously the main gate on the south wall. This section of wall was the newest portion of the fort, having been added by the Spanish cavalry unit, Compania Volante del Alamo (hence the name), who garrisoned the place around the turn of the century following Mission Valero's secularization. The Mexican Army never breached the gate from the outside and according to the existing Mexican Army maps there was depth of fortifications protecting it. For more on this see Jake Ivey's article "South Gate and its Defenses" in the *Alamo Lore and Myth Organization Newsletter*, December 1981.

40. This is apparently the same ford that was discussed in note 17.

San Luis Potsosi

At the outskirts of Béxar, the President-General ordered Colonel Miñón, with half the *cazadores,* to take the [San Fernando] church, being unaware that it was abandoned.[41] (McDonald and Young: 1)

de la Peña

The president, unaware upon entering Béxar that the [San Fernando] church[42] was abandoned, ordered Colonel Miñón to take it with half the *cazadores.*[43] (Perry:38)

Dimitt

Some distance out [of San Antonio]I met a Mexican who informed me that the town had been invested. After a short time a messenger overtook me, saying he had been sent by a friend of my wife to let me know that it would be impossible for me to return, as two large bodies of Mexican troops were already around the town. I then proceeded to the Rovia [Creek][44] and remained till 10 P.M. on the 25th. (Archives, TSL)

E. Esparza

The Alamo was decided upon by the mother as there her husband would be fighting for liberty. There they carried in their arms their most precious possessions—going back and forth many times, until at sunset the mother, Mrs. Anita Esparza, with her last bundles and her little daughter and four sons, passed across the bridge over the *acequia* into the courtyard of the Alamo just as the trumpet's blare and noise of Santa Anna's army was heard. (*San Antonio Light,* November 10, 1901)

* * * *

Santa Anna and his army arrived at about sundown and almost immediately after we sought refuge in the Alamo. Immediately after their arrival Santa Anna's personal staff dismounted on Main Plaza in front of the San Fernando Church. Santa Anna went into the building at the northwest corner of Main Plaza.[45] That building had been occupied by the Texians and before them by the soldiers of Mexico and still earlier by the soldiers of Spain. It had been a part of the presidio, or old fort, and the part where the officers had their headquarters.[46] The Texians had left this structure and gone over to the Alamo because the latter offered more advantages for defense. I have often heard it said that Santa Anna immediately upon his arrival in San Antonio dismounted in the west side of Military Plaza and hitched his horse to an iron ring set into the walls of the old building where the Spanish Governors dwelt and where the combined coats of arms of Spain and Austria form the keystone of the arch above its portal. This is not so. I saw Santa Anna when he arrived. I saw him dismount. He did not hitch the horse. He gave his bridle reins to a lackey. He and his staff proceeded immediately to the house on the northwest corner of Main Plaza. I was playing with some other children on the Plaza and when Santa Anna and his soldiers came up we ran up and told our parents who almost immediately afterward took me and the other children of the family to the Alamo. I am sure of this for I saw Santa Anna several times afterward and after I came out of the Alamo. (*San Antonio Express,* May 12, 1907)

* * * *

I went across town to see if I could spot the army coming. To my surprise, as I ran across the Main Plaza, I saw a splendid sight. A large army was

---

41. The *fusileros* had gone on to attack Concepción.

42. Santa Anna was being very cautious in taking San Antonio, still believing the Texians were going to try to defend the town.

43. Task organization must have been kept the same for the final assault. On March 6 Colonel Miñón was second in command of the provisional battalion of *cazadores.*

44. This was probably the Rosilla Creek on the road to Goliad.

45. This was the Yturri house.

46. Esparza is discussing two separate plazas. The old Presidio de San Antonio, then called Plaza de Armas, was one block west of where Esparza remembers seeing Santa Anna enter the building.

coming toward me on horseback and on foot. They wore red coats and blue trousers with white bands crossed over their chests.[47]

Pennants were flying and swords sparkling in the bright winter sun. Riding in front was Santa Anna, *el Presidente!* This man was every inch a leader. All the officers dismounted, but only the general tossed his reins to an aide with a flourish. I was very impressed.

Slipping away unnoticed, I ran to tell my parents that the army had arrived. No one had expected a forced march to cross the cold, arid plains of south Texas in winter. Santa Anna had done just that at the cost of the lives of a great many men and livestock. He intended to avenge the insult to his pride without a thought of the price.

At home, my family decided not to wait for the wagon. We gathered up a few clothes and bags of food.[48] (DRT Library, Alamo)

* * * *

When my father came my mother asked him what he would do. You know the Americans had the Alamo, which had been fortified a few months before by General Cós.

"Well, I'm going to the fort," my father said.

"Well, if you go, I'm going along and the whole family too." (*San Antonio Express,* November 22, 1902)

* * * *

When the trumpets of Santa Anna were heard, we had rushed to the Alamo. When father told her she had better go to a safer place, she said, "No; if you are going to die, I want to be near you!" We gathered up the few things we had—a *metate,*[49] two chairs, four skins, and some cooking utensils. In one bundle was my baby sister. My small brothers and I carried what we could. I was the oldest—Nine years.[50] (Driggs and King: 222)

Sutherland

We soon parted, Captain Lewis taking one direction, Smith and myself another. Thinking the Mexicans might have seen us going off and pursue us, we took the old Goliad road which runs directly south for some distance. After going about half a mile we turned due east into mesquite and chaparral brush, following the winding paths that lead through it. We crossed the Gonzáles road between the city and Powder House Hill, about one mile east of town. Turning eastward over the hill, we saw three men riding in the distance across the Salado [creek], about a mile and a half from us. We suspected that they might be a scouting party of the enemy, attempting to cut off anyone leaving the city and kept on our course, rather bearing around them to the left. (Sutherland: 23-24)

P. Díaz

The arrival of Santa Anna was announced by the firing of a gun from in front of the alcalde's home on Main Plaza. His [Santa Anna's] red flag was hoisted over the cathedral. I heard the gun fired from the plaza and saw the [red] flag floating from the plaza. When Santa Anna hoisted his red flag, it was his announcement that no quarter would be

---

47. Esparza was looking at mounted troops, most probably from the Presidential Escort of lancers under Capt. Miguel Aguirre of the Tampico Regiment (Woolsey 2: 224 and Perry: 123). The Mexican cavalry were issued . . .

> a tailcoat of scarlet *Querétaro* cloth (wool) with green collar, lapels and cuffs, coarse lining and white metal buttons, a pair of *Querétaro* cloth riding pants with antelope skin seat lining, cordovan bells at the bottom and [red] cloth strips at side seams . . . a helmet of tanned cowhide with a large brass shield, comb and chinstrap, wool plume and a crest of goat pelt. . . . (Nieto, Brown and Hefter, 51).

The lapels were omitted in the 1833 regulations, so it is possible a mix of uniforms occurred. The active cavalry wore the same uniform but the colors of red and green reversed. For more on the Mexican soldier see the above authors in *El Soldado Mexicano 1837-1847.*

48. Smith must have gotten too busy with his courier mission, or may have forgotten his promise to send a wagon. It is also possible that the Esparza family had left before a wagon could have arrived, or perhaps Smith had spoken too soon and there were no available wagons left to send.

49. A curved stone bowl with three legs, used for grinding corn.

50. The Esparzas who went to the Alamo were: José Gregorio Esparza, father; Ana Salazar Esparza, mother; Enrique Esparza; Manuel Esparza, about five; Francisco Esparza, younger than five; and Maria de Jesus Castro Esparza, ten years. There appears to be only one daughter born to the Esparza family. For more on the Esparzas, see Bill Groneman's *Alamo Defenders, A Genealogy: The People and Their Words.*

FIG. 3   THE BLOOD-RED BANNER

FIG. 3   THE BLOOD-RED BANNER

When Santa Anna ordered the blood-red banner raised on the bell tower of San Fernando Church, he was sending an unambiguous message to the Texian defenders observing it from the Alamo, nearly 1,000 yards to the east. For the Mexican Army, the banner signified, in William B. Travis' own words, "that the war is one of vengeance against rebels," and that they were "threatening to murder all prisoners and make Texas a waste desert." Aside from their cause, and the sense of honor that compelled them to stand and fight, the garrison now had an additional, perhaps more fundamental reason to resist: the preservation of their very lives.

The skull and crossbones depicted in the illustration are derived from the insignia on a banner drawn by Capt. José Juan Sanchez Navarro in his plan of the Alamo battle, as printed in his *La Guerra de Tejas; Memorias de un Soldado*. It flies above a sketch of the monument he proposed should be built to honor the Mexican soldiers killed in the March 6 attack. The monument inscription reads:

> "Don't look in vain, you who look upon this plan, / For, although badly drawn, it will inspire you / (If you bear in some way the name of Mexican / And desire that such a name not be lost) / To march to Texas, and with a strong hand / Make the base colonist bite the dust, / Until national honor, now outraged, / Will be with sword and fire well avenged."

This written expression corresponds to the message symbolized by the blood-red banner; and perhaps it was this very banner that Sanchez Navarro drew. (The monument was never built.)

The Mexican government had pronounced the rebellious Texians as pirates undeserving of mercy; and by this banner Santa Anna was making clear his intentions both to the enemy and to his own troops.

Skulls, bones, and death had been integral to the religion of the Aztec Mexicans, and the Spaniards brought over their own cultic preoccupation with death, largely borne out of their experience with the Black Plague of fifteenth-century Europe. That death motifs worked their way into the Mexican Army is not surprising: the Indians and peasants who filled its ranks well understood the macabre pomp and ceremony of funerals, and of the Day of the Dead and other religious holidays.[1] But battle emblems of skulls and bones had been adopted by fighting men from prehistoric times onward. A Prussian regiment of "Death's Head Hussars" followed Frederick the Great in the Seven Years' War; and, of course, seagoing European and American pirates of the seventeenth and eighteenth centuries almost universally flew the "Jolly Roger" flag. As late as the Mexican-American War of 1846-1848 some Mexican military units still carried grim flags or guidons bearing skulls and crossbones.[2] As recently as World War II, Hitler's SS units wore emblems of skulls and crossbones on their caps and uniforms.

Still, it must be mentioned that many of Santa Anna's soldiers, both officers and men, disapproved of his no-quarter tactic, on both humanitarian and political grounds. Indeed, many later blamed his cutthroat policy for losing Texas, by the wrath it aroused among the surviving white settlers.

One additional clue to the use of a blood-red banner with skull and crossbones appears in Henry McArdle's frequently reproduced 1905 oil, *Dawn at the Alamo*. At center top a Mexican soldier, shot, is falling backwards and letting go of a red flag with skull and crossbones decorating it. McArdle had been gathering, for several decades, much of his research data from a number of sources, including veterans of the Texian Revolution. Perhaps one of the latter remembered this flag, which nearly parallels what Navarro had drawn.

Lieutenant de la Peña noted that Santa Anna, upon entering Béxar, ordered Colonel Minon to seize the San Fernando Church with half of the *cazadores*. Evidently these nimble men also planted the banner atop the bell tower. How exactly it was "raised" is not known; most accounts refer to it as flying "from the top." There was a large metal crucifix at the apex of the small upper dome, and this might have provided the means of attachment. If some thought that this lent divine endorsement to the banner's meaning, it was no doubt an observation that was fully exploited.

Below the church, part of Main Plaza can be seen, with advance elements of the Mexican Army arriving: grenadiers, *cazadores*, cavalry, and artillerymen, all in their dress uniforms, along with covered artillery carts, mule-driven guns, and skirmishers sent forward to scour the town. In left background, beyond the curve of the river, sits the Alamo, from which the eighteen-pounder will soon respond, equally symbolically, to the raising of the banner.—GZ

shown those opposing him. This was well understood by those in the Alamo. They knew that unless Houston, on whom they vainly relied, sent them succor they were lost. (*San Antonio Express*, July 1, 1906)

E. Esparza

The red flag symbolizing "no Quarter" flew from the belfry of the [San Fernando] church in the military Plaza. It meant death to every man within the Alamo who had so defied Santa Anna.[51] (DRT Library, Alamo)

de la Peña

As the column entered the plaza, from the Alamo came a cannon shot from the eighteen-pounder; immediately the artillery commander was ordered to set up two howitzers and to fire four grenades, which caused the enemy to raise a white flag.[52] (Perry:38)

San Luis Potosi

They [Texians] raised a white flag, firing ceases . . . . (McDonald and Young: 1)

Dickenson

Enemy began throwing bombs into the Fort, but no [Texians] hurt till last day, i.e., the assault, except one horse killed. (Adjutant General Papers, TSL)

Loranca

We marched upon the place and were received by the fort with one or two cannon shots; those in the Alamo raising a red flag. (*San Antonio Express*, June 23, 1878)

Santa Anna

However, in spite of their [Texians'] artillery fire which they began from the fort, the troops of our country with the best of order have taken possession of this place and the traitors shall not again occupy it; for our part we have suffered the loss of a corporal and a *cazadore* killed and eight wounded.[53] (Woolsey, 2:168)

Loranca

Santa Anna then ordered a parley to be sounded, which was answered by the chiefs of the Alamo, and the President commissioned the Mexican Colonel Batres to confer with Bowie and Travis, both Colonels of the Texian forces holding the Alamo. This was on the 26th [*sic*, 23d] of February, 1836.

The President Santa Anna proposed to Travis and Bowie that they should surrender at discretion, with no guarantee than that their lives should be spared. The said Texian chiefs answered and proposed to surrender the fort on being allowed to march out with their arms and go join their government, as they had permitted the Mexican forces under Generals Cós and Filisola when they capitulated to the Texians at the Mission [San Francisco] de la Espada[54] and were allowed to march out with their arms, munitions of war, provisions, etc., and join the Mexican Army then in the field against Texas, and if this was not willingly conceded to

---

51. As soon as Colonel Miñón secured the plaza and the church, a red flag was hoisted from the church tower, plainly visible from 1,000 yards away in the Alamo.

52. The red flag must have been common knowledge to the Texian defenders. They immediately fired a round in response, toward the city. This was possibly fired from the eighteen-pounder at the southwest corner of the Alamo. The Mexican artillery immediately "dropped trail" and returned fire with the two howitzers. Grenade meant an exploding, as opposed to solid, ordnance. There was probably some confusion in the Alamo garrison and a decision to raise the white flag for a parley.

53. There is no other evidence of Mexican casualties during the taking of Béxar; however a good, well-aimed shot from the aforementioned gun could do this much damage with only one round.

54. He refers to the Battle of Béxar the previous December. The Alamo and Concepción were the only missions involved in the battle.

them, they would willingly take all chances of war. (*San Antonio Express*, June 23, 1878)

Bowie

James Bowie to the Commander of the Mexican Army of Texas:

> FORTRESS OF THE ALAMO: Because a shot was fired from a cannon of this fort at the time a red flag was raised over the tower of San Fernando, and because a little afterward they told me that a part of your army had sounded a parlay, which was not heard before the firing of the shot. I wish, Sir, to ascertain if it be true that a parley was called, for which reason I send my second aide, Benito Jameson, under guarantee of a white flag which I believe will be respected by you and your forces.
> God and Mexico. God and Texas.[55] (*SHQ* 37: 16)

de la Peña

The firing ceased and Bowie sent a written communication addressed to the commander of the invading troops of Texas, stating that he wished to enter into agreements. The president ordered a verbal answer that he would not deal with bandits, leaving them no alternative but to surrender unconditionally. Then he ordered the placement of the troops, and that they eat and rest, and summoned to Béxar the forces attacking Concepción. (Perry:39)

San Luis Potosi

. . . and one of them [Texians] came with a writ that said "Bowie to the Commander of the troops invading Texas."—that he wanted to [R.a.?] The President ordered the reply, by word, that "he did

not negotiate with bandits; that they had no means to escape, other than to surrender at discretion." Then he prepared the troops to attack—[giving orders] to eat, to rest, and he had brought to Béxar everyone whom he has ordered to march to Concepción. (McDonald and Young: 1-2)

Becerra

When the army arrived many inhabitants fled from the city, leaving everything behind them; most of them went into the country. This was late in February. General Santa Anna's army numbered about 4,000. He determined to take the Alamo by storm, but concluded to await the arrival of [Acting] General [of Brigade] [Eugenio] Tolsa with 2,000 men.[56] Santa Anna made the preparatory arrangements during the interval. (Beccera: 18)

E. Esparza

It took the whole day to move [our family] to the Alamo, and an hour before sundown we were inside the fort. There was a bridge over the [San Antonio] river about where [then]Commerce street crosses it, and just as we got to it we could hear Santa Anna's drums beating on Milam Square; and just as we were crossing the ditch going into the fort Santa Anna fired his salute on Milam Square.[57] (*San Antonio Express*, November 22, 1902)

* * * *

It was twilight when we got into the Alamo and it grew pitch dark soon afterward. All of the doors were closed and barred. The sentinels that had been on duty without [the fort] were first called inside [the walls] and then the openings closed. Some sentinels were posted up on the roof, but those were protected by the walls of the Alamo church and

55. The hastily fired round from the Alamo has caused at least Bowie to reflect on the situation. There could have been a Mexican proposal for a parley; at any rate Bowie does not seem as eager to bring on a fight as Travis may have been. Benito Jameson was actually Green B. Jameson, the engineer at least partially responsible for the Alamo defenses. For whatever reason, Bowie Mexicanized Jameson's name; perhaps he thought that it would show this was not an ethnic conflict. On the original document Bowie wrote, then lined through, "Dios y Mexico."

56. Beccera is probably confusing Tolsa's 2d Infantry Brigade with Acting General of Brigade Don Antonio Gaona's Brigade. The advance elements of Gaona's Brigade did not arrive until March 3.

57. This square is named for Ben Milam and was not established until later. It was then the Protestant cemetery near Campo Santo. More than likely it was not a salute the Mexicans were firing, but the four grenades.

FIG. 4   THE FLAG OF TRUCE

FIG. 4   THE FLAG OF TRUCE

In the late afternoon of February 23, 1836, Green B. Jameson, twenty-nine-year-old major of engineers of the Alamo garrison, rides out of the Texian fort holding a white flag of truce and bearing a message from James Bowie to determine if the newly arrived Mexican Army had called for a parley. Bilingual Col. Juan Almonte, Santa Anna's half-Tlaxcala Indian aide-de-camp, receives Jameson and reads Bowie's letter.

Almonte's garb is full dress, including bullion fringed epaulets, aigullettes, red silk waist-sash, and cane, the latter *de rigueur* among Mexican officers. His colonel's coat is based on an actual preserved relic of the campaign, that of Colonel Morales, who was captured at San Jacinto in April of 1836.[1]

To Almonte's left stands a captain of the grenadier company of Colonel Romero's Matamoras Permanente Battalion. Santa Anna had captured San Antonio only several hours earlier with his elite troops: three companies each of grenadiers and light infantry detached from the main battalions. A red pompom on his shako, with the flaming grenade badge on its front, denotes his grenadier status. His coat is dark blue, his trousers medium blue with a red stripe. His sword hangs by a black shoulder belt. He, too, carries a cane.

Green Jameson's dress is a civilian greatcoat (blanketcoats were also preferred winter garb in Texas), buckskin trousers, and boots. Only his sword marks him as a soldier. The horse he has ridden out on has been borrowed from a *Tejano* member of the garrison.

The Commerce (or Portrero) Street Bridge is suggested by William Bollaert's sketch of a new bridge built at the same location six years later.[2]

In the background, an avenue leads through the huts of Pueblo de Valero to its wider plaza, and then, just north of it, the Alamo (about 220 yards from the bridge).—GZ

---

the old convent building. We went into the church portion. It was shut up when we arrived. We were admitted through a small window. (*San Antonio Express*, May 12, 1907)

* * * *

As dusk fell, we arrived at the gate to find it bolted. Furious, Mama pounded on the gate and demanded that it be opened. When the sentries recognized Papa as being one of their best Mexican soldiers, they called him to a small side window. The soldiers pulled us up through the little window one by one and Papa handed in our bundles. (*San Antonio Express*, May 12 1907)

* * * *

I distinctly remember that I climbed through the window and over a cannon that was placed inside of the church immediately behind the window. There were several other cannon there. Some were [in] back of the doors. Some had been mounted on the roof and some had been placed in the convent. The window was opened to permit us to enter and it

was closed immediately after we got inside. (*San Antonio*, May 12, 1907)

* * * *

We all went into a small store room [sacristy] near the monastery. Here we slept on hay and under hay. With us were other Mexican mothers and children. The women helped by grinding corn and cooking it for the men. Mrs. Dickenson and her baby were with us. She seemed not to know what to do in this condition. I heard mother say *povrecita* and take the lady some food.[58]

We were too scared to think much of eating, but mother made some *atole*, a sort of mush, for all the children. She ground the corn and boiled it and almost poured it down our throats. Mother was a sensible woman and kept her head. Some of the other women were helpless. (Driggs and King: 222)

* * * *

There were a few other families who had gone in. Mrs. Alsbury and her sister, a Mrs. Victoriana, and family of several girls, two of whom I knew afterward, Mrs. Dickenson, Mrs. Juana Melton, a

---

58. *Povrecita* (*pobrecita*) is "poor baby." The twenty-one-year-old Susannah Dickenson has long been regarded as the "Mother of the Alamo"; however, *Señora* Esparza seems to have assumed the role.

FIG. 5   THE ESPARZA FAMILY ENTERS THE ALAMO

FIG. 5   THE ESPARZA FAMILY ENTERS THE ALAMO

Six and a half decades after the fall of the Alamo, when he was in his late seventies, noncombatant survivor Enrique Esparza granted the first of several newspaper interviews concerning his experience in the siege and battle; and, just before his ninetieth birthday, he gave his last one. For one so advanced in years, his recollections are surprisingly consistent enough in detail to support his claim that the events of 1836 were "burned into my brain and indelibly seared there."

By these accounts it can be gathered that his father, Gregorio, a Texian ally, had decided to remove his family from their house on North Flores Street and into the Alamo, just as Santa Anna's army was entering San Antonio. They may have made several trips with their bundles; but when at last the entire family was ready to enter the fort, "an hour before sundown," they found that "all the doors were closed and barred." Evidently this also meant that the drawbridge over the ditch at the lunette had been pulled up. In addition, access over the south palisade was not possible due to the barrier of abatis.

Instead, Enrique Esparza noted, they gained entrance via "the church portion," through "a small side window." In its condition in 1836, the Alamo church had no true "side window" except for one located near the northern end of the sacristy, on its east wall, a section of that room that no longer exists. A watercolor sketch of the rear of the church, made ca. 1848–1849 by Capt. Arthur T. Lee, shows this window, but his perspective is considerably distorted and the height of the ruins of the entire building is no less exaggerated.[1]

The sacristy wall as it then existed was only about eighteen feet high, with the bottom ledge of the window perhaps seven and a half feet from the ground. This would have been low enough for the Esparzas to have been pulled up by the soldiers within "one by one," as Enrique recalled, and perhaps his father stood on one of the two chairs they had brought along to help lift up his wife and children. Besides his parents Enrique had an older sister and three younger brothers, one of whom was still an infant.

"Immediately behind the window," remembered Esparza, a cannon was positioned. None of the Alamo plans, either Texian or Mexican, indicate a gun at this window; however, accounts by other survivors also tell of artillery pieces inside of other buildings that are also not seen on any plan, so it might well be that those plans show only exterior guns. A cannon at the sacristy window, sitting on a low ramp, would have abetted the three-gun cavalier battery in the church's chancel, some dozen feet above the ground; but this—like so much else in the Alamo story—remains mere speculation.

Part of the back of the church's front, or western, wall can be seen to right of center, as well as the flagpole positioned at its southwestern corner.—GZ

Mexican woman who had married an American, also a woman named Concepción Losoya and her son Juan, who was a little older than I.[59]

The first thing I remember after getting inside the fort was seeing Mrs. Melton making circles on the ground with an umbrella. I had seen very few umbrellas. (*San Antonio Express*, November 22, 1902)

* * * *

Within the Alamo courtyard were also other refugees who were saved—Mrs. [Juana Navarro] Alsbury and one child and sister, Gertrudes Navarro; Mrs. Concepción Losoya, her daughter and two sons; Victoriana de Salina and three little girls; Mrs [Susannah] Dickenson and baby, and an old woman named Petra. (*San Antonio Light*, November 10, 1901)

Almonte

. . . during the afternoon 4 grenades were fired at them. The firing was suspended in order to receive a messenger who brought a dispatch the contents of which appears in number one, and the answer which was given appears in number two.[60] I conversed with the bearer who was Jameson (G[reen]. B.) and he informed me of the bad state they were in at the Alamo, and he manifested a wish that some honorable conditions should be proposed for a surrender. Another messenger afterward came ([Albert] Martin) late a clerk in a house in New Orleans. He stated to me what Mr. Travis said, "that if I wished to speak with him he would receive me with much pleasure." I answered that it did not be-

59. The people gathered in this room were: the Esparza family, Juana Melton (wife of defender Eliel Melton and sister of defender Toribio Losoya), Concepción Losoya and her son Juan (mother and brother of the aforementioned defender), a Mrs. Victoriana with several daughters, Petra González, Trinidad Saucedo, and two Anglo sons of defender Anthony Wolf (Benjamin and Michael—both under twelve). For more on this see Groneman's *Roll Call at the Alamo* and *Alamo Defenders, a Genealogy: The People and Their Words* and Crystal Sasse Ragsdale's *The Women and Children of the Alamo*.

60. Bowie's letter was number one and Batres' response was number two.

FIG. 6   IN THE SHELTER OF THE SACRISTY

FIG. 6   IN THE SHELTER OF THE SACRISTY

During the siege of the Alamo, most of the women and children in the compound took up residence within the sacristy of the church, a strong room thirty-five feet long by fifteen wide, with two Moorish domes topping its eighteen-foot-high ceiling. Among these noncombatants were Mrs. Susannah Dickenson, in her early twenties, with her fifteen-month-old baby, Angelina, and Mrs. Ana Esparza and her five children. One of the latter was Enrique, who, years later, recalled how his mother "kept her head" while "some of the other women were helpless." Even Mrs. Dickenson "seemed not to know what to do in this condition." Mrs. Esparza brought food to her, and no doubt words of encouragement as the enemy bombardment shook the church.

Corn was one of the staples of the garrison, and one of the items the Esparza family brought into the Alamo was a *metate,* upon which kernels were mashed with a stone roller. The ground corn was then boiled into "*atole,* a sort of mush."

Enrique also remembered that hay comprised some of the beds in the sacristy; Mrs. Dickenson later noted that her own bed was a cot. The sacristy was also used as a partial storehouse for provisions, and as quarters for a few officers, no doubt including the artillerymen husbands of Mrs. Dickenson and Mrs. Esparza.

At least one domestic pet, a cat, was known to have been with the garrison. On the day of battle, it was shot by Mexican soldiers, who deemed it simply another "American."—GZ

come the Mexican Government to make any propositions through me, and that I had only permission to hear such as might be made on the part of the rebels. After these contestations night came on and there was no more firing.[61] (*SHQ* 48:16-17)

Batres

As Aide de Camp of his Excellency, the President of the Republic, I reply to you, according to the order of his Excellency, that the Mexican army cannot come to terms under any conditions with rebellious foreigners to whom there is no recourse left, if they wish to save their lives, than to place themselves immediately at the disposal of the Supreme Government from whom alone they may expect clemency after some considerations. God and Liberty. (*SHQ* 37:16)

Santa Anna

Confident that aid would come, Travis replied to my proposition of surrender, "I would rather die than surrender to the Mexicans!" (Crawford: 51)

de la Peña

When our commander in chief haughtily rejected the agreement that the enemy had proposed, Travis became infuriated at the contemptible manner in which he had been treated and, expecting no honorable way of salvation, chose the path that strong souls should choose in crisis, that of dying with honor, and selected the Alamo for his grave. It is possible that this might have been his first resolve, for although he was awaiting the reinforcements promised him, he must have reflected that he would be engaged in battle before these could join him, since it would be difficult for him to cover their entry into the fort with the small force at his disposal. (Perry:41)

Travis

[Excerpt from letter of the 24th]: The enemy has demanded a surrender at discretion, otherwise, the garrison are to be put to the sword, if the fort is taken—I have answered the demand with a cannon shot. . . . (*SHQ* 37:14)

---

61. The Texian cannon fired in response to the Red Flag, and the Mexican forces returned fire with four exploding rounds. Bowie on his own sent a courier, Jameson, out with a message. He met with Colonel Almonte. Travis, upon hearing Bowie had opened communication without him, sent his own messenger, Albert Martin, who also met with Almonte. During this meeting with Martin, Almonte delivers Santa Anna's response to Bowie's letter, offering only unconditional surrender. The Texians responded to "the demand with a cannon shot. . . ."

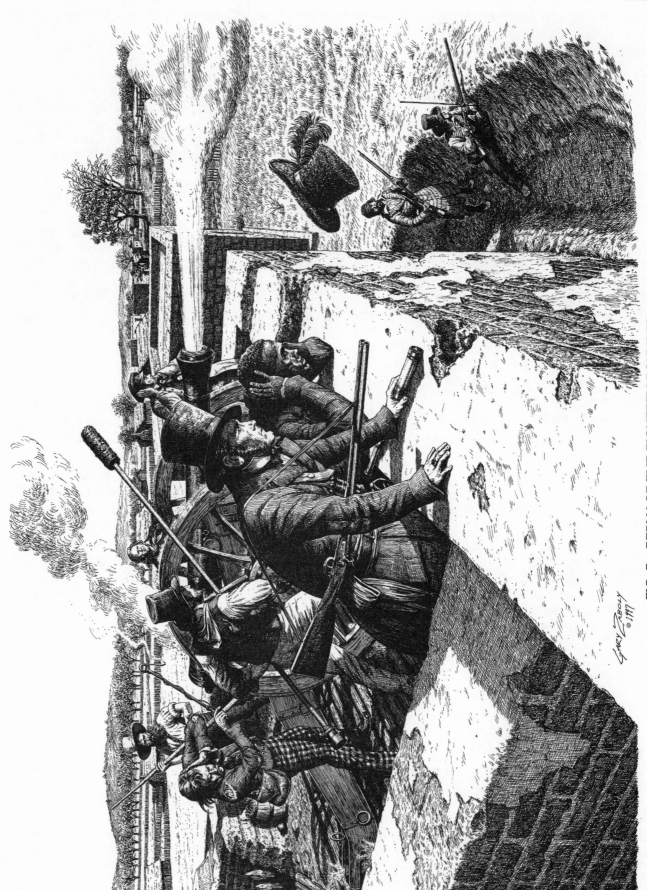

FIG. 7   REPLY OF THE EIGHTEEN-POUNDER

FIG. 7   REPLY OF THE EIGHTEEN-POUNDER

Late in the afternoon of February 23, 1836, the Alamo's eighteen-pound cannon, placed at the fort's southwestern corner, twice roared its contents at the Mexican Army as it entered and occupied San Antonio. The first round was fired after the enemy raised a red flag of no quarter on the tower of San Fernando Church; the second was ordered by Lieutenant Colonel Travis as an answer to Santa Anna's demand for unconditional surrender.

The iron-barreled eighteen-pounder was possibly the largest piece of ordnance in all the Southwest at that time, firing balls six pounds heavier than any gun with the Mexican Army. It had been shipped out of New Orleans in October of 1835, bound for Texas. At a stopover in the coastal town of Velasco, a blacksmith attached the barrel to a gun carriage equipped with wagon wheels.[1] The cannon finally arrived at San Antonio in December, following the surrender of General Cós' garrison.[2] Like most guns of its caliber, it probably had a length of nine feet and weighed in the vicinity of two tons.[3] However, the supply of cannonballs for all the Alamo guns was evidently insufficient for a protracted siege, judging by Travis' letter of March 3 to the president of the convention at Washington-on-the-Brazos, in which he requested, "without delay," "two hundred rounds of six, nine, twelve, and eighteen pound balls."

The illustration depicts the second firing of the eighteen-pounder on February 23. Lieutenant Colonel Travis, in foreground, wears only a sash around his overcoat as an emblem of rank (no evidence of his wearing a uniform during the siege has been found). His double-barreled shotgun hangs from one shoulder by a sling; over another is the belt of a shot pouch with twin dispensing tips. Next to him is his slave, Joe, who would survive the final battle and the next year run away from a second master.[4]

Nearly all of the men assigned to handle the Alamo guns were inexperienced in the service. In explaining the reasons for the eventual fall of the fort, Mexican Gen. Vicente Filisola noted that its defenders "did not have enough trained men to man the guns because good artillerymen cannot be just jumped up, as is done with rebellions."

In the scene, they are disposed somewhat according to the contemporary regulations of United States artillerymen: a man holding the straight sponge and rammer to the right of the barrel; the firer, holding a linstock with lit match; the gunner behind the barrel, holding a hand spike to maneuver the carriage; a man holding a priming wire (not seen) to prick the cartridge through the barrel vent; and the loader, who receives cartridge and ball from the gunner. If these were regular U.S. artillerymen, the firer would have his back to the gun, and the stances of all the men would be formal and rigid.

Just below the wall is a partially completed ditch in which two riflemen have been positioned to counter Mexican scouts or skirmishers approaching too closely. The standing man wears a hunting coat of ruffled calico, worn on the 1830s frontier almost as frequently as those of buckskin or linen.[5] (Travis kept picket guards outside the walls every night of the siege.)

About thirty feet south of the eighteen-pounder position stands a stone house that partially blocked the gun's field of fire in that direction. The house would also provide Colonel Morales' column with cover during the final assault on March 6. The huts of Pueblo de Valero stretch beyond it, and part of the Commerce Street bridge can be seen in right background.—GZ

E. Esparza

We had not been in there very long when a messenger came from Santa Anna calling on us to surrender. I remember the reply to this summons was a shot from one of the cannon on the roof of the Alamo. (*San Antonio Express*, May 12, 1907)

* * * *

One day Santa Anna demanded that the Texians surrender. Colonel Travis answered with a shot from one of the big cannons. Then Santa Anna ran up a blood red flag to the top of the tower of the Cathedral of San Fernando. Some one said that this

meant he would kill every one on the side of the Texians. The Texians did not seem to be excited. At night they would sing and dance. No fighting came for several days. (Driggs and King: 221)

* * * *

We heard that a messenger arrived from Santa Anna shortly after the window was closed behind us. He demanded unconditional surrender from the few men in the big, indefensible compound. Knowing that they could expect no mercy from the cruel general, the men in the Alamo replied with a shot from the cannon on the roof of the building where we had taken refuge. Santa Anna's answer was many cannon balls striking the walls of the church and convent. The exchange of shots, cheers, and jeers from men on both sides went on all night. The siege had begun. The date was February 23, 1836. (DRT Library, Alamo)

* * * *

Soon after the shot was fired I heard Santa Anna's cannon reply. I heard the cannon shot strike the walls of the church and also the convent. Then I heard the cannon within the Alamo buildings, both church and convent, fire repeatedly during the night. I heard the cheers of the Alamo gunners and the deriding jeers of Santa Anna's troops. (*San Antonio Express*, May 12, 1907)

Sutherland

On reaching the Salado River, my injured leg began to stiffen and to give me such pain that I thought of turning back and should have done so if Smith had not urged me on, believing that the enemy had by that time surrounded the fort, for a few minutes had passed since we had heard a cannon shot. After resting a moment and filling our gourds, bought from a Mexican whom we met for a dollar, we went on, continuing parallel with the road and about a mile from it. (Sutherland: 24)

Seguín

Santa Anna occupied the city of Béxar at about seven o'clock in the afternoon of the same day and immediately established the siege of the Alamo,

which at first was not rigorously kept as the sons of a widow named Pacheco, one of whom was named Esteban, took me my meals, and by them we were enabled to communicate with those citizens external to the Alamo.[62] (de la Teja: 194)

Almonte

In the night another small battery was made up the river near the house of [former governor] Veramendi.[63] I lodged in the house of Nixon, with Major [Fernando] Urissa and [Captain] Marcil [Miguel ?] Aguirre. An inventory of the effects taken was made, many curious papers were found. One John Smith, carpenter and cabinet maker, they say was the owner of the effects. I did not sleep all night, having to attend to the enemy and the property, the charge of which was entrusted to me; its value was about $3,000. (*SHQ* 48:16-17)

Beccera

The men laid on their arms during the night; and we fired one [cannon] shot which was answered by the Texians. Colonel [Acting General of Brigade Ventura] Mora was directed to take position north and east of the Alamo to prevent escape from the fort.[64] (Beccera: 18)

Yorba

When Santa Anna's army came they camped on the plains about the *pueblo* and a guard was put

---

62. Regardless of Mexican attempts it appears that the Texian line of communication remained open. Couriers and such went in and out of the mission the entire time with apparently little or no molestation.

63. The Veramendi Battery was the first Mexican artillery positioned for the siege. It must have been composed only of the two howitzers; the other six guns were still on the road to Concepción. The building backed against the San Antonio River, with a large yard area.

64. Mora was the commander of the cavalry. The mounted forces consisted of:

Dolores Cavalry Regiment	280
Vera Cruz Cavalry Squad	9
Tampico Cavalry	(?)
Coahuila Cavalry Company	30
Río Grande Presidial Company	50
Total	369

(Woolsey: 2:149-150)

The cavalry was split to cover the two most dangerous avenues for the Mexican Army. East were the Goliad and Gonzáles roads. To the north was the Old Mill Road. The Texians might either retreat or be reinforced on these routes.

about the Alamo fort. That was from the last day of February to March 4. (*San Antonio Express*, April 12, 1896)

Vargas

They camped in uncounted numbers, within the city, close to the Alamo and yet far enough away to escape the leaden hail which the Texians poured into them. (*San Antonio Light*, April 3, 1910)

Sutherland

After riding about sixteen miles, dark came upon us, when my pains now became so acute that I was forced to stop. We spread our blankets upon the ground, and ourselves upon them, and being somewhat relieved of my sufferings I was soon asleep. (Sutherland: 24)

E. Esparza

We slept little for the next twelve nights. Only 188 men, several slaves,[65] seven women and nine children had the hopeless task of delaying the Mexican army until Texians everywhere could rally to their aid. (DRT Library, Alamo)

---

65. The only documented African-Americans in the fort were Joe, who belonged to Travis, and John, who may have belonged to a local Anglo named DeSauque, or was possibly a free man. A possible third might be a Bettie. John died fighting. Joe later stated there were other Negroes besides himself in the Alamo. The Texians were generally Southerners and some were men of property and influence. For more on African-Americans who fought at the Alamo see Ron Jackson's "In the Alamo's Shadow," *True West*, February 1998.

1. Battery of two 8-pounders and a 5-inch howitzer begun early in the morning and finished in the afternoon.
2. Santa Anna reconnoiters the vicinity with the cavalry, at one point passing within musket shot of the Alamo.

DAY TWO

Wednesday
February 24, 1836

Prologue

THIS DAY BEGAN WITH each side attempting to organize the situation to its own benefit. The Mexican Army erected at least one more battery and conducted pre-combat inspections of the preferred companies as well as a detailed reconnaissance and topography.

The Texians found their well did not provide adequate water for the garrison. This forced them over the next several days to draw water from the eastern *acequia* or reservoir, leading to more skirmishes until the well could be improved. During the night the Texians sent out patrols and captured at least one *soldado,* and used him to help interpret Mexican movements. For the 24th, however, the Mexicans were content to prepare for combat and emplace artillery.

At some point Jim Bowie's illness entered its final stage. The garrison's surgeon referred to it as "a peculiar disease of a peculiar nature." Whatever it was—typhoid, tuberculosis, or some odd fever—Bowie collapsed entirely and turned complete command over to Travis. Travis' first act in command was to compose one of the more stirring pieces of American military literature. Of all his letters this one accorded the Texians the most recognition outside of Texas.

The idea of Texians leaving the Alamo and taking prisoners is interesting. At least one former Mexican *soldado* escaped execution on the final day claiming he was a Texian prisoner.

It is especially important at this point to examine each day by itself. The mechanics and effects of siege warfare take time to reevaluate.

de la Peña

On the 24th at nine o'clock his Excellency appeared and ordered that shoes be distributed in his presence among the preferred companies,[1] and that the frontal advance proceed immediately toward the Alamo and commence the firing, which had been interrupted the previous afternoon. A battery of two eight-pounders and a howitzer was properly placed and began to bombard the enemy's fortification. The enemy returned fire without causing us any damage. On this day, inventories were also taken of stock in the stores belonging to Americans.[2] At eleven, his Excellency marched with the cavalry in order to reconnoiter the vicinity. (Perry:39)

---

1. According to Filisola (Woolsey, 2:152), shoes were in short supply in the army. It makes sense that the preferred *cazadore* and *granadero* companies received resupply first. It further demonstrates their shortage by the fact that Santa Anna is personally supervising distribution. It is possible that these are not even issue items, but rather confiscated local inventories of various San Antonio cobblers and cordwainers.

2. This could be stock of Anglo businesspeople, i.e., Nat Lewis or John Smith.

San Luis Potosi

Location, Béxar. His Excellency S. E. [S. A.?] went out at nine o'clock in the morning. He oversaw the distribution of shoes to the preferred companies. Next, he led the advance to the Alamo and ordered [artillery] firing to begin—which had been suspended since the previous afternoon. A battery of two eight pounders and an howitzer were positioned and they began to batter the enemy fortification, which returned our fire; there were no misfortunes. The night before they [Texians] robbed from the battalion six pack mules.

We began to open up and inventory the contents of the American's stores. At eleven in the morning, His Excellency marched with the cavalry to reconnoiter the local [area]. (McDonald and Young: 2)

Yorba

Of course, I kept at home with my little boys and never stirred outside, for we women were all terribly frightened. Every eatable in the house, all the cows, lumber and hay about the place were taken by the [Mexican Army's] troops, but we were assured [by the *soldados*] that if we remained in the house no personal harm would come to us. (*San Antonio Express*, April 12, 1896)

Buquor

During the siege Mrs. Buquor says she and her family as well as the other citizens suffered severe hardships and were harshly treated by the Mexican [Army] soldiers from whom they had no protection. The Delgado family, consisting of her mother,

father, three sisters, four brothers and herself, she says was forced to give up their home, which is still standing on the river bank in the vicinity of the electric power house, to the Mexican soldiers. The members of the family sought refuge at the old [Jose Miguel] Arciniega home which stood on the street which now bears his name.[3] (*San Antonio Express*, July 19, 1907)

Vargas

I remember how they [Mexican Army] overawed all [of the *bexareños*], taking what they wanted with no thought of pay. They had come to suppress a rebellion and one way to do it was to take the worldly goods of the rebels. (*San Antonio Light*, April 3, 1910)

Almonte

Wednesday, very early this morning a new battery was commenced on the bank of the river, about 350 yards from the Alamo.[4] (*SHQ* 48:17)

Filisola

The day of the twenty-fourth we spent in reconnoitering the fortifications of the Alamo and the river crossings in order to prepare the operations that were to be taken in sequence until they overcame the colonists, adventurers or bandits that under such a mask had come from the United States to harass a friendly nation that had in no way offended them, which group now found itself shut up in the quarters of the Alamo.[5] (Woolsey, 2:170)

---

3. Arciniega was the former political chief of San Antonio (de la Teja: 75). The precise location of the home is unknown but Arciniega Street was the southernmost street in La Villita, next to the presumed ruins of the old Spanish military quartel.

4. This was the "river battery" and is the same one de la Peña described. The river battery was the first permanent battery the Mexican Army positioned and probably consisted of the Veramendi battery guns. Travis stated in his report on March 3, ". . . two howitzers (one a five and a half inch, and the other an eight inch) and a heavy cannonade from two long nine-pounders, mounted on a battery on the opposite side of the river, at a distance of four hundred yards from our walls. . . ." Navarro's map notes for this battery read ". . . one [battery] at the end of the city overlooking the [San Antonio] river and oriented to the west of the Alamo. It used an eight-pounder, a six pounder and a seven-pound [inch?] howitzer. They were at a distance of 200 *toesas* [approximately 400 yards] from the fort. . . ." On Navarro's map, however, he drew three cannon and one howitzer.

5. Santa Anna followed good military procedure and conducted reconnaissance to familiarize himself with the Area of Operations.

FIG. 8   THE BOMBARDMENT OF THE ALAMO

FIG. 8   THE BOMBARDMENT OF THE ALAMO

By March 3, according to Travis, "At least two hundred shells have fallen inside our works without having injured a single man." "Shells," in some accounts referred to as grenades, were essentially antipersonnel devices: hollow iron balls (from five and one-half to eight inches in diameter in the case of the Alamo siege, as reported by Travis), packed with black powder and lit with fuses. They were fired by howitzers or mortars which, unlike cannon, were angled for higher trajectories, thus allowing the shells to land and explode *behind* the walls of a besieged fort. Santa Anna's ordnance by March 3 included three howitzers[1]; the rest of his artillery were cannon, which threw solid shot of iron or brass directly against the perimeter walls to batter them down. These balls proved especially effective in demolishing considerable sections of the already fragile and ruinous north wall, forcing the Texian defenders to work night and day shoveling mounds of dirt against it to strengthen it.

Mexican Capt. José Juan Sánchez-Navarro later reported that the Texians had also dug trenches within the barracks and other buildings of the Alamo "to protect themselves from the shells and cannon balls of the artillery."[2] In fact, the defenders could walk casually about the compound only during breaks in the bombardment. The several Texians shown here, caught in the open during a particularly heavy shelling, seek whatever cover they can find in the sprawling compound, two of them crouching against a partially crumbled stone house along the west wall,[3] another man in the equally dubious shelter of the dry *acequia* that ran the length of the perimeter. Elsewhere, an earlier exploded shell has started a grass fire.

In the background stands the southernmost wall of the Texian fort, the low barracks building with its main gate; to the east, part of the log palisade can be seen, and directly to its left is the southwestern corner of the church, tricolor flag flying above. At far left, part of the tallest intact structure in the Alamo, the old convent building, is shown.[4]—GZ

Loranca

The bombardment was effectually commenced on the 27th [24th] of the same month. During this time the Mexican forces were joined by several bodies of infantry, making about four thousand men.[6] (*San Antonio Express,* June 23, 1878)

E. Esparza

The next morning after we had gotten in the fort, I saw the men drawing water from a well that was in the convent yard. The well was located a little south of the center of the square.[7] I don't know whether it is there now or not. (*San Antonio Express,* November 22, 1902)

Travis

To the people of Texas and all Americans in the world.[8] Fellow citizens and compatriots. I am besieged by a thousand or more of the Mexicans under Santa Anna—I have sustained a continual bombardment and cannonade for 24 hours[9] and have not lost a man. The enemy has directed a surrender at discretion, otherwise, the garrison are to be put to the sword, if the fort is taken. I have answered the demand with a cannon shot, and our flag still waves proudly from our walls—I shall never surrender or retreat. Then, I call on you in the name of Liberty, of patriotism and everything dear to the American character, to come to our aid, with all dispatch— The enemy is receiving reinforcements daily[10] and will no doubt increase to three or four thousand in

---

6. Loranca was only estimating the amount of *soldados* present and must be confused over the cannonade as well.

7. Later in the siege there were skirmishes over the *acequia* east of the Alamo; it is doubtful that this well provided enough water. The Texians finally built a second well. See map on page 122 for well locations.

8. This letter became the signal document of Texas' identification as more than a place or region of a continent. It was never voted on or passed into law, but it achieves the similar status of the United States Declaration of Independence. It, too, was not law, and like the U.S. Declaration of Independence, it identifies the American character.

9. Travis claimed the Mexican Army batteries never stopped firing during the night of the 23d, yet Mexican Army accounts disagree. The Mexican Army's cannon possibly let fly their four rounds or so over a long period of time to harass the Texians. Stretched over time and to the untrained ear this sounded like a "continual bombardment."

10. Travis probably saw, very early that morning, General of Brigade Ventura Mora returning with the artillery and *fusilero* companies from Mission Concepción. Unknown to Travis, these were not reinforcements but part of the same brigade. The first Mexican Army reinforcements arrived on March 3.

four or five days. If this call is neglected, I am determined to sustain myself as long as possible and die like a soldier who never forgets what is due to his own honor and that of his country—

VICTORY OR DEATH
William Barret Travis
Lt. Col. Com[man]d[an]t.

P.S. The Lord is on our side—When the enemy appeared in sight we had not three bushels of corn —We have since found in deserted houses 80 or 90 bushels and got into the walls 20 or 30 head of Beeves—Travis (*SHQ* 37:14)

Albert Martin

[Addition to Travis letter] To The People of Texas and All American send this to San Felipe by Express night and day since the above was written I have heard a very heavy cannonade during the whole day think there must have been an attack made upon the Alamo We were short of ammunition when I left hurry on all the men you can in haste.[11] (*SHQ* 37:307)

Alsbury

That during the siege of the Alamo she was ever ready to render and did render all the service she could towards nursing and attending upon the sick and wounded during said siege. . . . (Matovina: 33)

* * * *

Col. Bowie was very sick of typhoid fever. For that reason he thought it prudent to be removed from the part of the buildings occupied by Mrs. Alsbury. A couple of soldiers carried him away. On leaving he said: "Sister, do not be afraid. I leave you

with Col. Travis, Col. Crockett, and other friends. They are gentlemen and will treat you kindly."

She [Alsbury] says she does not know who nursed him, after he left the quarters she occupied, and expresses no disbelief in the statement of Madam Candelaria [that Candelaria was present during the siege]. "There were people in the Alamo I did not see." (Ford Papers: 122)

E. Esparza

Travis was a brave leader. He had been asked by Señor Bowie, who was ill, to take command.[12] Father would rather follow Bowie, because they were friends. I saw Señor Bowie while he was ill. The [Texian] soldiers let me go about among them. (Driggs and King: 221)

Almonte

It [the river battery] was finished in the afternoon, and a brisk fire was kept up from it until the eighteen-pounder and another [artillery] piece was dismounted.[13] The president reconnoitered on horseback, passing within musket shot of the fort.[14] According to a spy, four of the enemy were killed. At evening the music struck up, and went to entertain the enemy with it and some grenades.[15] In the night, according to the statement of a spy, 30 men arrived at the fort from Gonzàles.[16] (*SHQ* 48:17)

Saldana

One of the measures employed was that of constant alarms during the hours of the night. At intervals, when silence reigned over the Alamo and all was still in camp, the artillery would open, a great

---

11. Albert Martin carried Travis' letter and added his note to the back.

12. Until this date Travis and Bowie shared command. Apparently on the 24th Bowie succumbed to the final stages of his illness, generally believed to be tuberculosis or typhoid. This also explains his separation from the remainder of the garrison, and having his own *curandera*.

13. As this was the largest gun used in the siege, it makes sense for the Mexican Army to engage in counter-battery fire to dislodge it, especially if the gun had caused casualties the day prior.

14. Musket shot was close in work, about 100-150 yards.

15. Santa Anna throughout the siege used what today is called psychological operations. In an attempt to wear down his enemy, Santa Anna played music and bombarded the Alamo constantly. This sleep deprivation eventually affected morale and the Texians' will to resist.

16. Possible, though no other source mentions it.

shout would be raised by the besieging forces and this uproar, supplemented by volley of musketry, was intended to make the impression that a night assault had been planned, and also to make it appear to the beleaguered that their expected reinforcements, while trying to make their way into the Alamo, had become engaged with the enemy and were being destroyed. These continued—almost hourly—alarms throughout the night were supposed to keep every American in position ready to repel the attack, thus through loss of sleep and increasing anxiety unfitting him for the final struggle. (DeShields: 163)

E. Esparza

On the first night a company of which my father was one went out and captured some prisoners. One of them was a Mexican [Army] soldier, and all through the siege he interpreted the bugle calls on the Mexican [army] side, and in this way the Americans [were] kept posted on the movements of the enemy.[17] (*San Antonio Express,* November 22, 1902)

* * * *

One night father captured a Mexican [army soldier] who was prowling round, and kept him a prisoner. He was one of Santa Anna's soldiers. During the siege he would tell the Texians what the bugle call of the enemy meant. I heard that this poor fellow was afterwards killed because Santa Anna thought he was a deserter. (Driggs and King: 223)

Filisola

With this purpose in mind [to attack the next day] during the night two batteries were set up. . . . (Woolsey 2:170)[18]

Ortega

During the night of the 24th, two batteries commanding the Alamo were planted. . . . (DeShields: 156)

---

17. This statement suggests that some civilians were captured as well. A prisoner of the Texians makes sense, especially if the *Tejanos* captured him.

18. The batteries were probably the river and the La Villita battery. These supported the southern attack the next day. The number of cannon in the La Villita battery are problematic but probably contained the remainder of the Mexican Army's guns. In 1985-1986 a Mexican Army battery location was discovered just west of the intersection of E. Nueva and S. Alamo streets, near La Villita. From this location a battery would control the several road junctions, the west bank of the San Antonio River and the south wall of the Alamo. This earthwork could have been from either the Battle of Béxar or the Alamo siege. See Joseph H. Labadie's *La Villita Earthworks: A Preliminary Report of Investigations of Mexican Siege Works at the Battle of the Alamo.*

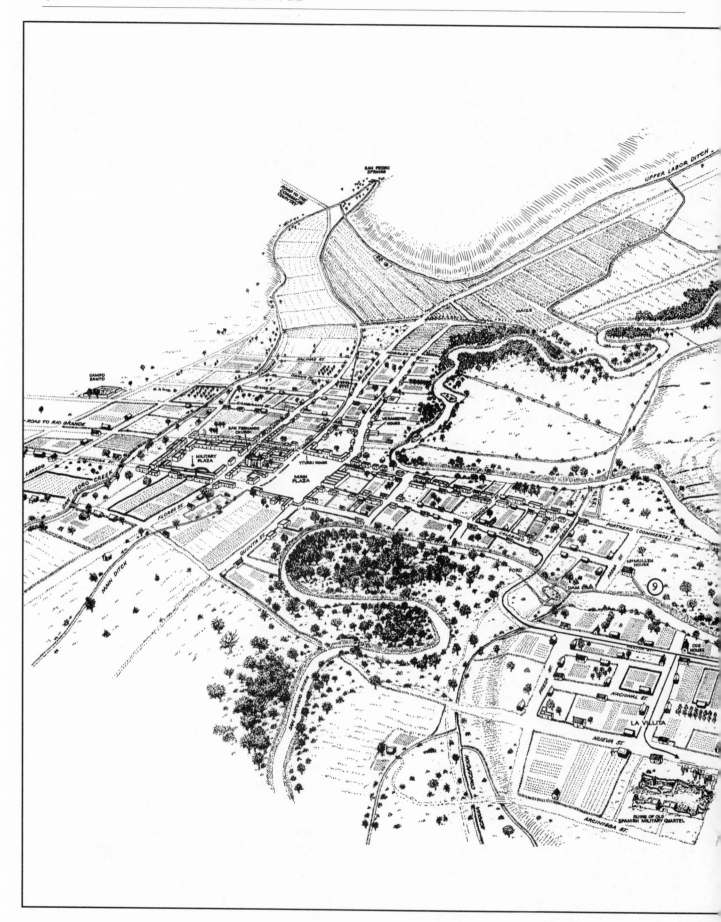

1. Three *cazadore* companies and the Matamoros Battalion attack through La Villita. Santa Anna personally directs the action.
2. Battery emplaced the previous night.
3A. 3B. Two entrenched camps built on the night of the 25th, occupied by the Matamoros Battalion.
4A. 4B. Cavalry posted on hills and roads to the east.
5. Texians burn huts closest to Alamo.
6. Repulsed Mexican charge, night of 25th.
7. Juan Seguín's escape route.
8. Nine deserters from the Alamo arrive at Mexican entrenchments.
9. Earthwork begun near McMullen house while La Villita attack was taking place.

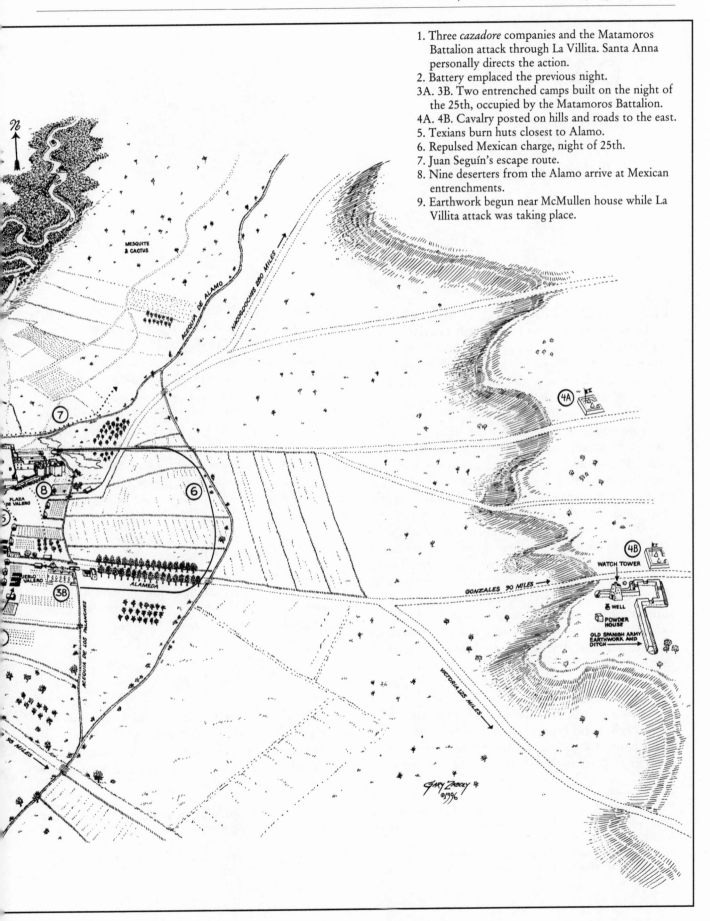

DAY THREE

Thursday
February 25, 1836

Prologue

THE 25TH OF FEBRUARY was an eventful day of the siege. Both forces were still confident but cautious. The siege, at this point, could have gone either way. The Mexicans attacked first with the task-organized battalion of *cazadores* and the Permanent Matamoros Battalion.

The attack position was in the vicinity of the river, probably between the river battery and the ford. The assault was personally commanded by General Castrillón with Santa Anna in the area. The column forded the river and attacked up through the *jacales* and outbuildings of Pueblo de Valero, apparently getting as close as fifty to one hundred yards.

While moving toward the Texian trenches the *soldados* discovered that some of the *jacales* were still occupied. In one they found a *señorita* and her mother. Santa Anna became enchanted with the *señorita* and arranged for a false marriage in order to consummate their relationship. The *soldados* were driven back from the pueblo into La Villita after about two hours, suffering light casualties. This engagement was not a victory for the Texians as it allowed the Mexicans to establish artillery and infantry entrenchments in both La Villita and the *alameda*.

During the fight the Texians dispatched men with torches and burned those buildings closest to the Alamo. Crockett was mentioned for the first time in dispatches. While holding no official posi-

tion his natural leadership abilities apparently caused men to look to him in times of need.

That evening a Texian council of war was held and Juan Seguín was dispatched to Houston with another plea for assistance. The Mexicans continued to improve and increase their positions.

The Alamo is generally famous only for its last ninety minutes; however, on the third day of the siege a 120-minute action was fought. This was an assault of two infantry battalions with artillery support. The Texians have not proven themselves too martial, but on this date they proved they could fight.

Ortega

. . . at dawn on the morning of the 25th these [cannon] opened fire on the garrison which in turn responded with vigor. (DeShields: 156)

de la Peña

On the 25th at nine-thirty his Excellency appeared at the [river] battery[1] and had the column of *cazadores* and the Matamoros battalion march to the other side of the river, he himself following.[2] Our

---

1. By this date there were at least three Mexican batteries in position, the Veramendi battery (one howitzer), the river battery 400 yards west of the Alamo in the bend of the San Antonio River (one howitzer, one 8-pounder and one 6-pounder) and the La Villita battery.

2. The column of *cazadores* indicates they were still task organized. The remaining six companies of the Matamoros Battalion bring the total number to nine companies for this attack, around 400-450 *soldados*.

soldiers fought within pistol range of the walls, and we lost two dead and six wounded. (Perry:39)

Caro

. . . His Excellency placed a battery of two cannon and a mortar within 600 paces of the fort [Alamo] and began a bombardment, taking possession at the same time of several small isolated houses that were to the left, [and south of the Alamo]. These were nearer to the enemy's position and were occupied by our troops who suffered the loss of several killed and wounded in the operation. Around the fortress there were ditches which were used by the enemy to fire upon our troops, while our soldiers, in order to carry out their [officer's] orders to fire, were obliged to abandon the protection the [jacale] walls afforded them, and suffered the loss of one or two men, either killed or at least wounded, in each attempt to advance. (Castañeda: 103-104)

San Luis Potosi

At nine-thirty o'clock His Excellency went to the [river] battery. He ordered the column of cazadores and the Matamoras Battalion to cross to our side of the river. While crossing, our soldiers were met [by] pistol fire from the [Texian] parapets. Epitacio Hernandez, [a] soldier from the 3rd [company], was wounded. (McDonald and Young: 2-3)

Almonte

Thursday—The firing from our batteries was commenced early. The General in Chief, with the battalion de cazadores, crossed the river and posted themselves in the Alamo—that is to say, in the houses near the fort.[3] A new fortification was commenced by us near the houses of McMullen.[4] In the random firing the enemy wounded four of the cazadores de Matamoros battalion, and two of the battalion of Jiménez, and killed one [fusilero] corporal and a [fusilero] soldier of the battalion of Matamoros. (SHQ 48:17-18)

Filisola

. . . the next day, the twenty-fifth, at dawn they [Mexican artillery] opened fire on the enemy parapets, which did likewise in the direction of our batteries.

The commander in chief, with the companies of cazadores from Jiménez and Matamoros crossed the river and took up a position in the houses and huts to the south of the Alamo about half a rifle shot's distance from the enemy parapets.[5] At the same time our men were digging a trench near Mr. [Mc]Mullen's house. In these operations, with the fierce fire from the enemy, we had one corporal and a cazadore from Matamoros killed, and four wounded, and two more wounded of those from Jiménez. (Woolsey, 2:170)

Beccera

The first movement was made by the Battalion Matamoros which crossed the river and took possession of some houses situated [south,] below the Alamo. Their mission was to collect timbers to build a bridge over the San Antonio River.[6] They were in charge of General Castrillón. The Texians fired on them. General Santa Anna and General Miñón went to the spot. During these operations an incident occurred not connected with military oper-

---

3. Houses near the fort were the jacales of Pueblo de Valero.
4. This was a supporting trench line for the river battery. On Navarro's map of the final assault he drew a large battery extending from the river bank to Portrero Street. This may have been the initial phase of a grand battery—all the cannon in one position. The 1836 McMullen house area is presently the location for the Hertzberg Circus Museum.
5. The Baker Rifle used by the cazadores was sighted at 200 yards. The "parapets" are the Texian trenchworks outside the walls. All the Mexican Army maps show some fortification, and from the accounts, the outerworks were manned.
6. Why, with a countryside full of woods and a town full of available lumber, would the Mexicans want to dismantle existing structures practically beneath the walls of the Alamo? There may have been several motives for the Mexican assault. Most probably it was for real estate instead of lumber. The Mexicans needed a lodgement on the Texian side of the river in order to establish siege operations. The main roads, either for ingress or egress, remained open to the colonies as well. After this date the Texians were fighting an encircling army and all roads were cut by the Mexicans by March 3. Entrenched encampments began this very night at the alameda and La Villita, followed shortly by several more.

FIG. 9　THE ATTACK FROM LA VILLITA

FIG. 9   THE ATTACK FROM LA VILLITA

"We will rather die in these ditches," wrote Col. James Bowie to Governor Henry Smith on February 2, 1836, "than give up this post to the enemy." In using the word "ditches," Bowie was not engaging in romantic symbolism, but referring to real conditions. Ditches and earthworks guarded more than a few streets within San Antonio de Bexar, as well as several exterior points, and they had been dug both inside and outside of the Alamo by General Cós' garrison in 1835. When the Texians occupied the latter post, they began to make additions and refinements; but their general unanxiety, and lack of sufficient manpower, made progress dangerously slow. Thus, by the time Santa Anna arrived—long before he was expected—on February 23, most of the Alamo's ditches and earthworks essentially still reflected the design and labor of Mexican Army engineers during the earlier campaign.

One such work was the lunette that extended for some sixty-five feet perpendicularly from the fort's south wall, covering the main gate. Evidence suggests that it was a five-sided structure, with embrasures for at least two cannon. Ingress and egress was obtained via an opening in its western side, with perhaps a rude draw-bridge (recalled by Enrique Esparza) lowered to cross the lunette's exterior ditch.

From the bottom of the ditch to the top of the lunette wall the measurement might have been over twelve feet high.[1] The width of the ditch was about nine feet, and its depth approximated five feet.[2] Extending eastward from the lunette ditch was a connecting trench just as wide but slightly shallower.[3] This stretched all the way to the chapel, forming an exterior ditch for the palisade breastwork.

These ditches bore the brunt of the Mexican attack on the morning of February 25. While Santa Anna had his engineers and artillerymen begin the construction of a battery position in the little suburb of La Villita, he sent forward a force of several hundred men, composed of the Matamoros Battalion and the detached companies of *cazadores.*

At the same time, the already established battery within the loop of the San Antonio River threw "balls, grape, and canister" (in Travis' words) against the Texian positions.

"Around the fortress," noted Ramon Caro, "there were ditches which were used by the enemy to fire upon our troops." Travis described this reply from the Alamo as "a heavy discharge of grape and canister . . . together with a well directed fire from small arms." This halted the Mexican advance, forcing the soldiers to take refuge within and behind the *jacales* of the little village. Caro says that they attempted to advance at least one more time, but were again stopped.

During the busy exchange of fire, according to Travis, "the Hon. David Crockett was seen at all points, animating the men to do their duty." Crockett had not participated in a battle for twenty-two years, but obviously the courage and spirit had not died in him. Nor had it died in Charles Despallier and Robert Brown, who sallied out to burn some of the huts shielding those enemy troops now within pistol range.

At the end of the affair the Mexicans drew back, having suffered, by most accounts, two dead and six wounded. Travis recorded that only "two or three of our men have been slightly scratched by pieces of rock." The skirmish heartened the small garrison, and made them proud, while Santa Anna had learned a lesson: he would never again attempt an advance in force during daylight hours. His next, and final assault, on March 6, would be in the form of a virtual sneak attack under cover of darkness.

The viewpoint of the illustration is from the connecting trench looking southward, through Plaza de Valero. A skirmish line of *cazadores* halts at the edges of the open space, trading fire with the defenders in their ditches. At right is the eastern wall of the lunette, and rushing along its ditch are men of the New Orleans Greys Company. While small arms crackle, the artillery of both sides roars and crashes. For many of the men involved this day marks their baptism of fire; and it proves to be a considerably hot, noisy, and turbulent little engagement, a testing ground for the uglier, supreme clash less than ten days away.—GZ

ations, which will be referred to in another place. (Beccera: 18-19)

Travis

Letter from William B. Travis to Maj. Gen. Sam Houston:

HEADQUARTERS, FORT OF THE ALAMO: Sir, on the 23rd of Feb. the enemy in large force entered the city of Béxar, which could not be prevented, as I had not sufficient force to occupy both positions. Colonel Batres, the Adjutant-Major of the President-General Santa Anna, demanded a surrender at discretion, calling us foreign rebels. I answered them with a cannon shot, upon which the enemy com-

menced a bombardment with a five inch howitzer which, together with a heavy cannonade,
has been kept up incessantly ever since. I instantly sent express to Colonel Fannin, at Goliad, and to the people of Gonzáles and San
Felipe. Today at 10 o'clock A.M. some two or
three hundred Mexicans crossed the river below
and came up under cover of the houses until
they arrived within virtual point blank shot,
when we opened a heavy discharge of grape and
canister on them, together with a well directed
fire from small arms which forced them to halt
and take shelter in the houses about 90 or 100
yards from our batteries. The action continued
to rage about two hours, when the enemy retreated in confusion, dragging many of their
dead and wounded.

During the action the enemy kept up a constant bombardment and discharge of balls,
grape, and canister. We know from actual observation that many of the enemy were wounded,
while we, on our part, have not lost a man. Two
or three of our men have been slightly scratched
by pieces of rock but have not been disabled. I
take great pleasure in stating that both officers
and men conducted themselves with firmness
and bravery. Lieutenant [Cleveland Kinloch]
Simmons of cavalry acting as infantry, and
Captains [William R.] Carey, Dickenson and
[Samuel] Blair of the artillery, rendered essential
service, and Charles Despallier and Robert
Brown gallantly sallied out and set fire to houses which afforded the enemy shelter, in the face
of enemy fire.[7]

Indeed, the whole of the men who were
brought into action conducted themselves with
such heroism that it would be injustice to dis-
criminate. The Hon[orable]. David Crockett
was seen at all points, animating the men to do
their duty. Our numbers are few and the enemy
still continues to approximate his works to ours.
I have every reason to apprehend an attack from
his whole force very soon; but I shall hold out to
the last extremity, hoping to secure reinforcements in a day or two. Do hasten on aid to me as
rapidly as possible, as from the superior number
of the enemy, it will be impossible for us to keep
them out much longer. If they overpower us, we

fall a sacrifice at the shrine of our country, and
we hope posterity and our country will do our
memory justice. Give me help, oh my country!
Victory or death!

> W. Barret Travis
> Lt. Col. Com[manding] (*SHQ* 37:28)

Filisola

Our fire ceased in the afternoon with the conclusion of the movements that had been decided
upon for the moment by the commander in chief.
The latter, wishing to step up the action of the taking of the Alamo, that same day issued the . . . order
to General Gaona, commander of the first infantry
brigade. (Woolsey, 2:170-171)

E. Esparza

I remember Crockett. He was a tall, slim man,
with black whiskers. He was always at the head. The
Mexicans called him *Don Benito*.[8] The Americans
said he was Crockett. He would often come to the
fire and warm his hands and say a few words to us in
the Mexican language. I also remember hearing the
names of Travis and Bowie mentioned, but I never
saw either of them that I know of.[9] (*San Antonio
Express,* November 22, 1902)

* * * *

Crockett seemed to be the leading spirit. He
was everywhere. He went to every exposed point
and personally directed the fighting. Travis was
chief in command, but he depended more upon the
judgement of Crockett and that brave man's intrepidity than upon his own. Bowie, too, was brave and
dauntless, but he was ill. Prone upon his cot he was
unable to see much that was going on about him and
others were too engrossed to stop and tell him. (*San
Antonio Express,* May 12, 1907)

---

7. The Texians deduced that the pueblo provided a great deal of cover for the *soldados*, and, by burning the *jacales*, denied the
soldados cover and cleared the fields of fire.

8. According to the *Velasquez Spanish and English Dictionary*, *Benito* is the term for a Benedictine friar. Why Crockett would
be called *Benito* is unknown. Possibly he was attempting to "go native" and introduced himself by what he thought was his name in
Spanish. Perhaps Crockett resembled a local priest.

9. The challenge of using accounts recorded years after the fact involves issues such as this. Esparza mentioned both of these
men several times in numerous accounts. Conflicting remembrances cast doubt on all the Esparza interviews.

* * * *

Then came the days of terrible fighting. It was all so frightful—but what could one do except just watch and wait.

Señor Crockett seemed everywhere. He could shoot from the wall or through the portholes. Then he would run back and say something funny. He tried to speak Spanish sometimes. Now and then he would run to the fire we had in the court yard where we were to make us laugh. (Driggs and King: 223)

* * * *

I heard the few Mexicans there call Crockett *"Don Benito."* Afterwards I learned his name was David, but I only knew him as *"Don Benito."* (*San Antonio Express*, May 12, 1907)

Dickenson

I heard him [Crockett] say several times during the eleven days of the siege, "I think we had better march out [of the Alamo] and die in the open air; I don't like to be hemmed up!"[10] (Morphis: 175)

E. Esparza

After the first day there was fighting every day. The Mexicans had a cannon somewhere near where [then Quinta] Dwyer Avenue now is and every fifteen minutes they dropped a shot into the fort.[11] (*San Antonio Express*, November 22, 1902)

* * * *

One thing that frightened me was the cannon the Texians brought. They placed these big guns on top of the thick walls and pointed them every way. The noise they made was terrible to me.

Santa Anna had many men and much "thun-der." I mean powder. The Indians called it "thunder." A man told my mother he was like a king with much power and many servants. It was said he ate from plates of silver and gold. I could not believe that, but I have read from books it is true. He was very proud. He said that the Texians could not get away from him. A Mexican woman told this to the men at the Alamo. (Driggs and King: 220-221)[12]

* * * *

The Mexican soldiers had been drafted to fight, forced to march in freezing winds for four hundred miles. They needed a foe on whom to vent their anger and frustration. Cannon balls pounded the fort for days with little effect. Texian sharpshooters were picking off Mexican soldiers with disconcerting regularity. (DRT Library, Alamo)

Beccera

During the operations preparatory to the storming of the Alamo I mentioned that the battalion Matamoros was under fire while collecting timbers for a bridge, and that Generals Castrillón, Miñón, and Santa Anna went to them. General Castrillón was in charge of the battalion[s], and directing the work. Many of the timbers were taken from houses. The General entered a house, and found a lady and her daughter. The girl was beautiful. The General asked the mother what she was doing there and if she was not afraid. She told him it was her home, and she had no other place to go; that she was not afraid. She was well bred and intelligent, though poorly clad.

General Castrillón related what had happened to the president. Santa Anna was in a great fever to see the pretty girl. He told General Castrillón he wanted her, and asked him to carry a message to her mother. Castrillón replied that he was ready to obey any legitimate order coming from General Santa

---

10. This whole passage has been about Crockett. There is no evidence that these thoughts or events about him took place this day. Travis mentioned him in his letter as being "animating" and perhaps this is the way the rest of the garrison noticed Crockett as well.

11. There was no identifiable battery there. However, it was the location Juan Díaz gave for the artillery park. An artillery park was basically an administrative or marshaling area for the guns. Perhaps this was where Esparza remembered seeing cannon, or when he stole glances over the walls he saw parked limbers and caissons.

12. There is continuing evidence of this "woman" or "spy" who appeared and reappeared on either side of the walls. Apparently, Esparza did not know her or he would have stated her name.

FIG. 10   SANTA ANNA'S CONCUBINE

FIG. 10   SANTA ANNA'S CONCUBINE

The poorer citizens of San Antonio lived in *jacales,* huts of various sizes and composition but most often made of standing mesquite logs and the roof made of bundles of prairie grass tied to a framework of poles. In South Texas, they were generally twelve feet wide by eighteen to twenty-four feet long, and fifteen feet high at center, sometimes with one or two windows, and sometimes without any. The floor was either naked packed earth, or covered with grass.[1]

Early in the siege of the Alamo, Santa Anna took possession of the small collection of *jacales* and adobe huts east of the city proper, across the San Antonio River, traditionally called La Villita. The *jacales* provided the Mexicans with ready-cut timbers, mainly for use in the construction of a military bridge. Evidently many of the huts had been abandoned at the outset of the siege. In one, however, Gen. Manuel Fernandez Castrillón and Col. José Miñón discovered the widow of a Mexican soldier, and her beautiful daughter. Despite the skirmishing and exchanges of cannon fire in the neighborhood, the two women would not leave, the mother asserting that "she was not afraid."

Though he informed Santa Anna of the attractive daughter, Castrillón demurred from being a party to any romantic intrigues of his commander; thus Colonel Miñón was appointed the go-between. The mother refused to allow her daughter to enter into any relationship with Santa Anna unless it was marriage. Machiavellian to the core, the *generallissimo* (already married though he was) arranged a fraudulent ceremony conducted by an impostor priest. The new young "wife," according to Sergeant Beccera, "in due course of time became the mother of a son."—GZ

Anna, as the president of Mexico and the commander-in-chief of the army, but in that particular case he begged to be excused, and requested the President to employ someone else.

General Santa Anna commanded the lady and her daughter to be taken to his quarters; and General Miñón executed the order. He delivered Santa Anna's message to the mother. She replied that she was a respectable lady of good family, and had always conducted herself with propriety; that her deceased husband was an honorable man, and commanded a company in the Mexican service; that President Santa Anna was not her president, and could not get her daughter except by marriage. She was not only inflexible, but defiant. Miñón reported accordingly. He informed Santa Anna he had a man in his command who was well educated, a great rascal, and capable of performing all sorts of tricks, even the impersonating of a priest. The man was sent for and was ready to do the bidding of His Excellency. He went to a priest and, in the name of General Santa Anna, President of Mexico, asked for and received vestments and all also necessary to celebrate a nuptial ceremony according to the rites of the Roman Catholic Church.

The obsequious pseudo-priest consented to solemnize the marriage in General Santa Anna's quarters. The wedding took place late in February. The honeymoon lasted until the army marched for the Guadalupe River. The deceived and trusting girl was sent to San Luis Potosi in the carriage of General Miñón. She was placed in the care of a very respectable family. In due course of time she became the mother of a son. I do not know when she ascertained that General Santa Anna was already a married man and the father of a family, and that she had been made the victim of a foul and rascally plot. The information came too late, yet its effects must have been crushing upon the unfortunate girl. (Beccera: 25-27)

Alsbury

She says the name of the girl General Santa Anna deceived by a false marriage was [———]. (Ford Papers: 124)[13]

Buquor

During the siege, Mrs. Buquor says she saw General Santa Anna many times and she bears testi-

---

13. This sounds amazing, but there must be a ring of truth to it if a noncombatant inside the Alamo knew of it. But what's more, the family must have still been prevalent in ante-bellum Béxar to have the name stricken from the Ford Papers.

FIG. 11   THE REPULSED ATTACK

FIG. 11   THE REPULSED ATTACK

Almost nothing is known of the Mexican attempt against the "rear of the fort" on the third night of the siege, except for Travis' mention of it in his letter to Jesse Grimes dated March 3. Travis noted that the attackers were "received gallantly by a discharge of grape shot and musketry, and they took to their scrappers immediately."

Travis' idea of the "rear" of the Alamo is problematic: it might refer to the north wall, or to the corrals on the east, both tempting targets because of their comparatively low heights. Since most Mexican activity taking place on February 25 in the form of skirmishing, entrenching, encamping and patrolling, was to the south and east of the fort, it is to be assumed that "rear" applies to the east, as shown in the illustration.

Elements of the Matamoros Battalion might have been sent against the two corrals, whose walls probably stood in places as low as six feet and in others no higher than ten. The northern corral, used as a cattle pen, has often been depicted as walled by pickets rather than stone or adobe. It must be remembered, however, that the maps of both Sánchez Navarro and Labastida show this as a stone wall, as does the Jameson plat and index. The U.S. Army plans of 1846 and 1848 also indicate that this wall had been built of stone (by then it was demolished).

According to Navarro, the Texians had gun emplacements in the northeastern corners of both corrals, on platforms perhaps as low as a foot high, and firing through embrasures to the north and, it is to be presumed, the east. (Labastida indicates one gun only, firing "barbette"—over the walls).

A discharge of deadly, scattering grapeshot, accompanied by volleys of small arms, evidently was sufficient to discourage further attempts that night against this sector. There is no list of Mexican casualties, if any indeed had been suffered.—GZ

mony to his well known penchant for amours in that she related how he seized a young girl living near her home and held the maiden captive during his stay in the city. (*San Antonio Express*, July 19, 1907)

Almonte

Our fire ceased in the afternoon. In the night two batteries were erected by us on the other side of the river in the *alameda* of the Alamo—the battalion of Matamoros was also posted there,[14] and the cavalry was posted on the hills to the east of the enemy, and in the road from Gonzáles at the Casa Mata Antigua.[15] At half past eleven at night we retired. The enemy, in the night, burnt the straw and wooden houses in their vicinity, but did not attempt to set fire with their guns to those in our rear.[16] A strong north wind commenced at nine at night. (*SHQ* 48:17-18)

San Luis Potosi

The division had two dead and six wounded from the night they put up the [breast] works to cover the line that was put in the billet by orders of Colonel Morales. (McDonald and Young: 2-3)

Travis

[Letter from March 3] . . . You have no doubt seen my official report of the action of the 25th ult. in which we repulsed the enemy with considerable loss; on the night of the 25th they made another attempt to charge us in the rear of the fort,[17] but we received them gallantly by a discharge of grape shot and musketry, and they took to their scrappers[18] immediately. (*SHQ* 37:24-25)

---

14. This was an entrenched encampment. By positioning an infantry battalion in the *alameda* the Mexican army effectively controled the road to Gonzáles and the colonies.

15. The slaughter house. This was an old building next to the Powder House Hill.

16. This was most likely another trip to destroy more cover for the Mexicans. The houses in the rear must mean those houses that protected the La Villita battery.

17. This appears to have been another attack by either the cavalry or the Matamoros Battalion. The eastern area of the Alamo battlefield was the most fought over. There was an *acequia* and a small reservoir. This could have been an early attempt by the Mexicans to control this water resource.

18. Does "scrappers" mean "scarppers" as in "escarpments"? Escarpments were the front slopes or glacis of fortifications.

Seguín

On the 28th [25th] the enemy commenced the bombardment, meanwhile we met in a council of war, and taking into consideration our perilous situation, it was resolved by a majority of the council that I should leave the fort and proceed with a communication to Colonel Fannin, requesting him to come to our assistance. I left the Alamo on the night of the council. [19] (de la Teja: 107)

* * * *

Finding ourselves in such a desperate situation, Colonel Travis resolved to name a messenger to proceed to the town of Gonzáles and ask for help, thinking that Sam Houston was then at that place. But, as to leave the fortification at such a critical moment was the same as to encounter death, Santa Anna having drawn as it were a complete circle around the Alamo, no one would consent to run the risk, making it necessary to decide the question by putting it to a vote; I was the one elected. Colonel Travis opposed my taking this commission, stating that as I was the only one that possessed the Spanish language and understood Mexican customs better, my presence in the Alamo might become necessary in case of having to treat with Santa Anna. But the rest could not be persuaded and I must go. I was permitted to take my orderly, Antonio Cruz [y Arocha], and we left at eight o'clock at night after having bid good-bye to all my comrades, expecting certain death. (de la Teja: 194)

* * * *

He [Seguín] was shut up in the Alamo by the encircling lines of Santa Anna's army, and was the fourth and the last messenger sent out by Travis for aid,[20] Major Red [John W. Smith] being the only [other] one so sent whose name he could recall. The message was verbal, directing Col. Fannin, at la Bahia, Goliad to us, to march to his rescue. His egress from the beleaguered Alamo was under friendly cover of darkness, and was accompanied by great danger as the fort was entirely surrounded.

Bombs were bursting all around. However, he made his way stealthily through the Mexican lines on foot, and often upon all fours. A horse was provided at a ranch. . . . (de la Teja: 191-192)

Cruz y Arocha

Colonel Juan Nepomeceno Seguín escaped from the Alamo [during] the night by the *acequia*. Cruz was waiting for him with a horse from a *jacale* [on the] west side in front of the church. (Matovina: 27)

E. Esparza

Captain Seguín was also sent for help. I saw him go. The way I remember was he rode *Señor* Bowie's horse. We were afraid he could not get by Santa Anna's soldiers. They were getting closer and closer to the Alamo. Afterwards I heard that the Captain was stopped by them, but he said he was a Mexican rancher. This was true; and they let him go. (Driggs and King: 221)

de la Peña

During the night some construction was undertaken to protect the line that had been established at la Villita under orders of Colonel Morales.[21] (Perry:39)

Filisola

During the night two trenches were constructed adjoining the houses located in the cottonwood grove of the Alamo for the infantry.[22] The Matamoros battalion was established in them for their defense, and the cavalry posted itself on the hills to the east of the fort on the road to the town of

---

19. The council was on the 25th, not the 28th. Only the true volunteer spirit of North America would try to resolve military affairs via committee.

20. Untrue. The last known courier from the Alamo was James Allen on March 5 or 6. See Lord's *A Time to Stand*, p. 205.

21. The Mexicans withdrew from the assault on the pueblo but occupied the La Villita area along with the *alameda*.

22. This was the *alameda*.

Gonzáles and in the vicinity of the former *Casa Mata*. This operation was completed at eleven-thirty at night, and during that time the enemy burned the hay and the wooden houses that were near them or within their reach; a brisk norther blew up. The Alamo from then on was surrounded by our troops, with only the north side open. (Woolsey, 2:171)

Ortega

A brisk fire was maintained by both sides during the day until late in the evening firing ceased and a deep silence fell upon the town and fortress. During the night, two entrenchments were constructed along the *alameda* of the Alamo and, while details of men were working on these entrenchments, nine men came over from the fortress and asked to be conducted into the presence of Santa Anna. As the General was asleep at that hour and no one cared to disturb his slumbers these men were held under guard until morning. These men spoke Spanish sufficiently fluent to make their wants known[23] . . . but it is well attested that they told . . . where fifty American rifles had been left in town by Travis' men, besides other belongings, all of which were seized by the Mexicans. (DeShields: 156)

Santa Anna

Fifty rifles of the rebel traitors of the North, have fallen in our possession, and several other things, which I shall have delivered to the general commissary of the army as soon as it arrives, so that these forces may be equipped, and the rest will be sold and the proceeds used for the general expenses of the Army. (Chariton: 279)

---

23. Interesting. This sounds as if they were Anglo defenders.

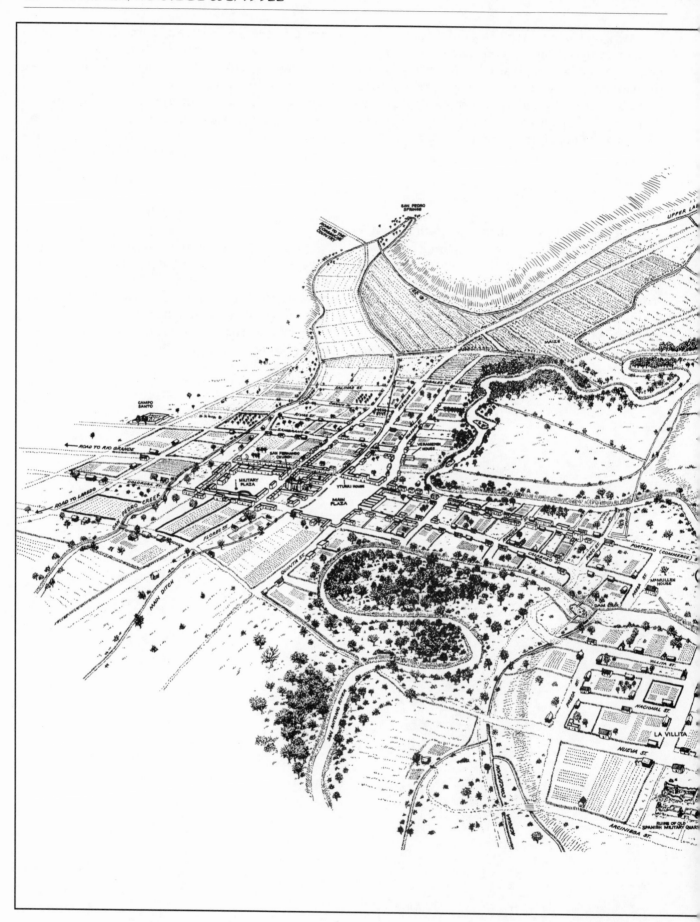

1. Early morning skirmish.
2. Texians sally for wood and water.
3. Matamoros Battalion sent to assist in guarding approaches to east and north.
4. Small work begun above the Alamo.
5. Texians sally out at night to burn more huts and attempt to obtain wood and water.
6. Colonel Bringas' advance and retreat.

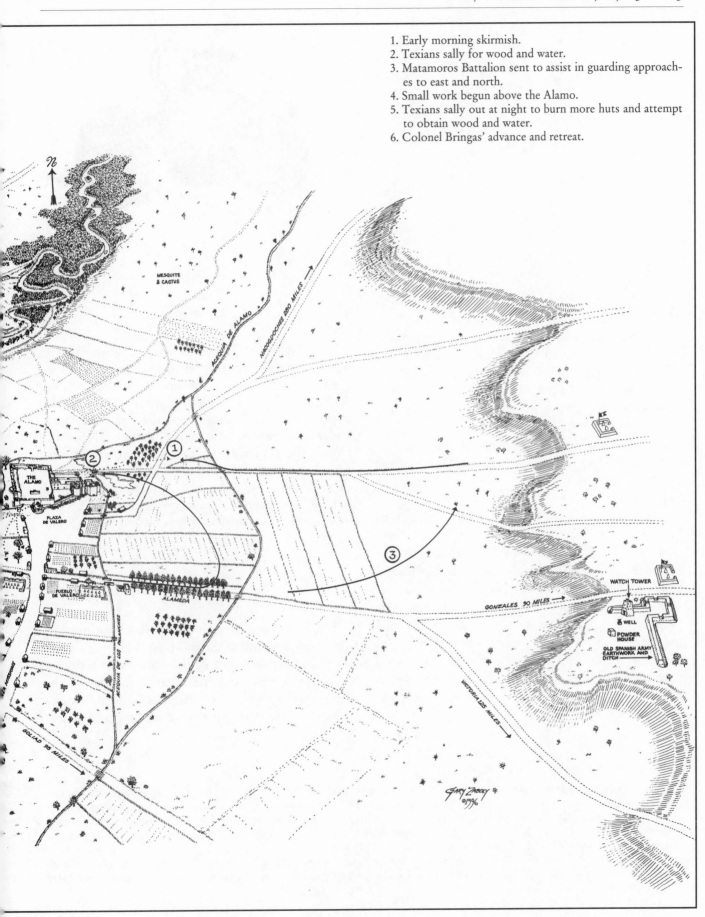

DAY FOUR

Friday
February 26, 1836

Prologue

A NORTHER BLEW IN. The garrison water situation worsened and precipitated a skirmish in the early hours near the *acequia* east of the Alamo. The Texians were repulsed and a larger battle started as a result. *Soldado* casualties were a little worse than before. This was probably due to the four cannon the Texians had oriented east en barbette.

During the evening the Texians again tried to gather water from the *acequia*. The riflemen of the provisional *cazadore* battalion kept the Texians at bay.

At this point in the siege it becomes difficult to believe that the Texians weren't suffering any casualties. At the end of the fourth day three separate skirmishes/battles had already occurred. The legend of the Texian sharpshooter with his rifle versus the Mexican with his twenty-five-year-old import is probably reversed. The *cazadore* battalion carried the best military rifle of the day, and it is doubtful that the average colonist, who was a farmer, mechanic, or businessman long before he was a soldier, carried anything other than a shotgun or smoothbore musket.

Almonte

Friday—The Northern wind continued very strong; the thermometer fell to 39 degrees, and during the rest of the day remained at 60 degrees. At daylight there was a slight skirmish between the enemy and a small party of the division of the east, under command of General [Ramírez y] Sesma.[1] During the day the firing from our cannon was continued. The enemy did not reply, except now and then. . . . In the course of the day the enemy sallied out for wood and water, and were opposed by our marksmen.[2] The northern wind continues. (*SHQ* 48:18)

Filisola

On the twenty-sixth the norther continued to blow strongly, and in the morning there was a small skirmish between some of the enemy that ventured outside the walls and the advance sentries of the eastern line under the command of General Ramírez y Sesma. Our artillery fire continued, and it was

---

1. General of Brigade Ramírez y Sesma appears to have commanded both the task organized battalion of *cazadores* and the cavalry at least during this portion of the siege. This attack was possibly to further develop any successes that were made during the previous night. Initially the Texian lines extended outside the walls, and Sesma might have been directing a series of shaping attacks to force all the defenders into the box. Or possibly the two attacks on the 25th and those on the morning of the 26th were merely sorties to test for weakness in the Alamo defense.

2. The well does not seem to have been providing enough water for the garrison; otherwise the Texians would not be challenging the Mexican pickets over water. The skirmishes that are developing between Sesma and the Alamo could only be over water.

FIG. 12   THE NORTHER OF FEBRUARY 26

FIG. 12   THE NORTHER OF FEBRUARY 26

Texian sharpshooters posted atop the cement-floored *convento* roof take a midday break to drink a little of the Alamo's dwindling coffee supply. They need the warmth: beginning last night and continuing all day a cold norther has blown, plummeting the temperature. The wind chill factor has made it feel even colder to the exposed riflemen, who often sleep at their posts.

One man at left wears an India-rubber overcoat, a garment of fairly recent invention designed for foul weather. In 1834, David Crockett himself was presented with a gift of an India-rubber hunting coat when he visited a Massachusetts factory specializing in items, from shoes to cloaks, made by this process.[1]

The seated man to his left wears a blanket coat, a very common garment on the Texas frontier, often worn by rangers. A blanket has also been used to make a guncase for the rifle at far left. The standing man has belted and draped a Mexican *serape* around him, much as an eastern Indian would wear his match-coat blanket.

The jagged, uneven parapet of the convent roof averaged thirty-three inches in height. Sandbags, and ox hides filled with earth, have been piled up along the top of it to protect the men from Mexican rifle bullets. Despite popular depictions of the siege, the men of the garrison were only rarely seen by Santa Anna's army; sniping was proving hazardous to both sides.

Beyond the corner of the convent roof stands the Alamo church, with part of the flagpole that rises from its southwestern corner; and extending to the right of it is the palisade of stakes and earth that protect the inner courtyard. The abatis of fallen trees lies just outside the palisade.

In middle distance are the ruins of several *Tejano* huts, burned the night before in the Texians' daring sally, as well as one of the still-standing huts that will also be torched in another sally on the night of the 26th.

Beyond the huts, over 250 yards from the Alamo, is the cottonwood-lined *alameda,* and nearby is one of the two entranched camps built by the Mexican Army the previous night to house and protect the Matamoros Battalion.

At far left is Powder House Hill, with its prominent *garita,* where another Mexican detachment would soon be posted.—GZ

---

answered only by a shot now and then from their guns. (Woolsey, 2:171)

Becerra

The next day two companies were sent to make a reconnaissance. They went within range of the deadly [Texian] rifle[s]; thirty *[soldados]* were killed within a few minutes.[3] General Castrillón requested General Santa Anna to withdraw them, if he wished to save any of their lives; the order [to withdraw] was given. The main body of the army was still on the south [west] side of the river, but the battalion Matamoros [at the *alameda*] was still under fire. The Texians kept up a steady fire [on us] all day, with little effect.

That night the battalion Matamoros was sent to reinforce Colonel Mora, and to more effectively cover the approaches north and east of the Alamo. They were replaced by Colonel Romero's command.[4] A small work was commenced above the Alamo. (Beccera: 19)

Filisola

During the night they [Texians] burned some other straw huts that were built against the [Alamo] walls and tried to obtain water and some wood. They were prevented from doing so by our advance sharpshooters.[5] (Woolsey, 2:171)

---

3. This was part of Ramírez y Sesma's dawn skirmish. Thirty deaths hardly seems likely; however, if the Texian batteries in the rear of the chapel found their mark, it could have been devastating.

4. The battalion was moved further east and north to reinforce the cavalry. This could have been in the vicinity of the Nacogdoches Road. Colonel Romero *was* the Matamoros Battalion's commander; it doesn't make much sense for him to have replaced himself. Becerra may be confusing the Matamoros Battalion under Romero with the *cazadore* battalion under Morales.

5. The Baker rifle was finding its mark.

FIG. 13   MORNING SKIRMISH IN THE EAST

FIG. 13   MORNING SKIRMISH IN THE EAST

In the cold morning of February 26, a number of Texian defenders made a sally beyond the walls, possibly to obtain wood and water, as Almonte noted another sally they would make later that day. In the morning venture they were confronted by "a small party," in Almonte's words, of soldiers of General Sesma's division. No doubt a number of the defenders covered the wood and water gatherers while they went about their work, although how successful they were is not known. Mexican riflemen would have countered the Texian rifles, perhaps from surrounding brush, ditches, or the orchard lying northeast of the fort, just beyond the ponds. Mexican cavalry might have made a charge to help drive the defenders back into their compound.

The Mexican accounts are slightly conflicting. Sergeant Becerra tells of two companies of Santa Anna's men sent within rifle range of the Alamo, on a reconnaissance, of which thirty were killed by Texian fire. Filisola says that Mexican advance sentries were the ones engaged. The germ of the truth no doubt lies hidden somewhere in all this testimony.—GZ

Almonte

At night the enemy burnt the small houses near the parapet of the battalion of San Luis,[6] on the other side of the river. Some sentinels were advanced. (*SHQ* 48:18)

---

6. This battalion may have been in La Villita entrenchments.

Caro

During one of our charges at night, His Excellency ordered Colonel Juan Bringas to cross a small bridge with five or six men. He had no sooner started to carry out his instructions than the enemy opened fire upon this group and killed one man. In trying to cross the bridge, the colonel fell into the water and saved himself only by a stroke of good luck. (Castañeda: 104)

FIG. 14   THE BURNING OF THE *JACALES*, FEBRUARY 26

Though members of the Alamo garrison had sallied out during the Mexican attack of February 25, setting afire some of the *Tejano* huts Santa Anna's soldiers had intended to use for cover, many more had not been burned. That night Travis launched another hut-burning operation; and did so again the next night. The results of the latter attempt are not entirely clear, however.

Filisola states that the Texians "burned some other straw huts that were built against the walls"; Almonte records that they "burnt the small houses near the parapet of the battalion of San Luis."

The position of the latter "parapet" (probably one of the "entrenched encampments" Travis noted in his March 3 letter) is not precisely known, either. One conclusion is that it was located near the junction of Nueva Street and the road to the lower missions.[1] An archaeological excavation in the early 1980s found an L-shaped ditch here, unearthing both military and civilian debris.[2] If this indeed was part of the San Luis "parapet," the sally was a very bold one, taking the Texians some 600 yards beyond the Alamo's south wall, as well as past the Mexican trenches, and possibly batteries, along the *alameda*. The sally might have been made after the Matamoros Battalion was removed from their *alameda* trenches that very same night, and before the trenches were reoccupied by other units.

Ramon Caro reported that a squad of Mexican soldiers made a charge across a small bridge in the night, and were turned back by Texian fire. This could have been either the Commerce Street bridge, or the smaller plank bridge by the dam—both within range of a Texian sally against La Villita.

The scene depicts a rifleman, in foreground, pouring priming powder from a small horn into the touch hole of his weapon, while next to him a musketman fires in the direction of the river. A corral wall, made of mesquite logs held by upright posts, serves as a handy breastwork. In middleground the roof of a *Tejano* hut is set fire to; such a hut, made of plank, stone, logs and straw, was one of many types painted by later San Antonio resident Theodore Gentilz.[3]

Some of the Texians in the sally might have been mounted, as shown here. Alamo couriers arrived and left on horseback; the Gonzales contingent, entering the fort on March 1, were entirely mounted. It is to be supposed that a sally requiring speed and surprise would certainly benefit from at least some of its number riding out.—GZ

FIG. 14   THE BURNING OF THE *JACALES*, FEBRUARY 26

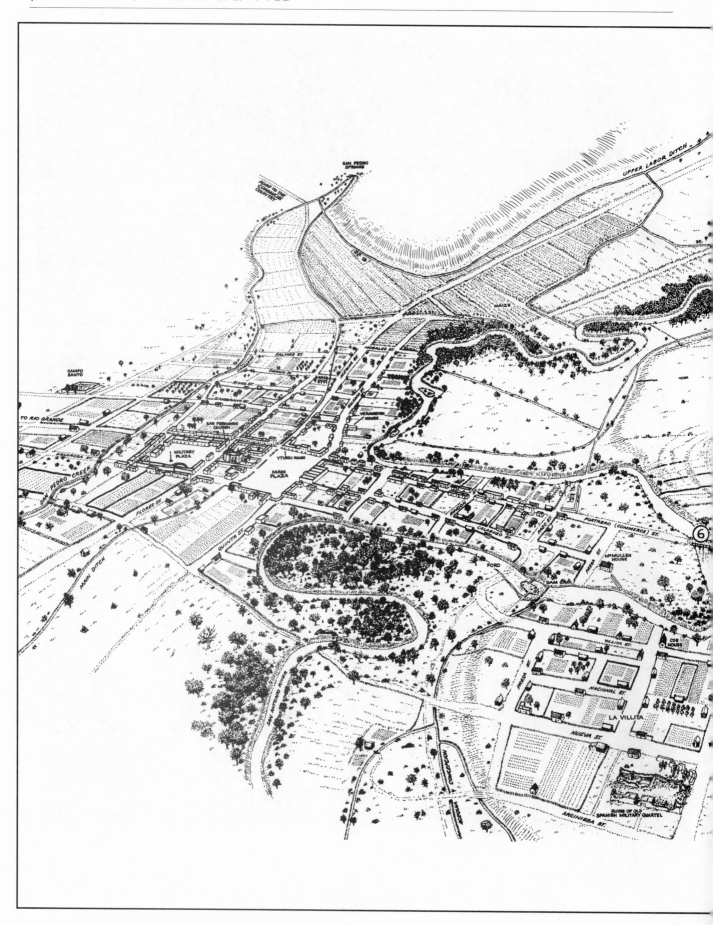

1. Mexican forage party sent to *ranchos* of Seguin and Flores.
2. Matamoros Battalion reoccupies *alameda* entrenched camps.
3. Abortive attempt to cut off water supply to Alamo ditch.
4. Small work built nearer to the Alamo, on the ditch.
5. Reconnoitering presidial troopers fired upon.
6. Colonel Bringas' advance and retreat.

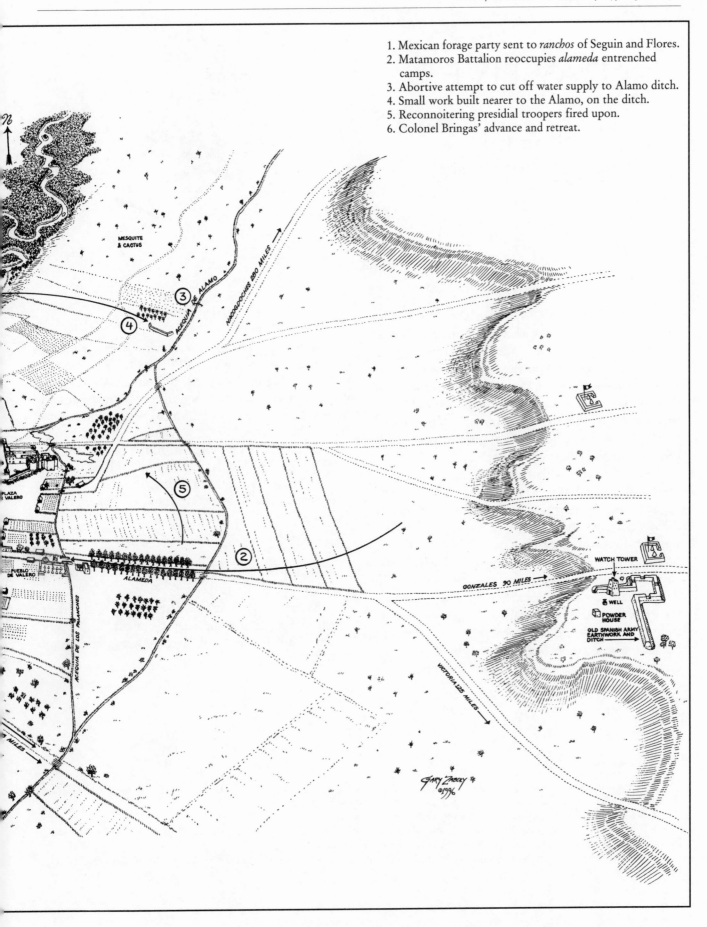

DAY FIVE

Saturday
February 27, 1836

Prologue

THE MEXICAN ARMY began the 27th as the Texians had on the 23d, with a search for provisions. The town was diminished and perishables were in short supply. Foraging details were sent out to local *Tejano ranchos* to obtain them. The skirmishes over the eastern *acequia* came to an end with the water flow cut off by the Mexican Army north of the mill on the San Antonio River. The Texians would have to make do with their well water.

The Matamoros Battalion was repositioned to the south of the Alamo. Once back in La Villita they began work again on the entrenchments. Santa Anna inspected them after completion and found the fortifications unsatisfactory. Work continued on the position through the night. The Texians discovered the working party and kept fire on them all day. General Gaona received Santa Anna's orders of the 25th to send three battalions as quickly as possible to Béxar. He did not forward any siege artillery because Santa Anna had not requested it. Santa Anna sent reports to Mexico City announcing his conquest of Béxar.

Almonte

Saturday—The northern wind was strong at day break, and continued all the night. Thermometer at 39 degrees. Lieutenant Manuel Menchacho was sent with a party of men for the corn, cattle and hogs at the *rancho*[s] of [Erasmo] Seguín and [Francisco] Flores [de Abrego y Valdes].[1] It was determined to cut off the water from the enemy on the side next to the old [Zambrano] mill.[2] There was little firing from either side during the day. The enemy worked hard to repair some entrenchments.[3] (*SHQ* 48:19)

E. Esparza

At first we got our water from the ditch in front of the Alamo.[4] Later the enemy cut off this supply and we had to use an old well. (Driggs and King: 222-223)

* * * *

---

1. These *ranchos* neighbored each other and were some miles south and east of San Antonio (Jackson: 18). Foraging began on the fifth day. Interesting is their choice of rebel *Tejano* Seguín's *rancho* for the supplies.

2. He must mean that portion of the Alamo *acequia* nearest the mill.

3. These were Texian fortifications outside the Alamo, on the south and possibly the east side. It is difficult to imagine the Mexican siege guns being devastating enough to damage the interior breastworks.

4. By front he must mean west. Ramírez y Sesma's forces in the east must have forced the Texians to begin using the western branch of the *acequia*.

When we got into the Alamo, which was before access to the ditch had been entirely cut off by the soldiers of Santa Anna, such occurrence had been foreseen and forestalled by the inmates of the Alamo chapel. They had already sunk a well in the church and the water therefrom was then being drunk by the occupants instead of the water from the ditch. (*San Antonio Express*, May 19, 1907)

Beccera

The next day the battalion Matamoros was sent to reoccupy position in front of the Alamo. Various movements were made in succession, brisk skirmish fighting occurred, the Texians were invested, and losses were inflicted on the Mexican army. When the small work was finished and inspected it did not suit the commanding General.[5] He ordered another to be constructed nearer the Alamo, under the supervision of General Amador.[6] (Beccera: 19)

Filisola

On the twenty-seventh there was some fire from both sides, and Lieutenant Menchaca of the Presidio [de Río Grande] guard was dispatched with a [foraging] party to the ranches of Seguín and Flores to obtain corn, cattle and hogs. An attempt was made to cut off the water to the rebels on the side of the old mill, but that was not possible. It was noted that they were working incessantly on opening up a ditch on the inside of the parapet with the intention of enlarging it and giving more resistance against our artillery. However, this operation was more harmful than useful to them. Since they had no walkway it was necessary for them on the day of the assault to stand up on it in order to fire with their guns, and thus they presented an immense target for our fire. In the afternoon the enemy became aware of the presidio group as they reconnoitered the points of the line and the opened fire upon it. (Woolsey, 2:171)

Beccera

The [*soldado*] working party took advantage of the night to commence. The Texians discovered them and kept up a heavy fire on them all night. They completed the little fort in due time. Fire was opened from it upon the Alamo. (Beccera: 19)

Filisola

During the night the [Mexican] government was advised of the capture of the city [of San Antonio] in the terms that are included here. That same day General Gaona in Charco de la Peña received the [President's] order of the twenty-fifth to advance with the three battalions mentioned there, and these were immediately put on forced march to Béxar. (Woolsey, 2:171)

Santa Anna

[Letter from] Antonio López de Santa Anna to D. Vicente Filisola, second in command.

GENERAL HEADQUARTERS OF Béxar: On the 23rd of this month I occupied this city after some forced marches from the Río Grande, with General Joaquín [Ramírez] y Sesma's division composed of the present battalions of Matamoros and Jimínez, the active battalion of San Luis Potosi, the regiment of Dolores, and eight pieces of artillery.

With speed in which this meritorious division executed its marches in eighty leagues of road, it was believed that the rebel settlers would not have known of our proximity until we should have been within rifle shot of them; as it is they only had time to hurriedly entrench themselves in Fort Alamo, which they had well fortified, and with a sufficient food supply. My objective had been to surprise them early in the morning of the day before but a heavy rain prevented it.

---

5. Since the Matamoros Battalion was originally posted in the La Villita vicinity, "front" as used here is interpreted as south of the Alamo, back in La Villita. Santa Anna apparently wanted La Villita battery moved closer to the Alamo. For whatever reason, he was hesitant to move any more infantry on the east side of the river. Possibly he may have needed to use the remaining battalions to secure his line of communication west toward Presidio del Río Grande.

6. General of Brigade Juan Valentin Amador, Cuban born and a former Spanish Royalist officer, was one of the many general grade staff officers with Santa Anna. Amador wrote Santa Anna's final order for the attack on March 6.

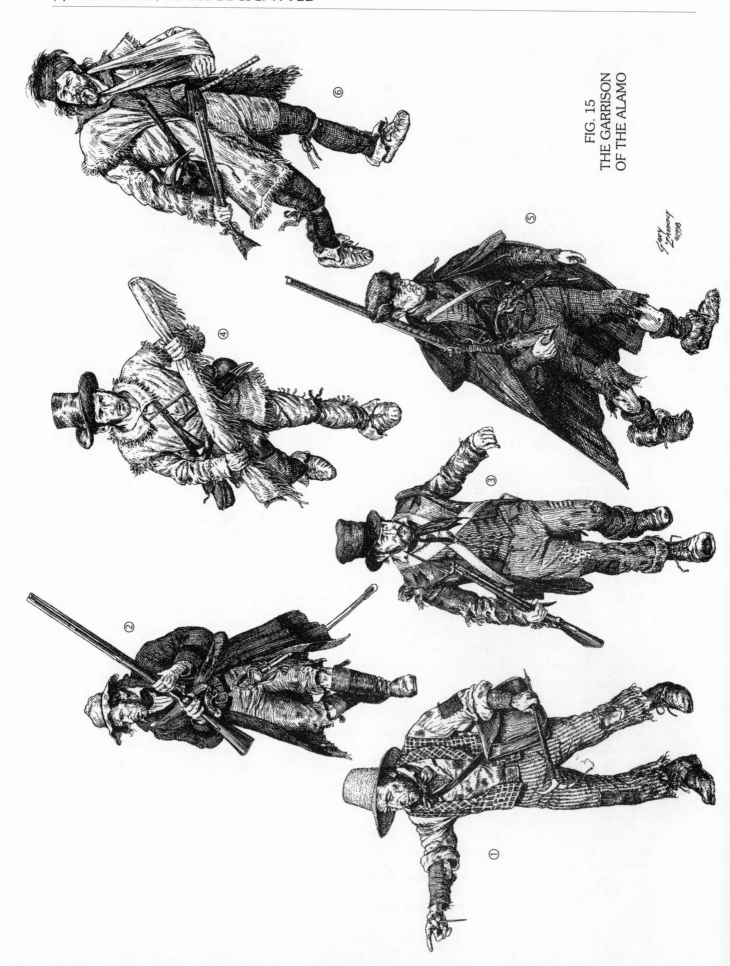

FIG. 15
THE GARRISON
OF THE ALAMO

FIG. 15   THE GARRISON OF THE ALAMO

1.) **Gunner**—Nineteenth-century artillerists were trained to fire cannon with understrength crews. At the Alamo, the condition already existed long before Santa Anna arrived. This gunner has the dual duty of ventsman and firer. With the priming wire hooked over his right thumb he pricks a hole into the rammed powder bag, through the cannon's vent. From his pouch he then takes a priming tube—in essence a quick fuse—and inserts it into the vent. Finally, he fires the gun with the lit length of match attached to the fork of his linstock. His attire is all civilian, from his high-crowned straw hat to the muddy brogans on his feet, but his belt plate is of United States Artillery issue. A relic of such a plate has been found at the site of a Mexican Army camp, occupied during the post-San Jacinto retreat from Texas. This suggests that it had been an item of plunder, taken from either the Alamo or Goliad.

2.) **Cavalryman**—Lack of funds kept the "regular" Texian cavalry un-uniformed during the course of the Revolution. Extended outdoor wear was the alternative: a blanketcoat, as shown here, of grey, green or white; a hunting shirt of linen or buckskin; or a sturdy roundabout jacket. This private also wears a narrow-brimmed felt hat and buckskin breeches that have shrunk several inches from his shins due to constant exposure to wet and cold weather. A black cloth neckstock and leather riding boots give him a pseudo-military appearance. He no doubt considered himself lucky to own a saber; and his gun was double-barreled, a favored weapon of horsemen. A double shot belt hangs from his right shoulder, and a pistol is carried in his waistbelt.

3.) **Musketman**—A volunteer from either Texas itself or one of the United States, this man carries a Mexican Brown Bess musket captured the year before at San Antonio, as well as its companion cartridge box and bayonet. Otherwise he is a true citizen soldier, wearing a battered tall hat, tail coat, single-breasted waistcoat, broadfall trousers, and brogans. Although the rifle was the preferred weapon of many revolutionists, bayonets were considered more effective arms in the face of Mexican cavalry. In fact, in the years following San Jacinto, muskets became the standard arm of the infantry of the Republic of Texas.

4.) ***Tejano Ranchero***—Based primarily on the visual evidence found in a ca. 1828 eyewitness drawing of a "Ranchero de Texas" by Lino Sanchez y Tapia, this *Béxareño* native wears a fringed buckskin shirt, tall hat with upturned brim, and carries his rifle in a fringed buckskin case. William Bollaert, in San Antonio in 1843, observed that they also wore—while herding cattle and horses, or hunting deer, buffalo, or mustangs—leggings and Indian moccasins. At San Jacinto, one of Juan Seguin's men was reported to have killed twenty-five Mexican soldiers with his Bowie knife (*Richmond Enquirer*, July 1, 1836). Generally, *Béxareño* men of this period considered full mustaches and beards unfashionable.

5.) **New Orleans Grey**—From a number of eyewitness accounts one can conclude that one or both companies of New Orleans Greys entering Texas in late 1835 came dressed in grey jackets and pants (arguably surplus fatigue clothing of the United States Army, purchased in merchant shops of New Orleans), cloaks, and sealskin caps (and perhaps a number of U.S. Army forage caps). They were armed primarily with rifles, pistols, and Bowie or butcher knives, though some probably carried muskets. Accouterments included bullet pouches or cartridge boxes, powder horns, canteens, and knapsacks. Sealskin caps, with the fine inner fur left on, were highly water-resistant, and are generally depicted in nineteenth-century art with brims and ear flaps. This private has resorted to cutting his pants to patch his campaign-ravaged uniform. His worn-out shoes are long since thrown away, replaced now with crude, undressed oxhide moccasins.

6.) **Backwoodsman**—Buckskin hunting shirts were not uncommon on the early white Texas frontier. They appear in descriptions of settlers, rangers, hunters, tree cutters, and some militiamen. In fact, buckskin was even considered very stylish attire, with many Texian men appearing at weddings and other social occasions in elaborately fringed outfits. Unlike most of his comrades, however, this Alamo defender is a real "decivilized" woodsy, accustomed to wearing hunting clothes much of the time. A poor emigrant from rougher parts east of the Sabine, he has long since accustomed himself to the wild and variegated landscape of Texas. His trousers, like his shawl-caped hunting shirt, are also of buckskin, but his plain shirt is of red flannel. Indian leggings of wool protect his legs from thorns and underbrush, and simple deerskin moccasins cover his feet. A handkerchief is worn turban-style on his head, like many southeastern Indians. He carries a small squirrel rifle, a tomahawk in his sash, a powder horn and bullet pouch, and a patch knife in a sheath on the latter's strap.—GZ

Nothwithstanding their artillery fire, which they began immediately from the indicated fort, the national troops took possession of this city with the utmost order which the traitors shall never again occupy; on our part we lost a corporal and a scout dead, and eight wounded. When I was quartering the corps of the division a bearer of the flag of truce presented himself with a paper, the original which I am enclosing for your Excellency, and becoming indignant of its content I ordered an aide, who was nearest to me, to answer it, as it is expressed by the copy that is also enclosed.

Fifty rifles of the rebel traitors of the north, have fallen into our possession, and several other things, which I shall have delivered to the general commissary of the army as soon as it arrives, so that these forces may be equipped; and the rest will be sold and the proceeds used for the general expense of the army.

From the moment of my arrival I have been busy hostilizing the enemy in its position, so much so that they are not even allowed to raise their heads over the walls, preparing everything for the assault which will take place when at least the first brigade arrives, which is now sixty leagues away. Up to now they still act stubborn, counting on the strong position which they hold, and hoping for much aid from their colonies and from the United States, but they will soon find out their mistake. After taking Fort Alamo, I shall continue my operations against Goliad and the other fortified places, so that before the rains set in, the campaign shall be absolutely terminated up the Sabine River, which serves as the boundary line between our republic and the one of the north. . . . God and Liberty. (Chariton: 279-280)

Filisola

Since the supplies that had been brought from Río Grande by the first division were about to be exhausted, the commander in chief sent the following communication to General Filisola who was with the rear guard of the army. (Woolsey, 2:171)

Santa Anna

[Letter] Antonio López de Santa Anna to D. Vicente Filisola, second in command.

GENERAL HEADQUARTERS OF Béxar: Most Excellent sir: In a separate note your Excellency will see the state of the first division facing the enemy and the need that there is for Your Excellency to order that the army brigades march with all haste since up to this time they are moving very slowly.

Your Excellency will give orders to the quartermaster general to gather together all supplies and set out on the march, avoiding delays that would be prejudicial to the service of the nation since these troops are very short on supplies.

Your Excellency will also have sent forward under escort and with forced marches the payroll with the commissary, for there is urgent need for money.

With the money Your Excellency will also arrange to send two packs of salt since there is not a single grain here, and it is greatly needed.

I charge Your Excellency to work efficiently and diligently, which is your wont to do, so that these orders may be carried out as all of them are urgent.

God and Liberty.

General Headquarters in Béxar.

February 27, 1836.—Antonio López de Santa Anna.—His Excellency Don Vicente Filisola, second in command of the army of operations. (Woolsey, 2:172)

E. Esparza

While I was walking around about dark I went near a man named Fuentes who was talking at a distance with a [Mexican?] soldier. When the latter got nearer he said to Fuentes, "Did you know they had cut the water off?"[7]

The fort was built around a square. I remember the main entrance was on the south side of the large

7. Antonio Fuentes was one of the *Tejanos*. Quite possibly Filisola was incorrect and the Mexicans were successful in cutting the water off to the Texians. At any rate, the Texians believed the Mexicans had accomplished it.

enclosure. The quarters were not in the church, but on the south side of the fort, on either side of the entrance, and were [in] part of the convent. There was a ditch of running water [in] back of the church and another along the west side of Alamo Plaza. We couldn't get to the latter ditch as it was under fire and it was the other one that Santa Anna cut off. (*San Antonio Express*, November 22, 1902)

Almonte

In the night a courier extraordinary was dispatched to the city of Mexico, informing the Government of the taking of Béxar and also to Generals [José] Urrea, Filisola, Cós and Vital Fernandez. No private letters were sent. (*SHQ* 48:19)

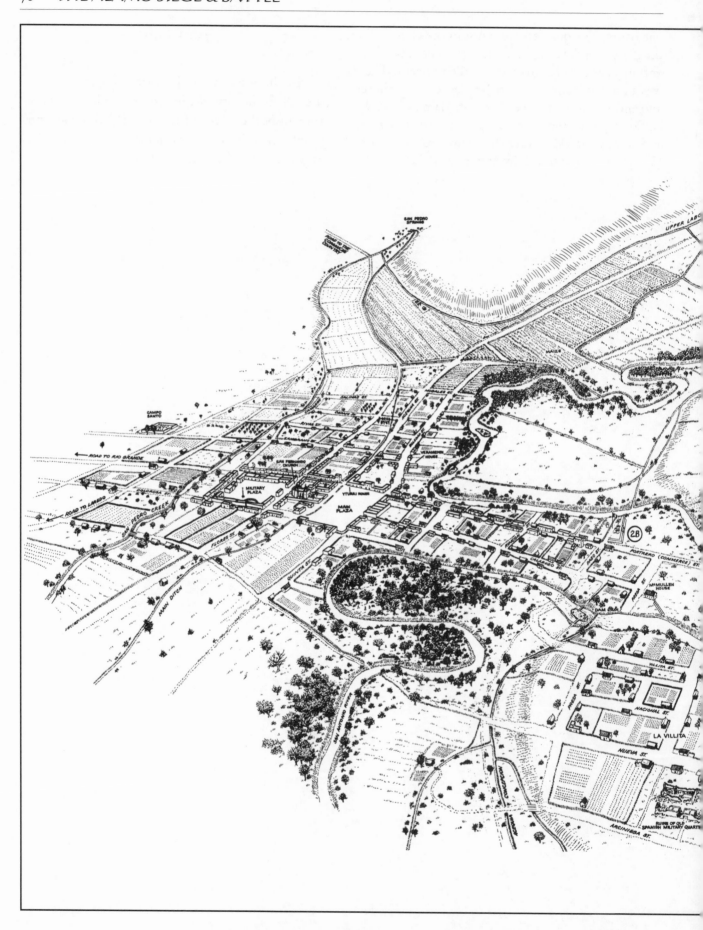

1. News received by Mexicans of Texas reinforcements coming from Goliad.
2A. 2B. 2C. Mexican batteries continue firing all day.

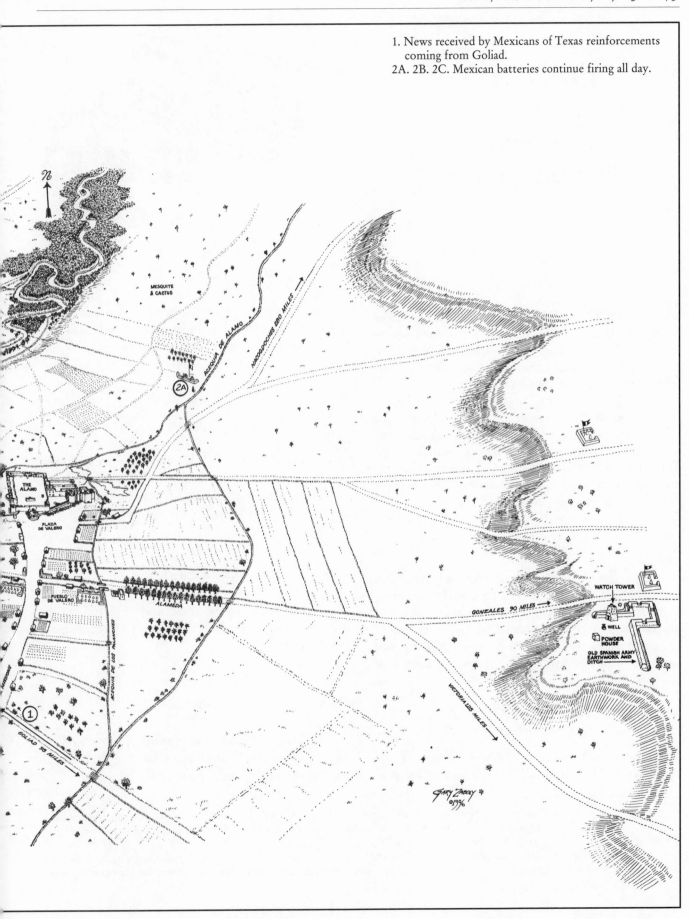

DAY SIX

Sunday
February 28, 1836

Prologue

RUMORS AND INTELLIGENCE informed the Mexican Army that 200 Texian reinforcements were en route from Goliad. The *soldados* prepared to meet them. The siege continued. Crockett conducted his famous concert with the fiddle.

According to the original plan the Texian forces from Goliad were to join the garrison at the Alamo around March 1. Fannin made an abortive attempt to reinforce the Alamo garrison on February 27 but turned back. It appears that his advance guard made it as far as the Cibolo River crossing and remained there until March 3.

Santa Anna

The self-styled "General," Samuel Houston, said to the celebrated Travis, in a letter we intercepted: "Take courage and hold out at all risks, as I am coming to your assistance with two thousand men and eight well-manned cannon." We did not hesitate to take advantage of this information that fell into our hands. (Crawford: 51)

Almonte

Sunday—The weather abated somewhat. Thermometer at 40 degrees at 7 A.M. News was received that a reinforcement to the enemy was coming by the road from la Bahia, in number 200. It was not true.[1] The cannonading was continued. (*SHQ* 48: 19)

Filisola

On the twenty-eighth news was received that two hundred men from Goliad were due to arrive to aid those against the Alamo, and the cannon fire continued all day long. (Woolsey, 2:172)

Candelaria

Crockett played the fiddle, and he played it well, if I am a judge of music. (*San Antonio Light*, February 19, 1899)

Dickenson

Colonel Crockett was a performer on the violin, and often during the siege took it up and played his favorite tunes.[2] (Morphis: 174-175)

---

1. There were columns en route to the Alamo, both from Gonzales and Goliad. The Goliad column eventually turned back except possibly for their advance guard. For more on this see Jakie L. Pruett and Everett B. Cole, Sr., *Goliad Massacre: A Tragedy of the Texas Revolution.* There may have been more columns than are now known.

2. The only evidence for this concert is the Long Barracks' museum at the Alamo. As part of the display a very brief day-by-day outline describes the siege and on this date the music was supposed to have occurred. No other source for the concert on the 28th has been located.

FIG. 16
THE SOLDIERS OF
SANTA ANNA

FIG. 16   THE SOLDIERS OF SANTA ANNA

1.) **Presidial Trooper**—Most contemporary depictions of Mexican presidial troopers in the late 1820s show soldiers attired in formal uniforms of blue-faced red or grey pantaloons, and wearing low-crowned black hats with wide bands of white. Lino Sanchez y Tapia's ca. 1828 watercolor, however, painted on the spot in Texas, reveals a somewhat different dress for a presidial on actual frontier field service. His dark blue jacket has red facings, but it sports three vertical rows of white metal buttons instead of just one. He seems to be wearing blue breeches rather than pantaloons, and fringed leather "botas" cover his shins. His hat is black with a high crown. Like a Texas *ranchero,* a fringed gun case protects his rifle, carbine, or short musket. No cartridge box *bandolier* is seen in Sanchez's rendition; instead the trooper probably carried his ammunition in a waistbox hanging in front. Also like a *ranchero,* a quirt would have been a necessity for a long patrol across the prairie.

2.) *Soldadera*—An untold number of women had followed Santa Anna's army into Texas: wives, mistresses, mothers, sisters, amateur nurses, prostitutes. They were an unofficial auxiliary corps in themselves, attending to a host of duties, from mending clothing to preparing meals; and many of them tugged their children along. They also had to be *lavanderas* (laundresses) and not long after the Battle of the Alamo one *lavandera,* probably washing the blood from a *soldado*'s uniform, spotted a Texian survivor hiding under a small bridge. She reported him to the nearest soldiers, and he was summarily executed.

3.) **Pioneer, Sapper Battalion**—The sappers *("zapadores")* were specialist troops trained as miners (i.e., trench, battery, and fort builders), pontooners (bridge-builders), and pioneers (men assigned to clear the trail of obstructions in advance of a marching army). How professional the sappers were in the Texas campaign is not fully known, though de la Pena, one of their officers, spoke highly of them, as did Santa Anna (de la Pena: 13, 44). In the Alamo assault they also served as pure soldiers, part of the reserve force sent in to buttress the other columns. This soldier, in marching kit, belongs to the battalion's pioneer company. An apron of white or buff leather covers his uniform. He wears a pragmatic barracks cap instead of the usual sapper's shako with its red brush pompon. Short gaiters prevent mud and pebbles from getting into his shoes. He carries a pioneer's felling axe, but remains armed with a musket (its muzzle protected from the rain with a stopper of fringed colored wool) and either a short sword or a sapper's machete. Black facings with red piping often distinguished Mexican sappers. Their epaulettes were red, and pants medium blue with a red stripe on each side.

4.) **Fusilier, Activo Battalion**—A private of one of the Active Militia battalions, he wears the 1832 dark blue contract tailcoat with front red lapels and facings, and white trousers. Yellow raquettes and cords on his shako mark him as a fusilier, as does the long tricolor (or in some cases red) pompon. His musket is an English import: a Brown Bess Indian Pattern model dating from the Napoleonic wars. Six fusilier companies were included in each Mexican battalion: they comprised the solid backbone of the army. The Activos were no doubt the most poorly equipped of the battalions. This fellow wears sandals instead of shoes. Jaunty hanging sideburns were grown by some soldiers. Regular ("Permanente") fusiliers dressed à la the 1833 contract: a single-breasted blue coatee with red facings and piping, and medium blue pants with red stripes.

5.) **Grenadier, Camp Attire**—Recently found evidence indicates that among the items issued to the Mexican infantryman, in 1833 at least, were a dress coat and two jackets. One jacket was of wool, the other of linen. The latter is assumed to have been white, and worn for fatigue duty; the woolen one was probably dark blue and plain in tailoring, used for marching or wearing in camp. This regular grenadier wears the plain blue jacket with his regulation middle blue trousers edged with red stripes. His dress coat would have been much like a permanente fusilier's, though the cords and raquettes on his shako were red instead of yellow, and its pompon was round and red. Card-playing, especially monte, was a favorite off-duty diversion of the Mexican *soldado.*

6.) **Rifleman**—Each battalion had a company of *cazadores,* or light infantry, and the best marksmen of these troops were generally armed with British Baker Rifles (when available). Baker accouterments included black leather cartridge box and strap, powder horn, small waistbelt bag containing loose balls and flints, and a sword bayonet. Green cords and raquettes, a green round pompon on their shakos and sometimes green epaulettes and facings, distinguished light troops. Pants were frequently grey. Brass bugle horn

(Continued on next page)

devices on shakos and cartridge box flaps also denoted them. Like the grenadiers, they were elite troops, trained to fight in skirmish order; and they proved the only effective response the Mexian Army had to Texian sharpshooters. Santa Anna saw to it that, of all his troops, his preference companies were well equipped with good shoes (de la Pena: 39).

7.) **Fatigue Dress**—This card-playing soldier is dressed entirely in white linen or cotton fatigue clothing; even his shako (its ornaments removed) is covered by a bag, which might have been water-proofed with oil. A bandana is worn under the shako, and a black stock around his neck: both served to absorb sweat. His jacket is collared and cuffed with red; in the 1820s red shoulder wings were also worn. A red sash holds his pants in place. In Texas this outfit was essentially the Mexican infantryman's working dress, but it was also favored when acutally campaigning in the sultrier tropics to the south.

8.) **Artilleryman**—Dark blue coats with dark red facings distinguished Mexican artillerymen. Yellow exploding grenades decorated their collars and epaulettes, and their buttons were imprinted with them as well. Their trousers were middle blue with red stripes, and the raquettes and cords and pompon of their shakos were dark red. They generally carried swords to help defend their guns in the event of an enemy charge, and light carbines, with short bayonets, were their favored firearms.

9.) **Cavalryman**—A private of the regular Dolores Regiment, this trooper wears a scarlet tailcoat of 1832 vintage (i.e., lapelled rather than single-breasted, the latter design introduced in the 1833 contract), with green facings; and gray riding pants with black buckskin lining and red stripes on the sideseams. His helmet is of tanned cowhide, with a brass shield, comb, and chinstrap, and a black goat pelt crest. A side socket held a tricolor wool plume on dress occasions. A white leather shoulder strap holds a cartridge pouch at his back as well as a secondary belt and clip from which a short carbine hangs. A sword is attached to his waistbelt, and a nine-foot lance with red pennant completes his armament (aside from pistols carried in saddle holsters). As trails in Texas were dusty, this trooper has tied a handkerchief around his neck to cover his nose and mouth when riding. Both helmet and pennant were usually covered on the march.—GZ

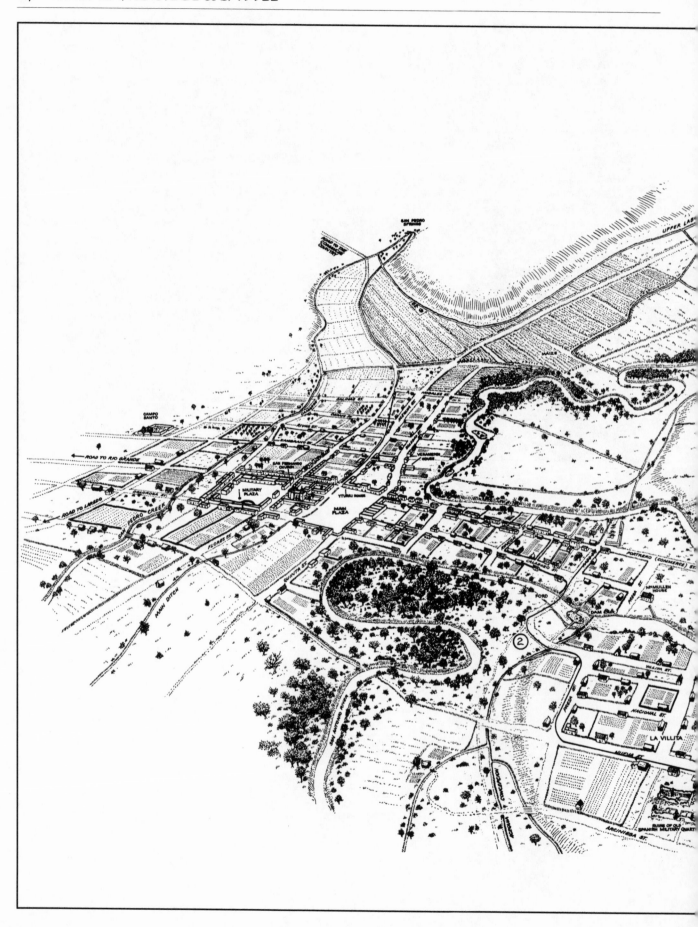

1. Jimenez Battalion posted east of the Alamo.
2. Santa Anna reconnoiters.
3. General Sesma marches with Dolores Cavalry and a detachment from the Jimenez Battalion to intercept reported Texian reinforcement coming from Goliad.

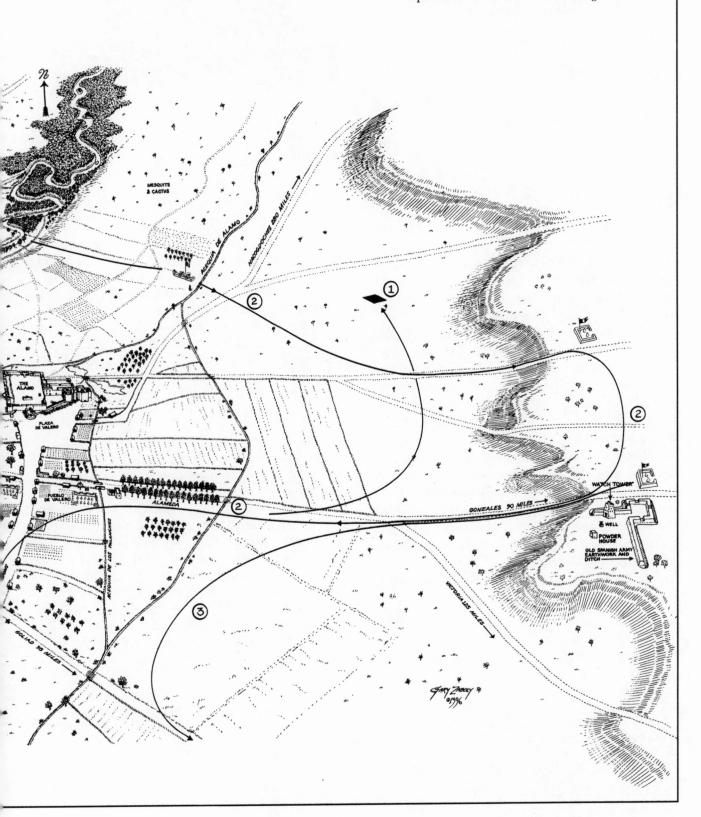

DAY SEVEN

Monday
February 29, 1836

Prologue

SANTA ANNA ORDERED detachments from the Jiménez Battalion and the cavalry, both task-organized under Ramírez y Sesma, to advance down the Goliad Road. He directed them to attack the believed Texian reinforcements at dawn for better surprise, and reminded Ramírez y Sesma that there would be no prisoners during this war.

At about this time in the siege the Mexicans proposed an armistice of three days. The Texians accepted it, and for the next three days hostilities calmed down a bit. Both Bowie and Travis seemed to let everyone in the garrison know about the truce, and several *Tejanos* left the Alamo during the abated hostilities.

There is nothing in any secondary source that has ever suggested an armistice. The general belief has always been that the Texians would prefer to die outright rather than accept any sort of a truce from the Mexican Army. In actuality it could have been the Texians who proposed an armistice. Both Bowie and Travis called for one on the first day, and Travis had discussed the possibility during the council of war on the 25th.

Almonte

Monday,—The weather changed—thermometer at 55 degrees in the night; it commenced blowing hard from the west. In the afternoon the battalion of Allende took post at the east of the Alamo. The President reconnoitered. One of our soldiers was killed, about that time Gen. [Ramírez y]Sesma left the camp with the cavalry of Dolores and the infantry of Allende to meet the enemy coming from La Bahia or Goliad to the aid of the Alamo. Gen'l Castrillón on [officer of the] guard.[1] (*SHQ* 48:19)

Santa Anna

My esteemed friend [Ramírez y Sesma]. Having been informed of the news that you have sent me [regarding Texian reinforcements],[2] I have this to say: It is a very good idea for you to go out in search of the enemy since they are so close by. However, I consider it necessary for you to take with you the Jiménez battalion, and at the same time ten boxes of cartridges for your guns; ammunition always stands one in good stead. Try to fall on them at dawn in order that you may take them by surprise. In this war you know that there are no prisoners.[3] Your

---

1. The Allende Battalion was not present with *any* of the invading columns. He must have meant the Jiménez Battalion.

2. On the 28th Santa Anna wrote of captured Texian correspondence claiming reinforcements. By the looks of this, Ramírez y Sesma may have been the commander who provided the document.

3. Santa Anna must have been challenged on this quite often to find it necessary to repeat it. The orders lack very much guidance at all, except "with regard to the taking of prisoners."

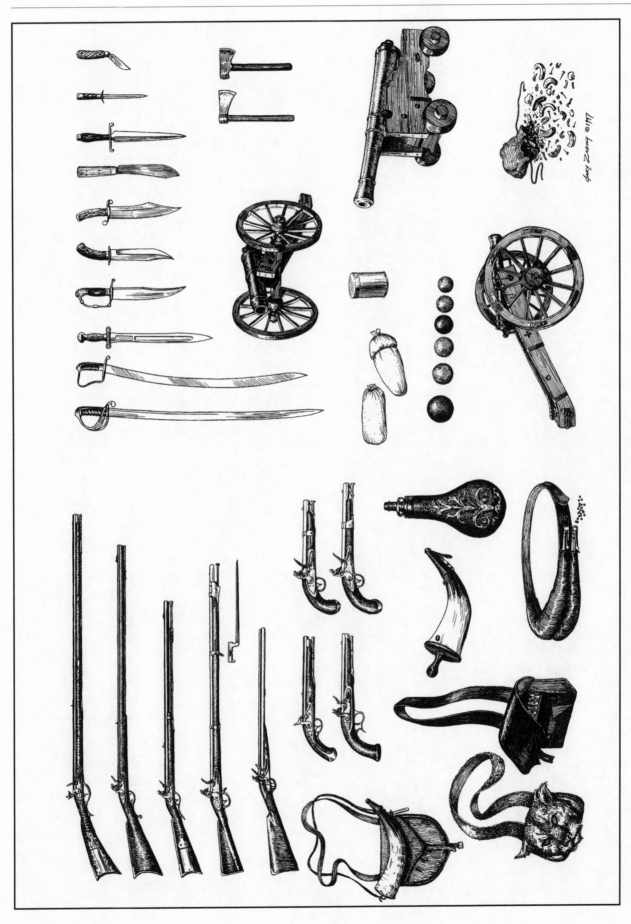

FIG. 17   TEXIAN WEAPONS AND AMMUNITION

FIG. 17   TEXIAN WEAPONS AND AMMUNITION

In describing the weapons of the Texas Army at the siege of San Antonio in the fall of 1835, Lt. Col. Frank W. Johnson recalled years later that "there was scarcely a musket and bayonet in the army; the principal arms were rifles with a few double-barreled shot-guns."[1] After the surrender of General Cós, several hundred Mexican muskets, and thousands of rounds of musket cartridges, were incorporated into the Texian ranks; but the rifle remained the most dependable arm.

Virtually all of the men of Texas, including those of the merchant and political classes, found the time every now and then to hunt, either to augment their larder or for the mere recreation it afforded. Even Stephen Austin, the colony's leader, donned hunting attire to have his full-length portrait painted in 1833: dark linen rifle shirt held in place with a waistbelt or sash, moccasins on his feet, his weapons a long rifle, small belt axe, antler-handled knife, with bullet pouch and powder horn under his right arm. Next to him sits his hunting dog.[2]

On display in the Alamo chapel museum is a rifle said to have been taken out of the post-battle debris by a local *Tejano*. Its manufacture is attributed to the gunshop of Jacob Dickert of Lancaster, Pennsylvania. It is 65 inches long, its barrel 45 inches, and it fired a .55-caliber ball. It weighs 8¼ pounds.[3]

The second rifle shown is often called the Southern "poor boy," indicating a rudimentary construction (even to the elimination of a patch bax). David Crockett owned at least one of this type, bringing it into Texas in 1835 and trading it to Andy Thomas; it was later converted to percussion.[4]

The third weapon is a Model 1815 U.S. Flintlock Rifle, made at the Harpers Ferry Armory in Virginia. The first model was produced in 1803 and had a 31¾" to 33½" barrel. The 1815 version had a 36" barrel, and was probably the model decided upon by Texas' General Council on November 27, 1835, which called for the purchase of "300 yagers with three-foot barrels."[5] A yager, from the German *jager*, referred to a short rifle; in this case, the Harpers Ferry was nine inches shorter in the barrel than the Dickert, and thus handier to use on horseback. A Texas veteran of the Grass Fight decades later remembered that his gun then was "a Harperferry yauger. The lock was tide on with a buck skin string and the stock and barrel was tide up to geather with buckskin string."[6]

The fourth longarm is a Model 1816 U.S. Flintlock Musket, made by both the Springfield and Harpers Ferry armories. This had a 42" barrel, steel ramrod, and bayonet. It was the type later reproduced by Tryon Son and Company of Philadelphia for Republic of Texas Infantry.[7]

The double-barreled shotgun was fairly ubiquitous in revolutionary Texas. Most were flintlocks, but doubtless a few percussion models were on hand. Travis was firing a double-barreled gun seconds before he was killed in the final battle of the Alamo.

The percussion pistol depicted is one of a pair once owned by Stephen Austin.[8] Below it is the pistol of Texas veteran Alphonso Steele, from a photograph taken in his elder years that evidently displays the weapons and accouterments he used during the Revolution.[9]

"Navy pistols" were carried into Texas by the New Orleans Greys, possibly the 1826 model seen here, manufactured by Simeon North of Middleton, Connecticut.[10] "200 pairs of horseman's pistols" were authorized for purchase by the November 27, 1835, General Council, and these might have been like the North 1819 pistol, designed for cavalry, shown here.

The hunting bag and powder horn at far left come from the Alphonso Steele photograph. Below it is a type worn by a "gigantic" Texian captain observed at San Jacinto by New Orleans Grey Herman Ehrenberg, and described by him as "a bullet pouch . . . made out of the head of a leopard, in which eyes of red cloth had been inserted, to bring out, by contrast, the beauty of the skin, and was suspended from a strap of brown untanned deer-hide."[11]

Cartridge boxes might have been like the ca. 1808 U.S. Army model seen here, with a little leather pocket opening in front. Made of black leather, it accommodated thirty-eight cartridges in a drilled wooden block that sat above a tiny tray of three compartments holding extra cartridges, flints, and oil rags.[12]

The powder horn is a U.S. government contract model. It has a screw-out plug serving as a measure, and a brass spring-loaded cap to dispense the powder. Powder flasks like the ca. 1790–1800 English brass model seen here were also used, mainly by shotgunners. The leather shotgun belt below it carries buckshot, its two brass spouts loading both barrels of a shotgun simultaneously.

The first sword shown is a dragoon saber; this model was later adopted by Republic cavalry units.

(continued on next page)

Next is a ca. 1810–1830 U.S.-made government sword for all three branches of services. It is large and durable, with a single-edged blade. "200 Sergeants' swords" were also among the items ordered—or at least decided upon—for the use of the army by the Council. In the mid-1830s these were actually short Artillery swords, brass-hilted and double-edged, which the U.S. ordnance directed for the use of non-commissioned officers. These were carried by American infantry sergeants until 1840.

Many Bowie knives have vied for the honor of *the* Bowie knife, but the first one shown here, with sword-hilt, can be seen in the only known portrait painting of Jim Bowie by George P. A. Healy, ca. 1831-34. The relic itself surfaced near Monterrey, Mexico, in the 1930s. It was made by Daniel Searles of Baton Rouge, Louisiana, and bears the name Juan Seguin.[13] If Bowie gave or sold this knife to Seguin, it was one of possibly several that *Tejano* citizens received from him. To the right of this specimen is a knife Bowie is said to have presented to Don Augustín Barrera in 1835.[14] Next is a Bowie with a 12-inch blade and stag hilt made in 1830 and said to have been used in early Texas.[15]

Butcher knives were in common use; 1,000 of them were ordered by the Council. The "Arkansas toothpick" was primarily a throwing knife, but also saw service in duels and battles. Next to it is a dirk probably carried by a San Antonio *Tejano* in both the 1823 and 1835 revolutions.[16] Pocketknives, or clasp-knives, did duty both as tools and weapons; this one is an English import ca. 1830.[17]

The left-hand belt-axe is a U.S. Army type of the very early 1800s.[18] At right is a tomahawk of the Fort Meigs pattern, oft-seen on the Appalachian and midwestern frontiers.

Directly below the swords and knives is an iron-barreled, twelve-pound "gunade." These stocky pieces, somewhat longer than the similar carronades, were originally used aboard merchant ships; and this relic, now on display at the Alamo grounds, had first seen service in the siege of Bexar in 1835. During the siege of the Alamo in February and March of the following year, the gunade was emplaced on a low ramp almost midway of the west wall.

The next artillery piece is a brass gun on a garrison carriage, derived from naval-type carriages. The term "brass" is generally interchangeable with "bronze" during this period, the alloys varying and often leaning to actual bronze; but the term "brass" was most often used, whether scientifically correct or not.[19]

The third gun, at lower left, is an iron six-pounder on a field carriage. Above it are solid cannonballs of either iron or brass, depicting most of the calibers available in the Alamo's arsenal. (A few powder-filled shells were also available.) A sealed example of canister is nearby.

At lower right is "langrage"—a mix of chopped-up horseshoes, bits of metal, nails, etc., tied together in a bag and fired like grape or canister. Sergeant Becerra, for one, recalled that the Texians fired "with pieces of iron and nails."—GZ

most affectionate friend, who sends you greetings. . . . (Woolsey, 2:172-173)

reinforcements that he had been told were coming to the aid of that place. (Woolsey, 2:172)

Filisola

On the twenty-ninth the Jiménez battalion was ordered to establish itself to the right of the cavalry, or to the left of the road that runs from the town of Gonzáles, in order to surround and enclose even more the Alamo. During the night General [Ramírez y] Sesma moved in, leaving the field covered, with the approval of the commander in chief. He marched with a detachment of the Jiménez battalion and another from the Dolores regiment in the direction of Goliad,[4] expecting to meet up with the [Texian]

Santa Anna

Before undertaking the assault and after the reply given to Travis who commanded the enemy fortification, I still wanted to try a generous measure, characteristic of Mexican kindness, and I offered life to the defendants [of the Alamo] who would surrender their arms and retire under oath not to take them up again against Mexico. Colonel Don Juan Nepomuceno Almonte, through whom this generous offer was made, transmitted to me their reply which stated that they would renew fire at a given hour. (Castañeda: 14)

---

4. This reconnaissance left part of the Gonzales Road open, possibly allowing a route in for the reinforcements of the 1st.

E. Esparza

But after about seven days fighting there was an armistice of three days, and during this time Don Benito [Crockett] had conferences every day with Santa Anna. [Juan] Badillo, the interpreter, was a close friend of my father's, and I heard him tell my father in the quarters that Santa Anna had offered to let the Americans go with their lives if they would surrender, but the Mexicans would be treated as rebels.

During the armistice my father told my mother she had better take the children and go, while she could, to safety. But my mother said: "No, if you're going to stay, so am I. If they kill one, they can kill us all." Only one person went out during our armistice, a woman named Trinidad Saucedo. (*San Antonio Express,* November 22, 1902)

* * * *

One day when I went to where Bowie was lying on his cot I heard him call those about him and say: "All of you who desire to leave here may go in safety. Santa Anna has just sent a message to Travis saying there will be an armistice for three days to give us time to deliberate on surrendering. During these three days all who desire to do so may go out of here. Travis has sent me the message and told me to tell those near me."[5] When Bowie said this quite a number left. Travis and Bowie took advantage of this occasion to send out for succor they vainly hoped would come to the Alamo and those within before it fell. William Smith and [Horace] Alsbury were among those who were sent for succor then. Seguín claimed also to have been so sent. Among the surnames of those I remember to have left during the time of this armistice were [Antonio?] Menchaca, Flores, Rodriquez, Ramírez, [Antonio

Cruz] Arocha, Silvero.[6] They are now all dead. Among the women who went out were some of their relatives. (*San Antonio Express,* May 12, 1907)

* * * *

Bowie asked my father if he wished to go when the armistice of three days was on. My father replied: "No. I will stay and die fighting." My mother then said: "I will stay by your side and with our children die too. They will soon kill us. We will not linger in pain." So we stayed. . . . (*San Antonio Express,* May 12, 1907)

Dickenson

He [Alsbury] left, unknown to witness,. . . . (Adjutant General Papers: TSL)

de la Peña

On the 29th the siege continued, and about seven-thirty at night the enemy killed a first-class private belonging to the first company of the San Luis Battalion, Secundino Alvarez, who on orders of the president had got in close to reconnoiter the Alamo. (Perry: 39)

San Luis Potosi

Around seven-thirty o'clock this night, the enemy killed Secudino Alvarez, of the 1st [Company], as he approached the Alamo by order of the President. (McDonald and Young: 3)

---

5. There does seem to have been a cessation or at least a slowing down of hostilities during this period. The Texians had expressed concern earlier in the siege over treating with Santa Anna. It is possible that the Mexicans offered this as a prospect to keep the Texians from a breakout attempt, where it might be even money on who could outrun who. The Texians could be entertaining the truce, all the more time for reinforcements to arrive from the colonies. It served both parties well—Mexican and Texian.

6. This is a large number of *Tejanos.* Travis' letter of March 3 claimed only three *Tejanos* remained in the compound. This could be over cause; the *Tejanos* were generally not separatists, but loyal Mexicans fighting for specific goals. It is also likely that ethnic tensions grew as the siege got tighter, and ignorance coupled with the first stages of exhaustion and stress began to play on emotions. At any rate a large portion of *Tejanos,* for whatever reason, decided they were in the wrong place and went over the wall during this period. It is also possible that some special amnesty was offered to them by the Mexican forces.

DAY EIGHT

Tuesday
March 1, 1836

Prologue

AT 1:00 A.M. THIRTY-TWO reinforcements arrived from the colonies, mainly from Gonzáles. The forces under Ramírez y Sesma advanced toward Goliad as far as the Tinja Creek and then returned to Béxar. The *soldados* constructed more trenches. The Texians, possibly responding to the armistice, fired two twelve-pound shots toward town, one of which hit Santa Anna's quarters. The temperature dropped again.

The phrase "32 Men from Gonzáles" is not accurate. At least two of those men were originally from the Alamo garrison, John Smith and Albert Martin. There could have been some men from the Goliad garrison as well. Of interest in Sutherland's account was the way the Texians made it into the Alamo. At one point they were received by a guide who spoke perfect English and offered to escort them into the fort. The Texians initially followed, but then decided to shoot him for a *soldado*. The man escaped.

Travis

. . . a company of thirty-two men from Gonzáles, made their way into us on the morning of the 1st inst, at three o'clock. . . .[1] (Foote, 1:219-222)

* * * *

. . . a company of 32 men from Gonzáles got in . . . (*SHQ* 37:24-25)

---

1. Sutherland stated he arrived at Gonzales on the afternoon of the 24th after he left the Alamo as a courier on the 23d. The following is his remembrance:

By Saturday [the 27th] we succeeded in getting twenty-five men who were placed under the command of Ensign [George] Kimble. These were principally from the town of Gonzales, men of families and her best citizens. They started for San Antonio on Saturday about two o'clock P.M., with John W. Smith acting as guide. On the Ciblo [Cibolo Creek] they increased their force to thirty-two, which number reached Béxar about one o'clock A.M. on Tuesday, March the first. On reaching the suburbs of the city they were approached by a man on horseback who asked in English, "Do you wish to go into the fort, gentlemen?" "Yes" was the reply. "Then follow me," said he, at the same time turning his horse into the lead of the company. Smith remarked, "Boys, it's time to be after shooting that fellow," when he put his spurs to his horse, sprung into the thicket, and was out of sight in a moment, before a gun could be brought to bear on him. Some supposed that this was General Wool, who was an Englishmen in the Mexican service.

The little band proceeded silently in single file, towards the fort, but were soon to be saluted again, though not in so friendly a manner. Notwithstanding Smith had taken the precaution to dispatch a messenger ahead, there seems to have been some misunderstanding as to the direction from which they should approach the walls, for the sentinel not being aware of their presence, fired upon them without hailing. The ball took effect in the foot of one of the men. The mistake was soon rectified, when all went in without further mishap. (Sutherland: 9-10)

Who was the mystery guide? General Wool was mentioned here (which may have been Col. Adrian Woll) and Dickenson remembered an Englishman, Colonel Black. There is no record of any English officers serving with this brigade, but staffs are odd organizations and sometimes personnel are overlooked when a record is produced of an event. Colonel Woll was the Quarter Master General for the army and did not arrive in Béxar until the afternoon of March 8. (Woolsey: 2:205)

1. A relief force of thirty-two men from Gonzáles arrives at the Alamo in the early morning hours.
2. Return of Dolores Cavalry to their posts.
3. Return of Jimenez Battalion to San Antonio.
4. Santa Anna reconnoiters to positions near mill.
5. Alamo's twelve-pound gunnade fires two shots; one hits Santa Anna's headquarters, the other falls beyond it.

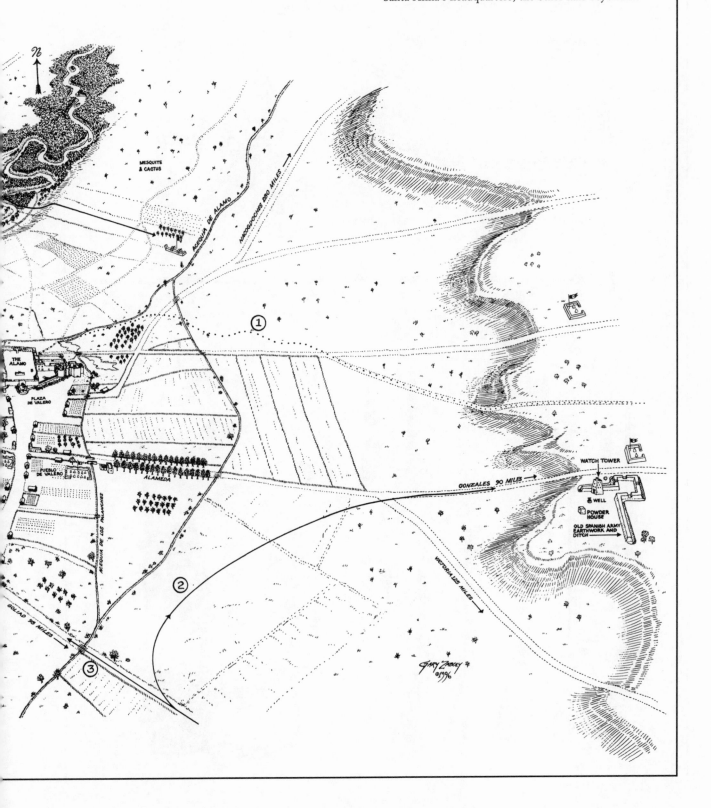

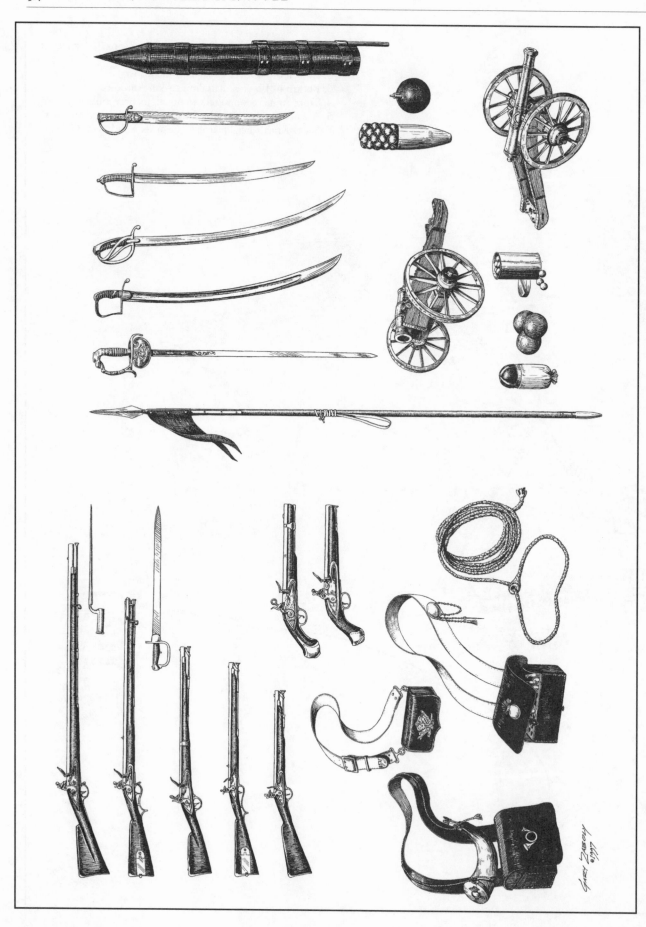

FIG. 18   MEXICAN WEAPONS AND AMMUNITION

FIG. 18   MEXICAN WEAPONS AND AMMUNITION

The sturdy workhorse of the British army of the eighteenth and early nineteenth centuries, the Brown Bess flintlock musket, was still seeing service in Mexico and Texas in the mid-1830s, and beyond, to the war between Mexico and the United States in 1846–1848. Surviving relics indicate that the Mexican Army had purchased primarily the 1809 India Pattern Brown Bess from England, and these were afterwards stamped on the lockplate with the eagle and snake of Mexico. It fired a .75-caliber lead ball, and came equipped with a socket bayonet having a nearly seventeen-inch blade.[1]

Scattered bits of evidence, both documentary and archaeological, also point to Mexico's purchase from England of the shorter and lighter Baker Rifle, born during the Napoleonic wars. Rifles were weapons for sharpshooters, and in Santa Anna's army these were the men of his companies of *cazadores* ("hunters"). Whether all *cazadores* were equipped with Bakers is not known. This rifle loaded a .625-caliber ball, and mounted a brass-hilted sword bayonet with a seventeen-inch doubleblade.

The *tercerola* was a short carbine for cavalry, originally manufactured in Spain; later models were made in Mexico itself. The specimen illustrated dates from 1815. It had no bayonet.[2]

In Mexican arms lists of the Texas campaigns of the period there are frequent references to "carbines." The types of carbines are not specified; but surmises can be made. J. C. Hefter, for instance, theorized that Baker Carbines might have been purchased along with the Baker Rifles.[3] The latter had thirty-inch barrels, while those of the carbines were but twenty inches.

An even shorter English-made carbine was the paget, with a sixteen-inch barrel; and this, too, probably saw service with Mexican cavalrymen.

The horseman's arms also included holstered pistols, perhaps like the late eighteenth-century Spanish model shown here,[4] or the English light dragoon pistol below it.[5]

It seems only logical that the stands of Baker Rifles shipped to Mexico were accompanied by Baker accouterments, such as the powder horn and cartridge box shown here. The trumpet badge signified "hunter," or light infantry. Rifle belts and box leather were generally black.

Cavalrymen had cartridge boxes for their arms slung over their backs. This example has a brass Mexican device on its flap.[6]

The grenadier's box has a brass flaming grenade adorning it. Its white leather shoulder belt holds an oval plate with brush and pick attached for cleaning the vent of the musket lock.

The rawhide lasso was a *ranchero's* tool, but in wartime the presidial and militia cavalry often used it to ensnare or trip enemy foot soldiers.[7]

A nine-foot lance was the favored arm of a charging horseman; red pennants were characteristic of many Mexican cavalry units.

The infantry officer's straight sword shown here is from a specimen in a private collection. It is of French manufacture, "Mexicanized" with eagle head and imprint on its hilt. On the blade is a blue and gold design, the decoration achieved via an arsenic process.

The 1796 British light cavalry saber can be seen in several Linati paintings. Another type used by light horsemen had a three-branch brass guard, this one based on a French model.

Grenadiers often carried short swords called "hangers." Presidial and militia cavalry favored short, wide-bladed *espada anchas;* this Mexican example has an iron shell guard sporting a floral motif, and a lightly engraved blade.[8]

Santa Anna brought several brass howitzers into Texas; at the Alamo siege they lobbed shells over the fort walls to explode within the perimeter. The brass eight-pound cannon fired solid shot, shell, grape or canister against both walls and attacking troops.

Some solid shot was affixed to a powder bag; otherwise both items were loaded one at a time. Most of the Mexican solid, or round, shot and canister balls were of brass. Cannister was just that: a metal can containing small balls, its lid welded on. When fired, the balls broke free in a lethal scattering. Grape was several layers of small balls tied together with string and cloth, and also sometimes affixed to a powder container; this acted much like canister.

There are a few references to rockets with Santa Anna's army, but their presence in San Antonio has been virtually overlooked in the scholarship until now. Shown here is an English Congreve rocket, approximately five feet long, with its side stabilizing stick. There were smaller sizes, and all could be armed with a variety of warheads: round shot, shells, grenades, and canister. There was even a type of flare in use in the British rocket ordnance,[9] which is significant, since rockets seemed to have signaled the March 6 assault on the Alamo.

E. Esparza

When Señor Smith came from Gonzáles with the band of men he had gathered, there was great shouting. The Texians beat drums and played on a flute. (Driggs and King: 223)[2]

Dickenson

Besieged were looking for reinforcements which never arrived.[3] (Adjutant General Papers, TSL)

Almonte

Tuesday—The wind subsided, but the weather continued cold—thermometer at 36 degrees in the morning—day clear. Early in the morning Gen. [Ramírez y] Sesma wrote from the mission de la Espada that there was no such enemy, and that he reconnoitered as far as the Tinja [creek], without finding any traces of them. The cavalry returned to [their] camp, and the infantry to this city.[4] At 12 o'clock the President went out to reconnoiter the [Zambrano] mill site to the northwest of the Alamo.

Lieut. Col. [Pedro de] Ampudia was commissioned to construct more trenches—in the afternoon the enemy fired two twelve-pound shots at the [Yturri] house of the President, one of which struck the house, and the other passed it.[5] Nothing more of consequence occurred. Night cold—thermometer 34 degrees Fahrenheit, and 1 degree *Reaumur*. (*SHQ* 48:19)

Santa Anna

They [Texians] decided on the latter course [not to surrender] and their decision irrevocably sealed their fate. (Castañeda: 14)

de la Peña

. . . for about sixty men did enter [the Alamo] one night, the only help that came [for the Texians]. They passed through our lines unnoticed until it was too late. (Perry: 41)

Filisola

However, since he [Ramírez y Sesma] had met no one [coming to reinforce the Texians] and had had no news whatsoever concerning the [Texian] troops, he returned to his post the next day, and the Jiménez Battalion was again a part of general headquarters.[6] (Woolsey, 2:173)

Caro

In the time intervening between our entrance into the city and the day set for the assault, the enemy received two small reinforcements from Gonzáles that succeeded in breaking through our lines and entering the fort. The first of these consisted of four men who gained the fort one night, and the second was a party of twenty-five who introduced themselves in the daytime. The entry of these reinforcements and the departure of messengers were witnessed by the whole army and need no particular proof. (Castañeda: 104)

---

2. The only recorded Texian reinforcements to arrive at the Alamo. The "Gonzáles Ranging Company of Mounted Volunteers" was led in by John Smith and Albert Martin. Smith would soon leave on courier duty again.

3. This is the obvious challenge with the Texian accounts. Noncombatant survivors left them who were not participatory in all ongoing events. It is quite reasonable that Dickenson did not remember or was even aware that some reinforcements arrived. The regrettable part is that some researchers discount all remembrances that may have been confused through the years or the eyewitnesses level of participation.

4. The Jiménez returned to Béxar and the cavalry to their bivouac east of the Alamo. The bivouac was probably in the vicinity of the powder house or the *alameda*.

5. This could have been the Texians' answer to Santa Anna's truce. With fresh reinforcements having arrived and probably promises of more en route, the Texians possibly felt confident.

6. When Ramírez y Sesma took the Goliad Road, he left the Gonzáles Road open for the reinforcements traveling from Gonzáles.

DAY NINE

Wednesday
March 2, 1836

Prologue

THE LARGEST EVENT ON March 2 was Texas' declaration of independence from the Republic of Mexico, at Washington-on-the-Brazos. The defenders of the Alamo had no way of knowing that this had occurred. Santa Anna hurried up the lead elements of Gaona's Brigade and ordered them to Béxar by noon of March 3. The Mexicans discovered a covered road within pistol shot of the Alamo, and posted the Jiménez Battalion on it.

Almonte

Wednesday—Commenced clear and pleasant thermometer 34 degrees—no wind. An aid of Col. [Francisco] Duque arrived [from Gaona's Brigade] with dispatches from Arroyo Hondo [River], dated 1st inst; in [Santa Anna's] reply, he was ordered to leave the river Medina, and arrive the next day at 12 or 1 o'clock. Gen. J.[oaquín] Ramírez [y Sesma] came to breakfast with the president. Information was received that there was corn at the farm of Seguín, and Lieut. Menchaca was sent with a party for it.[1] The President discovered, in the afternoon, a covered road within pistol shot of the Alamo, and posted the battalion of Jiménez there.[2] At 5 A.M. [Juan] Bringas went out to meet Gaona. (*SHQ* 48: 19-20)

Caro

His Excellency sent Colonel Bringas to meet the brigade of General Gaona with instructions for him to send, by forced marches, the picked companies [*granaderos* and *cazadores*] of his brigade. (Castañeda: 104)

de la Peña

. . . on the 2nd the *cazadore* from San Luis, Trinidad Delgado, drowned. . . . (Perry: 39)

San Luis Potosi

Cazadore Trinidad Delgado drowned while bathing in the river. (McDonald and Young: 3)

---

1. Col. Francisco Duque was the acting brigade commander for General of Brigade Gaona. He was forward on a reconnaissance; the remainder of the brigade would arrive the next day.

2. Pistol shot was close work, no more than fifty yards. The location of the hidden road remains a mystery. It is possible that the dense foliage on the northern side could have gone all the way to the wall.

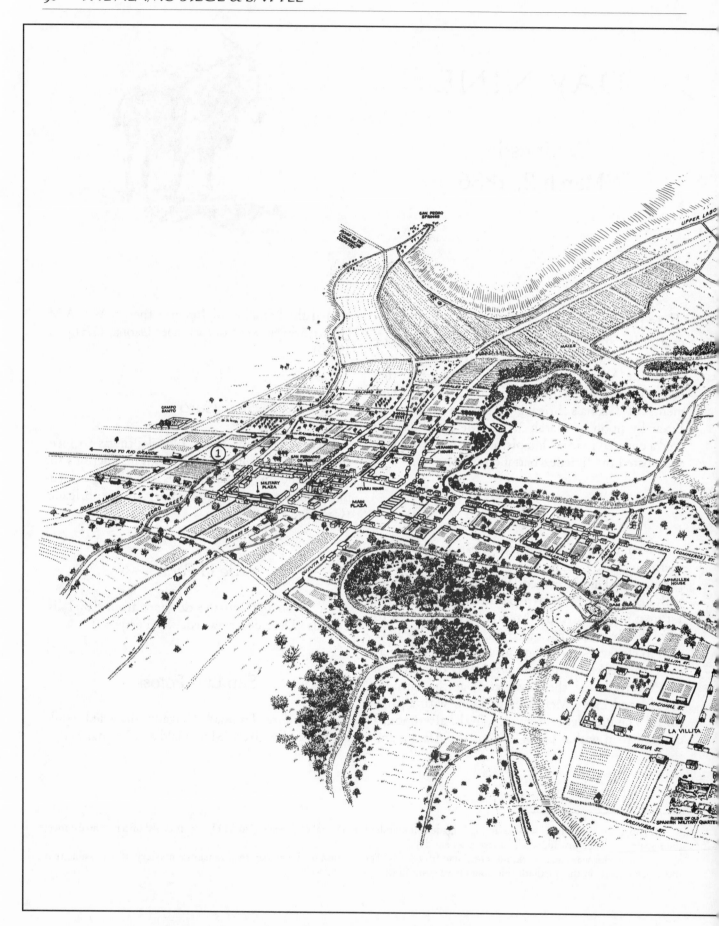

1. Dispatches arrive from General Gaona.
2. Lieutenant Menchaca of the Béxar presidial troops is sent to procure corn.
3. Santa Anna discovers a "covered road" within pistol shot of the Alamo (note: location is conjectural).
4. Jiménez Battalion posted to guard hidden road (location conjectural).

DAY NINE

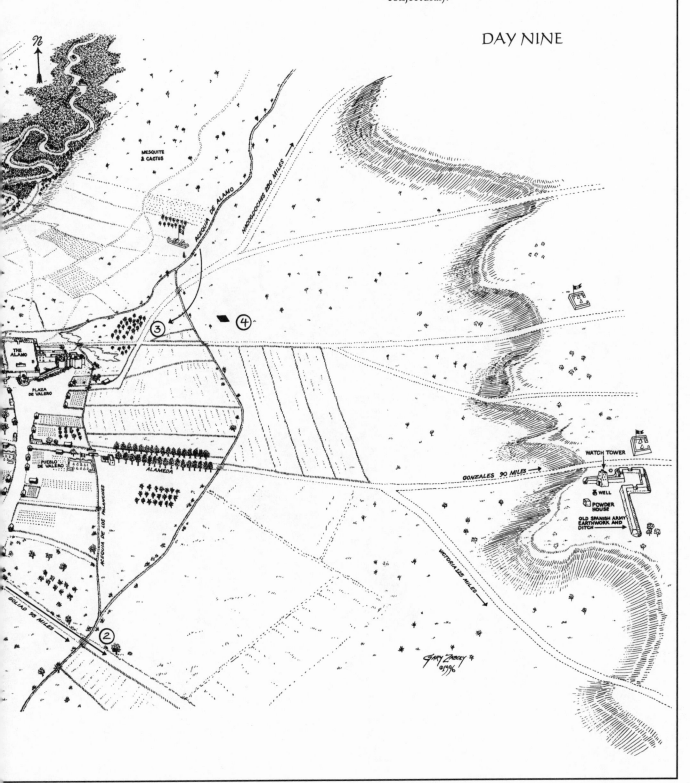

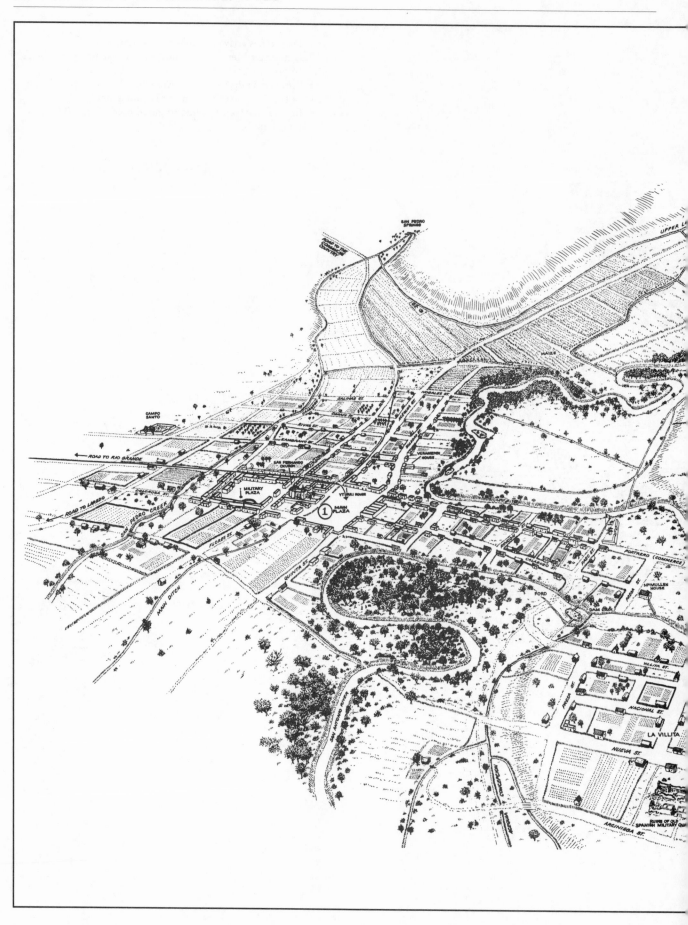

1. Arrival of Aldama, Toluca and Zapadore battalions, one cannon and one howitzer.
2. News arrives from Urrea of Johnson's defeat.
3. Arrival of James Butler Bonham.
4. Battery advances through Alamo ditch to within musket shot of fort.
5. Nighttime Texian sally at the sugar mill repulsed.

DAY TEN

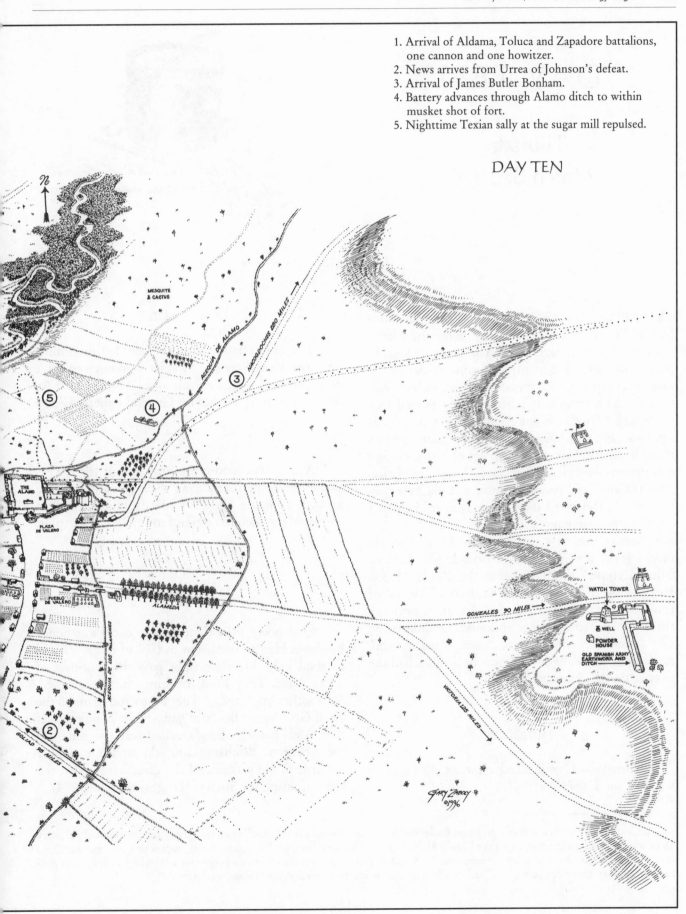

DAY TEN

Thursday
March 3, 1836

For God's sake hold out until we can assist you...

Prologue

AT APPROXIMATELY 11:00 A.M. James Bonham and possibly two other men entered the Alamo with news of reinforcements. The news, at least in part, contained a letter from the commander of the ranging companies and friend to Travis, Robert Williamson. The letter was positive and reported that sixty men were due in the Alamo from Gonzáles at any time, and that 600 more men were soon to be en route to Béxar. This good news set off a celebration and delivered an answer on Santa Anna's armistice. The Texians fired several cannon and muskets into the city. At this point the Texians believed help was coming; they were not willing martyrs.

Across the river the Mexican Army also received good news: General of Brigade José Urrea's column routed the Texians at the Battle of San Patricio on February 27. The lead elements of Gaona's Brigade arrived in San Antonio, bringing three more battalions of infantry. Undoubtedly, this ended the armistice for Santa Anna as well. Both sides had waited—and now both sides had the answer they had waited for.

Almonte

Thursday—Commenced clear, at 40 degrees, without wind. (*SHQ* 48:20)

Dickenson

The only outsiders who succeeded in coming into fort were three of our spies who entered three days before the final assault and all were killed [in the final assault]. (Adjutant General Papers, TSL)

* * * *

A few days before the final assault three Texians entered the fort during the night and inspired us with sanguine hopes of speedy relief, and thus animated the men to contend to the last.[1] (Morphis: 175)

E. Esparza

One brave man that did get back was Señor Bonham. He had been sent to Goliad to get Fannin to send help. He rode right past the sentinels of Santa Anna. They fired [on him], but he escaped. My mother knelt and said her beads and thanked the good God. Señor Bonham had a white handkerchief tied to his hat; this handkerchief was a sign he had seen Fannin. Bonham came through the danger unharmed. He was one of the great heroes that fell there fighting for liberty. (Driggs and King: 224)

---

1. One of these three was Bonham. James Butler Bonham probably separated himself from the Alamo garrison around February 16 to conduct land prospecting along the Cíbolo River. Legend has it that Bonham left and returned twice acting as a courier. There is no such evidence; the first time he is mentioned is March 3. It is likely that the other two people were traveling with him for protection and may have been part of the lead elements of the parties mentioned in the Williamson letter.

* * * *

After the first few days I remember that a messenger came from somewhere with word that help was coming. The Americans celebrated it by beating the drums and playing on the flute. (*San Antonio Express*, November 22, 1902)

Williamson

Gonzáles, March 1, 1836.

Dear Colonel Travis,

You cannot conceive my anxiety; today it has been four whole days that we have not the slightest news relative to your situation and we are therefore given over to a thousand conjectures regarding you. Sixty men have left this municipality, who in all probability are with you by this date. Colonel Fannin with 300 men and four pieces of artillery has been on the march toward Bèxar three days now.

Tonight we await some 300 [more] reinforcements from Washington[-on-the-Brazos], Bastrop, Brazoria, and S.[an] Felipe and no time will be lost in providing you assistance. As to the other letter of the same date let it pass, you will know what it meant; if the multitude gets hold of it, let them figure it out.[2]

Your true friend
R. L. Williamson

P.S. For God's sake hold out until we can assist you—I remit to you with Major Bonham's communication from the interim governor. Best wishes to all your people and tell them to hold on firmly by their "wills" until I go there.— Williamson.— Write us very soon.[3] (Velasques, *El Nacional:* March 21, 1836)

E. Esparza

The fighting began again and continued every day, and nearly every night. (*San Antonio Express*, November 22, 1902)

Almonte

The enemy fired a few cannon and musket shots into the city. I wrote to Mexico and to my sister, directed them to send their letters to Béxar, and that before 3 months the campaign would be ended. The General-in-Chief went out to reconnoiter. A battery was erected on the north of the Alamo within musket shot.[4] Official dispatches were received from Gen. Urrea, announcing that he had routed the colonists at San Patricio—killing 16 [Texians] and taking 21 prisoners.[5] The bells were rung. The battalions of Zapadores, Aldama, and Toluca arrived.[6] (*SHQ* 48:20)

---

2. Could Williamson have meant the "captured Houston correspondence" that Santa Anna wrote of around February 28?

3. Popular culture and Alamo lore encourages Bonham entering the Alamo on March 3, with news that no help would arrive. Bonham has been practically canonized for his choice of death over life, to tell his companions what was to become. This was not the case. The letter above from Williamson shows the news of March 3 to be grand news for the Texians that the garrison would be reinforced, and all would survive. The men in the Alamo at this point believed that they would be rescued; all they would have to do was hold out a bit longer. For more on this letter and on James Bonham see Thomas Ricks Lindley: "James Butler Bonham: October 17, 1835-March 6, 1836," *The Alamo Journal*, August 1988.

4. This was the northern battery and was the final battery emplaced. Not only was its function to bombard the Alamo from the north but also to deny Texian egress or ingress on the Nacogdoches Road.

5. This was an attack on a portion of the aborted Matamoros Expedition under Col. Francis W. Johnson. They were south of Goliad gathering horses.

6. These were the advance elements of the first brigade under General of Brigade Gaona. A courier from Santa Anna arrived at this brigade on February 27, directing Gaona to force march units north; the brigade was then still more than 120 miles away. Gaona sent the units listed below.

Col. Francisco Duque: Acting Commander		
Lt. Col. Agustín Amat	*Zapadores* Battalion	185 *soldados*
Lt. Col. Gregorio Uruñuela	Permanent Aldama Battalion	280 *soldados*
Col. Francisco Duque	Active Toluca Battalion	364 *soldados*
One cannon and one howitzer		
	Total	829 *soldados*

This brings the total number of Mexican forces in San Antonio to 2,370 *soldados*. The remainder of Gaona's Brigade were mostly inexperienced Active units. The Toluca had participated in the Zacatecas Campaign and was perhaps more experienced than even most Permanent Battalions. Gaona had larger cannon but did not send them "because they were not asked for . . ." (Santos: 69). The *zapadores'* branch mission was to support the engineers in the attack and defense of fortified places. They were organized into five companies. See: *Manual of Instructions for the Organization and Operations of the Army in War and Peace.*

FIG. 19   ADVANCING THE SAP

FIG. 19   ADVANCING THE SAP

The siege of the Alamo was to no small degree an episode of trench warfare. Within and immediately outside the walls the Texian defenders relied on a number of ditches to fight from as well as to duck into during enemy bombardments. The Mexicans also kept themselves fairly shielded in their entrenched encampments, behind earthen-walled batteries, and in trenches that systematically advanced those batteries.

On the night of March 4, Santa Anna's northeastern battery was moved closer to the fort via the convenient avenue of the Alamo *acequia*. (The *acequia* had been previously dammed by the Mexicans as much to deprive the Texians of an important water source as to be utilized as a ready-made "covered" road.)

When a position about 200 yards from the Texian stronghold was reached, an engineer lieutenant[1] began supervising construction of a sap leading away from the *acequia*. When a situation advantageous for an artillery emplacement was reached, construction of the battery itself was begun.

The manner of advancing a sap during a siege had not changed much since the mid-eighteenth century. Six-man parties of sappers worked in shifts. The chief of saps followed the engineer's marker line and placed gabions (wickerwork baskets of branches) along the line, toward the fort. To cover himself from enemy fire, he pushed before him, with sapper hooks, a large "sap roller"—a gabion thickly stuffed with bundles of sticks called fascines.[2] He also dug a little trench, and threw the dirt into the gabions.

The second man placed fascines atop the dirt-filled gabions, and widened and deepened the original trench, throwing more dirt into the gabions within his reach.

The third and fourth men continued to enlarge the trench. The fifth and sixth men staked the fascines in place and moved back and forth with tools, and brought forward fresh gabions and fascines. Sand bags, or "fortification sacks," were also stuffed between the gabions to buttress them.

After three or four gabions were in place, a new six-man party relieved them. Picket guards stood nearby. When completed, the trench might measure as high as seven feet, from floor to top of gabion wall, and about four and a half feet wide.

Most of the "zapadores" shown in the illustration wear their blue uniforms with black facings, and barracks or fatigue caps. One man at left works in a canvas fatigue jacket and has a bandana covering his head. Beards were long a tradition among sappers and pioneers, in armies in Europe as well as in the Americas.—GZ

San Luis Potosi

. . . on the 3rd day, the Aldama and Toluca battalions [and] of zapadores arrived. (McDonald and Young: 3)

de la Peña

. . . on the 3rd the zapper battalions [and the infantry battalions] from Aldama and Toluca arrived. (Perry: 39)

* * * *

On the third of March between eight and nine in the morning, after the troops had put on their dress uniforms, we marched toward Béxar, entering between four and five in the afternoon within sight of the enemy, who observed us from inside their fortifications. They calculated accurately the number of our forces, which differed by no more than a hundred men from their estimate; in the message Travis sent about this incident, he placed the number at around a thousand. There were 846 combatants [in the 1st Brigade column] which, with the commanders, officers and drivers came to that number. We entered Béxar just as the roar of cannon and martial music were announcing General Urrea's victory. (Perry: 37)

Beccera

On the third day of March Gen[eral of Brigade] Tolsa ['s units] arrived. The greatest activity prevailed in every department. . . . (Beccera: 19)

Nuñez

. . . the President ordered *zapas*[7] to be dug on the north, south and east of the Alamo, which were strongly garrisoned with troops, for the double purpose of preventing reinforcements from entering the Alamo and to cut the Americans off from water. This completed the cordon of troops which was drawn around the doomed Alamo. And right here, let me state that no ingress or egress could have been accomplished from the time our army regularly besieged the Alamo, and there was none, with the single exception of Don Juan Seguín and his company, who were permitted to leave. They were let go from the fact that they were Mexicans and we did not wish to harm them.[8] (*SHQ*, July 1990:74)

E. Esparza

One night there was music in the Mexican camp and the Mexican prisoner said it meant that reinforcements had arrived. (*San Antonio Express,* November 22, 1902)

Travis

Letter to:____ from Travis
COMMANDANCY OF THE ALAMO, Béxar:

In the present confusion of the political authorities of the country, and in the absence of the commander-in-chief, I beg leave to communicate to you the situation of this garrison. You have doubtless already seen my official report of the action of the 25th ul., made on that day to General Sam Houston, together with the various communications heretofore sent by express. I shall, therefore, confine myself to what has transpired since that date.

From the 25th to the present date, the enemy have kept up a bombardment from two howitzers (one a five and a half inch, and the other an eight inch) and a heavy cannonade from two long nine-pounders, mounted on a battery on the opposite side of the river, at a distance of four hundred yards from our walls. During this period the enemy has been busily employed in encircling us with entrenched encampments on all sides, at the following distance, to wit—in Béxar, four hundred yards west; in la Villita, three hundred yards south; at the powder house, one thousand yards east by south; on the ditch, eight hundred yards north.[9]

Notwithstanding all this, a company of thirty-two men from Gonzáles made their way into us on the morning of the 1st. inst, at three o'clock, and Col. J. B. Bonham got in this morning at eleven o'clock without molestation. I have so fortified this place, that the walls are generally proof against cannon-balls; and I shall continue to entrench on the inside, and strengthen the walls by throwing up dirt. At least two hundred shells have fallen inside our works without having injured a single man; indeed, we have killed many of the enemy. The spirits of my men are still high, although they have had much to depress them. We have continued for ten days against an enemy whose numbers are variously estimated at from fifteen hundred to six thousand, with Gen. Ramírez [y] Sesma and Col. Batres, the aide-de-camp of Santa Anna, at their head. A report was circulated that Santa Anna himself was with the enemy, but I think it is false. A reinforcement of one thousand men is now entering Béxar from the west, and I think it more probable that Santa Anna is now in town, from the rejoicing we hear. Col. Fannin is said to be on the march to this place with reinforcements; but I fear it is not true, as I have repeatedly sent to him for aid without receiving any. Col. Bonham, my special messenger arrived at la Bahia fourteen days ago, with a request for aid; and on the arrival of the enemy in Béxar ten days ago, I sent an express to Col. F[annin]. which arrived at Goliad on the next day, urging him to send us reinforcements—none have arrived [from Fannin]. I look to the colonies alone for aid; unless it arrives soon, I shall have to fight the enemy on his own

---

7. A *zapa* is a spade. "*Zapar*" is to mine or excavate. Possibly *zapas* was *soldado* slang for entrenchments.

8. Stephen Hardin, Ph.D, did an outstanding annotation for the Nuñez account in *SHQ*, July 1990.

9. Most of the Mexican artillery still seems to have been massed at the River Battery. Travis accounts for two cannon and two howitzers, presumably the batteries, at La Villita and the *alameda*, were outside his field of vision or may not have been active enough to draw his attention. It is also possible that the Mexicans had massed the guns at the river. The entrenchments were probably the ones discussed earlier; the McMullen house, near the Spanish Quartel in La Villita, and at the old Spanish fortification near the powder house.

terms. I will, however, do the best I can under the circumstances, and I feel confident that the determined valor and desperate courage, heretofore evinced by my men, will not fail them in the last struggle, and although they may be sacrificed to the vengeance of a Gothic enemy, the victory will cost the enemy so dear, that it will be worse for him than a defeat. I hope your honorable body will hasten on reinforcements, ammunition, and provisions to our aid, as soon as possible. We have provisions for twenty days for the men we have; our supply of ammunition is limited. At least five hundred pounds of cannon powder, and two hundred rounds of six, nine, twelve, and eighteen pound balls, ten kegs of rifle powder, and a supply of lead, should be sent to this place without delay, under a sufficient guard.

If these things are promptly sent, and large reinforcements are hastened to this frontier, this neighborhood will be the great and decisive battle ground. The power of Santa Anna is to be met here or in the colonies; we had better meet them here, than to suffer a war of desolation to rage in our settlements. A blood red banner waves from the [San Fernando] church of Béxar, and in the [entrenched] camp above us, in token that the war is one of vengeance against rebels; they have declared us as such, and demanded that we should surrender at discretion or this garrison should be put to the sword. Their threats have had no influence on me or my men, but to make all fight with desperation, and that high-souled courage which characterizes the patriot, who is willing to die in defense of his country's liberty and his own honor.

The citizens of this municipality are all our enemies except those who have joined us heretofore; we have but three Mexicans now in the fort; those who have not joined us in this extremity, should be declared public enemies, and their property should aid in paying the expenses of the war.[10]

The bearer of this will give you your honorable body, a statement more in detail, should he escape through the enemy's lines.

God and Texas!—Victory or Death!!

P.S. The enemy's troops are still arriving, and the reinforcements will probably amount to two or three thousand. (Foote, 2: 219-222)

* * * *

Do me the favor to send the enclosed to its proper destination instantly. I am still here, in fine spirits and well to do, with 145 men.[11] I have held this place for ten days against a force variously estimated from 1,500 to 6,000, and shall continue to hold it till I get relief from my country or I will perish in its defense. We have been miraculously preserved. You have no doubt seen my official report of the action of the 25th ult. in which we repulsed the enemy with considerable loss [to them]; on the night of the 25th they made another attempt to charge us in the rear of the fort, but we received them gallantly by a discharge of grape and musketry, and they took to their scrapers immediately. They are encamped in entrenchments on all sides of us.

All our couriers have gotten out without being caught and a company of thirty-two men from Gonzáles got in two nights ago, and Colonel Bonham got in today by coming between the powder house and the enemy's upper encampment[12] .... Let the Convention go on and make a declaration of independence, and we will then understand, and the world will understand, what we are fighting for. If independence is not declared, I shall lay down my arms, and so will the men under my command. But under the flag of independence, we are ready to peril our lives a hundred times a day, and to drive away the monster who is fighting us under a blood-red flag, threatening to murder all prisoners and make Texas a waste desert. I shall have to fight the enemy on his own terms, yet I am ready to do it, and if my countrymen do not rally to my relief, I am determined to perish in the defense of this place, and my bones shall reproach my country for her neglect. With 500 men more, I will drive [Ramírez y] Sesma beyond the Río Grande, and I will visit vengeance on the enemy of Texas whether invaders or resident Mexican enemies. All the citizens of this place that have not joined us are with the enemy fighting

---

10. This confirms Esparza's claim that a large number of *Tejanos* left the garrison. Other units do the same throughout the Texian Army, most notably at Goliad where *Tejano* Captain Guerra's Artillery Company left the Texian garrison at Goliad, and even joined the Mexican Army. See Pruett and Cole's *Goliad Massacre: A Tragedy of the Texas Revolution*, p. 63.

11. Unless the Texians have taken severe casualties they should have numbered around 180.

12. This could be either the powder house or the newly commenced northern trench.

against us. Let the government declare them public enemies, otherwise she is acting a suicidal part. I shall treat them as such, unless I have superior orders to the contrary. My respects to all friends, confusion to all enemies. God bless you. (*SHQ* 37: 24-25)

* * * *

Take care of my little boy. If the country should be saved, I may make for him a splendid fortune; but if the country be lost and I should perish, he will have nothing but the proud recollection that he is the son of a man who died for his country. (*The Texas Monument*, March 31, 1852)

Milsaps

BÉXAR: My Dear, Dear Ones, We are in the fortress of the Alamo, a ruined church that has most fell down. The Mexicans are here in large numbers they have kept up a constant fire since we got here. All our boys are well and Capt. [Albert] Martin is in good spirits. Early this morning I watched the Mexicans drilling just out of range they were marching up and down with such order. They have bright red and blue uniforms[13] and many cannons.

Some here at this place believe that the main army has not come up yet. I think they are all here even Santa Anna. Col. Bowie is down sick and had to be to bed. I saw him yesterday and he is still ready to fight. He didn't know me from last spring but did remember Wash.[14] He tells me that help will be here soon and it makes us feel good. We have beef and corn to eat but no coffee, [the] bag I had fell off on the way here so it was all spilt. I have not seen Travis

but 2 times since here he told us all this morning that Fannin was going to be here early with many men and there would be a good fight. He stays on the wall some but mostly to his room I hope help comes soon cause we can't fight them all. Some says he is going to talk some tonight and group us better for defense. If we fail here to get to the river with the children all Texas will be before the enemy we get so little news here we know nothing. There is no discontent in our boys, some are tired from loss of sleep and rest. The Mexicans are shooting every few minutes but most of the shots fall inside and no harm. I don't know what else to say they is calling for all letters, kiss the dear one for me be well and God protects us all.—Isaac

If any men come through there tell them to hurry with powder for it is short I hope you get this and know—I love you all. (DRT Library collection at the Alamo)

Alsbury

He [Bowie] had himself brought back two or three times to see and talk with her. Their last interview took place three or four days before the fall of the Alamo. She never saw him again, either alive or dead.[15] (Matovina: 45-46)

Almonte

The enemy attempted a sally in the night at the Sugar Mill, but were repulsed by our advance.[16] (*SHQ* 48:20)

---

13. Milsaps was looking at infantry and artillery. The uniform of the infantry was: *A tailcoat of [dark blue] Querétaro cloth with scarlet collar, lapels and cuffs, white piping, coarse lining and yellow metal buttons . . . a shako of tanned cowhide with brass plate and chinstrap, cotton cords and an elongated wool pompon . . .* (Nieto, Brown and Hefter, 51). Presumably the trousers were of sky-blue and white. The *cazadores* may have been issued frock coats, the *granadaros* probably wore the same as the line, with the appropriate insignia.

14. Alamo defender George Washington Cottle, another Gonzáles volunteer. His Uncle Jimmy fought at San Jacinto and as everyone yelled "Remember the Alamo!" he cried, "Remember Wash Cottle!" There is a good possibility that this letter is a fake. It did not appear until 1962 and is currently owned by the University of Houston. It came to the university through the collection of Dorman David, who allegedly forged several documents in his tenure as a collector. John Laflin, a notorious forger, was also operating in the Southwest during this time. There are some questions other than circumstantial, however. The phrase, "My dear, dear ones . . ." does not seem to be popular until about the mid-nineteenth century; it was also uncommon to sign only the first name in a letter during this time. The most damning evidence is the handwriting and certain phrases in other Laflin forgeries. For more on this and on John Laflin see *Texas Monthly*, March 1988.

15. Bowie, according to Alsbury, Milsap, and Esparza, had himself taken around to various parts of the mission. This was a morale factor. Bowie was well known and popular with the Texians.

16. Meaning Zambrano's Mill? This was possibly not a garrison sally, but more Texian reinforcements arriving.

DAY ELEVEN

Friday
March 4, 1836

Prologue

A MEXICAN COUNCIL OF WAR was called. The question was whether to hold the assault after the remainder of Gaona's Brigade arrived sometime around the seventh, or to attack as soon as possible. There would be no Texian prisoners. This declaration caused a rift in the officer corps, some of whom voiced strong opinion against execution of prisoners. The council adjourned with no resolution on the attack date; the only decision that came out of the council of war was that all prisoners were to be executed. The final decision on the assault would be made on March 5.

Late on the night of March 4 one or two *Tejanas* left the Alamo and informed the Mexican Army of the defenders' status, expected reinforcements, and possible surrender plans if no more Texians arrived. The *soldados* began movements for the final phase of the siege. The Mexican batteries moved closer and possibly consolidated from all positions into only two: the river battery and the northern battery now about 200 yards from the Alamo. There is a possibility of Texian reinforcements arriving sometime in the late hours.

Almonte

Friday—The day commenced windy, but not cold—thermometer 42 degrees. Commenced firing very early, which the enemy did not return. In the afternoon one or two shots were fired by them. A meeting of Generals and Colonels was held, at which Generals Cós, [Ramírez y] Sesma, and Castrillón were present; Generals Amador and Ventura Mora did not attend, the former having been suspended and the latter being in active commission.[1] Also present, Colonel Francisco Duque, battalion of Toluca—Uruñuela, battalion of Aldama—Romero, battalion of Matamoros—Amat, battalion of *Zapadores,* and the Major of the Battalion of San Luis. The colonels of battalion of Jiménez and San Luis did not attend, being engaged in actual commission. I was also called. After a long conference Cós, Castrillón, Uruñuela, and Romero were of the opinion that the Alamo should be assaulted—first opening a breach with two cannon and the two howitzers, and that they should wait the arrival of the two twelve-pounders expected on Monday the 7th. The President, Gen. Ramírez [y Sesma] and I were of opinion that the twelve-pounders should not be waited for, but the assault made. Colonels Duque and Amat, and the Major of the San Luis battalion did not give any definite opinion about either of the two modes of assault proposed.[2] In this state things remained—the General not making any definite resolution. (*SHQ* 48:20)

---

1. Amador may have been suspended as the chief of artillery because of Santa Anna's dissatisfaction with the La Villita Battery.
2. From Santa Anna's perspective there were more than enough *soldados* to do the job—2,700 to 180-250 were good odds. Besides, the Texians had already been reinforced at least once, and Santa Anna feared it could happen again. The Alamo needed to be taken as quickly as possible.

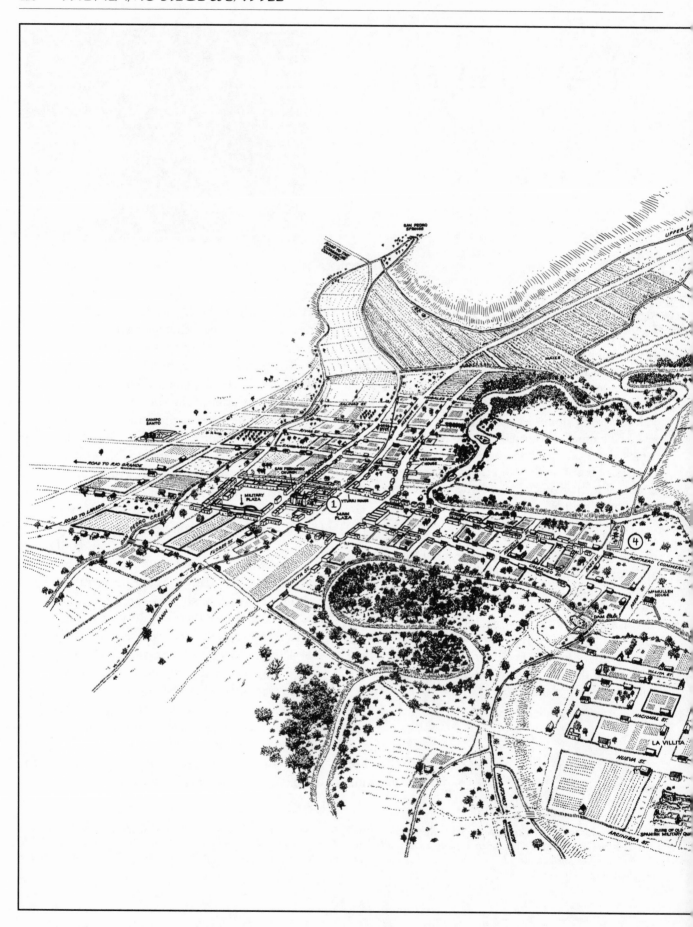

1. Council of war at Santa Anna's headquarters.
2. One or two *Tejano* women in the fort desert to Mexican lines.
3. North battery advances during the night of the 4th to within 200 yards of the wall; one howitzer added to it.
4. Third cannon is added to west battery.

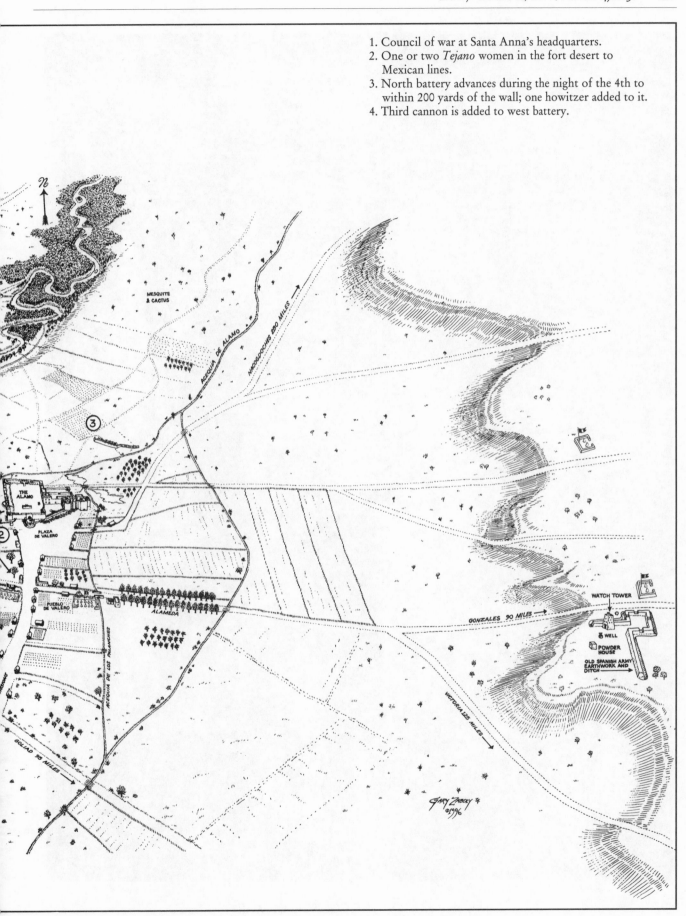

FIG. 20   THE COUNCIL OF WAR

FIG. 20   THE COUNCIL OF WAR

Issues of morality arose during Santa Anna's council of war with his officers on March 4. His opinion that the Alamo should be immediately assaulted evoked dissension from several of his officers, who argued in favor of waiting for two 12-pounders that would open a proper breach in the walls, and thus save lives. In addition, a number of them also protested against the commander-in-chief's decree that no prisoners were to be taken.

The illustration shows Santa Anna and ten of his officers in council in the general's headquarters, the Yturri house, located at the northwestern corner of Main Plaza. Sitting on the table is a map, drawn by engineer Col. Ygnacio de Labastida, showing the Alamo fortifications and the town of Béxar and environs.

General Castrillon is pleading against the no-prisoner order, voicing "principles regarding the rights of men, philosophical and human principles which did them honor," as de la Peña recorded. Santa Anna listens, but will not be dissuaded from his course.

To the left of Santa Anna stands Colonel Almonte; to his right, wearing the cavalry jacket seen in his only known portrait (a crude engraving), is General Cós, who also sports two gold rings in his ears. Other attendees included General Sesma, Colonels Duque, Romero, Salas, Uruñuela, and Amat, and the interim major of the San Luis Battalion.—GZ

Santa Anna

An assault would infuse our soldiers with that enthusiasm of the first triumph that would make them superior in the future to those of the enemy. It was not my judgement alone that moved me to decide upon it, but the general opinion expressed in a council of war, made up of generals, that I called even though the discussions which such councils give rise to have not always seemed to me appropriate. (Castañeda: 13-14)

de la Peña

During a council of war held on the 4th of March at the commander in chief's quarters, he expounded on the necessity of making the assault. Generals [Ramírez y] Sesma, Cós, and Castrillón, Colonels Almonte, Duque, Amat, Romero, and Salas, and the interim major of San Luis were present and gave their consent. The problem centered around the method of carrying it out. Castrillón, Almonte, and Romero were of the opinion that a breach should be made, and that eight or ten hours would suffice to accomplish this. Field pieces were coming up and Colonel Bringas, aide to the president-general, had left with the idea of activating them. It was agreed to call the artillery commandant[3] and to alert him to this, and although the artillery could not arrive for a day or so, that solution was still pending. When in this or some other discussion, the subject of what to do with prisoners was brought up, in case the enemy surrendered before the assault, the example of [Joaquín de] Arredondo[4] was cited; during the Spanish rule he had hanged eight hundred or more colonists after having triumphed in a military action, and this conduct was taken as a model.

General Castrillón and Colonel Almonte then voiced principles regarding the rights of men, philosophical and humane principles which did them honor. . . .

We had no officers of the engineer's corps who could estimate for us the strength at the Alamo and its defenses, because the section of this corps appointed for the army had remained in Mexico;[5] however, the sappers were not lacking in personnel

---

3. Lt. Col. Pedro de Ampudia was chief of artillery. It is odd that an attack planning session involving fixed fortifications would not have the artillerist present. (Woolsey, 2:154)

4. Commandant General Arredondo was a Spanish Royalist officer who defeated the Federalist rebels at the Battle of the Medina, August 18, 1813. The "example" discussed was Arredondo's execution of prisoners and sympathizers loyal to the Federalist cause. See: Schwarz, 109.

5. Incorrect. There were at least three engineer officers on staff: Lt. Col. Ignacio Labastida, Lt. Ignacio Berrespe, and Lt. Juan Ordones. (Woolsey, 2:154)

who could have carried out this chore and, further-more, information given by General Cós, by wounded officers after he had left at Béxar,[6] and by some townspeople of this locality was considered sufficient. The latter made clear to us the limited strength of the garrison at the Alamo and the short-age of supplies and munitions at their disposal. They had walled themselves in so quickly that they had not had time to supply themselves with very much. (Perry:43-44)

Filisola

In a staff meeting held for this purpose . . . sev-eral of the officers and leaders were of the opinion that they should have waited to have in hand the twelve-caliber pieces that were supposed to arrive on the 7th or 8th. (Woolsey, 2:174)

Loranca

On the 4th of March the President Santa Anna called a council of war to consider the mode of as-sault of the Alamo, and they decided to make the as-sault on the 6th, at daybreak, in the following man-ner: On the north, Col. Don Juan Baptisto Morales with the battalion *"Firmas,"*[7] of San Luis Potosi; on the west, Col. Don Mariano Salas, with the battalion of Aldama; on the south, Col. José Vicente Miñón, with the battalion of infantry; on the east, a squad-ron of lancers, flanked by a ditch, to cut off the retreat at the time of the assault. These lancers were commanded by Gen. Don Joaquín Ramírez y Ses-ma. (*San Antonio Express,* June 23, 1878)

Almonte

In the night the north parapet was advanced toward the enemy through the water course. A lieu-tenant of engineers conducted the entrenchment.[8] A messenger was dispatched to Urrea. (*SHQ* 48:20)

Filisola

On that same evening about nightfall it was re-ported that Travis Barret, commander of the enemy garrison, through the intermediary of a woman, proposed to the general in chief that they would surrender arms and fort with everybody in it with the only condition of saving his life and that of all his comrades in arms. However, the answer had come back that they should surrender uncondition-ally, without guarantees, not even of life itself, since there should be no guarantee for traitors. With this reply it is clear that all were determined to lose their existence, selling it as dearly as possible. Conse-quently they were to exercise extreme vigilance in order not to be surprised at any time of the day or night. (Woolsey, 2: 176-177)

Dickenson

. . . the two women escaped [from the Alamo] to the enemy and betrayed our situation about two days before the assault—(Adjutant General Papers, TSL)

* * * *

. . . A Mexican woman deserted us one night, and going over to the enemy, informed them of our inferior number.[9] (Morphis: 175)

---

6. A number of wounded *soldados* were left with the Texians in San Antonio after the December battle. According to Filisola: "In Bexar they [Cós' forces] had to leave some officers and soldiers who were wounded and that were in no shape to take the road. Among the former were First Assistant Don José María Mendoza, Captain of the 2nd Nuevo Leon [Presidial] compa-ny, Don Francisco Rada, and Second Lieutenant Don Ignacio Solio, who volunteered to remain to take care of them. Of the soldiers we have no knowledge either as to who they were or how many." (Woolsey, 2:96-97)

7. *"Firmas"* means standing, solvent.

8. According to the Navarro map the various battery locations were consolidated by this time, with four cannon and two how-itzers at the northern battery, now 250 yards away from the north wall, and the remaining three cannon and one howitzer emplaced at the river battery. The northern battery possibly began by cutting the Nacogdoches Road, and was advanced nightly to the *ace-quia* confluence.

9. It could be either Juana Alsbury, Trinidad Saucedo, or lost to history. Whoever it was not only left but convinced the Mexican Army to attack quickly. It was this piece of intelligence that probably convinced Santa Anna to launch his attack on the 6th rather than waiting for the 7th.

DAY TWELVE

Saturday
March 5, 1836

Prologue

BASED ON THE INFORMATION provided by the *Tejana(s)*, Santa Anna issued his order for an attack on March 6. The plan called for four assault and one reserve columns.

Preparations for combat began immediately. The columns bedded down at twilight on the 5th. The bombardment intensity increased, especially from the northern battery. Sometime during the afternoon of the 5th, the column commanders and Santa Anna conducted a reconnaissance of the attack positions and approaches.

At some point another messenger got through to the defenders and told them that no more help was coming. Around dusk Travis gathered the garrison and told them their options. Texian sentries were posted and the garrison went to sleep. It is doubtful they expected the assault to happen as soon as the next morning. At midnight all column formations began moving toward their attack position around the Alamo.

The report of the *Tejana(s)* probably accelerated the assault timetable by around forty-eight hours for the Mexicans. Until then it appeared that the assault was waiting until March 7.

Urissa

One night past midnight, when Santa Anna and Castrillón were planning an assault, Santa Anna declared that none [of the Alamo defenders] should survive. It was then inevitable that the fort could hold out but little longer, and Castrillón was persuading the commander to spare the lives of the men [of the Mexican Army]. Santa Anna was holding in his hand the leg of a chicken which he was eating and, holding it up, he said: "What are the lives of [our] soldiers than so many chickens? I tell you, the Alamo must fall, and my orders must be obeyed at all hazards. If our soldiers are driven back, the next line in their rear must force those before them forward, and compel them to scale the walls, cost what it may." After eating, Santa Anna directed me to write out his orders, to the effect that all companies should be brought out early, declaring that he would take his breakfast in the fort [Alamo] the next morning. His orders were dispatched, and I retired. (*Texas Almanac*, 1859: 62)

Santa Anna

The time has come to strike a decisive blow upon the enemy occupying the Fortress of the Alamo. Consequently, His Excellency has decided that, tomorrow morning, at 4:00 A.M. the columns to attack shall be stationed at musket-shot distance from the first entrenchments,[1] ready for the charge, which shall commence, at a signal to be given from the bugle, from the northern battery.

---

1. About 100 yards from the Texian trenches.

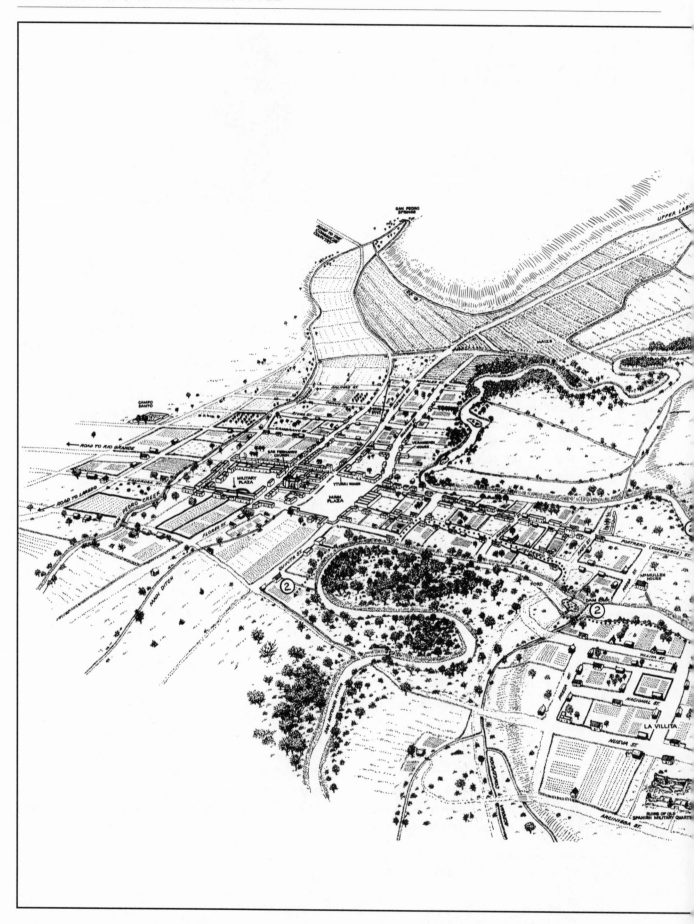

1. Newly placed north battery begins "brisk fire" from two howitzers and four cannon.
2. Escape route of Louis Rose as suggested by W. P. Zuber.
3. Mexican generals survey points of attack for the following day.

The first column will be commanded by General Don Martín Perfecto Cós, and in his absence, by myself. The permanent Battalion of Aldama, except the company of *granaderos*, and the three right center [*fusilero*]companies of the Active Battalion of San Luis, will comprise the first column. The second column will be commanded by Colonel Don Francisco Duque, and in his absence, by General Don Manuel Fernández Castrillón; it will be composed of the Active Battalion of Toluca, except the company of *granaderos*, and the three remaining center [*fusilero*] companies of the Active Battalion of San Luis.

The third column will be commanded by Colonel José María Romero, and in his absence, by Colonel Mariano Calas; it will be composed of the Permanent Battalion of Matamoros and Jiménez.

The fourth column will be commanded by Colonel Juan Morales, and in his absence, by Colonel José Miñón; it will be composed of the *cazadore* companies of the Battalion of Matamoros and Jiménez, and of the Active Battalion of San Luis. His Excellency the General-in-Chief will, in due time designate the points of attack, and give his instructions to the commanding officers.

The reserve will be composed of the Battalion of Engineers and the five [*granadero*] companies of the Battalion of Matamoros, Jiménez, and Aldama, and the Active Battalions of Toluca and San Luis.

The reserves will be commanded by the General-in-Chief, in person, during the attack; but Colonel Agustín Amat will assemble this party, which will report to him, this evening, at 5:00 o'clock to be marched to the designated station.

The first column will carry ten ladders, two crowbars, and two axes; the second, ten ladders; the third, six ladders; and the fourth, two ladders.

The men carrying ladders will sling their guns on their shoulders, to be enabled to place the ladders wherever they may be required.

The companies of *granaderos* will be supplied with six packages of cartridges to every man, and the center companies with two packages[2] and two spare flints. The men will wear neither overcoats nor blankets, or anything that may impede the rapidity of their motions. The commanding officers will see that the men have the chin-straps of their caps down, and that they are wearing either shoes or sandals.

The troops composing the columns of attack will turn in to sleep at dark, to be in readiness to move at 12 o'clock at night.

Recruits deficient in [training] instructions will remain in their quarters. The arms, principally the bayonets, should be in perfect order.

As soon as the moon rises, the center [*fusilero*] companies of the Active Battalion of San Luis[3] will abandon the points they are now occupying on the line, in order to have time to prepare.

The cavalry, under Colonel Joaquín Ramírez y Sesma, will be stationed at the *alameda*, saddling up at 3 o'clock A.M. It shall be its duty to scout the country, to prevent the possibility of an escape.

The honor of the nation being interested in this engagement against the bold and lawless foreigners who are occupying [against] us, His Excellency expects that every man will do his duty, and exert himself to give a day of glory to the country and of gratification to the Supreme Government, who will know how to reward the distinguished deeds of the brave soldiers of the army of Operations.[4] (Potter: 56-57)

---

2. United States Army cartridge packs of the era were ten rounds.

3. These companies were never mentioned during the siege. They must have been at a separate location from the remainder of the army. As stated earlier, the companies were probably guarding supplies or securing the lines of communication west and south.

4. This is the Operations Order for the attack, in short:

1st Column
General Còs

Aldama Permanent battalion	Six *fusilero* and one *cazadore* companies
San Luis Active Battalion	1st, 2nd and 3rd *fusilero* companies
10 ladders, 2 crowbars and two axes	

2d Column
Colonel Duque/General Castrillón

Active Toluca Battalion	Six *fusilero* and one *cazadore* companies
Active San Luis Battalion	4th, 5th and 6th *fusilero* companies
Ten ladders	

3d Column
Col. José María Romero

| Permanent Matamoros Battalion | Six *fusilero* companies |

Almonte

Saturday—The day commenced very moderate—thermometer 50 degrees—weather clear. A brisk fire was commenced from our north battery against the enemy, which was not answered, except now and then an increase in fire to weaken attack points of northern columns. At mid-day the thermometer rose to 68 degrees—the President determined to make the assault; it was agreed that four columns of attack were to be commanded by Generals Cós, Duque, Romero, and Morales, and second in command, Generals Castrillón, Amador and Miñón. For the purpose the points of attack were examined by the commanding officers, and they came to the conclusion that they should muster at 12 o'clock tonight and at 4 o'clock tomorrow morning the attack should be made. (*SHQ* 48: 22-23).

de la Peña

. . . on the 5th the order was given for the assault. Some [of the officers], though approving this proposal in the presence of the commander in chief, disagreed in his absence, a contradiction that reveals their weakness; others chose silence, knowing that he would not tolerate opposition, his sole pleasure being in hearing what met his wishes, while discarding all admonitions that deviated from those wishes. None of these commanders was aware that there were no field hospitals or surgeons to save the wounded, and that for some it would be easier to die than to be wounded, as we shall see after the assault.[5]

Travis's resistance was on the verge of being overcome; for several days his followers had been urging him to surrender, giving the lack of food and the scarcity of munitions as reasons, but he had quieted their restlessness with the hope of quick relief, something not difficult for them to believe since they had seen some reinforcements arrive. Nevertheless, they had pressed him so hard that on the 5th he promised them that if no help arrived on that day they would surrender the next day or would try to escape under cover of darkness; these facts were given to us by a lady from Béxar, a Negro who was the only male who escaped, and several women who were found inside and were rescued by Colonels Morales and Miñón. The enemy was in communication with some of the Bèxar townspeople who were their sympathizers, and it was said as a fact during those days that the president-general had known of Travis's decision, and that it was for this reason that he precipitated the assault, because he wanted to

---

Permanent Jimènez Battalion
Six ladders

Provisional *Cazadore* Battalion

Two ladders

Zapadores Battalion
Provisional *Granadaro* Battalion

Cavalry

Six *fusilero* companies

4th Column
Col. Juan Morales
Cazadore companies from the Jiménez, Matamoros and San Luis Battalions

Reserve
General Santa Anna/Ltc Agustín Amat
Granadaro companies from Matamoros, Jiménez, Aldama, Toluca, and San Luis battalions

Cavalry
General Ramírez y Sesma/General Mora
Dolores Regiment
Veracrus Platoon
Coahuila Company
Río Grande Presidial Company

Even though the column objectives were not yet determined, apparently the first column under Cós was the main effort. This could have been as simple as family. Cós was disgraced by the Texians in December and this would allow him to purchase some of his honor back.

5. The Military Medical Corps was established on November 30, 1829. Regardless of this, the *soldados* probably relied more on the *curanderas* and captured Texian doctors for their succor. See Nieto, Hefter, and Brown's *Soldado Mexicano: 1837-1847*, Ferris and Hoppe's *Scalpels and Sabers: Nineteenth Century Medicine in Texas*, and *Military Collector & Historian*, Spring 1996.

cause a sensation and would have regretted taking the Alamo without clamor and without bloodshed, for some believed that without these there is no glory.

Once the order was issued, even those opposing it were ready to carry it out; no one doubted that we would triumph, but it was anticipated that the struggle would be bloody, as indeed it was. All afternoon of the 5th was spent on preparations.

Four columns were chosen for the attack. The first, under command of General Cós and made up of the battalion from Aldama and three companies from the San Luis contingent, was to move against the western front, which faced the city. The second, under Colonel Duque and made up of the battalion under his command and three other companies from San Luis, was entrusted with a like mission against the front facing the north, which had two mounted batteries at each end of its walls. These two columns had a total strength of seven hundred men. The third, under command of Colonel Romero and made up of two companies of fusiliers from the Matamoros and Jiménez battalions, had less strength, for it only came up to three hundred or more men; it was to attack the east front, which was the strongest, perhaps because of its height or perhaps because of the number of cannon that were defending it, three of them situated in a battery over the church ruins, which appeared as a sort of high fortress. The fourth column, under command of Colonel Morales and made up of over a hundred *cazadores*, was entrusted with taking the entrance to the fort and the entrenchments defending it.

The *Zapadores* Battalion and five *granadero* companies made up the reserve of four hundred men. The commander in chief headed this column, according to the tenor of the secret order given for the assault, and its formation was entrusted to Colonel Amat, who actually led it into combat.

This was the general plan and although there were several minor variations proposed, almost all were cast aside.

Our commander made much of Travis's courage, for it saved him from the insulting intimation that the critical circumstances surrounding Travis would have sufficed to spare the army a great sacrifice. (Perry:43-46)

Filisola

. . . the commander in chief began to put into action his commands beginning on the night of the fifth of March to undertake the siege and capture of the Alamo if it were possible to surprise the enemy that were garrisoned there. To this end the general ordered that four attack columns commanded by their respective leaders—these all of unquestioned loyalty—should leave the city in greatest silence and order the operations to begin that same night. (Woolsey, 2:173)

Nuñez

. . . third day of the siege [since Nuñez arrived] resulted with very little variance from the first, to-wit; with heavy losses to our army. This so exasperated Santa Anna that he said, to use his own language, that he was losing the flower of his army, and to see the Alamo still hold out he became terribly enraged, and it was at this time that he made the fatal promise, which he so scrupulously carried out, that he would burn the last one of them when taken dead or alive. He immediately called a council of all his officers and proposed another attack on the Alamo in the evening of the third day's siege with his entire force. His cry was: "On to the Alamo." This was met by the officers and men that: "On to the Alamo was on to death."

A large majority of the officers were in favor of waiting until they could get more heavy cannon and perhaps by that time the garrison would be starved out and surrender and further bloodshed be avoided. But Santa Anna, with his usual impetuosity, swore that he would take the fort the next day or die in the attempt. So on Wednesday [Sunday], the 6th of March, 1836, and the fourth day of the siege[6] [since Nuñez arrived], was the time fixed for the final assault.

Each and everything pertaining to the final assault underwent the personal supervision of General Santa Anna, to the end that it would be successful. Three of his most experienced officers were selected to assist him in commanding the assaulting par-

---

6. In an attempt to give Nuñez's account the most doubtful benefit, the assumption is made that he arrived with the column on March 3, hence his "fourth day."

ties. General Vicente Filisola, his second in command, with a thousand picked men took charge of the assault on the east of the Alamo. General Castrillon with a like number, was placed on the south side. General Ramírez [y] Sesma was to have taken command on the west side next to the river, but seeing that President Santa Anna was determined to make the final assault the next day feigned sickness the evening before, and was put under arrest and started back to the capital. This part of the command then devolved on Gen. [Adrián] Woll, so there was no General [Ramírez y] Sesma in command of any portion of the army at the fall of the Alamo, nor afterwards. The troops on the north and northwest, 1,500 in number, were commanded by General Santa Anna in person. This made 4,500 men who participated in the engagement. In addition, to this, there was a fatigue party well supplied with ladders, crowbars and axes for the purpose of making breaches in the walls, or at any other vulnerable point. (*SHQ*, July 1990: 76-77)

Beccera

The plan of assault was formed and communicated to the commanders of corps and others, on the fifth. On the same day ammunition, scaling ladders, etc., were distributed. Everything was made ready for the storming. (Beccera: 19-20)

Yorba

We heard from the [Mexican] soldiers that not one of the imprisoned men had so much as returned a reply to the demand for surrender and that on the morning of the 6th of March 1836, Santa Anna was going to bring matters to a crisis with the beleaguered rebels. I never can tell the anxiety that we people on the outside felt for that mere handful of men in the old fort, when we saw around [the Alamo] hostile troops as far as we could see and not a particle of help for the Texians, for whom we few residents of the town had previously formed a liking. (*San Antonio Express*, April 12, 1896)

Coy

He was kept in the Mexican camp while preparations were made to attack the band of faithful heroes in the little church. With great avidity he saw the work go forward that was to destroy his comrades, to whom he should have brought word. He cursed the luck that had tied his hands in this important of all important hours. (*San Antonio Light*, November 26, 1911)

E. Esparza

We then had another messenger who got through the lines, saying the communication had been cut off and the promised reinforcements could not be sent.[7] (*San Antonio Express*, November 22, 1902)

Candelaria

One evening Colonel Travis made a speech to the soldiers in the Alamo. Mrs. Candaleria did not pretend to remember what he said, but she did remember that with his sword he drew a line on the floor, asking all who were willing to die for Texas to come over to his side. They all quickly stepped across the line but two men. One scaled over a wall and disappeared. The other man was James Bowie, who made an effort to rise, but failed, and with tears in his eyes, asked: "Boys, won't none of you help me over there?" Col. Davy Crockett and several others instantly sprang to the cot and carried him across. Mrs. Candelaria noticed Crockett drop on his knees and talk earnestly and in low tones to Colonel Bowie for a long time.

"At this time," said Mrs. Candelaria, "we all knew that we were doomed, but not one was in favor of surrendering." (*San Antonio Light*, February 19, 1899)

E. Esparza

Don Benito, or Crockett, as the Americans called him, assembled the men on the last day and

7. At some point the Texians' good news of March 3 is countered with reality. Either another courier group of reinforcements or at least one courier got in. A certain melancholy mode swept over the survivors when the last evening was remembered. Another group of reinforcements arriving will be discussed later.

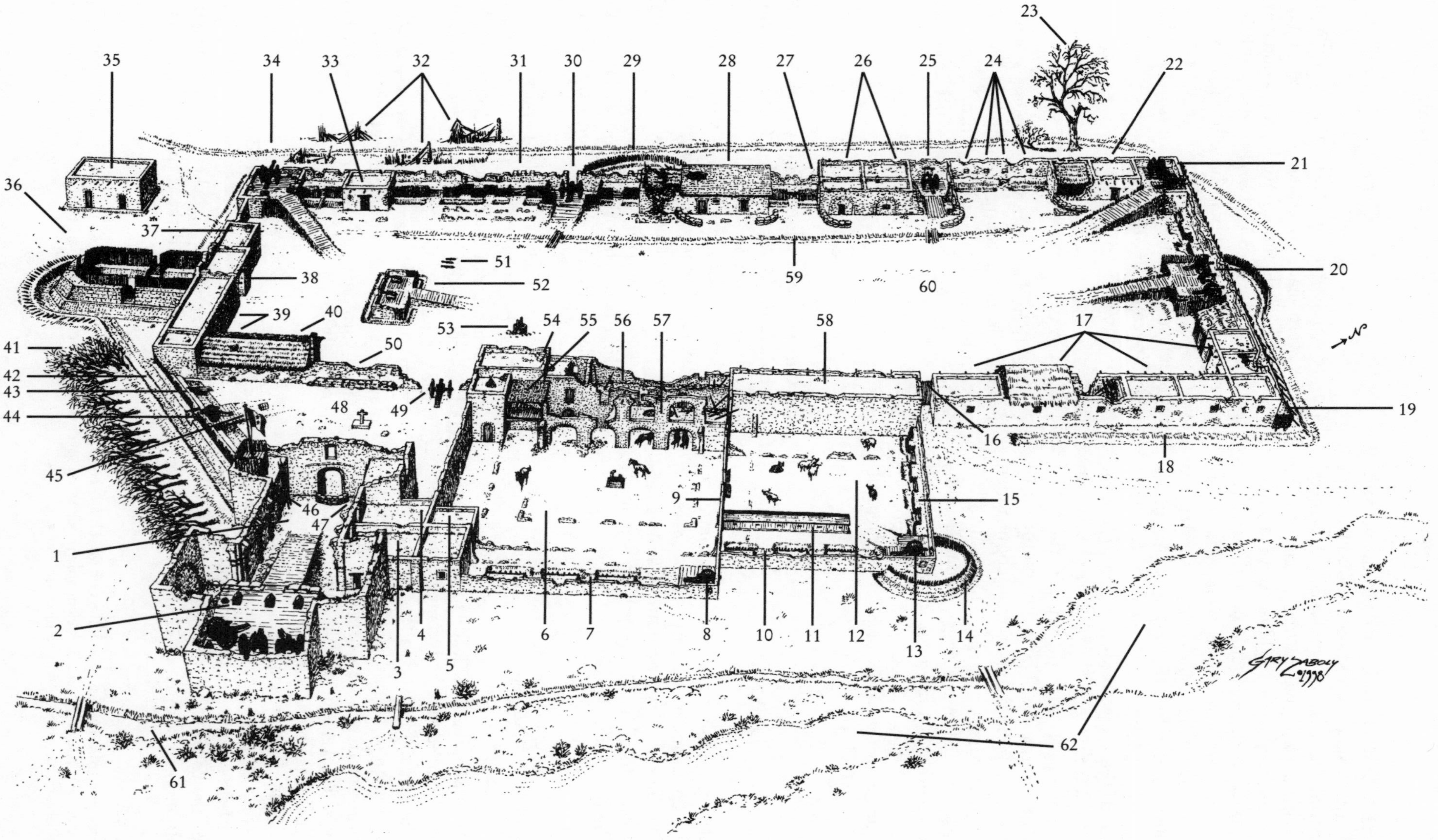

FIG. 21 THE ALAMO DURING THE SIEGE, FEBRUARY 23–MARCH 6, 1836

FIG. 21   THE ALAMO DURING THE SIEGE, FEBRUARY 23–MARCH 6, 1836

This drawing of the entire Alamo compound, with numbered keys describing individual positions and other features, has as its vantage point the rarely considered eastern side of the fort. As a result, the Alamo looks like a completely different place when compared to all previous reconstructions. The perspective also allows for an examination of important details heretofore neglected, overshadowed, or unseen.

By no means, however, does this illustration pretend to be definitive, or even mostly correct in every detail. It presents the fort as it *may* have looked, based on an interpretation of available evidence from a wide scattering of sources. The artist is very much aware that Alamo scholarship has jumped ahead by leaps and bounds in recent years, and fully expects much of what is presented here to be supplanted, or enhanced, by new evidence as it comes in.

Some of the most significant sources for uncovering fresh data on the physical Alamo of early 1836 are the two plans drawn by Capt. José Juan Sánchez-Navarro, his descriptive keys for both, and his drawing of the fort as viewed from San Antonio. If ever there was a Rosetta Stone in this field, these contemporary depictions comprise it. They warrant long hours of careful scrutiny and cross-referencing, coupled with the map of the Alamo and vicinity drawn by Mexican engineer Col. Ygnacio de Labastida.

These plans were not scientifically drafted. They are full of discrepancies, contain grotesque errors in wall-to-building relationships, and commit many sins of omission. It is in the *details* that they illuminate. These men were professional soldiers, and their plans reveal their concerns with military specifics, not precise architectural blueprints. Thus, in their keys, we are served with a variety of words seeped in a time when flintlocks and blackpowder still ruled the battlefield—words like *cavalier battery, abatis, banquette, ditch, esplanade, moat, sap, palisade, lunette, loophole,* and so on. This is the real, raw stuff, born out of the very time and place, not a memoir garbled by decades of emotional embellishment, bias, forgetfulness, and denial.

Navarro's two plans were most recently (and most clearly) reproduced in George Nelson's *The Alamo: An Illustrated History* (Dry Frio Canyon, Texas: Aldine Press, 1998), pp. 21-22. The printed indexes accompanying them are regrettably edited and incomplete (otherwise the book is an excellent visual source by a pre-eminent Alamo scholar). Earlier, complete translations of the battle plan appear in "A Mexican View of the Texas War: Memories of a Veteran of the Two Battles of the Alamo," *The Library Chronicle of the University of Texas* 4, no. 2 (Summer 1951); *A Mexican Officer's Report of the Fall of the Alamo* (Austin: University of Texas, Texana Program, 1965); and *At the Alamo: The Memoirs of Captain Navarro,* trans. C. D. Huneycutt (New London, Connecticut: Gold Star, 1988).

Unfortunately, we must return to the first publication of Sánchez-Navarro's *La Guerra de Tejas: Memorias de un Soldado,* ed. Carlos Sánchez-Navarro (Mexico City, 1938) to see the complete index for his "Vista y plano del Fuerte del Alamo," albeit in Spanish, and poorly reproduced. Still, the patient translator will find details which both complement and expand upon Navarro's battle plan and index.

Nelson's book also reproduces most of Labastida's map, in closeup and black and white, on pp. 23-24, while David Nevin's *The Texans* (New York: Time-Life "Old West" Series, 1975), pp. 82-83, prints the entire map in color.

Consult Nelson also, p. 18, for the "Plat of the Alamo as indexed by Green B. Jameson." The accompanying index is verifiably Jameson's, though the provenance of the map remains uncertain (the original has not been found). Some details here confirm Navarro and Labastida, while others provide completely new information.

Reuben M. Potter's flawed but important "Plan of the Alamo," originally published in 1878, was derived from personal observations he made in 1841, and then again in 1860, when he measured what remained of traceable walls. The version of both his plan and the monograph that contained it, *The Fall of the Alamo,* was consulted as it was printed on pp. 410-418 of Frank W. Johnson, *A History of Texas and Texans,* Vol. 1 (Chicago and New York: American Historical Society, 1914).

Additional depictions of a nearly contemporary nature were found in *Alamo Images: Changing Perceptions of a Texas Experience,* by Susan Prendergast Schoelwer and Tom W. Glaser (Dallas: De Goleyer Library and Southern Methodist University Press, 1985).

Articles appearing in issues of both the *Alamo Lore and Myth Organization Newsletter,* now defunct, and *The Alamo Journal,* which is still being ably and single-handedly published by William R. Chemerka, contained much that was useful and thought-provoking.

(Continued on next page)

Of all the unpublished works, Jake Ivey's *Mission to Fortress: The Defenses of the Alamo,* on file at the University of Texas at Austin, stands alone, an extremely incisive and exhaustive study of the Alamo's architectural evolution from religious edifice to revolutionary citadel. That this integral work in the literature remains unfinished and unpublished is almost criminal. No better single work on the Alamo's physical make-up has ever been penned.

Craig Covner is an equally adept Alamo scholar, out of whom someday a great book on the subject must surely be wrenched. Whenever I have raised a question to him on some obscure element of the architecture, Craig has never failed to provide an answer, or at the very least clues to lead one down the most likely avenue.

This drawing, then, is meant to significantly amplify and correct the version of the fort I made in 1993 for Stephen L. Hardin's *Texian Iliad: A Military History of the Texas Revolution, 1835–1836* (Austin, Texas: University of Texas Press, 1994)—evidence enough that five years, in the field of Alamo scholarship, is a very long time indeed.

Key to Numbers in Drawing:

1. Alamo church interior. Nearly fifty years earlier, the monks of Mission San Valero had given up their plans to complete the roofing of the church's nave, transept, and chancel for a number of reasons, including lack of sufficiently skilled Indian laborers. When the mission was secularized in 1793, only the arches over these sections of the cross-shaped interior had been completed.

2. High battery constructed by the engineers of General Cós during his occupation of the fort in the fall of 1835. To the Mexican Army it remained known as *Fortin de Cos* (Little Fort of Cos) during the Alamo siege in 1836.

The arches of the church had been pulled down, and considerable stone and adobe rubble had been gathered from here and elsewhere in the fort, to build both the high mound in the chancel and the inclined plane that sloped down toward the door. Wooden scaffolding completed the gun platform and ramp, which was set afire by the Mexican force that abandoned the Alamo over two months later. Three Texians guns stood here during the siege, making for a rather crowded area in which to maneuver them, with the added disadvantage that the platform slightly dipped toward its northern rim. The cannon were probably alternately pulled back for loading to allow each already loaded gun more space and flexibility in its aiming and firing.

3. Sacristy. The Labastida map indicates that this was an officers' quarters, while Sánchez-Navarro's key to his "Plano" notes that it was a storeroom for provisions. No doubt it served as both. Mrs. Dickenson's residence here during the siege suggests that the officers were probably of the artillery corps, as her husband was.

4. Large room, 21x25 feet, often called the "Monks' Burying Ground." This was evidently also both an officers' quarters and a storeroom. (The Alamo had a supply of over ninety bushels of corn; much of it must have filled this room.) It had no door opening into the nave of the church, as it does today; instead it was entered via a door from the sacristy, or from a narrow archway connecting the smaller room to its north.

5. Small room adjoining sacristy and Monks' Burying Ground. It had a small arched door in its west wall opening into the ruins of the monastery cloister (serving in 1836 as the Texians' horse corral) and was utilized as a quarters and storeroom.

6. Horse corral. This encompassed both the central convent garden, with its old well, and the surrounding spaces once occupied by a two-story square of cloistered walkways (the arches facing the garden) and monks' living quarters, called "cells." The foundations were probably still traceable in 1836, the majority of the structures having long since been demolished, mostly by the Spanish and Mexican troops occupying the mission after its secularization. Much of the stone probably provided sturdy substructures for the Alamo's gun platforms, and material to repair existing walls or to construct new ones.

7. The corral's east wall. The placement of this remains debateable. The map of the Alamo drawn by Francois Giraud in 1849, considered more reliable than most, positions the wall as shown here: aligned with the eastern face of the sacristy. Plans drawn at about the same time by the U.S. Army show a wall foundation about twenty feet more to the west, on a line approximate with the *western* wall of the sacristy. This discrepancy cannot be explained, unless the army's plans traced only the foundation of the exterior wall of the old cloister, while Giraud's indicated a makeshift wall built as a corral enclosure by post-mission military occupiers. The latter wall would have been torn down, along with all other walls considered defensible, when Santa Anna's garrison vacated the fort in May 1836.

(Continued on next page)

8. Cannon on a platform only a foot high, with embrasures cut into the wall, according to Navarro. The lowness of the platform was necessitated by the height of the wall itself, which probably reached only between six to ten feet.

9. Wall separating horse corral and cattle pen. This wall was all that remained of the northern wing of convent rooms.

10. Wall surrounding cattle pen. Navarro is the only source for its indentation, which must have been the case if the gun in the horse corral was to fire north through its own wall.

11. Latrines, or "communes," as indicated by Sánchez-Navarro in the key to his plan. Their doorways probably faced west. The latrines might have been topped with a peaked roof similar to the one on the latrine Seth Eastman drew, situated just a few yards north of the east end of the ruined Alamo church, in two rough sketches done in 1848 as preliminaries for eventual watercolors.

12. Cattle pen. The "20 or 30 heads of Beeves" Travis reported having gotten into the walls on February 23 must have thinned out considerably after just a few days, unless they were severely rationed. On March 3, however, Travis wrote that "we have provisions for twenty days for the men we have"; but the bulk of this food must have been the nearly two and a half tons of corn also requisitioned on February 23.

13. Cannon on a platform only a foot high, with embrasures cut into the wall, according to Navarro.

14. Semicircular palisade and ditch, serving as a defensive outerwork for this gun and probably as a bastion for riflemen and outguards.

15. Earthen banquettes (firing steps) and trenches, which Sánchez-Navarro deemed "poorly constructed . . . with which the colonists, thinking they were reinforcing part of the fort, weakened it." What he meant by this is unclear, unless the digging had somehow undermined and collapsed sections of these walls. Navarro's plan indicates that all of the free-standing walls of the Alamo had been "reinforced" with banquettes, and he draws them as half-rectangles along their interior. Some of these mounds were probably buttressed by wooden cribbing, though wood was a very scarce commodity for the defenders during the siege.

16. Gap in the wall, about five and one-half feet wide, covered by some sort of defensive work, perhaps a palisaded gate.

17. Barracks for the artillerymen, according to Labastida. Like most of the other barracks within the compound, these rooms contained trenches and semicircular parapets, some of the latter made of stretched ox hides filled with earth. De la Peña considered these interior works more a hindrance than a help to the defenders when the hand-to-hand fighting broke out within the barracks.

18. Exterior ditch extending north and west about halfway down the north wall, becoming semicircular in front of the wall's central battery. Labastida shows the straight part of the trench, Navarro its semicircular section.

19. Careful study of a good reproduction of Navarro's two plans reveals that the ruinous north wall was reinforced for its *entire length* by a timber-and-earth outerwork. The latter was clearly described by Filisola, and verified by de la Peña, as being made of narrow timbers placed horizontally upon each other, supported on the outside by straightly planted logs; and with dirt and rubble filling the gap between adobe wall and wood. Navarro added that this made the wall five feet thick; de la Peña recorded its height as being from eight to nine feet.

Previous Alamo histories, when discussing the critical attack on this wall, describe only a short section of it—as, for instance, a supposed breach—being covered by a timber outerwork; however, no evidence exists for such an abbreviated structure. Again, the facts, both written and visual, point to the wall's entire length being covered by wood, so brittle and crumbled the adobe must have been.

20. *Fortin de Teran,* a three-gun battery of eight-pounders, firing through embrasures, according to Labastida's map, and verified by de la Peña as having three guns (though Navarro shows only two here). On the ramp of this battery a wounded Colonel Travis "died like a soldier," wrote Navarro.

21. *Fortin de Condelle,* a two-gun battery firing through embrasures, according to Labastida. The so-called Jameson map also indicates two guns here, though Navarro shows three.

22. Officers' quarters, according to Labastida. Filisola notes that there were flat roofs on the rooms of the houses in the northwestern and northeastern sectors.

23. Large pecan tree. Navarro's drawing of the fort shows this tree with some of its limbs pruned—no doubt by exposure to artillery fire.

(Continued on next page)

24. Portholes in wall originally used for ground-based cannon to fire through, described in Jameson's key to his plan of January 18, 1836. By the time of the March 6 attack, however, the Texians had obviously moved these guns elsewhere, and largely blocked up the portholes. Nevertheless, the soldiers of Cos' column quickly hacked and pushed their way through them, at the same time also gaining entry at other points along the west wall.

25. Cannon on a low platform firing through a window. This might have been the "little fort" where Crockett's body was found. (See caption to Fig. 37: SANTA ANNA ORDERS THE EXECUTIONS.)

26. Officers' quarters, according to Labastida.

27. The wall from this point southward indented inward about eleven feet, due to misaligned construction during the mission period.

28. Headquarters of the Alamo, according to Jameson, and verified as an officers' quarters by Labastida; thus, Travis' quarters.

29. Semicircular palisade and outer ditch, serving the same purpose as #14.

30. Iron twelve-pound gunade, mounted on wagon wheels, placed on a low platform to fire through a hole cut in the adobe wall.

31. Crenellations: Navarro's drawing of the fort shows them along the west wall; perhaps he was merely stylizing the irregularities of the parapet. But in 1809, "834 varas of battlement" were ordered by the Spanish Army to renovate the Alamo walls, and they may have indeed survived here and there to 1836.

32. Ruins of Tejano *jacales* lying close to the walls, burned down by the defenders.

33. Artillery command post, according to Labastida. It also served as a warehouse containing iron tools and wood, and as an armory workshop (Navarro). Probably cannon were repaired here (which might explain the nearby three unmounted cannon tubes), such as the eighteen-pounder and another Texian gun after Mexcian guns dismounted them on February 24.

34. The iron-barreled eighteen-pounder, firing over the wall. Covering the approaches to this corner was an outside ditch, but it had been only partially completed.

35. Outlying stone building. Potter makes a possible reference to it when he noted "the old stone stable and huts that stood south of the southwest angle."

36. Lunette (also described as a "tambour") and exterior moat, with at least two cannon, defending the main gate. A careful study of the Navarro drawing reveals, for the first time, that the walls of the lunette were of either stone or adobe, not dirt, and most likely mortared. In fact, their construction probably dated back to the earlier Spanish or Mexican occupations. Behind the walls stands what appears to be a secondary defensive structure: a high palisade, high enough to deprive besiegers of a line of sight into the compound. The gate was on its western side, no doubt with a draw-ramp spanning the ditch. Within the walls were firing steps of earth for riflemen, the palisade being loopholed. Evidence of postholes within the lunette site has been found by archaeologists. A fraise of sharpened stakes might have edged the outer part of the moat.

For the most part, this reconstruction does not clash with the Labastida plan. Part of the palisade wall on the eastern side probably bent back to cover a section of the open gate; this, too, is suggested in Labastida. All in all, this exterior work was considerably more formidable than the U-shaped stake-and-earth breastwork previously thought to have stood here.

37. Officer of the Guard.

38. Main gate.

39. Rooms serving both as hospital wards and officers' quarters. In the room nearest the gate, James Bowie "died without resisting," according to Navarro.

40. Kitchens.

41. Abatis of felled trees, with branches probably sharpened and facing the enemy, to hinder an assault on the palisade. This type of outer defense was an old one. It was used frequently in the wars of the eighteenth century, and was still being used for fortification in America up through the Civil War.

42. Trench connected with lunette moat, and covering the palisade. Dirt from the trench was shoveled against the palisade to make a serviceable breastwork, buffering it against enemy artillery fire.

43. Palisade, drawn according to the conclusions of Jake Ivey: a single wall of vertical timbers about eight feet high, with an earthen firing step almost two feet high, and loopholes cut about four and one-half feet from the step. This agrees with archaeological work thus far done in this sector, although opinions differ. The dirt for the firing step came from an inner trench. Over this palisade a number of defenders attempted escape, once they realized how hopeless the battle was (Navarro).

(Continued on next page)

44. Single cannon and embrasure defending the palisade.

45. Tricolor flag with two stars, as drawn in Navarro's "Vista," and its existence confirmed in Almonte's journal entry of February 23. This raised platform obviously served as an observation post, and as a scaffolding for riflemen during the final battle.

46. Baptistry. Here the Texians stored part of their gunpowder supply. Noncombatants were gathered and herded into this room while the Mexicans carried out their final mopping-up of the church and compound.

47. Confessional room, also used as a powder magazine.

48. Inner courtyard, site of the old mission cemetery for Indian converts. Navarro drew this cross and foundation—not uncommon for churches of the Southwest—on his battle map, though it might have been merely symbolic.

49. Gun position noted on Navarro's battle plan.

50. So-called "low wall," separating inner courtyard from the fort's main plaza. In truth, by the evidence of post-battle sketches, this wall stood nearly as high as the doorways of the long barracks—perhaps about seven feet. A firing step might have been built on its eastern side to defend it from an enemy already invading the main plaza.

51. Three unmounted cannon barrels, probably destined for the nearby armory workshop (#33).

52. Two-gun platform covering the inner side of the main gate. It was partially built of adobe, and partially of stakes and earth.

53. Well dug by the defenders during the siege.

54. The old convent building. The second floor room was used as a hospital; the first floor room as an armory for small arms.

55. Shed covering an exposed floor, and a stairwell leading to the second floor of the convent. The exposed floor here had once been a corner of the arcaded gallery.

56. The second story of the "long barracks"—of which the convent was a part—mostly in ruins from both the 1835 Texian bombardment and the guns of Santa Anna in 1836.

57. Arcaded galleries, the second-story level almost obliterated. The ground floor provided a handy stable for the garrison's few horses.

58. Soldiers' barracks, once used as the mission granary building. A *"calabozo"* (jail cell) was located in its southern end, according to Navarro.

59. Waterless *acequia* built in mission days, its ends now covered by the dirt of fortifications that cut it off from its exterior water supply.

60. The Alamo's main plaza and parade ground.

61. A branch of the Acequia de Alamo, bringing irrigation water to surrounding farmland. During the siege the Mexicans lowered the water table here, or emptied it entirely, by cutting off the flow from the ditch in the north.

62. Two ponds, possibly deliberately dug as early as the mission days to ensure a nearby water source for livestock. When the Texians' well failed to deliver, they made sallies to collect water from either the *acequia* or the ponds.—GZ

told them Santa Anna's terms, but none of them believed that any one who surrendered could get out alive, so they all said if they would have to die anyhow they would fight it out. (*San Antonio Express,* November 22, 1902)

* * * *

At times Señor Travis looked very sad and stern. One day he said to Bowie, "Help will come." But help did not come. When he felt that they must fight it out alone, he gave his men a chance to say whether they would stay by him to the end. I saw him draw the line with his sword, and heard him say, "All who are willing to die, cross this line."

I think all jumped across. *Señor* Bowie said, "Boys, lift my cot across that line." My heart was in my mouth. My eyes were like coals of fire; but I would stay and listen. (Driggs and King: 224-225)

* * * *

Although too weak to stand upon his feet, when Travis drew the line with his sword Bowie had those around him bring his cot across the line. (*San Antonio Express,* May 12, 1907)

Dickenson

. . . the noble Travis called up his men, drew a line with his sword and said: "My soldiers, I am going to meet the fate that becomes me. Those who will stand by me, let them remain, but those who desire to go, let them go." (*San Antonio Express,* April 28, 1881)

* * * *

Colonel Travis called his well men and drew a line with his sword and said: "My soldiers, I am going to meet the fate that becomes me. Those who will stand by me let them remain, but those who desire to go, let them go—and who crosses the line that I have drawn—shall go." I came to the door of the room I had, the baptistery, and watched them. It was a most impressive scene. (Brogan: 87)

* * * *

On the evening previous to the massacre, Col. Travis asked the command that if any desired to escape, now was the time, to let it be known, and to step out of the ranks. But one stepped out. His name to the best of my recollection was Ross. The next morning he was missing. . . .[8] (Adjutant General Papers, TSL)

Rose

About two hours before sunset, on the third day of March 1836, the bombardment suddenly ceased, and the enemy withdrew an unusual distance. Taking advantage of that opportunity, Col. Travis paraded all of his effective men in a single file; and taking his position in front of the center, he stood for some moments apparently speechless from emotion. Then, nerving himself for the occasion, he addressed them substantially as follows:

"My brave companions—stern necessity compels me to employ the few moments afforded by this probably brief cessation of conflict[9] in making known to you the most interesting, yet the most solemn, melancholy, and unwelcome fact that perishing humanity can realize. But how shall I find language to prepare you for its reception? I cannot do so. All that I can say to this purpose is, be prepared for the worst. I must come to the point. Our fate is sealed. Within a very few days—perhaps a very few hours—we must all be in eternity. This is our destiny, and we cannot avoid it. This is our certain doom.

"I have deceived you long by the promise of help. But I crave your pardon, hoping that after hearing my explanation, you will not only regard my conduct as pardonable, but heartily sympathize with me in my extreme necessity. In deceiving you, I also deceived myself, having been first deceived by others.[10]

"I have continually received the strongest assurances of help from home. Every letter from the council and every one that I have seen from individuals at home, has teemed with assurances that our people were ready, willing, and anxious to come to our relief; and that within a very short time we might confidently expect recruits enough to repel any force that would be brought against us. These assurances I received as facts. They inspired me with the greatest confidence that our little band would be made the nucleus of an army of sufficient magnitude to repel our foes, and to enforce peace on our own terms. In the honest and simple confidence of my heart, I have transmitted to you these promises of help, and my confident hopes of success. But the promised help has not come and our hopes are not to be realized.

"I have evidently confided too much in the promises of our friends. But let us not be in haste to censure them. The enemy has invaded our territory much earlier than we anticipated; and their present

---

8. At some time on the evening of March 5, Travis may have assembled the garrison and told them what he believed was about to happen. Then in true federalist fashion he offered the defenders a choice: to stand and fight or leave. The decision was up to them. The accounts dealing with this event are presented here, but their validity is still challenged. Historians generally do not want to believe that something this melodramatic happened. There are three choices here:
    1). All are experiencing mass-hallucination;
    2). They are lying;
    3). They are telling the truth.
9. When the columns began displacing at sunset it is likely that the artillery fire ceased as well.
10. See Williamson's letter of March 3.

approach is a matter of surprise. Our friends were evidently not informed of our perilous condition in time to save us. Doubtless they would have been here by the time they expected any considerable force of the enemy. When they find a Mexican army in their midst, I hope they will show themselves true to their cause.[11]

"My calls on Col. Fannin remain unanswered, and my messengers have not returned. The probabilities are that his whole command has fallen into the hands of the enemy, or been cut to pieces, and that our couriers have been cut off.

"I trust that I have now explained my conduct to your satisfaction and that you do not censure me for my course. I must again refer to the assurances of help from home. They are what deceived me, and they caused me to deceive you. Relying upon these assurances, I determined to remain within these walls until the promised help should arrive, stoutly resisting all assaults from without. Upon the same reliance, I retained you here, regarding the increasing force of our assailants with contempt, till they outnumbered us more than twenty to one[12] and escape became impossible. For the same reason, I scorned their demand of a surrender at discretion and defied their threat to put every one of us to the sword, if the fort should be taken by storm.

"I must now speak of our present situation. Here we are, surrounded by an army that could almost eat us for breakfast, from whose arms our lives are, for the present, protected by these stone walls. We have no hope for help, for no force that we could ever reasonably have expected, could cut its way through the strong ranks of these Mexicans. We dare not surrender; for, should we do so, that black flag,[13] now waving in our sight, as well as the merciless character, admonishes us of what would be our doom. We cannot cut our way out through the enemy's ranks; for in attempting that, we should all be slain in less than ten minutes. Nothing remains then, but to stay within this fort, and fight to the last moment. In this case, we must, sooner or later, all be slain; for I am sure that Santa Anna is determined to storm the fort and take it, even at the greatest cost of the lives of his own men.

"Then we must die! Our speedy dissolution is a fixed and inevitable fact. Our business is not to make a fruitless effort to save our lives, but to choose the manner of our death. But three modes are presented to us. Let us choose that by which we may best serve our country. Shall we surrender, and be deliberately shot, without taking the life of a single enemy? Shall we try to cut our way out through the Mexican ranks, and be butchered before we can kill twenty of our adversaries? I am opposed to either method; for in either case, we could but lose our lives, without benefiting our friends at home—our fathers and mothers, our brothers and sisters, our wives and little ones. The Mexican army is strong enough to march through the country, and exterminate its inhabitants, and our countrymen are not able to oppose them in open field. My choice, then, is to remain in this fort, to resist every assault, and to sell our lives as dearly as possible.

"Then let us band together as brothers, and vow to die together. Let us resolve to withstand our adversaries to the last; and, at each advance, to kill as many of them as possible. And when, at last, they shall storm our fortress, let us kill them as they come! kill them as they scale our walls! kill them as they leap within! kill them as they raise their weapons and as they use them! kill them as they kill their companions! and continue to kill them as long as one of us shall remain alive.

"By this policy, I trust that we shall so weaken our enemies that our countrymen at home can meet them on fair terms, cut them up, expel them from the country, and thus establish their own independence, and secure prosperity and happiness to our families and our country. And, be assured, our memory will be gratefully cherished by posterity, till all history shall be erased, and all noble deeds shall be forgotten.

"But I shall leave every man to his own choice. Should any man prefer to surrender, and be tied and shot; or to attempt an escape through the Mexican ranks, and be killed before he can run a hundred yards, he is at liberty to do so.

"My own choice is to stay in this fort, and die for my country, fighting as long as breath shall remain in my body. This I will do even if you leave me alone. Do as you think best—but no man can die

---

11. Unknown to Travis, Urrea was already in their midst, with a sizable force.
12. Actually the number was about 2,370 to 180-250. See Santos, pp. 15, 69-71.
13. The flag was red, flying over both the San Fernando and probably the Casa Mata.

with me without affording me comfort in the moment of death."

Colonel Travis then drew his sword and with its point traced a line upon the ground extending from the right to the left of the file. Then, resuming his position in front of the center, he said, "I now want every man who is determined to stay here and die with me to come across this line. Who will be the first? March!"

The first respondent was Tapley Holland,[14] who leaped the line at a bound, exclaiming, "I am ready to die for my country!" His example was instantly followed by every man in the file, with the exception of Rose. Manifest enthusiasm was universal and tremendous. Every sick man that could walk arose from his bunk and tottered across the line. Col. Bowie, who could not leave his bed, said, "Boys, I am not able to go to you, but I wish some of you would be so kind as to remove my cot over there." Four men instantly ran to the cot and, each lifting a corner, carried it across the line. Then every sick man that could not walk made the same request, and had his bunk removed in like manner.

Rose, too, was deeply affected, but differently from his companions. He stood until every man but himself had crossed the line. A consciousness of the real situation overpowered him. He sank upon the ground, covered his face, and yielded to his own reflections. For a time he was unconscious of what was transpiring around him. A bright idea came to his relief; he spoke the Mexican dialect very fluently, and could pass for a Mexican and effect an escape. He looked over the area of the fort; every sick man's berth was at its wonted place; every effective soldier was at his post, as if waiting orders; he felt as if dreaming. He directed a searching glance at the cot of Col. Bowie. There lay his gallant friend. Col. David Crockett was leaning over the cot, conversing with its occupant in an undertone. After a few seconds Bowie looked at Rose and said, "You seem not to be willing to die with us Rose." "No," said Rose, "I am not prepared to die, and will not do so if I can avoid it." Then Crockett also looked at him, and said, "You may as well conclude to die with us, old man, for escape is impossible."

Rose made no reply, but looked up at the top of the wall. "I have often done worse than to climb that wall," he thought. Suiting the action to the thought he sprang up, seized his wallet of unwashed clothes, and ascended the wall. Standing on its top, he looked down within to take a last view of his dying friends. They were all now in motion, but what they were doing he heeded not. Overpowered by his feelings he looked away and saw them no more.

Looking down without, he was amazed at the scene of death that met his gaze. From the wall to a considerable distance beyond the ground was literally covered with slaughtered Mexicans and pools of blood.

He viewed this horrid scene but a moment. He threw down his wallet and leaped after it; he alighted on his feet, but the momentum of the spring threw him sprawling upon his stomach in a puddle of blood. After several seconds he recovered his breath, he arose and took up his wallet; it had fallen open and several garments had rolled out upon the blood. He hurriedly thrust them back, without trying to cleanse them of the coagulated blood which adhered to them. Then, throwing the wallet across his shoulders he walked rapidly away.

He took the road which led down the river around a bend to the ford, and through the town by the church. He waded the river at the ford and passed through the town. He saw no person in town, but the doors were all closed, and San Antonio appeared as a deserted city.

After passing through town he turned down the river. A stillness as of death prevailed. When he had gone about a quarter of a mile below the town his ears were saluted by the thunder of the bombardment, which was then renewed. That thunder continued to remind him that his friends were true to their cause, by a continual roar, with but slight intervals, until a little before sunrise on the morning of the sixth, when it ceased and he heard it no more.[15] (Zuber: 248-252)

---

14. Born ca. 1810 in Ohio, he was then from Grimes County, Texas. Holland fought in the Siege of Béxar the previous December and was probably an artilleryman. See Groneman, *Alamo Defenders*.

15. The Rose account is wrought with controversy, especially since Zuber was telling it three times removed and almost forty years later. It was discounted for years until it was discovered that Rose did exist and spent his final days in New Orleans. The possibility exists that Rose was in a reinforcement column that was chopped prior to the walls. For more on this and Zuber, see Walter Lord's *A Time to Stand*, and Janis Boyle Mayfield (ed.), *My Eighty Years in Texas*.

E. Esparza

Rose left after this armistice had expired and after the others had been sent for succor. Rose went out after Travis drew the line with his sword. He was the only man who did not cross the line. Up to then he had fought as bravely as any man there. He had stood by the cannon. Rose went out during the night. They opened a window for him and let him go. The others who left before went out of the doors and in the daytime. Alsbury left his wife and sister-in-law there. His sister-in-law afterward married a man named Cantu. She and Mrs. Alsbury stayed in the Alamo until it fell. They feared to leave, believing the Mexicans under Santa Anna would kill them. (*San Antonio Express*, May 12, 1907)

de la Peña

Night came, and with it the most somber reflections. Our soldiers it was said, lacked the cool courage that is demanded by an assault, but they were steadfast and the survivors will have nothing to be ashamed of. Each one individually confronted and prepared his soul for the terrible moment, expressed his last wishes, and silently and coolly took those steps which precede an encounter. It was a general duel from which it was important to us to emerge with honor. No harangue preceded this combat, but the example given was the most eloquent language and the most absolute order. Our brave officers left nothing to be desired in the hour of trial, and if anyone failed in his duty, if anyone tarnished his honor, it was so insignificant that his shortcomings remained in the confusion of obscurity and disdain. (Perry:45)

E. Esparza

At last came a night of quiet and the exhausted men fell into a deep sleep. (DRT Library, Alamo)

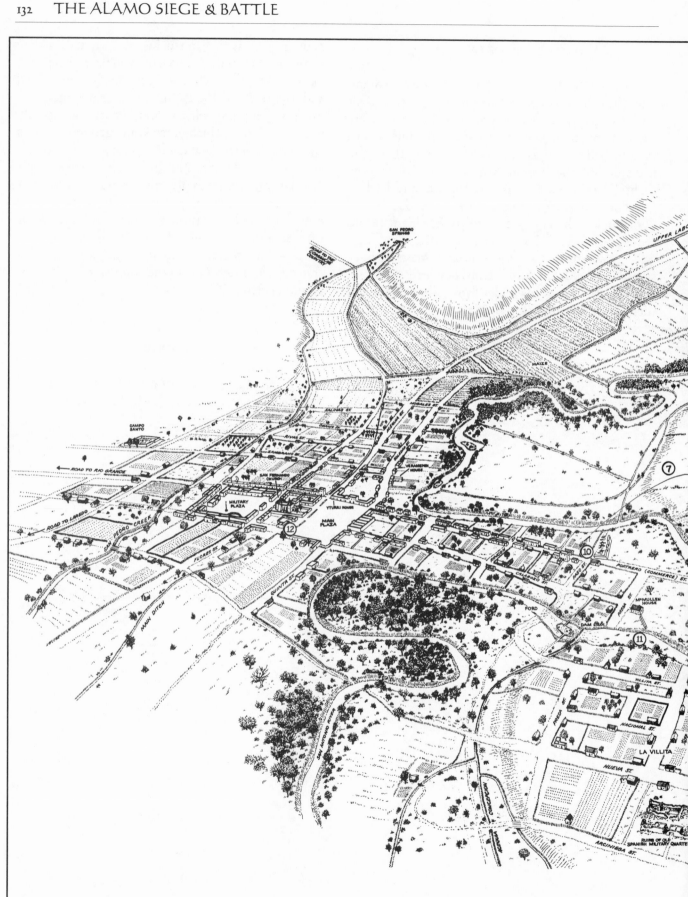

1. Duque's column and route of attack.
2. Cós' column and route.
3. Romero's column and route.
4. Morales' column and route.
5. Santa Anna and reserves and route.
6. Cavalry dispositions to intercept fugitives.
7. Rocket signal to commence the attack, in conjunction with bugle sounded at north battery.
8. Texian attempted escape routes.
9A. 9B. Funeral pyres for Texian dead.
10. Mexican wounded brought here.
11. Corpses of Mexican soldiers crowding river; others buried in Campo Santo.
12. Don Musquíz home, where Alamo refugee women and children were brought.

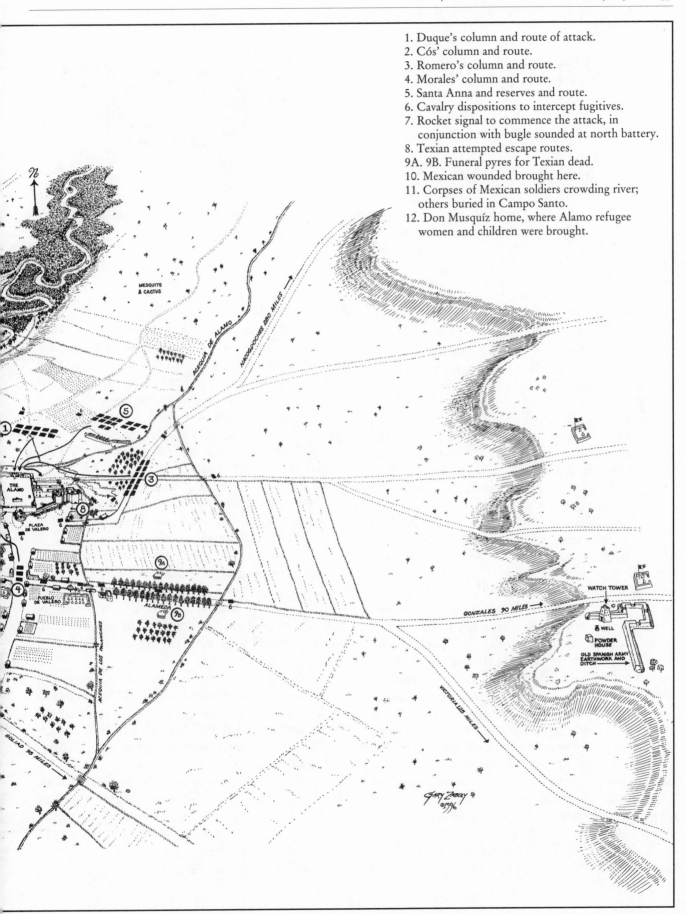

DAY THIRTEEN

Sunday
March 6, 1836

Prologue

AT AROUND midnight the Mexican Army stirred and awoke. The attack columns sleepily formed and moved toward their assault positions. Once in the positions they lay down again and attempted to get some more sleep. A little before sunrise at 5:00 A.M. a *soldado* from the second column could no longer wait, and the cry of "*Viva* Santa Anna!" broke silence of the still morning. Soon the cry was seconded by the rest of the column. Surprise then lost, Santa Anna ordered the rockets fired and the massed bands to sound the "*Atención, carga ó ataque*" and the "*degüello*."

All four Mexican columns surged forward. The Texians in their sleep were awakened by the thunder of hundreds of running feet and shouts for the Mexican Republic. The Texians posted outside the walls in the trenches breathed their last at their posts. It did not take long for the Texian gunners to fire their cannon into the onrushing columns. The *soldados* paid a high price for their noisy patriotism.

Due to the Texians' enfilade fire from their eastern batteries, the three northern columns shifted into one large formation and stalled at the base of the Alamo's north wall. Momentum lost, Santa Anna committed his reserve, and it was these *granaderos* and *zapadores* who succeeded in breaching the Texian northern defense and regaining the initiative. At the same time the *cazadore* battalion found success and breached the Texians' southwest corner. The Texians withdrew into the adobe apartments, the *convento*, and church.

Alamo Plaza was full of *soldados*, and the Texians poured a withering fire on them through loopholes in the buildings. The Texian batteries were abandoned by the Texian gunners, then captured and trained on the defenders' sanctuaries. The room-to-room fighting in the *convento* was the bloodiest yet of the morning. The northern columns cleared the adobe apartments and the *convento* while the provisional battalion of *cazadores* worked their way down the southern low barracks and into the church.

At about that point up to sixty Texians left the Alamo compound heading for the *alameda* at the Gonzáles Road. Awaiting them were Ramírez y Sesma's cavalry, who made quick work of the escape. By 6:30 A.M. the battle had ended. Santa Anna entered the fort along with his escort.

General Castrillón met him with at least five Texian survivors, one of which was David Crockett. Castrillón defended the men honorably, but Santa Anna would not hear of it. Several junior officers pulled their sabres and stabbed the survivors to death. According to all accounts, they died with dignity.

The noncombatant and dependent survivors were escorted by the *soldados* to the Músquiz house in Béxar where each was questioned, given two silver dollars, a blanket and then released. The Texian bodies were placed in two funeral pyres on either side of the *alameda*.

Each participant's account is designated with their column identifier where applicable. The accounts are broken into seven phases for reading ease:
Phase I—The assembly of forces
Phase II—The charge
Phase III—Inside the walls

Phase IV—The executions
Phase V—The escape
Phase VI—The aftermath
Phase VII—The numbers.

The legend is challenged in the area of execu-tion of Crockett, but more notably with the Texian escape attempt. This escape attempt explains the difference in the numbers of defenders and why there were three funeral pyres. Several Mexican par-ticipants witnessed the attempt and at least one assisted in the termination of the Texian escape.

Phase I:
The Assembly of Forces

de la Peña
(Column 2)

BEGINNING AT ONE O'CLOCK in the morn-ing of the 6th, the columns were set in motion, and at three [o'clock] they silently advanced toward the [San Antonio] River, which they crossed marching two abreast over some narrow wooden bridges.[1] A few minor obstacles were explored in order to reach the enemy without being noticed, to a point per-sonally designated by the commander in chief, where they stationed themselves, resting with weapons in hand.[2] Silence was again ordered and smoking was prohibited. The moon was up, but the density of the clouds that covered it allowed only an opaque light in our direction, seeming thus to con-tribute to our designs.[3] This half-light, the silence we kept, hardly interrupted by soft murmurs, the coolness of the morning air, the great quietude that seemed to prolong the hours, and the dangers we would soon have to face, all of this rendered our sit-uation grave; we were still breathing and able to communicate; within a few moments many of us would be unable to answer questions addressed to us, having already returned to the nothingness whence we had come; others badly wounded, would remain stretched out for hours without anyone thinking of them, each still fearing perhaps one of the enemy cannonballs whistling overhead would drop at his feet and put an end to his sufferings. Nevertheless, hope stirred us and within a few min-utes this anxious uncertainty would disappear; an insult to our arms had to be avenged, as well as the blood of our friends spilled three months before within these same walls we were about to attack.[4] Light began to appear on the horizon, the beautiful dawn would soon let herself be seen behind her gold-en curtain. (Perry:46-47)

Vargas

I did not fire a shot, neither did I storm the old fort when the Mexicans [*soldados*] rushed in to cut to pieces the last remnant of the gallant band. They did their own work, I refusing to go to the Alamo. For this they threatened execution when the day was won, but could not at that time waste a shell on me. One shell might mean victory or defeat. They used their shells on the Texians. (*San Antonio Light*, April 1910)

Nuñez
(Column 1)

The infantry were formed nearest the Alamo, as we made the least noise. The cavalry was formed

---

1. There are two known bridge locations. One was between Béxar and La Villita, the other was near the old mill. The cavalry, Matamoros, Jiménez and *cazadore* battalions were already on the Alamo side of the river and probably moved into position from their entrenched encampments.

2. The attack positions are unknown, but probably were the northern battery for the first, second, and reserve columns, some sort of fortification built by Ramírez y Sesma east of the Alamo for the third column, and the La Villita area for the fourth column.

3. According to Eric von Schmidt in *Smithsonian*, March 1986, this puts the available moonlight at about 88% with some minor obscurity from light cloud cover.

4. Battle of Béxar.

around on the outside of the infantry, with special orders from all commanders to cut down every one who dared to turn back.[5] (*SHQ*, July 1990:77)

Ben

Santa Anna ordered him [Ben] to have coffee ready for them all night; that both he and Almonte were conversing constantly, and did not go to bed; that they [Almonte and Santa Anna] went out about midnight, and about two or three o'clock returned together to the [Yturri?] house[6] that Santa Anna ordered coffee immediately, threatening to run him [Ben] through the body if it was not instantly brought; that he [Ben] served them [Santa Anna and Almonte] with coffee; that Santa Anna appeared agitated, and that Almonte remarked that "it would cost them much" that the reply was, "it was of no importance what the cost was, that it must be done." (Newell: 88)

Becerra

(Column 2)

During the night the troops were placed in position. About three o'clock on the morning of the 6th the battalion Matamoros was marched to a point near the river, and above the Alamo. At their rear were two thousand men under Gen. Cós.[7] Gen. Castrillón commanded this portion of the army.

Gen Tolza's [*sic*, Col. Morales'] command held the ground [south] below the Alamo. The troops were to march to the attack when the bugler at headquarters sounded the advance. The order delivered by Santa Anna to the commanders was to move in silence, and not fire a single shot until the trenches of the enemy had been reached. The Mexican troops thought little of the terrible ordeal through which they were about to pass. (Becerra: 20)

E. Esparza

If I had been given a weapon I would have fought likewise. But weapons and ammunition were scarce and only wielded and used by those who knew how. But I saw some there no older than I who had them and fought as bravely and died as stolidly as the adults. This was towards the end and when many of the grown persons within had been slain by the foes without. It was then that some of the children joined in the defense.[8]

The end came suddenly and almost unexpectedly and with a rush. It came at night and when all was dark save when there was a gleam of light from the flash and flame of a fired gun. Our men fought hard all day long. Their ammunition was very low.[9] That of many was entirely spent. Santa Anna must have known this, for his men had been able during the day to make several breeches in the walls.[10] Our men had fought long and hard and well. But their strength was spent. Many slept. Few there were who

---

5. This seems to echo Urissa's recollection and has been used, incorrectly, to vilify Santa Anna's need to abuse his own *soldados* in order for them to attack. The cavalry were posted in the *alameda*.

6. This would appear that Santa Anna is operating to a certain extent out of his command post established at the Yturri house in Béxar and later moved to the northern battery.

7. The Matamoros *fusileros* were with column three. Their attack position was east of the Alamo. Cós commanded the first column.

8. Esparza was possibly referring to the eleven- and twelve-year-old sons of Alamo defender Anthony Wolf, who were with the women and children and were killed by the *soldados*. There were other juveniles: William King, fifteen, John Gaston, seventeen, Galba Fuqua, sixteen; these young men were armed and probably treated by the garrison as adults. They were definitely treated by the *soldados* as such. See Groneman's *Alamo Defenders*.

9. Untrue. The Mexican Army's captured Texian ordnance inventory from the Alamo has recently come to light. In short there were remaining:

14,600 cartridges					
369	12 pound rounds	199	12 pound balls	129	12 pound grapeshot
226	8 " "	89	8 " "	83	8 " "
201	6 " "	198	6 " "	199	6 " "
109	4 " "	200	4 " "	99	4 " "
120	3 " "			20	3 " "
93	2 " "			19	2 " "

See: *Expediente* XI/481.3/1655, document 0039

10. Undoubtedly the walls were weakened by the siege, but to what extent is not known. It is unlikely there were any breeches in the walls.

were awake. Even those on guard beside the breeches in the walls dozed. The fire from the Mexicans had slacked and finally ceased. Those who were awake saw the Mexican foeman lying quietly by their campfires and thought they likewise slept. But our foes were only simulating sleep or if they slept, were awakened by their savage chief and his brutal officers.

After all had been dark and quiet for many hours and I had fallen into a profound slumber suddenly there was a terrible din. (*San Antonio Express*, May 12, 1907)

Caro

Early in the morning of the 6th the four attacking columns as well as the reserve took up their respective positions as assigned by the general order of the 5th, a copy of which was transmitted to the supreme government. From this it will be seen that our force numbered 1400 men in all.[11] (Castañeda: 104)

Mexican Soldier

(Column One)

The attack was made in four columns, led by General Cós, General [*sic,* Colonel] Morales [column four], Duque de Estrada [column two], and Romero [column three]. I watched under the immediate command of General Cós and will tell you what I saw. After a long wait we took our places at 3 o'clock A.M. on the south side [of the northern battery?], a distance of 300 feet from the fort of the enemy. (*El Mosquito Mexicano*, April 5, 1836)[12]

Filisola

The Mexican troops, at 4:00 A.M. on the 6th, were in their places as had been indicated in the instructions set forth. The artillery, as is gathered from the same instructions, was to remain inactive since they were not scheduled for anything, nor was it impossible in the darkness, and also according to the plans for the troops, to attack on four sides. There could be no artillery fire without blowing their [*soldado*] comrades to bits. Thus the enemy enjoyed the advantage of not enduring the artillery fire throughout the whole time of the attack.

Their [Texians] own artillery was ready and alert so that when the fatal trumpet sounded, there was no doubt that the ultimate scene was at hand—conquer or die. And if there had been any doubt, they were promptly disillusioned by the reckless shouting and *vivas* by the attacking columns as soon as they were seen. (Woolsey, 2:177)

Phase II:
The Charge

Almonte

SUNDAY—AT 5 A.M. the columns were posted at their respective stations. . . . and at half past 5 the attack or assault was made. (*SHQ* 48:23)

Ben

After drinking coffee, they went out, and I soon saw rockets ascending in different directions,[13] and shortly after I heard musketry and cannon, and

---

11. More likely around 1,700: column one—355; column two—395; column three—430; column four—125; reserve—390. See Santos, pp. 15, 69-71.

12. Walter Lord in *A Time to Stand* (p. 229) believes this author to be Navarro.

13. This is interesting. Rockets might indicate Congreve Rockets as used by the British Army in the peninsula against Napoleon and of U.S. national anthem fame. Frank W. Johnson in his *A History of Texas and Texans, Vol. 1* (p. 283) produces a dispatch from Austin to Bowie and Fannin during the siege of Béxar on October 31, 1835: "I wish you to send to Seguín's Ranch for some rockets that are there—two or three dozen. In Spanish they are called '*quetes*,' pronounced 'quates'—we may want them." The *soldados* raided this ranch on February 27. Additionally, the *Arkansas Gazette*, April 12, 1836 reported a Mexican Army deserters' claim that ". . . at between 3 and 4 o'clock, on the next morning, at a signal given by throwing up rockets from the town, the attack was simultaneously made on all sides of the garrison." It is possible there was a small rocket battery or section with the Army of Operations.

FIG. 22   SANTA ANNA AT THE NORTH BATTERY

FIG. 22   SANTA ANNA AT THE NORTH BATTERY

The north battery had been emplaced within musket range of the Alamo's north wall on the night of March 4, and was mounted with four cannon and two howitzers. When the attack began in the predawn dark of the 6th, Santa Anna and his staff officers kept themselves sensibly shielded behind this earthwork as hundreds of rifle and musket balls, as well as Texian artillery shot, shell, and scrap, erupted from the fort. Not far behind them stood the reserve column of grenadiers and *zapadores,* along with the massed bands from all the battalions.

A cannon has been pulled away from one of the battery's embrasures to allow Santa Anna a vantage point from which to study the battle's progress. Nearby sits one of the howitzers; this fired shells *over* the battery's gabion-and-earthen walls, and thus did not require an embrasure.

Santa Anna in his report to Mexico City later that day remarked that the "scene offered by this engagement was extraordinary," and that the Texian guns and small arms "illuminated the interior of the Fortress and its walls and ditches." Pale golden light over the eastern horizon, along with a moon partially hidden by clouds, enabled the attackers to see better as they made their way over the walls.

At lower left stand two junior "musicians," one of them holding a bell-bedecked *chinesco,* or "jingling Johnnie." At right a lieutenant colonel briefs a grenadier captain, whose men are about to reinforce the four main columns already attacking the enemy walls. The man in civilian garb is Ramon Caro, Santa Anna's personal secretary.—GZ

by the flashes I could distinguish large bodies of Mexican troops under the walls of the Alamo. I was looking out of a window in the town, about five hundred yards from the Alamo, commanding a view of it. The report of the cannon, rifles, and musketry, was tremendous. (Newell: 88-89)

Dickenson

On [the] morning of 6th March about daylight [the] enemy threw up signal rocket[14] and advanced and were repulsed. They [third column] rallied and made [a] second assault with scaling ladders, first thrown up in east side of fort. (Adjutant General Papers, TSL)

* * * *

The Mexican horde came on like a whirlwind. Organized into [four] divisions they came in the form of a semi-circle that extended from the northeast to the southwest. The strongest attack was [the first column] from about where the Military Plaza is, and from a division [of the forth column] that marched up from the direction of [La] Villita. Three times they were repulsed and the two cannon planted high on the ramparts [of the church?] carried dismay with their belches of fire and lead. The ill-fated end came and with it the horrors of which

even Crockett's vivid conception could not have dreamed. (*San Antonio Express,* April 28, 1881)

* * * *

Under the cover of darkness they approached the fortification and planted their scaling ladders against our walls just as light was approaching. They climbed up to the tops of our walls and jumped down within, many of them to immediate death.

As fast as the [*soldado*] front ranks were slain, they were filled up again by fresh troops. (Morphis: 175)

Yorba

The morning of Sunday—the 6th of March—ah! indeed, I could never forget that, even if I had lived many years more—was clear and balmy and every scrap of food was gone from my house and the children and I ran to the home of a good old Spanish priest so that we could have food and comfort there. There was nothing to impede the view of the Alamo from the priest's home, although I wished there was. The shooting began at six in the morning. It seemed as if there were myriad's of soldiers and guns about the stone building. There was volley after volley fired into the barred and bolted windows. Then the volleys came in quick succes-

---

14. Another reference to a rocket battery.

sion. Occasionally we heard muffled volleys and saw puffs of smoke from within the Alamo, and when we saw, too, Mexican soldiers fall in the roadway or stagger back we knew the Texians were fighting as best they could for their lives.

It seemed as if ten thousand guns were shot off indiscriminately as firecrackers snap when whole bundles of them are set off at one time. The smoke grew thick and heavy and we could not see clearly down at the Alamo, while the din of musketry, screams of crazy, exultant Mexicans increased every moment. I have never heard human beings scream so fiercely and powerfully as the Mexican soldiers did that day. I can compare such screams only to the yell of a mountain panther or lynx in desperate straits.

Next several companies of soldiers came running down the street with great heavy bridge timbers. These were quickly brought to bear as battering rams on the mission doors, but several volleys from within the Alamo, as nearly as we could see, laid low the men at the timbers and stopped the battering for a short time. Three or four brass cannon were loaded with what seemed to us very long delay and were placed directly in front of the main doors of the mission. They did serious work. Meanwhile, bullets from several thousand muskets incessantly rained like hail upon the building and went through the apertures that had been made in the wood barricades at the windows and doors. The din was indescribable. It did not seem as if a mouse could live in a building so shot at and riddled as the Alamo was that morning. (*San Antonio Express*, April 12, 1896)

Filisola

But such was the enthusiasm and excitement of those brave men to meet up with the enemies of the name and the government of their country, that it degenerated into a sad and overwhelming lack of discretion of the sort that is never committed with impunity on such occasions. One of the columns [second column] began to shout, "Long live the Republic!" in a loud voice. This cry immediately resounded in the air and awakened the drowsy vigilance of the Texians. Thus warned of the approach of our army, they prepared to make a desperate defense and began to train their artillery in such manner that their fire shortly played terrible havoc in our ranks.

Although the bravery and daring of our soldiers hastened to fill in the ranks, after a long while they began to become disorganized and perhaps would have retreated if General Santa Anna who was watching had not ordered the reserves into action. With their support, confidence and order were restored to our men, and the siege was begun. The enemy against whom it was directed strove to repel this attack with vigorous resistance and fire from all their arms. They were convinced that they had no other choice than to perish if only they could overcome us. (Woolsey, 2:173)

S. Rodríguez

... one morning about daybreak, I heard some firing and Pablo Oliveri, who was with us, woke me up. He said, "You had better get up on the house; they are fighting at the Alamo." We got up on the house and could see the flash of the guns and hear the booming of the cannon. (Matovina: 115)

J. Díaz

Díaz tells how he watched the progress of the battle from a distant point of vantage, how after the cannon had ceased to boom, he [Díaz] saw the six [*sic*, four] columns of Mexican soldiers form in line and go straight for the walls of the Alamo. He [Díaz] was not too far away to see the soldiers go scrambling up and up, only to be hurled back onto their comrades who, all undaunted, stepped into the breaches and fought their way to the top of the battle scarred walls. (*San Antonio Light*, September 1, 1907)

Ruiz

On the 6th of March at 3 o'clock P.M. [A.M.], General Santa Anna at the head of 4000 men advanced against the Alamo. The infantry, artillery, and cavalry had formed 1000 *varas*[15] from the walls of said fortress. The Mexican army charged and were twice repulsed by the deadly fire of Travis' artillery, which resembled a constant thunder. At the third charge the Toluca battalion [second column] commenced to scale the walls and suffered

---

15. A *vara* is approximately a yard.

severely. Out of 830 men only 130 of the battalion were left alive.[16] (*Texas Almanac*, 1850:56-57)

Coy

The attack commenced. With unholy joy, he saw the Mexican troops beaten back, only to surge forward again, overpowering the brave defenders by sheer weight of numbers. He longed to join his friends. (*San Antonio Light*, November 26, 1911)

Filisola

They [*soldados*] were hit by a hail of shrapnel and bullets that the besieged men let loose on them. The attackers at the first sound of the trumpet were all on their feet at their respective posts with their arms at the ready.

The three columns that attacked on the west [first column], north [second column] and east [third column], drew back or hesitated a little at the first fire from the enemy, but the example and the efforts of the leaders and officers soon caused them to resume the attack. They did so although the columns of the west [first column] and the east [third column][17] found no means of getting on top of the flat roofs of the small rooms whose walls formed the enclosure, by means of a move to the right and the left simultaneously and unorganized, both swung to the North so that the three columns almost merged into a single mass.[18] Whereupon, with their officers leading them on, they redoubled their efforts to mount the parapet on top of the wall

of that front line. They went over finally with General Juan V. Amador[19] being one of the first to reach the goal.

At the same time, to the South, Colonels José Vicente Miñón and Juan Morales [column four] with the columns skillfully took advantage offered by some small jacales with walls of stone and mud which were next to the angle corresponding to the West.[20] (Woolsey, 2:177)

Nuñez
(Column 1)

Everything being in readiness just at dawn of the day of the 6th of March, and the fourth day of the siege, all the bugles sounded a charge from all points. The division of our army on the west [column one] was the first to open fire. They fired from the bed of the river near where the opera house[21] now stands. The first fire from the cannon of the Alamo passed over our heads and did no harm; but as the troops were advancing the second one opened a lane in our lines at least fifty feet broad.(*SHQ* 1990:77-78)

Beccera
(Column 2)

On the morning of March 6, 1836 at four o'clock, the bugle sounded the advance from the small work near the Alamo.[22] The troops under Gen.

---

16. Ruíz was probably watching the north wall attack of the first and second columns. Possibly he was in the north battery with Santa Anna.

17. The west column was Cós, the east column belonged to Romero. This passage describes the columns shifting toward the north concurrently.

18. The three columns seem to be one mass of men under the Texians' north wall guns. The momentum of the charge, and the confusion of the Texian fire, probably caused a complete loss of command and control for the column commanders. At this point it was the sergeants and subalterns who were in control and pushed the *soldados* over the wall.

19. Juan Valentín Amador (1781-1851) was a Cuban born former Spanish Army officer.

20. This was the provisional battalion of *cazadores* attacking from the south. Their support job was probably to fix the Texian defenders on the south side of the fort, to keep them from reinforcing the north wall assault and the Mexican main effort. This attack was still using the remaining *jacales* as cover, which was probably why this area was given to the *cazadores*. Light infantry did not fight as linear as the *fusileros*, and preferred the broken terrain. Morales would start to find success and begin securing a foothold of his own at the southwest corner.

21. The opera house was built in the late 1890s and was just south of the Alamo's west wall. He was probably confusing the second column with firing from the fourth column.

22. The massed bands of the battalions were all gathered with Santa Anna at the north battery.

FIG. 23   THE ADVANCE OF MORALES' COLUMN

FIG. 23   THE ADVANCE OF MORALES' COLUMN

Assigned to seize the entrance to the Alamo, in the fort's south wall, as well as the lunette and trenches defending it,[1] Col. Juan Morales led the smallest of the four Mexican columns that morning, composed of three *cazadore* companies from the Matamoros, Jimenez, and San Luis battalions, totaling about 100 men.[2] Col. José Miñón was second in command. The movements of this column were poorly documented, but it is almost certain that the palisade east of the low barracks was *not* its objective, as suggested by some historians. The palisade was hardly a weak position: at least one gun stood there, and the wall had a firing step for riflemen. There was a trench in front of it and, beyond that, an abatis of fallen trees. Any attempt to storm these obstacles would have resulted in significant casualties.

Whether Morales and his men attempted to take the lunette in a frontal assault is not known; instead, Filisola places them behind the cover of "small jacales with walls of stone and mud" near the southwest corner. These allowed the column to advance virtually undetected to the corner itself, where, "by a daring move," in Filisola's words, "they seized the cannon which was placed on a platform." Evidently, the Texian gunners had their attention shifted to the massive onslaughts against the west, north and east walls, where penetrations were already being made.

The illustration depicts Colonel Morales at the head of his column,[3] behind the stone building that stood thirty to thirty-five feet south of the southwest corner. In the predawn greyness they wait for the precise moment to spring upon the unsuspecting gunners. Two ladders went with this column. Santa Anna had ordered all ladder-carriers to sling their longarms, and all soldiers' shako chin-straps to be down; but one man here has lost his shako, perhaps by a piece of grapeshot or scrap iron from an Alamo cannon. It is likely that not all of the *cazadores* carried rifles; several probably had Brown Besses sawed down by half a foot or so for lighter handling, while others had *tercerolas*, or even carbines.—GZ

Castrillón moved in silence.[23] They reached the fort, planted scaling-ladders, and commenced ascending; some mounted on the shoulders of others; a terrific fire belched from the interior; men fell from the scaling-ladders by the score, many pierced through the head by balls, others felled by clubbed guns. The dead and wounded covered the ground. After half an hour of fierce conflict, after the sacrifice of many lives, the column under Gen. Castrillón succeeded in making a lodgement in the upper part of the Alamo. It was sort of outwork. It think it is now used as a lot or a courtyard.[24] (Beccera: 20-21)

Mexican Soldier
(Column 1)

Here we remained flat on our stomachs until 5:30 (it was cold) when the signal to march was given by the President from the battery between the north and east. Immediately, General Cós cried, "For-

ward," and placing himself at the head of the attack, we ran to the assault, carrying scaling ladders, picks and spikes. Although the distance was short, the fire from the enemy's cannon was fearful. We fell back; more than forty men fell around me in a few moments. One can but admire the stubborn resistance of our enemy, and the constant bravery of all our troops. It seemed every cannon or ball or pistol shot of the enemy embedded itself in the breast of our men who without stopping cried: "Long live the Mexican Republic! Long live General Santa Anna!" I can tell you the whole scene was one of extreme terror. . . . (*El Mosquito Mexicano*, April 5, 1836)

Navarro
(Column 1)

Long live our country, the Alamo is ours! Today at five in the morning, the assault was made by four columns under the command of General

---

23. This is confusing. All of Becerra's comments prior to the final battle seem to dictate that he was a member of the Matamoros Battalion, or from one of the *cazadore* companies of the Vanguard Brigade. Once he begins on the sixth, however, all his remembrances deal with column two, which contained neither unit. The column organizations were based on Santa Anna's own orders of the fifth; it is possible, though, that further task organizations went on after the order was published and that some of the Matamoros Battalion was substituted for the San Luis, or an extra *cazadore* company was added.

24. "Courtyard" could mean the area between the east and west walls, or the corral on the eastern side of the *convento*.

FIG. 24   CÓS ATTACKS THE WEST WALL

FIG. 24   CÓS ATTACKS THE WEST WALL

The column attacking the Alamo from the northwest, under Gen. Martín Perfecto de Cós, had been greeted with terrific fire from the Texian guns emplaced along that front; and, as the columns of Duque and Romero milled and massed under the north wall in momentary confusion, Cós found his left flank also being hit—in this case by misdirected fire from the Toluca companies with Duque. Somehow his column had maintained its attack formation through all this and, in an effort to save both it and the overall assault, he led it in an oblique movement to the right, against the northern half of the west wall. José Juan Sánchez-Navarro, who was with Cós' column, drew a map delineating this movement. It clearly shows Cós attacking in three lines, each line representing two ranks of men, with officers positioned before and behind each line. Cós had approximately 300 men under his command: six companies of the Aldama Permanente fusiliers, the Aldama *cazadore* company, and three companies of the San Luis Activo fusiliers. Thus, each line was composed of three companies, with about forty-five men per rank, the company of *cazadores* advancing before all in skirmish formation.

Cós' maneuver almost certainly made the difference in the overall assault on the Alamo. It must have been obvious to the Texian garrison that Santa Anna was concentrating his main thrust against the ruinous north wall with its timber outerwork, and defenders must have flocked to reinforce it at the expense of the other walls. As a result, Cós' attack against the west met with thin or uneven resistance; and once the north wall defenders saw their left flank perforated, they had little choice but to retreat into their second line of defense within the fort buildings (or jump the walls and attempt escape).

A letter from a Mexican soldier[1] in *El Mosquito Mexicano* of April 5, 1836, noted that "we carried ladders, beams, bars, pick-axes, etc." The use of beams by Santa Anna's soldiers was confirmed sixty years later, in the memoir of Béxar resident Eulalia Yorba, who remembered how, during the attack, "several companies of soldiers came running down the street with great heavy bridge timbers," to batter down the fort's doors and gates. At least two doors, or posterns, were located along the west wall, and through them, and "going up ladders, and batteries, through embrasures and even one on top of the others," as the *El Mosquito Mexicano* letter reported, Cós' men overran the wall.

Their success did not come without a price: Manuel Loranca recalled how "a whole company of the Battalion Aldama, which made the attack on the point toward San Antonio," had been "swept off" by one of the two Alamo guns firing through holes along the west wall.

The illustration depicts the moment when Cós' northernmost of his three lines, under his direct command, breaks against the wall to begin its "forcible entry." In the foreground charges an Aldama fusilier; to his right an Aldama rifleman begins climbing one of the remaining ladders of the original ten assigned to Cós' column. At lower left is a wounded soldier with a crowbar; next to him a fusilier sergeant urges on the second rank. Another soldier wields a pick-axe, breaking down a window blocked up with stones and adobe bricks. The wall in this area was less than ten feet high and possibly as low as eight; many Mexicans were able to scale it by simply climbing the shoulders of their comrades. Those Texians who attempted to mount the parapet to fire at the enemy at the base of the wall, "could not remain for a single second without being killed," according to Filisola.

Cós himself might have led the attack on horseback, as shown here. Commanders were generally mounted when leading their troops into battle (although this was no doubt a flexible rule when assaulting fortified positions). One report of the February 25 attack from La Villita noted that "Cós was defeated, and fled, leaving his horse in possession of the Texians,"[2] although if any officer's horse had then been captured, it was not Cós'—he didn't arrive in San Antonio until March 2.—GZ

Cós and colonels Duque, Romero and Morales. His Excellency the President commanded the reserves. The firing lasted half an hour.[25] Our *jefes*, officers, and troops, at the same time as if by magic,[26] reached the top of the wall, jumped within, and continued fighting with side arms. (Navarro: 150-151)

de la Peña

A bugle call to attention was the agreed signal and we soon heard that terrible bugle call of death, which stirred our hearts, altered our expressions, and aroused us all suddenly from our painful meditations. Worn out by fatigue and lack of sleep, I had

25. Navarro was probably referring to the firing outside of the walls taking this long.

26. Here Navarro describes the coming together of the three columns and the reserves, forcing the lodgment on the north wall of the Alamo.

FIG. 25   DECIMATION OF THE TOLUCA CHASSEURS

FIG. 25   DECIMATION OF THE TOLUCA CHASSEURS

Of all the Mexican units taking part in the assault on the Alamo, the *activo* Toluca Battalion chalked up the highest casualty rate of all. It comprised the bulk of Col. Francisco Duque's column,[1] which aimed its attack against the center of the north wall (where Travis stood with three eight-pounders). The light infantry ("chasseurs," or *cazadores*) of the Toluca Battalion preceded the main column in two skirmish lines; most of them were probably armed with Baker rifles.

As Duque's column neared the walls, its already shredded ranks faced seemingly redoubled Texian rifle and artillery fire. Noted Enrique de la Peña, "It could be observed that a single cannon volley did away with half the company of chasseurs from Toluca."[2] This volley might have been a hail of grapeshot, scrap iron (shrapnel), or an exploding shell. Subsequent blasts hit the main column itself, downing many fusiliers and even wounding Colonel Duque.—GZ

just closed my eyes to nap when my ears were pierced by this fatal note. A trumpeter of the zappers, José María González, was the one who inspired us to scorn life and welcome death.[27] Seconds later the horror of this sound fled from among us, honor and glory replacing it.

The columns advanced with as much speed as possible; shortly after beginning the march they were ordered to open fire while they were still out of range, but there were some officers who wisely disregarded the signal. Alerted to our attack by the given signal, which all columns answered, the enemy vigorously returned our fire, which had not even touched him but had retarded our advance. Travis, to compensate for the reduced number of the defenders, had placed three or four rifles by the side of each man, so that the initial fire was very rapid and deadly. Our columns left along their path a wide trail of blood, of wounded, and of dead. The bands from all the corps, gathered around our commander, sounded the charge; with a most vivid order and enthusiasm, we answered that call which electrifies the heart, elevates the soul, and makes others trem-

ble. The second column, seized by this spirit, burst out in acclamations for the Republic and for the president-general.[28] The officers were unable to repress this act of folly, which was paid for dearly. His attention drawn by this act, the enemy seized the opportunity, at the moment that light was beginning to make objects discernible around us, to redouble the fire on this column, making it suffer the greatest blows. It could be observed that a single cannon volley did away with half the company of *cazadores* from Toluca, which was advancing a few paces from the [second] column; Captain José María Herrera, who commanded it, died a few moments later and Vences, its lieutenant, was also wounded. Another volley left many gaps among the ranks at the head, one of them being Colonel Duque [second column], who was wounded in the thigh; there remained standing, not without surprise, one of the two aides to this commander, who marched immediately to his side, but the other one now cannot testify to this.[29] Fate was kind on this occasion to the writer, who survived, though Don José María

27. This call is undoubtedly "Attention" followed by the "Charge." Candelaria also stated a third call was blown that morning, the "*Degüello*." The *degüello* was an old Moorish call and meant "to slit the throat." This was a reminder to the *soldado* that no quarter was to be given.

28. This would seem that it was Castrillón's column that violated the noise discipline that morning rather than the legend that all the columns sounded the "*vivas*."

29. Duque in July wrote:

"That I was appointed to command the second attack column in the assault of the Alamo. I went to receive the final orders of the general-in-chief, and I presented to him that although [de la] Peña was destined to be with the reserve column, I had so much confidence in him and desire that he would accompany me in the attack. His Excellency consented to my request and [de la] Peña confirmed that it was a good idea.

"He [de la Peña] advanced with the enthusiasm that is so characteristic of him, and he was very calm and cool at the head of the attacking column. When I was wounded in the vicinity of the enemy parapets, he was the only one of my assistants who was able to command in order to summon the leader who was appointed to succeed me.

"[de la]Peña, then without fear of danger to himself, went from one end of the enemy line to the other extreme end to meet up with General Manuel Fernández Castrillón, who was coming with the rear guard of the reserve column. He [de la Peña] informed him, notified him, in time, that I would be out of combat because of my wound." (Borroel: 19)

FIG. 26   ASSAULTING THE NORTH WALL

FIG. 26   ASSAULTING THE NORTH WALL

Disaster loomed for Santa Anna's troops at the base of the north wall. Two of his columns—Duque's and Romero's—converged there by happenstance, forming a mass of humanity that began faltering from disorganization and heavy losses. They were faced by a log outerwork, eight to nine feet high, that covered the brittle adobe wall, and composed, in Filisola's words, of timbers "five or six inches thick placed horizontally and supported by the outside part with some straight legs, also of wood." Dirt filled much of the space between timber and adobe.

The first Mexicans to climb this outerwork "were thrown down by bayonets already waiting for them behind the parapet, or by pistol fire," wrote de la Peña. Many others were shot down by the blind fire of their own comrades; and in the general panic and confusion the outcome of the battle hung in the balance.

Santa Anna clearly saw that the issue was doubtful, and sent in 400 troops—all his reserves. The sheer momentum of this additional force carried the attackers up and over the north wall, while General Cós' column was escalading the west wall. The thin line of Texians could no longer rely on their courage and fighting ability to hold back the tide: they were simply overpowered by numbers, and those who survived the rush fell back into the compound.

The illustration shows the mix of soldiery under the wooden wall: fusiliers of the Activo regiments of Toluca and San Luis, grenadiers, *cazadores,* and, at left, bearded *zapadores,* who gave a good accounting of themselves in the battle (de la Pena himself being wounded). A fusilier corporal strikes at a slow-moving soldier with a wooden switch; the soldier wears a red-white-and-green bull's-eyed shako more common in the 1820s. In the foreground, one soldier sports red shoulder wings, also typical of the earlier decade, while next to him another man wears his canvas fatigue jacket in place of a lost tailcoat.—GZ

Macotela, captain from Toluca was seriously wounded and died shortly after.

It has been observed what the plan of attack was, but various arrangements made to carry it out were for the most part omitted; the columns had been ordered to provide themselves with crow-bars, hatchets and ladders, but not until the last moment did it become obvious that all this was insufficient and that the ladders were poorly put together.

The columns, bravely storming the fort in the midst of a terrible shower of bullets and cannon-fire, had reached the base of the walls, with the exception of the third [column], which had been sorely punished on its left flank by a battery of three cannon on a barbette [at the apse of the church] that cut a serious breach in its ranks[30] since it was being attacked frontally at the same time from the height of a position, it was forced to seek a less bloody entrance, and thus changed its course toward the right angle of the north front. The few poor ladders that we were bringing had not arrived, because their bearers had either perished on the way or had escaped. Only one [ladder] was seen of all those that were planned. General Cós [first column], looking for a starting point from which to climb, had advanced frontally with his column to

where the second and third [columns] were. All united at one point, mixing and forming a confused mass. Fortunately, the wall reinforcement on this [north wall] front was of lumber, its excavation was hardly begun, and the height of the parapet was eight or nine feet; there was therefore a starting point, and it could be climbed, though with some difficulty. But disorder had already begun; officers of all ranks shouted but were hardly heard. The most daring of our veterans tried to be the first to climb, which they accomplished, yelling wildly so that room could be made for them, at times climbing over their own comrades. Others, jammed together, made useless efforts, obstructing each other, getting in the way of the more agile ones and pushing down those who were about to carry out their courageous effort. A lively rifle fire coming from the roof of the barracks and other points caused painful havoc, increasing the confusion of our disorderly mass. The first to climb were thrown down by bayonets already waiting for them behind the parapet, or by pistol fire, but the courage of our soldiers was not diminished as they saw their comrades falling dead or wounded, and they hurried to occupy their places and to avenge them, climbing over their bleeding bodies. The sharp reports of the

30. This refers to the third column attacking east against the corral area and coming under fire from the church battery. The withering fire from this battery forced their attack toward the north wall and entwined them with the other columns.

FIG. 27   ADJUTANT BAUGH AWAKENS COLONEL TRAVIS

FIG. 27   ADJUTANT BAUGH AWAKENS COLONEL TRAVIS

March 5 had been a long and busy day for the Alamo garrison, who had spent it in repairing and strengthening the battered fort; and this work lasted well into the night. By the time the Mexicans were ready to attack, even the sentinels, both within and without the walls, had fallen asleep (or were killed), for they gave no alarm.

The officer of the day, thirty-three-year-old Adjutant John J. Baugh, had just begun making his rounds when he heard or observed the enemy launching their assault. He burst into Travis' quarters and awakened both Travis and Travis' slave Joe with the cry, "The Mexicans are coming!"

Grabbing his shotgun and sword, and telling Joe to bring his own gun, Travis ran to take a position at the central cannon platform along the north wall. There he was abruptly put out of action with a Mexican ball to the head.

Baugh had arrived in Texas as first lieutenant of the second company of New Orleans Greys, commanded by Capt. Thomas Breece, in November of 1835. Now, nearly four months later, he wears mostly civilian clothing and hat in place of the tattered Greys uniform and cap that had suffered considerable campaigning and fighting. (The only remnant of that uniform is his cloak.) The likelihood is that he carried a lantern to make his rounds. In the sky behind him, a Mexican signal rocket explodes—more than one might have been fired that early morning hour—ordering the columns to attack.

Travis' headquarters was in one of the two surviving rooms of the house once occupied by Capt. Alexandro Trevino, of the presidial company of San Antonio. It was presumably back into this room that Joe retreated following his master's death. Among the items the Mexicans eventually found while looting the captured fort was a pair of deerskin saddlebags bearing the name "W. B. TRAVIS."—GZ

rifles, the whistling of bullets, the groans of the wounded, the cursing of the men, the sighs and anguished cries of the dying, the arrogant harangues of the officers, the noise of the instruments of war, and the inordinate shouts of the attackers, who climbed vigorously, bewildered all and made of this moment a tremendous and critical one. The shouting of those being attacked was no less loud and from the beginning had pierced our ears with desperate, terrible cries of alarm in a language we did not understand.

From his point of observation, General Santa Anna viewed with concern this horrible scene and, misled by the difficulties encountered in the climbing of the walls and by the maneuver executed by the third column, believed we were being repulsed; he therefore ordered Colonel Amat to move in with the rest of the reserves.[31] The *Zapadore* Battalion, already ordered to move their columns of attack, arrived and began to climb at the same time. He

then also ordered into battle his general staff and everyone at his side.[32] This gallant reserve merely added to the noise and the victims, the more regrettable since there was no necessity for them to engage in the combat. Before the Sapper Battalion, advancing through a shower of bullets and volley of shrapnel, had a chance to reach the foot of the walls, half their officers had been wounded. . . . Something unusual happened to this corps; it had as casualties four officers and twenty-one soldiers, but among these none of the sergeant class, well known to be more numerous than the former.

A quarter of an hour had elapsed [since the attack began], during which our soldiers remained in a terrible situation, wearing themselves out as they climbed in quest of a less obscure death than that visited on them, crowded in a single mass; later and after much effort, they were sufficient numbers to reach the parapet, without distinction of ranks. (Perry:47-50)

31. From his vantage point at the north battery, Santa Anna must have assumed that his columns were meeting with disaster at the base of the north wall. Unbeknownst to Santa Anna, the fourth column supporting the attack was gaining a foothold on the southwest corner, so Santa Anna, fearing defeat, committed his reserves against the north wall. The momentum of this caused the columns to succeed in breaching the north wall defenses.

32. According to Filisola, Gen. Juan Amador was the first to reach the top of the north wall. Amador must have entered the assault at this point. The momentum of the three columns must have been choked at the bottom of the wall for a staff officer of the reserves to be the first on top of the wall.

Caro

At daybreak and at the agreed signal our whole force moved forward to the attack. The first charge was met with a deadly fire of shot and shell from the enemy, the brave colonel of the Toluca Battalion, Francisco Duque, being among the first who fell wounded.

His [second] column wavered as a result of his fall, while the other three columns were held in check [by the Texian fire] on the other fronts. His Excellency, seeing the charge waver, gave orders for the reserve to advance. The brave General Juan Valentín Amador, General Pedro Ampudia, Colonel Esteban Mora,[33] and Lieutenant-Colonel Marcial Aguirre succeeded in gaining a foothold on the north side where the strife was bitterest, which encouraged the soldiers in their advance and resulted in their capture of the enemy's artillery on that side. (Castañeda: 105)

Santa Anna

. . . they [columns] moved forward in the best order and with the greatest silence, but the imprudent huzzas of one of them awakened the sleeping vigilance of the defenders of the fort and their artillery fire caused such disorder among our columns that it was necessary to make use of the reserves. (Castañeda:15)

Joe

The garrison was much exhausted by incessant watching and hard labor. They had all worked until a late hour on Saturday night, and when the attack was made sentinels and all were asleep, except one man, Capt. [John J.] Baugh, who gave alarm. There were three picket guards without the fort, but they too, it is supposed, were asleep and were run upon and bayonetted, for they gave no alarm.

Joe was sleeping in the room with his master[34] when the alarm was given. Travis sprang up, seized his rifle and sword, and called to Joe to follow him. Joe took his gun and followed. Travis ran across the Alamo and mounted the wall, and called out to his men, "Come on, boys, the Mexicans are upon us and we'll give them hell." He discharged his gun;[35] so did Joe. In an instant Travis was shot down. He fell within the wall, on the sloping ground, and sat up. The enemy twice applied their scaling ladders to the walls, and were twice beaten back. But this Joe did not well understand, for when his master fell he ran and ensconced himself[36] in a house from which he says he fired on them several times, after they got in. On the third attempt they succeeded in mounting the walls,[37] and then poured over like sheep. (Gray: 137-138)

✻ ✻ ✻ ✻

The servant of the lamented Travis, says his master fell near the close of the siege. That the Texians had picket guards stationed some hundred yards around the Alamo, and upon its walls; that on Sunday morning about 3 o'clock the guard upon the wall cried out, "Col. Travis, the Mexicans are coming!" Whether the picket guards were asleep or killed is not known; they were not heard, if they sounded any alarm.[38] The Mexicans were encamped around the Alamo, out of reach of its cannon. Col. Travis sprang from his blanket with his sword and gun, mounted the rampart, and seeing the enemy under the mouths of the cannon with scaling ladders, discharged his double barreled gun down upon them and was immediately shot, his gun falling upon the enemy and himself within the fort. The Mexican General leading the charge mounted the wall by means of a ladder, and seeing the bleeding Travis, attempted to behead him; the dying Colonel raised his sword and killed him! The Negro then hid in one of the apartments of the fort. . . . (*Memphis Enquirer*, April 14, 1836)

✻ ✻ ✻ ✻

---

33. This was probably the Mora that Joe saw Travis kill; Col. Esteban Mora, rather than Ventura Mora.

34. In the fort's headquarters, almost midway along the west wall.

35. Travis probably carried a double-barreled shotgun. He believed this was the best weapon for cavalry.

36. Joe might very well have returned to his headquarters room, or perhaps to one of the apartments on the east wall of the fort near Alsbury's room.

37. There is no sense to three coordinated assaults on the north wall. It was most likely that the Mexicans lost command and control once the columns had reached the foot of the wall. Joe could be recounting noise of the surging and shifting of the columns and the rising and falling of gunfire and is mistaking this for separate assaults.

38. These sentries could have either dozed and been caught up in the rush or purposely killed by a detachment of *cazadores* or *zapadores*, prior to the assault.

DAY THIRTEEN: March 6, 1836   153

And when the attack was made, which was just before daybreak, sentinels and all were asleep, except the officer of the day who was just starting on his round. There were three picket guards without the fort; but they too, it is supposed, were asleep and were run upon and bayonetted, for they gave no alarm that was heard. The first that Joe knew of it was the entrance of Adjutant Baugh, the officer of the day, into Travis' quarters, who roused him with the cry—"the Mexicans are coming!" They were running at full speed with their scaling ladders, towards the Fort, and were under the guns, and had their ladders against the wall before the Garrison were aroused to resistance. Travis sprung up, and seizing his rifle and sword, called to Joe to take his gun and follow. He mounted the wall and called out to his men—"Come on, Boys, the Mexicans are upon us, and we'll give them Hell." He immediately fired his rifle—Joe followed his example. The fire was returned by several shots, and Travis fell, wounded, within the wall, on the sloping ground that had recently been thrown up to strengthen the wall. There he sat, unable to rise. Joe seeing his master fall and the Mexicans coming over the wall, and thinking with Falstaff[39] that the better part of valor is discretion, ran, and ensconced himself in a house, from the loop holes of which he says he fired on them several times after they had come in.[40] (*Frankfort Commonwealth*, May 25, 1836)

Alsbury

They saw very little of the fighting. While the final struggle was progressing she [Alsbury] peeped out, and saw the surging columns of Santa Anna assaulting the Alamo on every side, as she believed. She could hear the noise of the conflict—the roar of the [Texian] artillery, the rattle of the small arms—the shouts of the combatants, the groans of the dying, and the moans of the wounded. (Ford: 122a)

E. Esparza

At last there came fire and guns and bayonets with many men. The soldiers of Santa Anna scaled the walls to be met by the fighting Texians. It was early morning. I ran out to the courtyard from a deep sleep. I was fastened to the ground.[41] The Texians killed many of Santa Anna's men, but more and more kept coming up the ladders. My father was killed. The brave Travis while shooting a cannon was shot down. I wish I could tell you all the great bravery of these few Texians fighting against that host. It would take great words like in your Bible and in your songs. I do not know these words. Santa Anna's men broke down the outside wall and came into the courtyard. (Driggs and King: 225)

* * * *

On the last night my father was not out, but he and my mother were sleeping together in headquarters. About 2 o'clock in the morning there was a great shouting and firing at the northwest corner of the fort, and I heard my mother say: "Gregorio, the soldiers have jumped the wall. The fight's begun." He got up and picked up his arms and went into the fight. I never saw him again. We could hear the Mexican officers shouting to the men to jump over, and the men were fighting so close that we could hear them strike each other. (*San Antonio Express*, November 22, 1902)

* * * *

At dawn the Mexican forces attacked. The infantry were forced to advance over the bodies of their own dead and wounded by the swords of the mounted cavalry at their backs. They found weak places and poured over the walls like sheep, regardless of the horrendous losses. (DRT Library, Alamo)

* * * *

Cannon boomed. Their shot crashed through the doors and windows and the breeches in the walls. (*San Antonio Express*, May 12, 1907)

---

39. John Falstaff from Shakespeare's *Henry IV*, who decided that discretion was the better part of valor.

40. The Texians, to their credit, did prepare the buildings for better defense with gabions, lunettes, palisades, and loopholes. It is a pity they weren't thinking more about offense.

41. This was probably the corral on the northeast side of the church, as it would have been easiest for him to get to from the church.

Candelaria

During the fight he [Bowie] was unable to sit up longer than for a few minutes at a time. When the fighting grew hot, he asked his faithful nurse [Candelaria] to assist him in raising himself to a window.[42] He would aim deliberately, and after firing, fall back on his cot and rest.

Colonel Travis was the first man killed. He fell on the southeast side, near where the Menger Hotel [now] stands.[43] The Mexican infantry [fourth column] charged across the plaza [de Valero] many times and rained musket balls against the walls, but they always were made to recoil.[44] Up to the morning of March 6, the cannon had done us very little damage, though the [Mexican] batteries never ceased firing. Colonel Crockett frequently came into the room and said a few encouraging words to Bowie.

On the morning of March 6, 1836, General Santa Anna prepared to hurl his whole force against the doomed fort. The *degüello* was sounded, and Mrs. Candelaria said that they all very well understood what it meant, and every man prepared to sell his life as dearly as possible. The [Texian] soldiers, with blanched cheeks and looks of fearless firmness, gathered in groups and conversed in low tones. Colonel Crockett and about a dozen strong men stood, with their guns in their hands, behind the sand bags at the front. The cot upon which Bowie reposed was in the room on the north side[45] [of the gate building] within a few feet of the position occupied by Crockett and his men. These two brave

spirits frequently exchanged a few words while waiting for the Mexicans to begin the battles.

I sat by Bowie's side, and tried to keep him as composed as possible. He had high fever, and was seized with a fit of coughing every few moments. Colonel Crockett loaded Bowie's rifle and a pair of pistols and laid them by his side. The Mexicans ran a battery of several guns out on the *plaza* [de Valero] and instantly began to rain balls against the sand bags.[46]

It was easy to see that they [in the fourth column] would soon destroy every barricade from the front door, and Crockett assured Bowie that he could stop a whole regiment from entering. I peeped through a window and saw long lines of infantry, followed by dragoons, filing into the plaza [de Valero], and I notified Colonel Crockett of the fact. "All right," he said. "Boys, aim well." The words had hardly left his lips before a storm of bullets rained against the walls and the very earth seemed to tremble beneath the tread of Santa Anna's legions. The Texians made every shot tell and the *plaza* [de Valero] was covered with dead bodies. The assaulting columns recoiled, and I thought we had them beaten, but hosts of officers could be seen waving their swords and rallying the hesitating and broken columns.[47]

They charged again, and at the time when within a dozen steps of the door, it looked as if they were about to be driven back, so terrible was the fire of the Texians. Those immediately in front of the great door were certainly in the act of retiring when a column that had come obliquely across the *plaza*

---

42. Bowie was more than likely kept in the gate building or low barracks building. There were windows to the outside, and it is possible that there was enough left open to peep through at the area south of the Alamo, and Bowie could have seen the *cazadore* battalion's attack.

43. The Menger Hotel was built in the 1850s and is just south of the Alamo's palisade and church area. According to Joe, Travis died on the north wall.

44. Candelaria seems to have been describing the battalion of *cazadores*' attack against the south wall. She has often been confused, given her terminology of "plaza" as meaning inside the walls. She was almost definitely describing the plaza as the Plaza de Valero, or open area between the south wall and where Pueblo de Valero began—precisely where the *cazadores* started their attack.

45. By "front" and "door" Candelaria has been interpreted as discussing the chapel defense. Based on the above notes, however, she was calling the gate area "front" and "door," and by "sandbags" she was describing the intricate defense works shown on numerous period maps in front of the gate or door. She was possibly confusing Crockett in the darkness with another defender. According to Sutherland, Crockett had been assigned by Travis to defend the palisade wall running from the gate to the chapel, though Crockett could have moved to the gate defenses for this battle.

46. No other account discusses this, yet it was possible for the La Villita battery to limber up and move forward. Doubtful but possible, especially if the Mexican cannon had been massed at the northern battery.

47. Could be the initial *cazadore* attack was interrupted by the tambour battery in front of the gate, and was forced to shift to the west. Only two of the Texian batteries were en barbette and had enfilade fire capabilities: the church and tambour batteries. It makes sense that the attacks against both of these well-placed positions were unsuccessful and caused the columns to shift.

[de Valero] reached the southwest corner of the Alamo, and bending their bodies, they ran under the [south] wall to the door.[48] It looked as if 100 bayonets were thrust into the door at the same time, and a sheet of flame lit up the Alamo. (*San Antonio Light*, February 19, 1899)

Dickenson

Under the cover of darkness they [*soldados*] approached the fortifications and planted their scaling ladders against our walls just as light was approaching, they climbed up to the tops of our walls and jumped down within, many of them to immediate death.

As fast as the [*soldado*] front ranks were slain, they were filled up again by fresh troops. (Morphis: 175)

Buquor

Here [in the Arciniega home] they were forced to dig and seek refuge in a cellar where they were safe from the bullets which swept the streets of the city at the moments of attack. Childhood's idea of humor has not wholly departed from the now aged woman, for she laughed slightly as she remembered the efforts of an aged blind woman to get into the cellar and the woman's fall into the same just in time to avoid a bullet which whistled by. (*San Antonio Express*, July 19, 1907)

Vargas

Back in the camp I heard the roar of artillery. Shrieks of shell mingled with groan of dying; soldiers mutilated and torn stumbled into camp to be bound up; dozens and scores were dragged in with gaping wounds through which their lifeblood had trickled; ever and anon the cry of *"Muerte a los Tejanos"*[49] echoed; carnage and a hell of battle reigned; Mexicans were mowed down as though a scythe passed. (*San Antonio Light*, April 3, 1910)

P. Díaz

. . . on the fateful morning of March 8 at two o'clock [A.M.] began the last act in the terrible tragedy, when the Mexicans made a night attack upon the chapel and with crowbars and ladders scaled the walls and began the hand-to-hand encounter which ended in the massacre of all the brave little band who so desperately fought for their lives. (*San Antonio Light*, October 31, 1909)

Loranca
(Cavalry)

The assault took place at 3:30 A.M. on the 6th, and was so sudden that the fort had only time to discharge four of the eighteen weapons which it had.

The Fort Alamo had only one entrance, which was on the south, and the approach was made winding to impede the entrance of the cavalry. The Mexican infantry, with ladders, were lying down at musket-shot distance, awaiting the signal of assault, which was to be given from a fort about a cannon shot [north-]east of the Alamo, where the President Santa Anna was with the music of the Regiment of Dolores and his staff to direct the movements. In the act of assault a confusion occurred, occasioned by darkness, in which the Mexican troops opened fire on each other.[50] A culverin, or 16 pound howitzer, fired from the fort, swept off a whole company of the Battalion Aldama [first column], which made the attack on the point toward San Antonio.

---

48. This piece may validate Candelaria's claims. Here she appears to be describing a part of the *cazadores* fixing the defenders of the south wall and another element moving west and breaching the southwest corner of the compound.

49. "Death to the Texians."

50. Interesting that fratricide would be recorded in 1836. The best chance for this fratricide to have occurred was when the *cazadores* entry and northern columns breached the walls simultaneously, and both were inside the compound apart from each other. Possibly this could be columns one and two engaging each other outside the walls.

FIG. 28   THE FIRING FROM THE BARRACKS ROOF

FIG. 28   THE FIRING FROM THE BARRACKS ROOF

In the process of taking the north wall, the Mexicans had to deal not only with those Texians defending it, but with additional fire turning their way as they began to pour into the compound. "A lively rifle fire coming from the roof of the barracks and other points," wrote de la Peña, "caused painful havoc, increasing the confusion of our disorderly mass." How long it was before the rooftop defenders were overcome, or were themselves forced down into the barracks, can only be surmised.

The condition of the long barracks on March 6 is not precisely known. Post-battle sketches show a somewhat craggy and fractured rooftop. According to Enrique Esparza, Mexican "shot and shells tore great holes in the walls. They also sawed out great jagged segments of the walls of both the convent and the church. The roof of the convent was knocked in, the greater part of it falling . . . nearly one-half of the walls of the convent were knocked off." (Previous damage to the convent walls had been done by deliberately aimed Texian guns during the siege of Cós' garrison in 1835.)

It might be, then, as shown in the illustration, that much more of the convent stood than subsequent histories and reconstructions have allowed—perhaps even parts of the second-story arcade.

In left foreground a rifleman in buckskins is forced to hammer his ramrod home with a rock, so jammed has the barrel become from constant loading and firing. His fur cap is made from a fox pelt, with the tail attached to the top of the crown rather than below it. At right, a *Tejano* in a serape, his head wrapped in a bandana, fires at Mexicans making inroads on the east.

In left background, the north wall has by now been entirely overrun. A cannon round strikes into the heart of the troops, who are milling and reforming under the intense crossfire. Years later R. M. Potter penned the recollection of Gen. Juan Bradburn, who had told him that "a small piece on a high platform . . . was wheeled by those who manned it against the large area after the enemy entered it. Some of the Mexican officers thought it did more execution than any gun which fired outward; but after two effective discharges it was silenced, when the last of its cannoneers fell under a shower of bullets."[1] The location of this "small piece" is not known.—GZ

Phase III:
Inside the Walls

Becerra
(Column One)

THIS SEEMING ADVANTAGE was a mere prelude to the desperate struggle which ensued. The doors of the Alamo building were barricaded by bags of sand as high as the neck of a man, the windows also. On the top of the roofs of the different apartments were rows of sandbags to cover the besieged.

Our troops, inspirited by success, continued the attack with energy and boldness. The Texians fought like devils. It was short range—muzzle to muzzle—hand to hand—musket and rifle—bayonet and Bowie knife—all were mingled in confusion. Here a squad of Mexicans, there a Texian or two. The crash of firearms, the shouts of defiance, the cries of the dying and the wounded, made a din almost infernal. The Texians defended desperately every inch of the fort—overpowered by numbers, they would be forced to abandon a room; they would rally in the next and defend it until further resistance became impossible.[51]

Gen. Tolza's [fourth column] command forced an entrance at the door of the church building.[52] He met the same determined resistance without and within. He won by force of numbers, and at great cost of life.

---

51. This was the room-to-room fight in the *convento*. From the looks of it, the rooms of the convent building were connected, by either hallways or doors and a gabled arcade or patio on the east side. This allowed the Texians to continue with a spirited defense once the *soldados* breached the compound, no doubt causing higher casualties to the *soldados*—but in the end only slowing their progress up a bit.

52. General Tolza arrived on March 10. He is probably referring to one of the battalions under Duque from General Gaona's (confusing him with Tolza) command that arrived on March 3. Gaona himself arrived on March 7. Which battalion, Aldama with column one, Toluca with column two, or the *zapadores* with the reserves, is anyone's guess.

There was a long room on the ground floor [of the *convento*]—it was darkened. Here the fight was bloody. It proved to be the hospital. The sick and wounded fired from their bed and pallets. A detachment of which I had command had captured a piece of artillery. It was placed near the door of the hospital, doubly charged with grape and canister and fired twice. We entered and found the corpses of fifteen Texians. On the outside we afterwards found forty-two dead Mexicans.

In the main building, on the ground floor, I saw a man lying on a bed—he was evidently sick.[53] I retired without molesting him, notwithstanding the order of Gen. Santa Anna to give no quarter to the Texians. A sergeant of artillery[54] entered before I had left the room—he leveled his piece at the prostrate man; the latter raised his hand and shot the sergeant through the head with a pistol. A soldier of the Toluca regiment [second column] came in, aimed his gun at the invalid, and was killed in similar manner. I then fired and killed the Texian. I took his two empty pistols and found his rifle standing by the bed. It seemed he was too weak to use it.

The Alamo, as has been stated, was entered at daylight—the fighting did not cease until nine o'clock. (Becerra: 21-24)

de la Peña
(Column Two)

Another one of these officers, young [José María] Torres [reserve column], died within the fort at the very moment of taking a [Texian] flag. He died at one blow without uttering a word, covered with glory and lamented by his comrades. (Perry:49)

Navarro
(Column One)

By six-thirty there was not an enemy left. I saw actions of heroic valor I envied. The women and children were saved. Travis, the commandant of the Alamo died like a hero; Bowie, the braggart son-in-law of Veramendi, died like a coward. The troops were permitted to pillage.[55] The enemy have suffered a heavy loss; twenty-one field pieces of different caliber, many arms and munitions. (Navarro: 150-151)

Mexican Soldier
(Column One)

After some three quarters of an hour of the most horrible fire, there followed the most awful attack with hand arms. . . . Poor things—no longer do they [Texians] live—all of them died, and even now I am watching them burn to free us from their putrification. Their leader named Travis, died like a brave man with his rifle in his hand at the back of a cannon, but that perverse and haughty James Bowie died like a woman, in bed, almost hidden by the covers. Our loss was terrible in both officers and men. (*El Mosquito Mexicano*, April 5, 1836)

Joe

The battle then became a melee. Every man fought for his own hand, as he best might, with butts of guns, pistols, knives, etc. As Travis sat wounded on the ground General [Esteban] Mora, who was passing him, made a blow at him with his sword, which Travis struck up, and ran his assailant through the body, and both died on the same spot. This was poor Travis's last effort.

---

53. As of January 15, eight Texians were in the infirmary. This late in a twelve-day siege a high percentage of defenders would have been wounded and placed in the hospital.

54. Why would an artilleryman be involved in a ground assault? It was not for numbers; Santa Anna did not even commit all his infantry. It could have been to have expert cannoneers available once the Texian guns were captured, to use the guns against the Texians.

55. This was not uncommon. From Henry V's siege of Hafleur to the many sieges of the peninsula, and Nathan Bedford Forrest's assault on Fort Pillow, troops were believed to be uncontrollable after a breach was effected. Quite often this was used to motivate the soldiers, telling them of the money and women inside that would be theirs. No doubt the Mexican officers encouraged this; Señora Esparza tells of being robbed as do Almonte and Alsbury. The Mexican *soldado* has unfairly been held accountable for the pillage and slaughter of the Alamo; their behavior was typical of nineteenth-century siege warfare.

The handful of Americans retreated to such covers as they had, and continued the battle until one man was left, a little, weakly man named Warner, who asked for quarter.[56] He was spared by the soldiery, but on being conducted to Santa Anna, he ordered him to be shot and it was done. Bowie is said to have fired through the door of his room, from his sick bed. He was found dead and mutilated where he lay. The Negroes, for there were several Negroes and women in the fort, were spared.[57] (Gray: 137-138)

* * * *

The enemy three times applied their scaling ladders to the wall; twice they were beaten back. But numbers and discipline prevailed over valor and desperation. On the third attempt they succeeded, and then they came over "like sheep." As Travis sat wounded, but cheering his men, where he first fell, General [Esteban] Mora in passing aimed a blow with his sword to dispatch him—Travis rallied his failing strength, struck up the descending weapon, and ran his assailant through the body. This was poor Travis' last effort. Both fell and expired on the spot. The battle now became a complete melee. Every man fought "for his own hand," with gun-butts, swords, pistols and knives, as he best could. The handful of Americans, not 150 effective men, retreated in such cover as they had, and continued the battle until only one man, a little weakly body, named Warner, was left alive. He, and he only, asked for quarter. He was spared by the soldiery; but, on being conducted to Santa Anna, he ordered him to be shot, which was promptly done. So that not one white man, of that devoted band, was left to tell the tale.

Bowie is said to have fired through the door of his room, from his sick bed. He was found dead and mutilated where he had lain. The body of Travis too, was pierced with many bayonet stabs. The despicable Colonel Cós [first column], dashed his dastard sword in the dead body. Indeed, Joe says, the sol-diers continued to stab the fallen Americans until all possibility of life was extinct. Captain Barragán[58] was the only Mexican officer who showed any disposition to spare the Americans. He saved Joe, and interceded for poor Warner, but in vain. There were several Negroes and some Mexican women in the fort. They were all spared. One only of the Negroes was killed—a woman—who was found lying dead between two guns. Joe supposes she ran out in fright and was killed by a chance shot. Lieutenant Dickenson's child was not killed, as was first reported. The mother and child were spared and sent home. The wife of Dr. Alsbury, [Juana Navarro Alsbury] and her sister, Miss Navarro, were also spared and restored to their father, who lives in Béxar. (*Frankfort Commonwealth*, May 25, 1836)

Alsbury

At the time when the place was stormed and carried by the enemy, she and an only sister and a Mrs. [Susannah] Dickenson were the only females in the garrison. That all the property she had, to wit, her clothing, money and jewels were seized and taken by the enemy. (Matovina: 33)

* * * *

The firing approximated where she was, and she realized the fact that the brave Texians had been overwhelmed by numbers. She asked her sister to go to the door and request the Mexican soldiers not to fire into the room, as it contained women only. *Señorita* Gertrudis opened the door; she was greeted in offensive language by the soldiers. Her shawl was torn from her shoulder, and she rushed back into the room. During this period Mrs. Alsbury was standing with her one-year-old son strained to her bosom, supposing he would be motherless soon. The soldiers then demanded of *Señorita* Gertrudis: "Your money and your husband." She replied, "I have neither money nor husband." About this time

56. There was no Warner known to have been at the Alamo. There was a Henry Warnell, the only known defender to have escaped the carnage, though not intact. Warnell died of his wounds in Nacogdoches in June. He was a small man; therefore, it is possible that Warnell, wounded and pleading, was hidden away by some of the Mexican officers and allowed to escape. See Groneman's *Alamo Defenders*.

57. See Jackson in *True West*.

58. Probably Manuel Rudocindo Barragán, commander of the Río Grande Presidial company, or another Barragán who commanded the escort company. Since both Barragáns were with the cavalry, Joe was probably discovered well after the battle ended. During the siege of Béxar in December, Captain Barragán withdrew his presidials to the Río Grande, abandoning the battle. See Woolsey, 2:92.

FIG. 29   THE RETREAT TO THE LONG BARRACKS

FIG. 29   THE RETREAT TO THE LONG BARRACKS

Following the mass Mexican penetrations of the north and west walls, the surviving defenders retreated to their second line of defense: the barracks and other buildings lining Alamo Plaza. Most of the Texians raced pell-mell into these positions; but a few, according to de la Peña, "remained in the open, looking at us before firing, as if dumbfounded at our daring."

One Texian was mistaken for Travis. This unknown soldier, wrote de la Peña, "was seen to hesitate, but not about the death that he would choose. He would take a few steps and stop, turning his proud face toward us to discharge his shots; he fought like a true soldier. Finally, he died, but he died after having traded his life very dearly. . . . He was a handsome blond, with a physique as robust as his spirit was strong."

As things turned out, it was unfortunate for the Texians that they had not placed cannon within or atop the long barracks, converting it into a "citadel" within the fort proper, for they might have then succeeded in stopping the Mexican attack. (Captain Sánchez-Navarro acknowledged this in the index to his plan of the Alamo.) Instead, within the buildings, they retired behind parapets of hides held by stakes and filled with dirt, or ducked into entrenchments in the floor, or fired their weapons through loopholes and windows.

Since the Alamo's artillery pieces remained unspiked when their gunners abandoned them, or were killed, it was a foregone conclusion that the Mexicans would shortly turn them against the doors of the barracks, huts, and chapel; and this, indeed, is what happened. With the doors thus breached, "a horrible carnage took place." More than a few Texians attempted to surrender in the course of this indoor fighting, but it was too late for that: the battle had hopelessly degenerated into a cauldron of frenzied extermination.—GZ

a sick man ran up to Mrs. Alsbury and attempted to protect her. The soldiers bayoneted him at her side. She thinks his name was Mitchell.[59]

After this tragic event a young Mexican [defender], hotly pursued by soldiers, seized her by the arm, and endeavored to keep her between himself and his assailants. His grasp was broken and four or five bayonets plunged into his body, and nearly as many balls went through his lifeless corpse. The soldiers broke open her trunk and took her money and clothes; also the watches of Colonel Travis and other officers.

A Mexican officer appeared on the scene. He excitedly inquired: "How did you come here? What are you doing here anyhow? Where is the entrance to the fort?" He made her pass out of the room over a cannon standing near by the door. He told her to remain there, and he would have her sent to President Santa Anna. Another officer came up and asked: "What are you doing here?" She replied: "An officer ordered us to remain here, and he would have us sent to the President." "President! The devil. Don't you see they are about to fire that cannon? Leave." They were moving when they heard a voice calling, "Sister." To my great relief *Don* Manuel Peréz came to us. He said: "Don't you know your own brother-in-law?" I answered: "I am so excited and distressed that I scarcely know anything." *Don* Manuel placed them in charge of a colored woman belonging to Colonel Bowie and the party reached the house of *Don* Angel Navarro in safety.[60]

Mrs. Alsbury says to the best of her remembrance she heard firing at the Alamo till twelve o'clock that day. (Ford: 122-124)

de la Peña
(Column Two)

The terrified defenders withdrew at once into quarters placed to the right and the left of the small area that constituted their second line of defense. They had bolted and reinforced the doors, but in order to form trenches they had excavated some places inside that were now a hindrance to them. Not all of them took refuge, for some remained in the open, looking at us before firing, as if dumb-

59. This could have been either Edwin T. Mitchell or Napoleon B. Mitchell. Of note, Edwin's brother Dewarren would be one of the Texians executed by the *soldados* at Goliad on Palm Sunday. See Groneman's *Alamo Defenders*.

60. This meeting must have occurred outside the walls as Mrs. Alsbury was being escorted into Béxar.

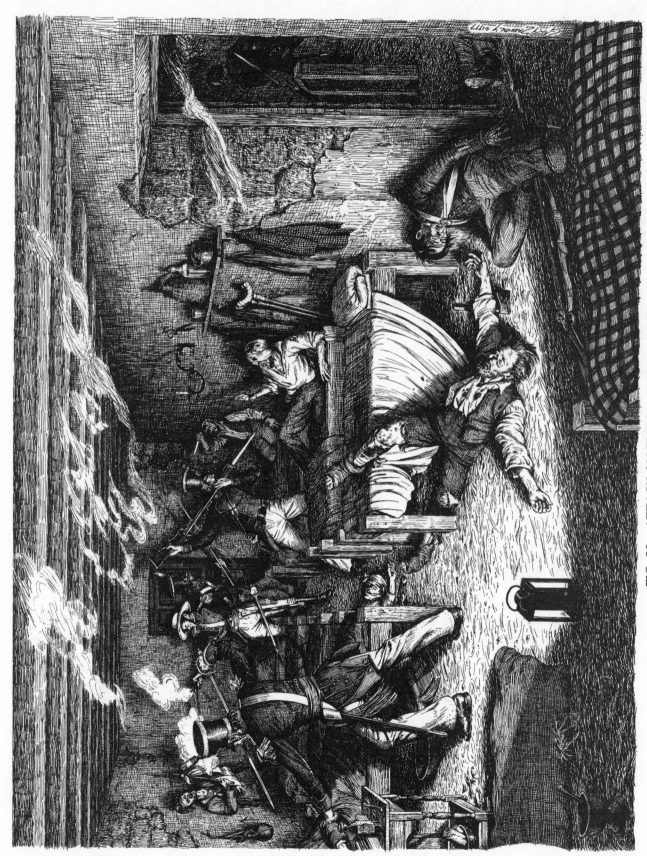

FIG. 30 ATTACK ON THE HOSPITAL PATIENTS

FIG. 30 ATTACK ON THE HOSPITAL PATIENTS

During the siege of the Alamo, two places were known to have been used by the defenders as hospitals: a section of the low barracks, just east of the main gate, and the second floor of the old *convento* building.[1] In fact the latter location had been first established as a hospital in 1805, to serve the sick troopers of the Flying Company of San Carlos de Parras del Alamo. By 1807 it contained thirty beds fully equipped, and at least three rooms.[2]

Available evidence suggests that the northernmost room of the *convento* had lost most if not all of its roof during the Texian bombardment of Cós' garrison in the fall of 1835. Immediately south of this, the largest room of the second story—27 feet long by 12½ wide—had remained relatively damage-free, and thus continued to be used as a hospital by the men under Travis and Bowie in 1836. A door led to a smaller room on the east, and to the landing of a stairwell. These stairs descended to the corridor of one of the remaining arcaded galleries, at the western edge of the horse corral.

If the ceiling of this main room had been constructed like that of the old granary section of the long barracks, it would have consisted of hewn cedar timbers placed two feet apart, with cedar boards laid over them, and two feet of cement poured over these to form the roof.[3]

Virtually nothing is known of the occupancy of this second-floor room during the siege and battle of the Alamo. Sergeant Becerra places a hospital room on the ground floor of the church, with fifteen patients; and these the Mexicans blasted with one of the Alamo cannon stuffed with grape and canister. Becerra told his account thirty-nine years after the event, so he might have mistakenly recalled the low barracks hospital for a room in the church. How many patients were roomed in the *convento*'s upper story can only be surmised. A dozen bunks and mattresses might have narrowly fit within it; perhaps several more were in the smaller room. The remaining sick and wounded would have been housed in the low barracks, where James Bowie was also warded. All told, some twenty defenders might have been confined to these hospital rooms during the final battle.[4]

The illustration is meant to convey the possible situation on the *convento*'s second floor: limited, feeble, or no resistance (or even an attempt at surrender) from the patients there, and the Mexican soldiers methodically slaughtering them with bullet, bayonet, and sword. The officer in the non-regulation hat is suggested by the narrative of sapper lieutenant de la Peña, who noted that he and Heredia, another officer, made the assault in "white hats." He also records that he had had a "presentiment" that this would make him a mark for Texian riflemen.[5] Why, then, would he choose to enter battle with such a distinctive headgear? It might have been for a very practical reason—to allow his own men to keep track of him through the early morning darkness and heavy smoke of combat.—GZ

founded at our daring. Travis was seen to hesitate, but not about the death that he would choose. He would take a few steps and stop, turning his proud face toward us to discharge his shots; he fought like a true soldier. Finally he died, but he died after trading his life very dearly.[61] None of his men died with greater heroism, and they all died. Travis behaved as a hero; one must do him justice, for with a handful of men without discipline, he resolved to face men used to war and much superior in numbers, without supplies, with scarce munitions, and against the will of his subordinates. He was a handsome blond, with a physique as robust as his spirit was strong.

In the meantime Colonel Morales [fourth column] with his *cazadores*, having carried out instructions received, was just in front of us at a distance of a few paces, and rightly fearing that our fire would hurt him, he had taken refuge in the trenches he had overrun trying to inflict damage on the enemy without harming us. It was a good thing that [the]other [three] columns could come together in a single front, for because of the small area the destruction among ourselves could be partially avoided; nevertheless, some of our men suffered the pain of falling from shots fired by their comrades, a grievous wound indeed, and a death even more lamentable.[62] The soldiers had been overloaded with ammunition, for the reserves and all the select companies carried

61. This was probably not Travis, if Joe is to be believed. It could have been one of a dozen men; more than likely it was Baugh trying to regain command and control after the breach occurred.

62. Fratricide occurred as the northern columns breached and ran into elements from the *cazadores* who had also effected a breach. The *cazadore* breach was unknown to the northern columns, hence the casualties.

FIG. 31   TAKING THE SOUTHWEST CORNER

FIG. 31   TAKING THE SOUTHWEST CORNER

Because it numbered little more than 100 men, Colonel Morales' column is sometimes dismissed in Alamo histories as a mere feint; but its mission was no less critical than those assigned to the other assault columns. In fact, the small number of soldiers belied their superior professionalism: the *cazadores* were better trained, better equipped and better clothed than the rest of Santa Anna's army. They were elite troops specializing in open-order, irregular tactics, unlike the linear formations of the fusiliers and grenadiers. Thus, it might be said that this little attack column was as formidable as any of the larger ones that morning.

Springing from the cover of the *jacales* beyond the Alamo's southwest corner, Morales' men, in "a daring move" (Filisola), climbed the wall and captured the eighteen-pound Texian gun emplaced there. Aside from the enormous volume of battle smoke that must have compromised their field of vision, the Texian gunners were probably preoccupied with the Mexican incursions into the other parts of the compound. The eighteen-pounder would have been wheeled around to fire a round or two at the waves of enemy troops to the north; and undoubtedly the artillerymen were swiftly killed or driven away by Morales' sudden rush.

The *cazadores* next seized the main gate and lunette, and occupied the ditches adjacent to these points, as much to stay out of the fire of the other Mexican columns as to exchange shots with the Texians retreating to, or already within, the barracks and other buildings.

The platform upon which the eighteen-pounder stood was actually the top of an earthen mound that filled the ruins of a former Tejano carpenter's shop. The mound extended beyond the room's eastern wall to the line of ruined arcade that once ran the length of all the rooms built against the west wall in mission days. A long ramp led down from the platform into the Alamo's plaza.[1] —GZ

seven [packs of] rounds apiece. It seems that the purpose of this was to convey the message to the soldier not to rely on his bayonet, which is the weapon generally employed in assault, while some of the *cazadores* support the attackers with their fire; however, there are always errors committed on these occasions, impossible to remedy. There remains no consolation other than regret for those responsible on this occasion, and there were many.

Our soldiers, some stimulated by courage and others by fury, burst into the quarter where the enemy had entrenched themselves, from which issued an infernal fire. Behind these came others who, nearing the doors and blind with fury and smoke, fired their shots against friends and enemies alike, and in this way our losses were most grievous. On the other hand, they turned the enemy's own cannon to bring down the doors to the rooms, or the rooms themselves; a horrible carnage took place, and some were trampled to death. The tumult was great, the disorder frightful; it seemed as if the furies had descended upon us; different groups of soldiers were firing in all directions, on their comrades and on their officers, so that one was as likely to die by a friendly hand as by an enemy's. In the midst of this thundering din there was such confusion that orders could not be understood, although those in command would raise their voices when the opportunity occurred. Some may believe that this

narrative is exaggerated, but those who were witnessing will confess that this is exact, and in truth, any moderation in relating it would fall short.

It was thus time to end the confusion that was increasing the number of our victims, and on my advice and at my insistence General Cós [first column] ordered the fire silenced; but the bugler Tamayo of the *zapadores* [reserve column] blew his instrument in vain, for the fire did not cease until there was no one left to kill and around fifty thousand cartridges had been used up. Whoever doubts this, let him estimate for himself, as I have done, with data that I have given.

Among the defenders there were thirty or more colonists; the rest were pirates, used to defying danger and to disdaining death, and who for that reason fought courageously; their courage, to my way of thinking, merited them the mercy for which, toward the last, some of them pleaded; others, not knowing the language, were unable to do so. In fact, when these men noted the loss of their leader and saw that they were being attacked by superior forces, they faltered. Some, with an accent hardly intelligible, desperately cried, "Mercy, valiant Mexicans"—others poked the points of their bayonets through a hole or a door with a white cloth, the symbol of cease-fire, and some even used their socks. Our trusting soldiers, seeing these demonstrations, would confidently enter their quarters, but those

FIG. 32   SEÑORA CANDELARIA ATTEMPTS TO SAVE JIM BOWIE

FIG. 32   SEÑORA CANDELARIA ATTEMPTS TO SAVE JIM BOWIE

In her later years San Antonio resident Señora Candelaria (better known to history as "Madam" Candelaria), was frequently interviewed about her presence within the Alamo during the siege and battle. Although that presence has been questioned by some other noncombatant survivors, as well as by many subsequent historians, many of the details she gave have the ring of authenticity.

Claiming to have been nursing Bowie on the morning of March 6, in one account she said that he was already dead by the time the Mexican soldiers burst into his sickroom in the low barracks. In a later interview she described Bowie as resisting with pistols. In both accounts she maintained that she was wounded by the Mexican bayonets, and had the scars to prove it.

The illustration depicts *cazadores* from Colonel Morales' column—which had seized the main gate and lunette after surmounting the southwest corner—entering the room with their Baker sword bayonets at the ready. One soldier, evidently lacking a proper shako, wears his barracks cap, or bonnet du police.

Whether or not Bowie was already dead by this point, Señora Candelaria's entreaties to spare him were quickly spurned by the blood-lusting blades of cold English steel.—GZ

among the enemy who had not pleaded for mercy, who had no thought of surrendering, and who relied on no other recourse than selling their lives dearly, would meet them with pistol shots and bayonets. Thus betrayed, our men rekindled their anger and at every moment fresh skirmishes broke out with renewed fury. The order had been given to spare no one but the women and this was carried out, but such carnage was useless and had we prevented it, we would have saved much blood on our part.

An unfortunate father with a young son in his arms was seen to hurl himself from a considerable height, both perishing at the same blow.[63] (Perry: 50-52)

Filisola

By a daring move they [fourth column] seized the cannon which was placed on a [the southwest] platform, as were all the others in the enclosure. They made their way into the fortified area of the quarters, assisting the efforts of General Amador. He had made use of the enemy's own artillery and turned them towards the doors of the small inner rooms in which the rebels had taken cover. From there they opened fire on the [Texian] troops who were coming down from the parapet to the patio or plaza of the aforesaid enclosure so that all were finally killed by shrapnel, bullets and bayonets. Our losses were great and deplorable. (Woolsey, 2:177)

Santa Anna

I felt that delay would only hinder us and ordered an immediate attack. The filibusters, as was their plan, defended themselves relentlessly. Not one soldier showed signs of desiring to surrender, and with fierceness and valor they died fighting. Their determined defense lasted for four hours and I found it necessary to call in my reserve forces to defeat them. (Crawford: 51)

Caro

The enemy immediately took refuge in the inside rooms of the fortress, the walls of which had been previously bored to enable them to fire through the holes. Generals Amador and Ampudia trained the guns upon the interior of the fort to demolish it as the only means of putting an end to the strife.

On the opposite side, where there was another entrance to the enemy's stronghold, the resistance was equally stubborn, but Colonels Juan Morales and José Miñón, commanding the [fourth] attacking column, succeeded in overcoming it. (Castañeda: 105)

Candelaria

Santa Anna made the attack on March 6. The Alamo was filled with Texians, a number of women

63. There were several eyewitnesses to this suicide. In the nineteenth century he was believed to be Dickenson with his son. Now it is believed to be defender Thomas Wolff and one of his sons. See Groneman's *Alamo Defenders*.

being among them. Colonel Bowie died in my arms only a few minutes before the entrance to the Alamo by the [Mexican] soldiers. I was holding his hand in my lap when Santa Anna's men swarmed into the room where I was sitting. One of them thrust a bayonet into the lifeless head of Colonel Bowie and lifted his body from my lap. As he did so the point of the weapon slipped and struck me in the jaw. (*San Antonio Express*, March 6, 1892)

Nuñez
(First Column)

At this time our cannon had battered down nearly all the walls that enclosed the church, consequently all the Americans had taken refuge inside the church, and the front door of the main entrance fronting to the west was open. Just outside of this door Colonel Travis was working his cannon. Our troops rallied and returned a terrible fire of cannon and small arms. After this the cannonading from the Alamo was heard no more. It is evident that this discharge killed Travis, for then the front door was closed and no more Americans were seen outside. By this time the court yard, the doors, the windows, roof and all around the doomed Alamo became one reeking mass of armed humanity.[64] Each one of us vied with the other for the honor of entering the Alamo first. Just at sunrise a lone marksman appeared on top of the church and fired. A colonel was struck in the neck by this shot and died at sundown. This the officers took as an evidence that the Americans had opened a hole in the roof themselves. This proved to be true, for almost in the next moment another American appeared on top of the roof with a little boy in his arms, apparently about three years old, and attempted to jump off, but they were immediately riddled with bullets, receiving a deadly fire from the top of the roof, when it was discovered that the Americans had constructed a curious kind of ladder, or gangway of long poles tied

together with ropes and filled up on top with sticks and dirt. This reached from the floor on the inside of the church to over the top edge of the wall, to the ground on the outside.[65] As soon as this discovery was made Santa Anna ordered his entire division[66] to charge and make for the gangway and hole in the roof. But most of the soldiers who showed themselves at this place got not into the Alamo, but into another world, for nearly every one of them was killed. We then found out that all the Americans were alive inside of the church. During the entire siege up to this time we had not killed even a single one, except Colonel Travis and the man and boy referred to, for afterwards there were no new graves nor dead bodies in an advanced state of decomposition discovered. (*SHQ*, July 1990: 77-80)

* * * *

By this time the front door was battered down and the conflict had become general.[67] The entire army came pouring in from all sides, and never in all my life did I witness or hear of such a hand to hand conflict. The Americans fought with the bravery and desperation of tigers, although seeing that they were contending against the fearful odds of at least two hundred to one, not one single one of them tried to escape or asked for quarter, the last one fighting with as much bravery and animation as at first. None of them hid in rooms nor asked for quarter, for they knew none would be given. On the contrary, they all died like heroes, selling their lives as dear as possible. There was but one man killed in a room, and this was a sick man in the big room on the left of the main entrance. He was bayoneted in his bed. He died apparently without shedding a drop of blood. The last moments of the conflict became terrible in the extreme. The soldiers in the moments of victory became entirely uncontrollable and, owing to the darkness of the building and the smoke of the battle, fell to killing one another, not being able to distinguish friend from foe. General Filisola was the first one to make this discovery. He

---

64. This is confusing and does not add much to Nuñez's credibility. Perhaps he was remembering the battle after the walls were breached. More likely he has confused Travis with someone else; he seems to be discussing the battle from the fourth column perspective in the south, which is where the gate was—the only "door"—and which had a cannon defending it. Given the order of battle, however, he should have been with a northern column; perhaps he was not intending to deceive but was merely relating the story from a *compadre's* viewpoint instead of his own. Or the order of battle, so often repeated, was modified as de la Peña stated.

65. This was the church battery's ramp.

66. The division was the reserves that Santa Anna commanded.

67. The front door was the gate. Those *cazadores* who breached the southwest corner swung around and opened the gate for those still outside.

reported to General Santa Anna, who at once mounted the walls. Although the voice of our idolized commander could scarcely be heard above the din and roar of battle, his presence together with the majestic waving of his sword sufficed to stop the bloody carnage, but not until all buglers entered the church and sounded a retreat did the horrible butchery entirely cease.[68] (*SHQ*, 1990:80-81)

Yorba

Next we saw ladders brought and in a trice the low roof of the church was crowded with a screaming, maddened throng of men armed with guns and sabers. Of course we knew then that it was all up with the little band of men in the Alamo. I remember that the priest drew us away from the window and refused to let us look longer, notwithstanding the fascination of the scene. We could still hear the shouts and yells and the booming of the brass cannon shook the priest's house and rattled the window panes. (*San Antonio Express*, April 12, 1896)

E. Esparza

The Texians went to the second wall [in front of the church] fought them back. They clubbed with their rifles, and stabbed with their Bowie knives. At last the few Texians that were left drew back into the monastery and shot the enemy as they came into the courtyard.

The women and children had hidden themselves where they could. I crawled under the hay. I would open my eyes and shut them again. I could not keep myself from looking and hearing. The awful sights still come to my eyes and the sounds ring in my ears. The soldiers of Santa Anna came on thick as bees. Inch by inch they gained ground, but for every Texian they killed, five of them fell. Poor fellows—many of them cared not to fight. It was the will of their tyrant leader. Mexico builds not one statue to Santa Anna. It is a lesson to all. He was a self-seeking, cruel ruler.

I did not stay in the courtyard. I was afraid. Long before this I had heard Señor Bowie tell Señor Smith, "We must hold the Alamo. We must keep Santa Anna back from Gonzáles. If we don't even the women and children will be murdered." I had kept close to Señor Bowie. He knew my language and I could feel his strength. Though he was ill I felt he would yet find a way to overcome Santa Anna. When he and the other brave fighters were slain fear seized me.

I hid with other frightened children and their mothers. Some of Santa Anna's men shot into the room. One boy was killed, but the rest of us escaped alive.[69] We could see little in the dark corner where we had huddled. As soon as it was light enough, some of the soldiers came searching through the rooms.

One of them put his bayonet against my mother and said, "Where is the Texian's money?"

"If they had money, find it," she said. The soldier struck her and I screamed. An officer appeared and ordered the soldier to go and leave the women and children alone. (Driggs and King: 225-227)

* * * *

The noise and confusion prevented men from telling friend from foe. Soldiers swarmed over us in hand-to-hand fighting. After emptying their guns, they used them as clubs or killed with knives or bayonets. Two small boys and an older American boy beside me were killed, although unarmed. My father's body fell from the high cannon he was firing to the ground at my feet.[70] My mother fell to her knees beside him, holding my baby sister in her arms. My brothers and I crowded behind her, clinging to her skirts in fright. (DRT Library, Alamo)

* * * *

Then men rushed in on us. They swarmed among us and over us. They fired on us in volleys. They struck us down with the *escopetas*.[71] In the dark our men groped and grasped the throats of our foe-men and buried their knives into their hearts.

By my side was an American boy. . . . As they

---

68. Doubtful. Santa Anna probably did not enter the fort until the battle was over.

69. This boy was possibly the other Wolff child. Oddly all the Hispanic women and children survived while only one Anglo woman and child were spared. As often as the Texians are accused of prejudice, it appears as strong in the *soldados*.

70. Esparza's father manned the cannon on the apse at the rear of the church. Esparza quite possibly saw his father's body after the fight, but it would be improbable given Esparza's location in the sacristy for his father to have landed at his feet.

71. Probably the third model India pattern Tower musket.

FIG. 33   ROMERO'S COLUMN BREAKS INTO THE HORSE CORRAL

FIG. 33   ROMERO'S COLUMN BREAKS INTO THE HORSE CORRAL

According to the plan and key of Capt. José Juan Sánchez-Navarro, fusiliers of Colonel Romero's column seized the two Texian gun positions in the northeastern corners of the cattle and horse corrals. Of the engagements that took place in this sector, almost nothing is known, except that, as elsewhere in the Alamo compound, the Texians were eventually forced back from their positions to either seek shelter in the barracks, or to attempt to escape by jumping over the walls.

The scene as illustrated is hypothetical: soldiers of the New Orleans Greys fire by platoons as they retire (the actual positions of the Greys during the battle is not known). That the Greys—aside from the artillerymen—might have offered the only true disciplined resistance, in formal military terms, is a real possibility. Doubtless they had had some training in the current Manual of Arms; and they had proved their mettle in the capture of San Antonio the previous December, displaying "throughout the undaunted bravery of disciplined regulars."[1]

One might reasonably assume that the Greys in the Alamo, experienced as they were in house-to-house fighting against Mexican troops, probably chose to fight it out within the long barracks, or any other position assigned to them.—GZ

reached us he rose to his feet. He had been sleeping but, like myself, he had been rudely awakened. As they rushed upon him he stood calmly and across his shoulders drew the blanket on which he had slept. He was unarmed. They slew him where he stood and his corpse fell over me. My father's body was lying near the cannon which he had tended. My mother with my baby sister, was kneeling beside it. My brothers and I were close to her. I clutched her garments. Behind her crouched the only man who escaped and was permitted to surrender. His name was Brigido Guerrero.[72]

As they rushed upon us the Mexican soldiers faltered as they saw a woman. My mother clasped her babe to her breast and closed her eyes. She expected they would kill her and her babe and me and my brothers. . . .

Brigido Guerrero pled for mercy. He told them he was a prisoner in the Alamo and had been brought there against his will. He said he had tried to escape and join Santa Anna's men. They spared him. They led him out, an officer going with him.

The old convent had been used for barracks by Bowie, Travis, and Crockett's men and was so used until the besiegers had driven them to seek final refuge in the chapel after a number of breaches had

been made in the convent wall. Communication was constantly kept up between the Convent and the church buildings. This was done through a door connecting them. I was in the convent several times but stayed most, and practically all of the time in the church, as it was considered safest.

Travis spent most of his time directing the firing from the roof of the church.[73] He too, seemed not only dauntless but sleepless. He encouraged the gunners. Whenever a good shot was made with the cannon he commended them. He told them where to aim and where to fire efficaciously, the cannon fire from the roof of the church being most of the time under his direct personal supervision. Crockett and he both, however, looked after the cannonading from the convent as well, both making repeated visits to that locality and at frequent intervals.

Bowie, although ill and suffering from a fever, fought until he was so severely wounded that he had to be carried to his cot, which was placed in one of the smaller rooms on the north side of the church.[74] Even after he was confined to his cot he fought, firing his pistol and occasionally his rifle at the enemy after the soldiers of Santa Anna had entered the church and some of them got into his room. He loaded and fired his weapons until his foes closed in

72. Brigido Guerrero was a former *soldado* who arrived in Texas in 1832 or 1835. Possibly during the siege of Béxar he deserted or was captured by the Texians. During the church fight Guerrero managed to convince the *soldados* that he was a prisoner of the Texians. He was believed and repatriated. See Groneman's *Alamo Defenders*.

73. Travis fought at one of the Texian north wall batteries. Dickenson commanded the church battery.

74. Bowie most likely was kept in the low barracks or gate building. At this date Bowie was a desperately ill man, and probably would not have been kept in a large damp room with approximately sixteen or so noncombatants. If he was tubercular he was also extremely contagious. Lastly, Bowie's position could have allowed him a private room.

FIG. 34   MOPPING UP RESISTANCE IN THE CHURCH

FIG. 34   MOPPING UP RESISTANCE IN THE CHURCH

Whatever structure the Texians had built to defend the doorless church entrance—whether it was an earth-and-stake breastwork, a barricade of sandbags, or a parapet of ox-hides filled with earth—it was almost certainly demolished by a Texian cannon turned around by the Mexicans. (Evidence of artillery damage to the ornamented portal clearly shows in post-battle sketches of the facade by Seth Eastman and Edward Everett.)

Once inside the building, Santa Anna's soldiers were confronted with a long, wooden ramp stretching up to a platform of earth and wood about twelve feet high, built by General Cós in 1835. Both platform and ramp had as their foundations the amputated arches of the old church—a necessary sacrilege that war's expediency had demanded of Cós' engineers.

Atop the platform were three Texian guns, but some of the gunners had already abandoned them or had died in the abortive defense of the doorway. A few ran into rooms of the church where noncombatants huddled, or attempted to escape by jumping over the high limestone walls. A mere handful kept resisting from the "pitch dark" eastern end of the church, according to Enrique Esparza, who added that the Mexican soldiers "seemed to fear to go there even after firing from the Constitutionalists from there had ceased. Santa Anna's men stood still and fired into the darkness until someone brought lanterns."

In the wake of the battle, shoe-deep pools of blood made a crimson swamp of the church floor—an observation later shared by Felix Nuñez, Señora Candelaria, and Eulalia Yorba.

Before the Mexican Army vacated the Alamo in May 1836, a month after Santa Anna's defeat at San Jacinto, the fort's extant defenses were torn down, and the wooden portions of the ramp and platform were burned, leaving only the earth-and-rubble mound beneath.—GZ

on him. When they made their final rush upon him, he rose up in his bed and received them. He hurled his sharp Bowie knife into the breast of one of them as another fired the shot that killed him. He was literally riddled with bullets. I saw his corpse before we were taken out of the building.

Mrs. Alsbury and my mother were among those who nursed and ministered to his wants. Mrs. Alsbury was near him when he was killed, while my mother and I were in the large main room of the church, and by the cannon near the window where my father fell. Nearly one-half of the walls of the convent were knocked off. Although I don't remember to have seen anyone killed in the convent, because I was not in there when they were, I am told and believe that many of the defenders of the Alamo perished there. (*San Antonio Express*, May 12, 1907)

* * * *

It was so dark that we couldn't see anything, and the families that were in the quarters just huddled up in the corners. My mother's children were near here. Finally they began shooting through the dark into the room where we were. A boy who was wrapped in a blanket in one corner was hit and killed.[75] (*San Antonio Express*, November 22, 1902)

Dickenson

The struggle lasted more than two hours when my husband rushed the church where I was with my child, and exclaimed: "Great God, Sue, the Mexicans are inside our walls! All is lost! If they spare you, save my child!"

Then, with a parting kiss, he drew his sword and plunged into the strife, then ranging in different portions of the fortifications.

Colonel Bowie was sick in his bed and not expected to live, but as the victorious Mexicans entered his room, he killed two of them with his pistols before they pierced him through with their sabres.

Colonels Travis and Bonham were killed while working the cannon, the body of the former lay on top of the church.[76]

Soon after he left me, three unarmed gunners who abandoned their useless guns came into the church where I was, and were shot down by my side. One of them was from Nacogdoches and named

---

75. *Soldados* fired blindly into a room as a method of fire by reconnaissance—the room was dark and potentially dangerous to the *soldados*.

76. By Joe's account Travis died at the north wall. Bonham was probably the one in the church.

FIG. 35   "GREAT GOD, SUE, THE MEXICANS ARE INSIDE OUR WALLS!"

FIG. 35   "GREAT GOD, SUE, THE MEXICANS ARE INSIDE OUR WALLS!"

In a scene worthy of Scott or Cooper at their most melodramatic, Capt. Almeron Dickenson burst into the Alamo's sacristy as the tide of battle turned, and spoke to his wife for the last time: "Great God, Sue, the Mexicans are inside our walls! All is lost! If they spare you, save my child."

In interviews given in her later life, Mrs. Dickenson said that her husband then returned to the fight, with either sword or gun—or both—in hand. When next she saw him, his bullet-riddled body was receiving the coup de grace of angry Mexican bayonets, and the sight of it made her faint.

During the siege, the twenty-six-year-old artillery officer, in peacetime a Gonzales blacksmith, doubtless spent much of his time repairing dismounted guns and carriages, or helping to patch up breaks in the walls. Mrs. Dickenson later recalled that the two of them also helped nurse the Alamo sick and wounded.

Though the sacristy was probably the safest room in the entire fort, the blood of several cornered male survivors would soon dampen its floors. Captain Dickenson evidently commanded the guns in the high cavalier battery of the church, and perished on or near the elevated platform.—GZ

Walker.[77] He spoke several times to me during the siege about his wife and four children with anxious tenderness. I saw four Mexicans toss him up in the air, as you would toss a bundle of fodder, with their bayonets, and then shoot him. (Morphis:175)

* * * *

Terrible fight ensued. Witness [Dickenson] retired into a room of the old church and saw no part of the fight—though she could distinctly hear it.

Col. Travis commanded the fort. The only man, witness [Dickenson] saw killed was a man named Walker from Nacogdoches, who was bayonetted and shot. She knew John Garnet[78] from Gonzáles, who she is certain was killed though she did not see it. (Adjutant General Papers, TSL)

* * * *

The blood of noble men was seeping into the ground and the bodies of heroes were lying cold in death. The last man to fall was Walker. He had often fired the cannon at the enemy. Wounded, he rushed into the room where I crouched on my cot with my baby clasped in my arms and took refuge in a corner opposite me. The Alamo had fallen and the hordes of Santa Anna were pouring over its ramparts, through its trenches, through the vaults. The barbarous horde followed the ill-fated Walker and shot him first, then stuck their bayonets in his body and lifted him up like a farmer does a bundle of fodder on his

pitchfork. An officer rushed to stop them; then they dropped the body. They were all bloody, and crimson springs coursed in the yard. Some say they did this to Bowie's body, but it was the dead body of Walker they raised on their bayonets. He was the last to be killed and they were drunk with blood. (*San Antonio Express*, April 28, 1881)

* * * *

On the day of the fall, Sunday, her husband kissed her good-bye in the morning, and she never saw him again.

Probably she [Dickenson] and the Mexican women, who were her companions, saw the bayoneting of the last American; when the shooting was over, a soldier crawled into the room where they were, not to seek refuge, but to carry out an order previously given, and generally understood, which was that if the garrison fell someone was to try to fire the powder supply; and this man named Evans, wounded and spent with weariness, was killed while making his painful way to the powder room.[79] (Maverick: 135-136)

Ruiz

When the Mexican army entered the walls, I with the political chief Don Ramón Músquiz and other members of the corporation, accompanied by the *Curate*,[80] Don Refugio de la Garza, who by Santa

---

77. Jacob Walker, an artilleryman, who probably worked the church battery. See Groneman's *Alamo Defenders*.

78. She was probably referring to defender John E. Garvin of Gonzáles. See Groneman's *Alamo Defenders*.

79. Maj. Robert Evans was the ordnance officer of the Alamo. Lore has it that Travis' final order was that the last defender blow up the magazine. There is no evidence for this order and it was just as possible that Evans was there in performance of duty as the ordnance officer. See Groneman's *Alamo Defenders*.

80. A priest or someone who renders first aid.

Anna's orders, had assembled during the night at a temporary fortification on Potero Street, with the object of attending the wounded, etc. As soon as the storming commenced we crossed the bridge on Commerce Street with this object in view, and about 100 yards from the same a party of Mexican dragoons fired upon us and compelled us to fall back on the river and place we occupied before. (*Texas Almanac:* 1850)

stood the garrison had all been killed. (*Texas Almanac:* 1859)

S. Rodríguez

The firing lasted about two hours. (Matovina: 115)

Urissa

I soon after heard the opening fire. By daybreak our soldiers had made a breach and I under-

San Luis Potosi

The active, defensive fire lasted twenty minutes. (McDonald and Young: 4)

Phase IV:
The Escape

Almonte

. . . and continued until 6 A.M. when the enemy attempted in vain to fly, but they were overtaken and put to the sword. (*SHQ* 48:23)

de la Peña

Those of the enemy who tried to escape fell victims to the sabers of the cavalry, which had been drawn up for this purpose, but even as they fled they defended themselves. (Perry: 55)

Beccera

On top of the church building I saw eleven Texians. They had some small pieces of artillery, and were firing on the cavalry and on those engaged in making the *escalado*.[81] Their ammunition was exhausted, and they were loading with pieces of iron and nails. The captured piece was placed in a position to reach them, doubly charged, and fired with so much effect that they ceased working their pieces. (Beccera: 22)

Loranca

Sixty-two Texians who sallied from the east side of the fort were received by the lancers and all killed. Only one of these made resistance; a very active man, armed with a double barrel gun and a single barrel pistol, with which he killed a corporal of the lancers named Eugenio. These were all killed by the lance, except one, who ensconced himself under a bush and it was necessary to shoot him.

There in front of the fosse were gathered the bodies of all who died by the lance, and those killed in the fort, and here they were ordered to be burned, and there being no room in the *campo santo* or burying ground, it being all taken up with the bodies of upwards of four hundred Mexicans, who were all killed in the assault. (*San Antonio Express,* June 23, 1878)

Ramírez y Sesma

Once the fire started and the [Texian] enemy was expelled from the first line of fortification as you saw, many of them thought they would be able to march away through the right side *fortin* and a considerable group that marched organized on the

---

81. From the Spanish *escalar*: to scale, to climb by the help of a ladder.

field trying to take advantage of the immediate vegetation. As soon as I saw this, I sent a company of the Dolores Regiment with my assistants Lieutenant Colonel Juan Herrera, Captain Cayetano Montero, the lieutenant from Dolores, *Don* Juan Palacios and a soldier José María Medrano, who would control the enemy on the side of the vegetation. To move them over there was a group of brave officers as well as the troop that was commanded. They were charged and pushed at blade point . . . and the desperate resistance they posed did not make our people hesitant.

Another group of about fifty men left then the fortress from the center *fortin* and I sent another group to campaign. These were the lancers of the Dolores Regiment under the command of Lieutenant Colonel Ramón Valera, Lieutenant Santos Carillo and soldier *Señor* Leandro Ramírez and *Don* Tomas Viveros, and since the [Texian] enemy saw their movement they took under their command a ditch and made a vigorous defense [of it], so strong that I had to command Lieutenant Francisco Molina to help in that corps, although they never hesitated I was afraid they would be repulsed, and sent the captain of [the] Río Grande [Company] *Señor* Manuel Barragán, and lieutenant of the same company *Señor* Pedro Rodríguez with fifteen men of the first regiment [?] to support them: all these officers executed the movement with such decision and exactness that some men that were protected in that position and who were ready to sell their lives at a very high price were overwhelmed in a few minutes and they were killed.

Then the captains breveted as lieutenant colonel for the Dolores Regiment Manuel Montellano, José

Jaso and soldier José Guijarro were destined to another campaign they had to undertake which as against those who left the fort through the left *fortin* and who were also killed, and these officers and the troop fought with courage that was not exceeded by their companions, very much like the rest of the cavalry under the command of General Ventura Mora, Colonel of the Dolores Regiment Major Venvenuto López, Captain Antonio Valez, Lieutenant Telesforo Carrion, and soldier Manuel Puis, who were ordered to cover the other flank of the fort, and this troop was also up to all our expectations.

Finally, your honor, the cavalry that has encircled the fort of the Alamo at a distance of fifteen steps, has been going around under enemy fire, and has complied with orders received, I can assure your honor that the troop that in this day has been under my command has gone beyond the call of duty. The desperate resistance of these men is emphasized by me to your honor, because it has been in the midst of risk that they have been dictating their orders, and they have witnessed more than anyone else all these facts. Enthusiastic work has been so general that it would be impossible to identify an individual without hurting others and thus I believe that the courageous officers that have concurred in this memorable case are so worthy of the consideration of the Supreme Government as they are of the gratitude of their fellow citizens . . .[82] (Secretaria de la Defensa, Archivo Historico Militar Mexicano)

Mexican Soldier

. . . or those who vainly sought safety in flight.[83]

---

82. Viewed from the *alameda*, the Alamo from the southwest corner to the apse of the chapel might appear as one long wall. "Fort" could be defined as "fortified." The whole Alamo was not. In Ramírez y Sesma's sight that morning perhaps the left fort was the tambour, the center the palisade, and the right the fortified area at the apse of the church.

83. It appears that near the end of the battle a large group of Texian defenders attempted a withdrawal. This is absolutely contrary to current Alamo interpretation, but the people above witnessed it. The attempts may have occurred either as part of a plan (doubtful, given the defenders' absolute inability to plan for anything) or possibly a spontaneous escape led by one of the officers after the *soldados* breached. There are large discrepancies in the Texian casualties which will be addressed in the next phase, but this escape attempt may account for the difference in numbers. Most notable among the accounts is that from Ramírez y Sesma and Loranca, both in the cavalry and both posted at the *alameda*. The cavalry also having the mission not to push frightened *soldados* forward but the prosecution of any fleeing Texians. Loranca even mentions Mexican cavalry casualties, as did Filisola. How would the cavalry have taken casualties several hundred yards away from the battle? Why did the Texian gunners on the church fire on the cavalry; surely they were more than occupied with Romero's column attacking the corral area, or with the *soldados* inside the compound. The answer is simple: A large body of Texians made a break for it, going in the only direction they knew, toward Gonzáles. They had no idea there was cavalry there because of the dark. The *soldados* from Morales' column had already shifted their attack to the southwest corner, so the road to the colonies looked clear. As soon as they made it over the wall and covered the open land, heading toward the *alameda* over the Gonzáles Road, the nearly 400 lancers of the cavalry struck. The lancers must have seen them approaching, and waited until the Texians could no longer seek the safety of the Alamo before riding at charge lance down upon them. With the escaping Texians probably low on ammunition, disorganized, exhausted . . . the eight foot lances must have finished it all very quickly. Apparently the Texian church battery under Dickenson and Bonham tried to help, and some cavalrymen were wounded and killed; still it must have only been a nuisance to them.

FIG. 36   INTERCEPTING THE FUGITIVES

FIG. 36   INTERCEPTING THE FUGITIVES

A substantial number of Alamo defenders—perhaps as many as one hundred—attempted to escape the mass slaughter they realized was inevitable once the Mexicans began flooding over the walls. They quit the fort in at least three separate bodies, according to General Sesma, whose cavalry stood waiting for just such an event approximately seventy feet from the walls.[1]

The skirmishes that followed between the fleeing Texians and the Mexican cavalry comprised an entirely separate phase of the Alamo battle, but one no less vicious than the action taking place within the compound.

Those who endeavored to escape via the east ("a considerable group," noted General Sesma) were intercepted by a company of Dolores Cavalry, and were flushed out of "the immediate vegetation" they tried to hold against their attackers.

Perhaps one of the Texians with this group was the "very active man" Manuel Loranca later recalled, "armed with a double-barrel gun and a single-barrel pistol, with which he killed a corporal of the lancers named Eugenio."

The identity, origin, fate, and dress of this "very active man" is not known. In the illustration he wears attire not uncommon in the border regions of the day: a blanket coat with dark blue selvage binding, a broad-leafed Spanish hat of beaver, and Indian-style leggings.[2] His shooting pouch is of a European pattern; and his massive Bowie is Sheffield-made, almost sixteen inches in overall length.[3]

The lancer corporal has charged his foe at the "Couch Lances!" position, the weapon held below his right breast and fixed between arm and body.[4]

Although these fleeing Texians were also defeated, with minimal loss to Santa Anna's horsemen, evidence suggests that several of them did succeed in escaping the battlefield and arriving in settlements many miles away, although most of them probably did not survive their wounds.—GZ

Phase V:
The Executions

Candelaria

Every man at the door fell by Crockett. I could see him struggling at the head of the column, and Bowie raised up and fired his rifle. I saw Crockett fall backward. The enraged Mexicans then streamed into the building, firing and yelling like mad men. (*San Antonio Light*, February 18, 1899)

Mexican Officer

. . . Kwokety [Crockett] was the last man slain and that he fought like an infuriated lion . . . his last stand was in a small room and with his gun in hand he brained every Mexican that tried to enter the door. He used his gun as a club until a shot from just without the door broke his right arm, and his gun barrel, the stock had been broken off, fell to the floor. Seeing this the Mexican soldiers made a rush into the room with fixed bayonets, but drawing a large knife with his left hand, he rushed upon his assailants and, parrying their thrusts, killed several before he was finally slain. (DeShields: 161)

Saldana

A tall man with flowing black hair was seen firing from the same place on the parapet during the entire siege. He wore a buckskin suit and a cap all of a different pattern entirely from those worn by his comrades. This man would kneel or lie down behind the low parapet, rest his long gun beside him and we all learned to keep at a good distance when he was seen to make ready to shoot. He rarely missed his mark and when he fired he always rose to his feet and calmly reloaded his gun, seemingly indifferent to the shots fired at him by our men. He had a strong, resonant voice and often railed at us, but as we did not understand English we could not comprehend the import of his words further than that they were defiant. This man I later learned was known as "Kwockey" [Crockett].

When the final assault was made upon the walls these men fought like devils. "Kwockey" was killed in a room of the mission. He stood on the inside to the left of the door and plunged his long knife into the bosom of every soldier that tried to enter. They were powerless to fire upon him because of the fact that he was backed up against the wall and, the doorway being narrow, they could not bring their guns to bear upon him. And, moreover, the pressure from the rear was so great that many near the doorway were forced into the room only to receive a deadly thrust from that long knife. Finally a well directed shot broke this man's right arm and his hand fell useless at his side. He then seized his long gun with his left hand and leaped toward the center of the room where he could wield the weapon without obstruction, felling every man that came through the doorway. A corporal ordered the passage cleared of those who were being pressed forward, a volley was fired almost point blank and the last defender of the Alamo fell forward dead. (DeShields: 163-164)

Caro

Among the 183 killed there were five who were discovered by General Castrillon [second column], hiding after the assault. He took them immediately to the presence of His Excellency who had come up by this time. When he presented the prisoners, he was severely reprimanded for not having killed them on the spot, after which he turned his back upon Castrillon while the soldiers stepped out of their ranks and set upon the prisoners until they were all killed. (Castañeda: 106)

Navarro
(First Column)

I was horrified by some cruelties, among others, the death of an old man named Cochran and of a boy about fourteen. (Navarro: 150-151)

Beccera
(First Column)

In another room I saw a man sitting on the floor among feathers. A bugler, who was with me, raised his gun. The gentleman said to him in Spanish: "Don't kill me—I have plenty of money." He pulled out a pocket-book, also a large roll of bank bills, and handed the latter to the bugler. We divided the money. While this was occurring another Texian made his appearance. He had been lying on the floor, as if resting. When he arose I asked: "How many is there of you?" He replied: "Only two." The gentleman, who spoke Spanish, asked for General Cós, and said he would like to see him. Just then General Amador came in. He asked why the orders of the president had not been executed and the two Texians killed. In answer the bugler exhibited his roll of bank bills and they were taken from him immediately by the general. In a few moments General Cós, General [Colonel]. Almonte, and General Tolza entered the room. As soon as General Cós saw the gentleman who spoke Spanish, he rushed to him and embraced him. He told the other generals it was Travis, that on a former occasion he had treated him like a brother, had loaned him money, etc. He also said the other man was Colonel Crockett. He entreated the other generals to go with him to General Santa Anna and join with him in a request to save the lives of the two Texians. The generals and the Texians left together to find Santa Anna. The bugler and myself followed them. They encountered the commander-in-chief in the courtyard with General Castrillón. General Cós said to him: "Mr President, you have here two prisoners—in the name of the Republic of Mexico, I supplicate you to guarantee the lives of both." Santa Anna was very much enraged. "Gentlemen Generals, my order was to kill every man in the Alamo," he said. "Soldiers, kill them." A soldier was standing near Travis and presented his gun at him. Travis seized the bayonet and depressed the muzzle of the piece to the floor and it was not fired. While this was taking place the soldiers standing around opened fire. A shot struck Travis in the back. He then stood erect, folded his arms and looked calmly, unflinchingly, upon his assailants. He was finally killed by a ball passing through his neck. Crockett stood in a similar position. They died undaunted, like heroes.

The firing was brisk for a time. It came from all sides. Gen. Santa Anna and most of the officers ran. General Castrillón squatted down—so did I. In this affair eight Mexican soldiers were killed and wounded by their comrades.

I did not know the names of two Texians, only as given by Gen. Cós. The gentleman he called

Crockett had on a coat with capes to it. (Beccera: 22-24)

Joe

Crockett and a few of his friends were found together, with twenty-four of the enemy dead around them. (Gray: 137)

* * * *

Crockett, the kind-hearted, brave Crockett, and a few of the devoted friends who entered the Fort with him, were found lying together, with 21 of the slain enemy around them. (*Frankfort Commonwealth*, May 25, 1836)

Ruiz

Toward the west and in a small fort opposite the city, we found the body of Colonel Crockett. (*Texas Almanac:* 1850)

E. Esparza

Crockett who, as I said before they called *Don Benito*, went often into the convent and stayed there for some time. But he was everywhere during the siege and personally slew many of the enemy with his rifle, his pistol and his knife. He fought hand to hand. He clubbed his rifle when they closed in on him and knocked them down with its stock until he was overwhelmed by numbers and slain. He fought to his last breath. He fell immediately in front of the large double doors which he defended with the force that was by his side. Crockett was one of the few who were wide awake when the final crisis and crash came. When he died there was a heap of slain in front and on each side of him. These he had all killed before he finally fell on top of the heap. (*San Antonio Express*, May 12, 1907)

Nuñez

(First Column)

To recount the individual deeds of valor, of the brave men who were slain in the Alamo, would fill a volume as large as the History of Texas; nevertheless there was one who perished in that memorable conflict who is entitled to a passing notice. The one to whom I refer was killed just inside of the front door. The peculiarity of his dress, and his undaunted courage attracted the attention of several of us, both officers and men. He was a tall American of rather dark complexion and had on a long *cuera*[84] and a round cap without any bill, and made of fox skin, with the long tail hanging down his back. This man apparently had a charmed life. Of the many soldiers who took deliberate aim at him and fired, not one ever hit him. On the contrary he never missed a shot. He killed at least eight of our men, besides wounding several others. This fact being observed by a lieutenant who had come in over the wall; he sprung at him and dealt him a deadly blow and in an instant he was pierced by not less than twenty bayonets. This lieutenant said that if all Americans had killed as many of our men as this one had, our army would have been annihilated before the Alamo could have been taken. He was about the last man that was killed.[85] (*SHQ*, July 1990)

Candelaria

He was one of the strangest men I ever saw. He had the face of a woman, and his manner that of a girl. I could never regard him as a hero until I saw him die. He looked grand and terrible, standing at the front door and fighting a whole column of Mexican infantry. He had fired his last shot, and had no time to reload. The cannon balls had knocked away the sand bags, and the infantry was passing through the breach. Crockett stood there, swinging something over his head. The place was full of smoke, and I could not tell whether he was using a gun or a sword. A heap of dead was piled at his feet, and the Mexicans were lunging at him with bayonets, but he would not retreat an inch. Poor Bowie could see it all, but he could not raise himself from the cot. Crockett fell and the Mexicans poured into the Alamo. (*San Antonio Light*, February 19, 1899)

Dickenson

I recognized Colonel Crockett lying dead and

---

84. A leather jacket.

85. The vast majority of Nuñez's account is muddled and confused at best. It is rarely quoted except for this passage, which seems to confirm that Crockett died as his admirers prefer.

mutilated between the church and the two story barrack building, and even remember seeing his peculiar cap lying by his side. (Morphis: 177)

Anonymous

Dear Sir:—The fall of the Alamo and the massacre must be fresh in the memory of every American. But I will relate one circumstance, detailed by an Eyewitness, not before known, that will at once establish (if not before established), the blood thirsty cruelty of the tyrant, Santa Anna. After the Mexicans had got possession of the Alamo, the fighting had ceased, and it was near day light, six Americans were discovered near the wall yet unconquered, and who were instantly surrounded and ordered by General Castrillón to surrender, and who did so under a promise of his protection, finding resistance any longer in vain—indeed, perfect madness,—Castrillón was brave and not cruel, and disposed to save them. He marched them up to that part of the fort where stood "His Excellency," surrounded by his murderous crew, his sycophantic officers. David Crockett was one of the six. The steady, fearless step, and undaunted tread, together with the bold demeanor of this hardy veteran—"his firmness and noble bearing," to give the words of his narrator, had a most powerful effect on himself and Castrillón. Nothing daunted he marched up boldly in front of Santa Anna, looked him steadfastly in the face, while Castrillón addressed "His Excellency," 'Sir, here are six prisoners I have taken alive; how shall I dispose of them?'[86] Santa Anna looked at Castrillón fiercely, flew into a most violent rage, and replied, 'Have I not told you before how to dispose of them? Why do you bring them to me?' At about the same time his brave officers drew and plunged their swords into the bosoms of their defenseless prisoners!! So anxious and intent were these blood thirsty cowards to gratify the malignity

of this inveterate tyrant, that Castrillón barely escaped being run through in the scuffle himself,-Castrillón rushed from the scene apparently horror struck—sought his quarters, and did not leave them for some days, and hardly ever spoke to Santa Anna after. This was the fate of poor Crockett, and in which there can be no mistake. Who the five others were, I have not been able to learn. Three wounded prisoners were discovered and brought before "His Excellency," and were ordered to be instantly shot. There are certain reasons why the narrator of these events should not be known. I will only repeat that he was an eyewitness. (*Frankfort Commonwealth*, July 27, 1836)

Loranca

After that we all entered the Alamo, and the first thing we saw on entering a room at the right was the corpses of Bowie and Travis. Then we passed to the corridor which served the Texians as quarters, and here found all refugees which were left. President Santa Anna immediately ordered that they should be shot, which was accordingly done, excepting only a Negro and a woman having a little boy about a year old. She was said to be Travis' cook. (*San Antonio Express*, June 23, 1878)

Filisola

In short, be that as it may, the place fell to the possession of the Mexicans, and its defenders were all killed. It is most regrettable that after the first moments of the heat of the battle there should have been atrocious authorized acts unworthy of the valor and resolve with which that operation was carried out, which forthwith left it with an indelible mark for history. These acts were denounced immediately by all who were disgusted upon witnessing

---

86. According to the Tornel Decree, which arguably legalized murder:
   All foreigners who may land in any port of the [Mexican] Republic or who enter it armed and for the purpose of attacking our territory shall be treated as pirates, since they are not subjects of any nation at war with the republic nor do they militate under any recognized flag.
   Foreigners who introduce arms and munitions by land or by sea at any point of the territory now in rebellion against the government of the nation for the purposes of placing such supplies in the hands of enemies shall be treated and punished likewise. (Young: 2)
   One can hardly blame the Mexican government for defending its borders or system of government, just as one cannot cast judgment on people fighting what they believed to be an oppresive rule. This decree by Mexican Secretary of War Tornel does not address legal Texas colonists but rather emphasizes "foreigners," i.e., adventurers from the United States, which for a large part the Texian revolutionaries were. It would be interesting if those executed were not colonists but, as the Mexicans termed them, "pirates."

them, and afterwards by the entire army who surely were not moved by any such feelings. They heard this with the horror and repugnance in keeping with the bravery and generosity of the Mexicans who can agree only with noble and generous actions. There were deeds that we refrain from relating because of the sorrow that the account of the events would cause us, and which with all good will and the honor of the republic we would wish had never existed. This is like others that preceded these while that poor imitation of a blockade or siege lasted. Although of a different sort and purely personal, they did not fail to scandalize and to cost a number of lives and wounded of the most inspired soldiers of the army. (Woolsey, 2:179)

Urissa

As I was surveying the dreadful scene before us, I observed Castrillón coming out of one of the quarters, leading a venerable-looking old man by the hand; he was tall, his face was red, and he stooped forward as he walked. The President stopped abruptly when Castrillón, leaving his prisoner, advanced some four or five paces towards us, and with his graceful bow, said, "My General, I have spared the life of this venerable old man, and taken him prisoner." Raising his head, Santa Anna replied, "What right have you to disobey my orders? I want no prisoners," and waving his hand to a file of soldiers, he said, "Soldiers, shoot that man," and almost instantly he fell, pierced with a volley of balls. Castrillón turned aside with tears in his eyes, and my heart was too full to speak. So there was not a man left. Even a cat that was soon after seen running through the fort, was shot, as the soldiers exclaimed: "It is not a cat, but an American." "What was that old man's name?" said I. "I believe," said he, "that they called him Coket." (*Texas Almanac* 1859:62)

Yorba

I remember seeing poor old Colonel Davy Crockett as he lay dead by the side of a dying man, whose bloody and powder-stained face I was washing. Colonel Crockett was about fifty years old at that time. His coat and rough woolen shirt were soaked with blood so that the original color was hidden, for the eccentric who must have died of

some ball in the chest or a bayonet thrust. (*San Antonio Express*, April 12, 1896)

Arocha

His [Antonio Cruz Arocha] wife *Doña* María Jesúsa Peña could see from a small window, everything or part of what was going on. After the first ceased Santa Anna entered through the south west door. Several Texians who were still hidden came towards him and kneeled, each one holding a small white flag. They were surrounded by the soldiers who hesitated to kill them, but as Santa Anna went by he nodded his head and made a meaning sign with his sword; they were immediately showered by bayonet stabs. (Gentilz Papers: DRT Library)

Santa Anna

When we entered the fortress we found few defenders still alive. We disposed of them instantly, after a brief interrogation which brought out some startling information. Of course we knew the stand-or-die order had been given long before our attack. And then I discovered the strange reason why this fort manned by very able fighters such as the famous Crockett and Bowie was so easily taken. No less than 30 of these men mutinied. This much was divulged by Crockett before he died. He died, however, before we could extract from him the manner in which the mutiny had been brought under control. But the mute answer to this question lay before us in the center of the fortress itself. A pile of bodies lay in the middle of the compound. All of these had been shot in the chest as if they had been executed. Those bodies that we found on the ramparts, however, showed the usual combat wounds in the usual variety, bullet holes in the head and face, saber cuts about the head and shoulders from our troops who scaled the walls, and so forth. I could only conclude that there had indeed been a mutiny, as Crockett had testified when he said, "If they had not mutinied we would have held you off from now until Armageddon." Clearly the mutiny had been put down by summary execution. It is quite possible that had it not been for this incident the battle would have gone against us. On the other hand, if the commander of these poor men had not issued his insane stand-or-die order, I would never have given the no-quarter signal, and these brave men

FIG. 37   SANTA ANNA ORDERS THE EXECUTIONS

FIG. 37   SANTA ANNA ORDERS THE EXECUTIONS

As the noise and smoke of the vicious and bloody Battle of the Alamo dissipated, Santa Anna entered the fort to make a tour of his conquest. At one point during this inspection, General Castrillon approached him with, as the varying Mexican accounts have it, anywhere from five to seven Texians who had laid down their arms on condition that their lives would be spared. Outraged that his order that no prisoners were to be taken alive had been ignored, Santa Anna, according to accounts by several eyewitnesses, flew into a rage, demanded that they be killed at once, and indignantly turned his back on the scene that followed.

A number of officers and soldiers standing nearby fell to the task in earnest, their swords, muskets and bayonets bringing a cruel end to the lives of these unfortunate survivors. Other officers, including Castrillon, were visibly shaken by the merciless butchery.

Most of the Mexican accounts of this incident mention David Crockett as being among those executed. Some contemporary American newspapers reported his execution as well, though many more had him fighting to the death with clubbed rifle and Bowie knife. The latter version might have been a wishful fabrication of the press; or it might very well have been the truth. If true, how does one reconcile the substantial Mexican execution testimony?

This controversy has spawned in recent years a number of books and articles endeavoring to dismiss the Mexican accounts of this incident as deliberate lies, or perhaps even modern forgeries, without success. That many of these books and articles are often poorly researched and written, sometimes puerile in logic, and generally irascible in tone, only serves to crack the foundations of the authors' already flimsy theories. Nevertheless, and despite all the excitably spilled ink, the Mexican accounts remain standing—like the proverbial Tartar who refuses to be captured.

As for *where* the executions took place, no certain spot up to this time has been pinpointed. Decades later Mrs. Dickenson claimed to have seen Crockett's body lying between the church and convent building; but because so much else of her testimony is erroneous or nebulous, sifting the facts from her faulty memory is sometimes impossible. (In one interview, for instance, she stated that Colonel Travis was killed "on top of the church," despite several pieces of solid evidence indicating his demise at the north wall.) Still, at least one new possibility can be submitted as a candidate for the actual site of Crockett's death.

In *Graham's Magazine* for January 1851, "Scenes in Texas . . . From the Reconnoisance of an Officer of the U.S. Army"—the author identified only as "T. W."—was published. These observations were made while the officer's company was stationed in San Antonio in 1848. After seeing the town and its citizens,

> We next visited the Alamo . . . By a broad archway through the centre of a fortress which fronts the south,[1] we entered an oblong square of some twelve acres extent, and turning obliquely to the left, we had passed all but the last of a long row of soldiers' quarters, which form a part of the western wall, when our guide exclaimed, "Here perished poor Crockett."

By T. W.'s directions, this position seems to have been the low cannon platform on the west wall built within a roofless room of the next-to-the-northernmost block of houses. One might casually suspect the "guide" of simply recounting a yarn of spurious local vintage, were it not for one important piece of verifying evidence.

San Antonio's *alcalde* at the time of the battle, Francisco Antonio Ruiz, helped identify the bodies of Travis, Bowie, and Crockett for Santa Anna, while preparations were being made to remove the Mexican dead from the field. In his memoir of that day, Ruiz correctly places Travis' body on the north wall, and Bowie's in one of the rooms "on the south side" (which coincides with Sánchez Navarro's plan and key to the fort and the action of March 6). "Towards the west," Ruiz added, "and in a small fort opposite the city, we found the body of Col. Crockett."[2]

"Small fort," or *"fortin"* in Spanish, seems to have been the term applied to most of the batteries within the Alamo by the Mexicans. Whether they sat on high platforms or low ones, they seem to have been deemed positions formidable enough to deserve the appelation. Perhaps it really only took a low stockade, or jerry-built wall of adobe bricks or sandbags enclosing such a battery, to call it a "fortin."

Thus we have for the first time a meshing of two pieces of evidence that quite agree with one another concerning the location of Crockett's body. Indeed, this site *is* "opposite the city," i.e., facing San

(Continued on next page)

Antonio. Crockett's body might indeed have been found there; but arguments over his death by combat as opposed to execution after surrender will almost certainly continue. It must be remembered, however, that if he *was* one of the prisoners executed, his survival of the battle proper was no shameful thing. The three surviving French legionnaires at Camerone in 1863, Lee at Appomattox in 1865, and the thousands of American soldiers who capitulated after a long defense of Bataan and Corregidor in 1942—to give just three examples—were no less heroic for choosing life to certain annihilation. By this reasoning, if Crockett indeed chose life, it serves no purpose to deny that he could have been capable of such a decision. (My great thanks to Kevin R. Young for bringing to my attention the heretofore unknown account of "T.W."—GZ)

would not have died in vain. If this officer was not a madman, he was a fool.[87] (Burke, *Men's Illustrated:* 40)

de la Peña

Shortly before Santa Anna's speech, an unpleasant episode had taken place which, since it occurred after the end of the skirmish, was looked upon as base murder and which contributed greatly to the coolness that was noted. Some seven men had survived the general carnage and, under the protection of General Castrillón, they were brought before Santa Anna. Among them was one of great stature, well proportioned, with regular features, in whose face there was the imprint of adversity, but in whom one also noticed a degree of resignation and nobility that did him honor. He was the naturalist David Crockett, well known in North America for his unusual adventures, who had undertaken to explore the country and who, finding himself in Béxar at the very moment of surprise, had taken refuge in the Alamo, fearing that his status as a foreigner might not be respected. Santa Anna answered Castrillón's intervention in Crockett's behalf with a gesture of indignation and, addressing himself to the zappers, the troops closest to him, ordered his

execution. The commanders and officers were outraged at this action and did not support the order, hoping that once the fury of the moment had blown over these men would be spared; but several officers who were around the president and who, perhaps, had not been present during the moment of danger, became noteworthy by an infamous deed, surpassing the soldiers in cruelty. They thrust themselves forward, in order to flatter their commander, and with swords in hand, fell upon these unfortunate, defenseless men just as a tiger leaps upon his prey. Though tortured before they were killed, these unfortunates died without complaining and without humiliating themselves before their torturers. It was rumored that General [Ramírez y] Sesma was one of them; I will not bear witness to this, for though present, I turned away horrified in order not to witness such a barbarous scene. Do you remember, comrades, that fierce moment which struck us all with dread, which made our souls tremble, thirsting for vengeance just a few moments before? Are your resolute hearts not stirred and still full of indignation against those who so ignobly dishonored their swords with blood? As for me, I confess that the very memory of it makes me tremble and that my ear can still hear the penetrating, doleful sound of the victims.[88] (Perry: 53-54)

---

87. See Groneman's *Eyewitness*, p. 208.

88. The evidence lends itself that Crockett was executed. The man was forty-nine years old and, contrary to popular culture, was not a frontiersman nor adventurer but a politician. Having fought for thirteen days and especially hard for the past ninety minutes to two hours, he was exhausted and possibly wounded. Believing himself to be well known, he surrendered to the Mexicans, expecting treatment as an official of the U.S. Instead, when brought before Santa Anna he was executed—not by firing squad but by being stabbed to death by swords.

Phase VI:
The Aftermath

de la Peña

This scene of extermination went on for an hour before the curtain of death covered and ended it; shortly before six in the morning it was all finished; the corps were beginning to reassemble and to identify themselves, their sorrowful countenances revealing the losses in the thinned ranks of their officers and comrades, when the commander in chief appeared. He could see for himself the desolation among his battalions and that devastated area littered with corpses, with scattered limbs and bullets, with weapons and torn uniforms. Some of these were burning together with the corpses, which produced an unbearable and nauseating odor. The bodies, with their blackened and bloody faces disfigured by a desperate death, their hair and uniforms burning at once, presented a dreadful and truly hellish sight. Quite soon some of the bodies were left naked by fire, others by disgraceful rapacity, especially among our men. The enemy could be identified by their whiteness, by their robust and bulky shapes. What a sad spectacle, that of the dead and dying! What a horror, to inspect the area and find the remains of friends!

The general then addressed his crippled battalions, lauding their courage and thanking them in the name of their country. But one hardly noticed in his words the magic that Napoleon expresses in which, which, Count Segur[89] assures us, was impossible to resist. The *vivas* were seconded icily, and silence would hardly have been broken if I, seized by one of those impulses triggered by enthusiasm or one formed to avoid reflection, which conceals the feelings, had not addressed myself to the valiant *cazadores* of Aldama [first column], hailing the Republic and them, an act which, carried out in the presence of the commander on whom so much unmerited honor had been bestowed, proved that I never flatter those in power.

To whom was this sacrifice useful and what advantage was derived by increasing the number of victims? It was paid for dearly, though it could have been otherwise had these men been required to walk across the floor carpeted with the bodies over which we stepped, had then been rehabilitated generously and required to communicate to their comrades the fate that awaited them if they did not desist from their unjust cause. They could have informed their comrades of the force and resources that the enemy had. (Perry: 53)

Filisola

In our opinion all that bloodshed of our soldiers as well as of our enemies was useless, having as its only objective an inconsiderate, childish and culpable vanity so that it might be proclaimed that Béxar had been reconquered by force of arms and that in the attack many men had died on both sides. As we have already stated, the defenders of the Alamo were ready to surrender with only the condition that their lives should be saved.

But let us suppose such an arrangement had not existed, what would those wretched men do or hope for with more than 5,000 men[90] surrounding them without means of resistance nor any means of escape by retreat, nor that any friendly force that might have caused the Mexicans to raise the siege to save them, without food to keep them alive in that indefensible location? Even though there had been more than enough of what we had indicated that they lacked, by merely placing twenty artillery pieces properly, that poor wall could not have withstood one hour of cannon fire without being reduced to rubble with the poor quarters inside. (Woolsey, 2:177-180)

89. Count Segur was a French general and imperial aide-de-camp to Napoleon. See Chandler's *The Campaigns of Napoleon: The Mind of History's Greatest Soldier.*

90. The total number of Mexican forces in Texas was around 6,019 (Santos:17).

FIG. 38   SANTA ANNA'S SPEECH

FIG. 38   SANTA ANNA'S SPEECH

Shortly after Santa Anna had ordered the execution of the surrendered garrison survivors, he "addressed his crippled battalions," in the words of José Enrique de la Peña, "lauding their courage and thanking them in the name of their country." Travis' slave, Joe, literally a captive audience to the speech, observed that the Mexican troops "were formed in hollow square, and Santa Anna addressed them in a very animated manner."

Joe's remark that the *generalissimo* was "dressed very plainly—somewhat 'like a Methodist preacher,'" suggests that Santa Anna probably wore an undress military frock coat much like the one Carlos Paris painted him wearing, in that artist's ca. 1834 oil, "The Battle of Tampico."[1] The color of the coat appears to be the same green as the green in the Mexican flag directly behind him in the painting; traditionally, this national green was of a middle hue. The coat is lined with red, and has gold lace around collar and cuffs.

While he might have worn a bicorn with tricolor plumes attached, our illustration shows him in the *sombrero* he sometimes also wore, according to at least two nearly contemporary prints. A division general's blue sash circles his waist, and he leans on a fashionable cane.

His use of the Alamo's small interior redoubt (covering the main gate) for a podium is a supposition; but it would have made him visible to all his gathered troops. At least two Texian guns were positioned here.

To his immediate left is a black orderly, possibly Ben (remembered in history as Santa Anna's cook), who went into the fort in the battle's wake to help identify the Alamo's dead leaders. The precise dress of such an orderly is not known; the figure here is attired much like General Arista's orderly, in a painting made about ten years later.[2] His coat is a middle blue, with red collar and cuffs; his vest white; and a gold band encircles the crown of his black hat. To Santa Anna's right is a staff trumpeter of the light cavalry, who kept close to the general to immediately relay orders and signals.[3]

De la Peña's description of the battlefield as Santa Anna saw it is terse but graphic: a "devastated area littered with corpses, with scattered limbs and bullets, with weapons and torn uniforms. Some of these were burning together with the corpses, which produced an unbearable and nauseating odor . . . What a sad spectacle . . . What a horror!" Ever the severe critic of his commander-in-chief, de la Peña chided him for lacking in his speech "the magic that Napoleon expresses in his, which . . . was impossible to resist."—GZ

Urissa

At about eight o'clock I went into the fort and saw Santa Anna walking to and fro. As I bowed, he said to me, pointing to the dead: "These are the chickens. Much blood has been shed, but the battle is over; it was but a small affair." (*Texas Almanac* 1859: 62)

Almonte

. . . and only five women, one [former] Mexican soldier and a black slave escaped from instant death. (*SHQ* 48:23)

Ruiz

Half an hour elapsed when Santa Anna sent one of his aide-de-camps with an order for us to come before him. He directed me to call on some of the neighbors to come with carts to carry the [*soldado*] dead to the cemetery and to accompany him as he desired to have Colonels Travis, Bowie, and Crockett shown to him.

On the north battery of the fortress lay the lifeless body of Colonel Travis on the gun carriage, shot only through the forehead. Colonel Bowie was found dead in his bed in one of the rooms on the south side.

Santa Anna, after all the Mexicans were taken out, ordered wood to be brought to burn the bodies of the Texians. He sent a company of dragoons with me to bring wood and dry branches from the neighboring forest. About three o'clock in the afternoon they commenced laying the wood and dry branches upon which a pile of dead bodies was placed; more wood was piled on them and another pile brought, and in this manner they were arranged in layers. Kindling wood was distributed through the pile, and about 5 o'clock in the evening it was lighted.

The dead Mexicans of Santa Anna were taken

to the graveyard, but not having sufficient room for them, I ordered them to be thrown into the river, which was done that same day.

The gallantry of the few Texians who defended the Alamo was really wondered at by the Mexican army. Even the generals were astonished at their vigorous resistance, and how dearly victory was bought.

The Generals who, under Santa Anna, participated in the storming of the Alamo were Juan Amador, Castrillón, Ramírez [y] Sesma, and Andrado. (*Texas Almanac:* 1850)

Becerra

General Santa Anna directed Colonel [Ventura] Mora to send out his cavalry to bring in wood. He ordered that they should make prisoners of all inhabitants they might meet, and force them to pack wood to the Alamo. In this manner a large quantity of wood was collected. A large pile was raised. It consisted of layers of wood and layers of corpses of Texians. It was set on fire. The bodies of those brave men, who fell fighting that morning, as men have seldom fought, were reduced to ashes before the sun had set. It was a melancholy spectacle.[91]

There was an order to gather our dead and wounded. It was a fearful sight. Our lifeless soldiers covered the grounds surrounding the Alamo. They were heaped inside the fortress. Blood and brains covered the earth and the floors, and had splattered the walls. The ghostly faces of our comrades met our gaze, and we removed them with despondent hearts. The killed were generally struck in the head. The wounds were in the neck, or shoulder, seldom below that. The firing of the besieged was fearfully precise. When a Texas rifle was leveled on a Mexican he was considered as good as dead. All this indicates the dauntless bravery and the cool self-possession of the men who were engaged in a hopeless conflict with an enemy numbering more than twenty to one. They inflicted on us a loss ten times greater than they suffered. The victory of the Alamo was dearly bought. Indeed the price in the end was well nigh the ruin of Mexico.

During the evening we buried our dead.[92] These were sad duties which each company performed for its fallen members. How many never again responded at roll call; it was a day of bitter strife, of sadness and sorrow. A triumph which bore bitter fruits.

Our wounded were placed in houses, and properly cared for. (Beccera: 172)

Candelaria

All was silent now. The massacre had ended. One hundred and seventy-six of the bravest men that the world ever saw had fallen, and no one asked for mercy. I walked out of the cell, and when I stepped on the floor of the Alamo the blood ran in my shoes. (*San Antonio Light*, February 19, 1899)

Nuñez

After all the firing had ceased and the smoke cleared away, we found in the large room to the right of the main entrance three persons, two Mexican women named Juana de Melton and La *Quintilla*[93] and a Negro boy, about fifteen or sixteen years old who told us that he was the servant of Colonel Travis. If there had been any other persons in the Alamo they would have been killed, for General Santa Anna had ordered us not to spare either age nor sex, especially of those who were American or of American descent.

On the floor of the main building there was a sight which beggared all description. The earthen floor was nearly shoe-mouth deep in blood and weltering therein laid 500 dead bodies, many of them still clenched together with one hand, while the other held fast a sword, a pistol or a gun, which betokened the kind of conflict which had just ended.

General Santa Anna immediately ordered every one of the Americans to be dragged out and burnt. The infantry was ordered to tie on the ropes, and the cavalry to do the dragging. When the infantry commenced to tie the ropes to the dead bodies they could not tell our soldiers from the Americans,

---

91. This would be one of the funeral pyres. The other two would be in the location of the *alameda* near the Dolores Cavalry. The funeral pyres are confusing. Seguín later in life mentioned three piles of ash. The *Plaza de Valero* was probably the first, the other two at the *alameda*.

92. This occurred in the *Campo Santo*.

93. A *quintilla* is a metrical composition of five verses. Perhaps this was a nickname for one of the survivors.

from the fact that their uniforms and clothes were so stained with blood and smoke and their faces so besmeared with gore and blackened that one could not distinguish the one from the other. This fact was reported to Santa Anna and he appeared at the front and gave instructions to have every face wiped off and for the men to be particular not to mistake any of our men for Americans and burn them, but to give them decent sepulture. He stood for a moment gazing on the horrid and ghastly spectacle before him, but soon retired and was seen no more.

After we had finished our task of burning the Americans a few of us went back to the Alamo to see if we could pick up any valuables, but we could not find anything scarcely, except their arms and a few cooking utensils and some clothing. I found Colonel Travis's coat, which was hanging on a peg driven to the wall just behind the cannon and from where his dead body had just been dragged away. In the pockets I found some papers that resembled paper money or bonds of some kind. His cannon was standing just as he had left it with its mouth pointing west and not towards the Alamo plaza. We did not use Colonel Travis' cannon, nor even our own, because cannons were almost useless on the day that we made the final assault. (*SHQ*, July 1990: 77-84)

Yorba

Along about nine o'clock, I should judge, the shouting and swearing and yelling had ceased, but the air was thick and heavy with blue powder smoke. A Mexican Colonel came running to the priest's residence and asked that we go down to the Alamo to do what we could for the dying men.

Such a dreadful sight. The roadway was thronged with Mexican soldiers with smoke and dirt begrimed faces, haggard eyes and wild, insane expression. There were twelve or fifteen bodies of Mexicans lying dead and bleeding here and there and others were being carried to an adobe house across the way. The stones in the church wall were spotted with blood, the doors were splintered and battered in. Pools of thick blood were so frequent on the sun-baked earth about the stone building that we had to be careful to avoid stepping in them. There was a din of excited voices along the street and the officers were marshaling their men for moving to camp.

But no one could even tell you of the horror of the scene that met our gaze when we were led by the sympathetic little colonel into the old Alamo to bandage up the wounds of several young [*soldado*] men there. I used to try when I was younger to describe that awful sight, but I never could find sufficient language. There were only a few Mexicans in there when we came and they were all officers who had ordered the common soldiers away from the scene of death and—yes—slaughter, for that was what it was. The floor was literally crimson with blood. The woodwork all about us was riddled and splintered by lead balls and what was left of the old altar at the rear of the church was cut and slashed by cannon ball and bullets. The air was dark with powder smoke and was hot and heavy. The odor was oppressive and sickening and the simply horrible scene nerved us as nothing else could.

The dead Texians lay singly and in heaps of three or four, or in irregular rows here and there all about the floor of the Alamo, just as they had fallen when a ball reached a vital part or they had dropped to their death from loss of blood. Of course we went to work as soon as we got to the mission at helping the bleeding and moaning men who had only a few hours of life left, at most; but the few minutes that we looked upon the corpses all about us gave a picture that has always been as distinct as one before my very eyes.

So thick were the bodies of the dead that we had to step over them to get [near] a man in whom there was still life. Close to my feet was a young man who had been shot through the forehead. He had dropped dead with his eyes staring wildly open and, as he lay there, seemingly gazed up into my face. (*San Antonio Express*, April 12, 1896)

San Luis Potosi

At ten o'clock the troops began to march back to Béxar. (McDonald and Young: 4)

E. Esparza

When it was broad daylight, the families were sent to the home of Don Músquiz at the southwest corner of Main Plaza. A servant there gave us coffee and tamales. We were very hungry. That afternoon we were taken before Santa Anna. He had his headquarters on the Plaza. I saw a pile of silver on the table where he sat.

Mrs. Dickenson was more excited than any of the other women. My mother was very quiet and very sad, but not afraid of Santa Anna. I was scared. The Texians had told me that he would cut off my ears if he ever caught me. I did not cry out, but I clung to my mother. Santa Anna, I remember, was dressed up very fine and he had a pleasant voice; but he looked angry. He thought us traitors. He was kind to Mrs. Dickenson, at least his voice sounded different when he spoke to her.

He asked the Mexican women, "Why do you fight your countrymen?" "They are not our countrymen," my mother answered, "we are Texians." "I suppose if I let you go you will raise your children to fight Mexico." "Yes," my mother said. Her sorrow over the death of my father had made her not afraid to die, I think. "You ought to have your ears cut off," he replied. This made me and the other children scream. "Get the mob out!" Santa Anna said. "Give each woman two dollars and a blanket." The officer led us away. As we were going out he said in a low voice, "Vamonos."[94] We did.

Mrs. Dickenson sat there before Santa Anna when we left. She was crying. Señor Travis had a Negro slave named Joe, who was also standing there. We heard afterwards that Santa Anna sent Mrs. Dickenson on a horse to Gonzáles with Joe to help her along. Deaf Smith and some of Houston's scouts met her on the way. After hearing the sad story from her, some of them hurried on to Gonzáles with the news.

We stayed in San Antonio with my uncle. He had taken no part in the war. He was too old. Uncle found my father's body among the slain and buried it.[95] It took three days for the soldiers of Santa Anna to gather up their dead and bury them.

I heard that they did burn the bodies. Later, when Santa Anna had been defeated, I learned that Captain Seguín had come to San Antonio and gathered up the ashes of these brave men and given them burial near the spot where they had died fighting for freedom. Alcalde Ruiz helped to burn and bury many of the bodies.

I heard Guerrero, an old man, tell that the names were Fuentes, Losoya, Jiménez, and my father; also Captain Badilla of Nacogdoches. Guerrero was there too, I was told, but escaped because he said he was a prisoner of the Texians. It is a sin for a man to carry a lie to his grave. (Driggs and King: 227-230)

* * * *

Some soldiers grouped the women and children together and herded them to the front of the chapel where there were others. We passed the room where Bowie had lain on his cot, desperately ill. His body was covered with blood and hideously mutilated. He had been tossed from his cot to the floor, but a pile of Mexican bodies said he sold his life dearly.

Gathered at the front, the Mexican soldiers continued firing into the bodies and walls for a long time, until lanterns were brought to check for survivors. The last I saw of my father was when a lantern was held over his body and the bodies of the dead all about the cannon he had tended. (DRT Library, Alamo)

* * * *

After the dreadful ninety-minute slaughter, the Texians were piled on stacks of wood to be burned. My uncle asked for permission to locate his brother's body. He alone was permitted a Christian burial because the family were "good Mexicans." My mother told me to forget the horror of all that I had seen, but to remember that no one who had been in the battle had had one thing to gain, and only the Texians who died were even remembered. (DRT Library, Alamo)

* * * *

They took my mother, her babe, my brothers and I to another part of the building where there were other women and children huddled. Another of the women had a babe at her breast. That was Mrs. Dickenson. There was an old woman in there. They called her Doña Petra. This was the only name I ever knew her by. With her was a young girl, Trinidad Saucedo, who was very beautiful. Mrs. Alsbury and her sister were there also and several other women, young girls and little boys. I do not remember having seen Madam Candaleria there. She

---

94. Meaning "Well, go on."
95. Esparza also claimed that the uncle who buried his father did fight for Santa Anna.

may have been among the women and I may not have noticed her particularly. She claimed to have been there and I shall not dispute her word. I did not notice the women as closely as I did the men.

After the soldiers of Santa Anna had got in a corner all of the women and children who had not been killed in the onslaught, they kept firing on the men who had defended the Alamo. For fully a quarter of an hour they kept firing upon them after all of the defenders had been slain and their corpses were lying still. It was pitch dark in the eastern end of the structure and the soldiers of Santa Anna seemed to fear to go there even after firing from the Constitutionalists from there had ceased. Santa Anna's men stood still and fired into the darkness and until some one brought lanterns.

The last I saw of my father's corpse was when one of them held his lantern above it and over the dead who lay about the cannon he had tended.

But to return to the story of the fall of the Alamo. After all of the men had been slain, the women and children were kept huddled up in the church's southwest corner in the small room to the right of the large double door of the church as one enters it. A guard was put over them. They were held there until after daylight when orders were given to remove them. We were all marched off to the house of *Señor* Músquiz. Here all of the women were again placed under guard. Músquiz owned a *suerte*[96] on South Alamo Street not very far from where Beethoven Hall now is. My mother and father were well acquainted with the Músquiz family. At about 8:00 we became very hungry, up to then not having been given any food. My mother, being familiar with the premises, began to look about for food for herself and children as well as her other comrades. While she was doing so Músquiz told her that it was dangerous for her to be moving about and leaving the place and the room in which she was under guard. She told him she did not care if she was under guard or not, she was going to have something to eat for herself, her children, and her companions whom she intended to feed if Santa Anna did not feed his prisoners.

Músquiz admonished her to silence and told her to be patient and he would get some food from his own store. After urging my mother not to leave the room, Músquiz disappeared and went to his pantry, where he got quite a quantity of provisions and brought them to the room in which the prisoners, some ten or a dozen in number, were and distributed the food among them. There was some coffee as well as bread and meat. I recollect that I ate heartily, but my mother very sparingly. We were kept at Músquiz's house until 3:00 in the afternoon when the prisoners were taken to Military Plaza.

We were halted on the plaza and in front of the place where Wolfson's store now is.[97] Mrs. Alsbury and her sister, Mrs. Gertrudis Cantu, were the first ones to be taken before Santa Anna. He questioned them and after talking with them for a few minutes, discharged them from custody and they left. Mrs. Cantu afterwards removed to the Calaveras where she married and resided up to the time of her death.

Mrs. Dickenson, the wife of Lieutenant Dickenson, the woman I told you, like my mother, had a babe at her breast, was the next to be summoned before Santa Anna. He spent some time in questioning her after which he dismissed her.

My mother was next called before the dictator. When she appeared before him my baby sister pressed closely to her bosom, I with my brother followed her into his presence. My brother was clinging to her skirt, but I stood to one side and behind her. I watched every move and listened to every word spoken. Santa Anna asked her name. She gave it. He then asked, "Where is your husband?" She answered, sobbing: "He's dead at the Alamo." Santa Anna asked where the other members of the family were. She replied that a brother of my father's, she was informed, was in his [Santa Anna's] army. This was true. My father had a brother whose name was Francisco Esparza, who joined the forces of Santa Anna. It was this brother who appeared before Santa Anna later and asked permission to search among the slain for my father's corpse. The permission was given. My uncle found my father's body and had it buried in the *Campo Santo* where Milam Square is now. I did not get a chance to see it before it was buried there as the burial, as all others incident to that battle, was a very hurried one. It was probably that my father was the only one who fought on the side of the Constitutionalists, and against the forces of the dictator, whose body was buried without having first been burned. Santa Anna released my mother. He gave her a blanket

96. Piece of property.
97. Wolfson's was on the corner of Main and Commerce.

FIG. 39   SEÑORA ESPARZA MEETS SANTA ANNA

FIG. 39   SEÑORA ESPARZA MEETS SANTA ANNA

In one of the rooms of the Yturri house, Santa Anna's headquarters, groups of noncombatant survivors are taken before the general one by one on the afternoon of March 6. One group is composed of Señora Esparza and her children: her sons, Enrique (about eight years old), Francisco and Manuel (both five), daughter Maria (ten), and an infant baby.

On the table before Santa Anna was a pile of blankets and an impressive supply of silver dollars. When he asked Señora Esparza about her husband, Alamo defender Gregorio Esparza, she told him, sobbing, that he was in the fort, dead. Santa Anna gave her a blanket and two dollars, and told her she was free.

Little Enrique never forgot the impression the *generalissimo* made on him that day. Decades later he recalled that Santa Anna "had a hard and cruel look and his countenance was a very sinister one."

The silver dollars might well have been American coins found within the Alamo. The cash-starved, heavily indebted Mexican Army was as obsessed with finding money within the fort as with capturing it that morning; and this obsession is verified in many accounts. Doubtless much of the coinage seized quickly found its way, however reluctantly, back to El Presidente.—GZ

and two silver dollars as he dismissed her. I was informed that he gave a blanket and the same sum of money to each of the other women who were brought from the Alamo before him.

I noticed him closely and saw he was the same officer I had seen dismount on the Main Plaza about sundown on the night when I went into the Alamo. After our release we went back to our home and my mother wept for many days and nights. I frequently went to the Main Plaza and watched the soldiers of Santa Anna and saw him quite a number of times before they marched away towards Houston where he was defeated. He had a very broad face and high cheek bones. He had a hard and cruel look and his countenance was a very sinister one. It has haunted me ever since I last saw it and I will never forget the face or figure of Santa Anna. (*San Antonio Express,* May 12, 1907)

* * * *

Santa Anna gave each of the women two silver pesos, or Mexican "dobe" dollars when he ordered their release.

After this we went to look for the body of my father and my brother, but when we got to the Alamo again all of the bodies had been removed and taken to the *alameda*. They were put in two piles, one on each side of the *alameda* and burned. All of the dead killed in the siege who were defenders of the Alamo were burned, both Mexicans and

Americans, and my father and brother were among them, but we could not find them in either pile, for the soldiers would not let us get close enough to examine or claim them.

They [*soldados*] set fire to them and burned them. My mother placed her *mantilla*[98] before her face and ran screaming from the scene, dragging me by the hand with her. After the bodies were burned we went back several times to the two places until all of the fragments had been removed and the ashes had been scattered in every direction. (*San Antonio Express,* March 26, 1911)

* * * *

The families, with the baggage, were then sent under guard to the house of Don Ramón Músquiz, which was located where Frank Brother's store now is, on Main Plaza.[99] Here we were given coffee and some food and were told we would go before the President at 3 o'clock. On our way to the Musquiz house we passed up Commerce street and it was crowded as far as Presa Street with soldiers who did not fire a shot during the battle. Santa Anna had many more troops than he could use. At 2 o'clock we went before Santa Anna. His quarters were in a house which stood where L. Wolfson's store now is. He had a great stack of silver money on a table before him, and a pile of blankets. One by one the women were sent into a side room to make their declaration, and on coming out were given $2 and a

---

98. A standing hair comb.
99. This is now a parking lot.

blanket. While my mother was waiting her turn, Mrs. Melton, who had never recognized my mother as an acquaintance, and who was considered an aristocrat, sent her brother, Juan Losoya, across the room to my mother to ask the favor that nothing be said to the President about her marriage with an American. My mother told Juan to tell her not to be afraid. Mrs. Dickenson was there, also several other women. After the President had given my mother her $2 and blanket, he told her she was free to go where she liked. We gathered what belongings we could together and went to our cousin's place on North Flores Street, where we remained several months. (*San Antonio Express,* March 7, 1905)

* * * *

My uncle told me afterward that Santa Anna gave him permission to get my father's body and that he found it where the thick of the fight had been. (*San Antonio Express,* November 22, 1902)

* * * *

No tongue can describe the terror and horror of that fearful last fight! The women and children were paralyzed with terror and faint from hunger when the Mexican soldiers rushed in after the fall of the Alamo. A poor paralytic unable to speak to them and tell that he was not a belligerent was murdered before their eyes, as was a young fellow who had been captured sometime previous and continued in the Alamo. Brigidio Guerrero, a youth, was saved as he managed to say he was not a Texian, but a Texian prisoner.

A Mexican officer, related to some of the refugees, arrived just in time to save the women and children—but they were subjected to terrible usage and horrible abuse. Finally, someone obtained safe conduct for them at about two o'clock on the morning of the 7th to the house of Governor [Ramón] Músquiz on Main Plaza. Here the famished prisoners were served with coffee by the Músquiz domestics. At daylight they were required to go before Santa Anna and take the oath of allegiance. Each mother was then given a blanket and two dollars, by Santa Anna in person. The only two who escaped this additional humiliation were the two daughters of Navarro [Juana Alsbury and Gertrudis Cantú] who were spirited away from Músquiz's house by their father [uncle]—José Antonio Navarro. The body of Esparza's father, who was butchered with other Texians, was obtained by his

brother [Francisco] who was in the Mexican Army and was buried in the San Fernando *Campo Santo* [cemetery] and thus he has the distinction of being the only Texian who escaped the funeral pyre. (*San Antonio Light,* November 10, 1901)

Villaneuva

After the Fall of the Alamo I went there and among the dead bodies of those lying inside of the rooms I recognized the body of Gregorio Esparza; I also saw the dead bodies of Antonio Fuentes, Toribio Lasoya, Guadalupe Rodriguez and other Mexicans who had fallen in the defense of the Alamo, as also the bodies of Colonel Travis, Bowie, Crockett and other Americans that I had previously known. I saw Francisco Esparza and his brothers take the body of Gregorio Esparza and carry it off towards the *Campo Santo* for interment, the bodies of the Americans were laid in a pile and burnt. (Matovina: 35-36)

Guerrero

. . . he [Guerrero] was one of those who entered the Alamo under Colonel Travis in February 1836, that he was one of the defenders of that place by the Mexican Army [when] he saw that there was no hope left, he had the good fortune of saving his life by concealing himself, he and perhaps one other man an American being the only survivors of that awful butchery. (Matovina: 36)

F. Esparza

After the fall of the Alamo I applied and obtained permission from General Cós to take the body of my brother [Gregorio Esparza] and bury it. I proceeded to the Alamo and found the dead body of my brother in one of the rooms of the Alamo. He had received a ball in his breast and a stab from a sword in his side. I, in company with two of my brothers, took his body and we proceeded and interred it [in] the burying ground [*Campo Santo*] on the west side of San Pedro Creek, where it still lies. My brother, at the taking of Béxar [in December 1835] was under the command of Colonel Juan

N. Seguín and Captain Don Manuel Flores and a member of the company. (Matovina: 34)

E. Esparza

Santa Anna gave each of the women two silver pesos, or Mexican "dobe" dollars when he ordered their release.

After this we went to look for the body of my father and my brother, but when we got to the Alamo again all of the bodies had been removed and taken to the *alameda*. They were put in two piles, one on each side of the *alameda* and burned. All of the dead killed in the siege who were defenders of the Alamo were burned, both Mexicans and Americans, and my father and brother were among them, but we could not find them in either pile, for the soldiers would not let us get close enough to examine or claim them.

They [*soldados*] set fire to them and burned them. My mother placed her mantilla before her face and ran screaming from the scene, dragging me by the hand with her. After the bodies were burned we went back several times to the two places until all the fragments had been removed and the ashes had been scattered in every direction. (*San Antonio Express*, March 26, 1911)

Dickenson

At this moment a Mexican officer came into the room and addressing me in English, asked: "Are you Mrs. Dickenson?" I answered, "Yes." Then said he, "If you wish to save your life, follow me." I followed him, and although shot at and wounded, was spared.

As we passed through the enclosed ground in front of the church, I saw heaps of dead and dying. The Texans on an average killed between eight and nine Mexicans each. . . .[100]

In the evening the Mexicans brought wood from the neighboring forest and burned the bodies of all the Texians, but their own dead they buried in the city cemetery across the San Pedro. (Morphis: 175-177)

* * * *

After the fall she [Dickenson] was approached by a Col. Black[101] (an Englishman) and an officer in the Mexican service who sheltered her from Mexican injury and took her in a buggy to Mr. Músquiz, a merchant in town, where she stayed till next day when she was conducted before Santa Anna who threatened to take her to Mexico with her child; when Almonte, his nephew, addressing his English, pleaded for witness, saying he had been educated in N[ew].O[rleans]. and had experienced great kindness from Americans. Witness was thus permitted to depart to her home in Gonzáles.

After her removal to Músquiz, she expressed a wish to visit the scene of carnage, but was informed by the people of the house that it would not be permitted as the enemy was then burning the dead bodies—and in confirmation thereof, she was shown a smoke in the direction of the Alamo. She knew Colonel Bowie and saw him in the fort, both before and after his death. He was sick before and during the fight, and had even been expected to die.

Colonel Crockett was one of the 3 men who came into the Fort during the siege and before the assault.[102] He was killed, she believes.[103] (Adjutant General Papers, TSL)

* * * *

I left the Alamo on horseback carrying my baby in my arms. I went first to the Musquiz House where I had lived before the Alamo Siege. Then from there I rode alone with my baby towards Gonzáles. Out on the Salado [Creek] I met Colonel Travis'

---

100. The Texians on average killed less than one *soldado* each.

101. There is no known record of Colonel Black's service with this brigade.

102. This is odd. Why would Crockett have left in the first place? Could this have been to guide in reinforcements from the colonies? Who were these three men with him, an advance party from the reinforcements Williamson spoke of? According to a deed and affidavit signed by Crockett, he was at the Cibolo Crossing on March 3. Crockett supposedly made an X as he was too sick to sign his full name. For more on this and the possibility of increased Texian defenders see *Texas Monthly*, December 1993. Unusual, but could Crockett have gone out to attempt a link-up with reinforcements? Was it Crockett who brought in the final group the evening of the 4th/5th? This is more than a lost memory years later; the San Luis journal detailed the same situation.

103. Odd that in at least one account Dickenson details Crockett's final scene, yet here seems unsure as to his demise.

Negro servant [Joe] and he went with me. I was glad to see him. (*San Antonio Express*, February 24, 1929)

* * * *

One of the Mexican officers, always thought by Mrs. Dickenson to be General [Colonel] Almonte, Chief of Staff to Santa Anna, who spoke broken English, stepped to the door of the room in which the women were, and asked: "Is Mrs. Dickenson here?" As she feared to answer and kept quiet, he repeated: "Is Mrs. Dickenson here? Speak out, for it is a matter of life and death." Then she answered, telling who she was, and he took her in charge over to Main Plaza.

* * * *

Here [Músquiz's house] she and her child were held and cared for some days, when she was given a horse and a bag of provisions and told to go. (Maverick: 135–136)

Joe

The Negroes, for there were several Negroes and women in the fort, were spared. Only one woman was killed, and Joe supposes she was shot accidentally, while attempting to cross the Alamo.[104] She was found lying between two guns. The officers came around, after the massacre, and called out to know if there were any Negroes there. Joe stepped out and said, "Yes, here is one." Immediately two soldiers attempted to kill him, one by discharging his piece at him, the other with a thrust of the bayonet. Only one buckshot took effect in his side, not dangerously, and the point of the bayonet scratched him on the other. He was saved by Capt. Barrágan.[105] Besides the Negroes, there were in the fort several Mexican women, among them the wife of a Dr. ——— and her sister, Miss Navarro, who were spared and restored to their father, D. Angel Navarro, of Béxar. Mrs. Dickenson, wife of Lieut. Dickenson, and child, were also spared, and have been sent back into Texas. After the fight was over, the Mexicans were formed in hollow square, and Santa Anna addressed them in a very animated manner. They filled the air with loud shouts. Joe describes him as a slender man, rather tall, dressed very plainly—somewhat "like a Methodist preacher,"[106] to use the Negro's own words. (Gray: 137-138)

* * * *

. . . until the spirit of bravery was entirely quenched, when he heard a voice inquiring if there "were no Negroes here." The Negro replied, "yes, here's one," and came out; a Mexican discharged a gun at him, but did him no injury; another ran his bayonet at him, injuring him slightly, when the Mexican officer speaking English, interposed and saved him. This officer conversed freely with the Negro as also did Santa Anna; this general was there, and made the Negro point out Col. Travis, by which conversation he knew his master had killed the general leading the siege, as their blood had congealed together. The body of Col. Travis and his little, yet great band, were burnt by order of Santa Anna. (*Memphis Enquirer*, April 12, 1836)

---

104. Sadly the identity of this woman is lost to history. There was at least one more African-American man and woman, according to John Ford:

> On the morning of March 6, 1836, she [Bettie] was in the kitchen [of the Alamo] with a colored man, named Charlie; after the resitance of the defenders had ceased a detachment of Mexican soldiers entered the kitchen, Charlie attempted to secrete himself, was found and dragged out. The officer in charge of the men was very small. A soldier made a bayonet thrust at Charlie. The colored gentleman seized the little officer and held him before his own body as a shield—at the same time he backed into a corner. The soldier made many attempts to bayonet Charlie, and in every instance he skillfully covered himself with the diminutive officer. This lasted for several minutes. The soldiers began to relish the joke, and were laughing. The officer did not feel comfortable. He finally called for a parley. He promised to save Charlie's life, on condition that his precious little person should be safely deposited on the floor. Charlie acceded, and the treaty was faithfully observed.

Groneman, *Eyewitness:* 94-95.

105. Captain Barrágan commanded the escort company of lancers for Santa Anna. Joe's discovery must have been quite late in the operation for surely the escort company would not have been present without Santa Anna.

106. Santa Anna had been painted earlier in the decade (Paris: "The Battle of Tampico," 1829, Musso Nacional de Historia) wearing a plain dark frock coat with white vest and trousers. Since all known Mexican generals' uniforms in no way resemble an 1830s Methodist preacher, it can be assumed that Santa Anna again donned the plain dark frock coat.

Dickenson

I never saw my husband again after he went from me his gun in his hand to die for his country. I feared for my fate but was saved by an English Colonel in the Mexican Army. Through the intervention of Almonte I was permitted to leave the Alamo on horseback. Almonte said, "We are fighting men, not women." (*San Antonio Express*, February 24, 1929)

Joe

Joe was taken into Béxar and detained several days, was shown a grand review of the army after the battle which he was told, or supposes, was 8,000 strong. Those acquainted with the ground on which he says they formed think that not more than half that number could form there. Santa Anna questioned Joe about Texas, and the state of its army. Asked if there were many soldiers from the United States in the army, and if more were expected, and said he had men enough to march to the city of Washington. The American dead were collected in a pile and burnt. (Gray: 137-138)

* * * *

After the fight, when they were searching the houses, an officer called out in English, "Are there any Negroes here?" Joe then emerged from his concealment and said, "Yes, here's one." Immediately two soldiers attempted to dispatch him—one by discharging his piece at him, and the other by a thrust of the bayonet. He escaped with a scratch only from the steel, and one buckshot in his side which, however, did little damage. He was saved by the intervention of Captain Barragán, who beat off the soldier with his sword.

The slain were collected in a pile and burnt. (*Frankfort Commonwealth*, May 25, 1836)

J. Díaz

"I did not go to the plaza when the dead were burned," said Díaz. "I had no desire to see that great funeral pyre, but the odor of it permeated every part of the city. It was sickening, and for weeks and months people shunned the Alamo. Some of the men who went there during the cremation told us that the Texas and Mexican soldiers were all piled in a heap and burned together." (*San Antonio Express*, 1907)

Ben

It [burning] shortly died away, day broke upon the scene, and Santa Anna and Almonte returned, when the latter remarked that "another such victory would ruin them." They then directed me to go with them to the fort and point out the bodies of Bowie and Travis—whom I had before known—which I did. The sight was most horrid. (Newell: 88-89)

Buquor

She says that she did not see any of the Texas dead after the final attack but she plainly remembers seeing the smoke arising from the burning bodies of the Texians when their remains were destroyed in this way, a sacrificial fire on the altar of Texas liberty. (*San Antonio Express*, July 19, 1907)

P. Díaz

Finally, on the sixth day after a fierce fusillade, there was silence and I saw the red flag of Santa Anna floating from the Alamo where the Constitutional Flag before had been. Next I saw an immense pillar of flames shoot up a short distance to the south and east of the Alamo and the dense smoke from it rose high into the clouds. I saw it burn for two days and nights, and then flame and smoke subsided and smoldered. I left my retreat and came forth cautiously, coming along Garden Street to town. I noticed that the air was tainted with the terrible odor from many corpses and I saw thousands of vultures flying above me. As I reached the ford of the [San Antonio] River my gaze encountered a terrible sight. The stream was congested with the corpses that had been thrown into it. The *Alcalde*, [Francisco Antonio] Ruiz, had vainly endeavored to bury the bodies of the soldiers of Santa Anna who had been slain by the defenders of the Alamo. He had exhausted all of his resources and still was unable to cope with the task. There were too many of them. . . . Then, involuntarily I put my hands before my eyes and turned away from the river, which

I hesitated to cross. Hurriedly I turned aside and up *la Villita* and went to South Alamo [street]. I could not help seeing the corpses which congested the river all around the bend from Garden [Street] to way above Commerce Street and as far as Crockett Street is now. (*San Antonio Express,* July 1, 1906)

* * * *

Then fell a great silence in the gray dawn; the fight was over and drawn by curiosity to learn what was the outcome of the *"guerra,"* . . . the Mexicans dragged branches of trees and limbs of trees through the streets and made a funeral pyre in the *plaza* [*de Valero*] off to the [south] side of the Alamo. First a layer of wood and then a layer of other corpses until the pyre was completed. Pablo Díaz declared [this] was the work of Santa Anna, the Napoleon of the West. (*San Antonio Light,* October 31, 1909)

* * * *

. . . we saw a huge pillar of flames and smoke shooting up to a considerable height to the south and east of the Alamo. The dense smoke from this fire went up into the clouds and I watched it while the fire burned for two days and two nights. Then it subsided and smoldered.

I noticed that the air was tainted with a terrible odor from many corpses and that thousands of vultures were circling in the sky above us. They were hovering over the city and especially along and above the river's course. As I reached the ford of the San Antonio River at the old Lewis Mill site I encountered a terrible sight. The stream was congested with corpses that had been thrown into it.

[Francisco Antonio] Ruiz, the alcalde [mayor] at that time, had vainly striven to bury the dead soldiers of Santa Anna's command who had been slain in the struggle during the siege. After exhausting every effort and all of his resources, he was unable to give burial to but a very limited number, these principally being officers. Being unable to bury them in the earth he was compelled to dispose of them otherwise. He had them cast into the swiftly flowing stream. But they were so numerous that they choked up the stream, finding lodgement along the banks of the short curves and banks of that stream.

They obstructed the stream for some time until Ruiz was able to get a sufficient force to push the bodies away from the banks as they lodged against them and floated them down the stream for a considerable distance below, where they remained until devoured by the vultures and wolves.

I stopped and looked at the sickening sight, which made me shudder, and I became ill. I was told afterward that the sight and stench had even unseated Santa Anna himself so that he had complained and reprimanded Ruiz for not getting rid of the dead. Involuntarily, I put my hands before my eyes and turned away. But I could not, even then, help seeing the corpses. I turned away from the river which I hesitated to cross and went to the right, along the settlement of la Villita, but even then could not help seeing the corpses, for they lined the river's course and banks all the way from Crockett Street to more than a mile below [the town].

But while the bodies of the Mexican soldiers in the river was a revolting spectacle the one that met my vision later was even more gruesome. It filled me with the greatest horror. I had passed along *la Villita* to South Alamo Street and then north to the *alameda*. This was a broad and spacious place used as a promenade and also as a highway of ingress to and from the city on the east side of the river. On each side of the *alameda* was a row of large cottonwood trees. From them the place took its name of *alameda*. It commenced at about where St. Joseph's Church now stands, this having been the western extremity about half a block from South Alamo Street.

It was Santa Anna himself who had given orders to Ruiz to have the bodies of all who perished while defending the Alamo incinerated. By intuition I went straight to the place. I did not need a guide. The whole story was told by the spectacle I saw. The witnesses were silent but eloquent ones. They were charred skulls, fragments of arms, hands, feet, and other members of the bodies of the dead defenders. In carts the slain, among whom were Travis, Crockett, Bowie, Bonham and Jameson, as well as all of the others, had been removed from the Alamo mission, where they fell, to the *alameda*, where they were burned on two different pyres. These were about 250 yards apart and one was on each side of the *alameda*. The one on the north side was the smallest, while that on the south side was the largest. The latter was probably about twenty feet longer than the former. Both were about the same width—about eight or ten feet. Both pyres were about ten feet high when the flames were first kindled and the consuming of the corpses commenced.

In alternate layers the corpses and wood were placed. Grease of different kinds, principally tallow, was melted and poured over the two pyres. They were then ignited and burned until they burned out, leaving but a few fragments of different members. Most of the corpses were entirely consumed. (*San Antonio Express*, March 26, 1911)

Vargas

Rivers of blood flowed and the earth ran red. Texians—Americans—gave their lives willingly to the holy cause. I know as a Mexican and guarded by Santa Anna's men—bound up the wounds of the injured of his army and helped to bury the dead . . . the uncounted dead were piled in camp, while [a] sort of service was rendered the living by doctors aided by myself and others who, like me, had been impressed for this service. (*San Antonio Light*, April 3, 1910)

Chavez

There was an orchard very near the place where the bodies were burned on the south side of the *alameda* and it is stated that flames and sparks blowing in the fierce March wind that prevailed a part of the time during the incineration blew the flames into the orchard, injuring many and destroying some of the fruit trees, most of which died soon after.

This fact probably gave rise to the prevalent belief that obtained for many years, that after the bodies were burned none of the fruit trees in the neighborhood would bear and that they as well as the other cottonwood trees died soon after. (*San Antonio Express*, March 26, 1911)

* * * *

When we returned [from the ranch] the bodies of those [Texians] that had perished in the Alamo were still burning on two immense pyres on the old *alameda*. I went to look at them and the sight indelibly impressed itself upon my memory. One pyre occupied a position on the site of where the [then] new Haff building is. The other was diagonally across the street on what is now [was then] known as the lawn of the Ludlow house and the [then] recently built house adjoining it on the east. The

bodies burned for several days and the wood and tallow fuel used for consuming them was frequently replenished. I made several trips to the scene, which so fascinated me I could not stay away until all of the bodies had been consumed. They were all reduced to ashes except a few charred heads, arms and legs that were scattered about. These were gathered up and placed in a shallow grave where the Ludlow house lawn now is.

All of the [Mexican] officers and some of the privates of Santa Anna's army, according to *Don* [Juan] Antonio Chavez, were burned in the cemetery [*Campo Santo*] where Milam Park now is, but the slain Mexicans were so numerous it was thought the quickest and best way of getting rid of the bodies was by throwing them in the San Antonio River, then a swift and deep stream. There were so many bodies they choked its flow. Many of them lodged in the curves of the river. (*San Antonio Express*, April 19, 1914)

Coy

Looking hastily about him he saw that the [Mexican] camp was deserted. All the hangers-on [camp followers/*soldaderas*] had followed the line of soldiery. He [Coy] worked his hands against a stone until they parted. He made his way out of the camp, followed a well known path that led around the city, and in another hour he had arrived at a point in back of the chapel of the Alamo from where he could join his [Texian] comrades.

Only a bank of cottonwood trees [*alameda*] hid them [Texians] from his view. He forced his way through the underbrush. The Alamo lay before him. There were no signs of fighting. All was quiet. Only, before his eyes, then rose the heavy black cloud from a smoking pile.

It was the funeral pyre of his friends. (*San Antonio Light*, November 26, 1911)

Rodríguez

. . . during the siege of the Alamo the Mexican women in San Antonio remained indoors, praying, and when the final assault began on Sunday morning, every morning was on her knees pleading for the repose of the fallen, foes as well as friends. . . . one young woman who enamored of one of the garrison and who went into the Alamo when the carnage had ceased, found the object of her affection among the slain, folded his hands across his breast, wiped the grime from his pallid face, placed a small cross on his breast and, when ordered away, she dipped her handkerchief in his blood and carried it away in her bosom. (DeShields: 161-162)

Phase VII:
The Numbers

Caro

At the time of the assault, therefore, the enemy's force consisted of 183 men. (Castañeda: 104)

de la Peña

The Alamo was an irregular fortification without flank fires[107] which a wise general would have taken with insignificant losses, but we lost more than three hundred brave men. (Perry: 45)

San Luis Potosi

Immediately they began to gather the dead and wounded. There were two hundred thirty enemy dead in the clearing [between the walls]. Among them were the ringleaders—Bowie, commander of the Alamo, Travis, his second [in command], and Crockett, who had succeeded in entering [the Alamo] three night[s] ago. Of [Texian] wounded or prisoners there were none. (McDonald and Young: 4)

Loranca

. . . making a total of two-hundred and eighty-three persons, including a Mexican found among them, who it appears, had come from La Bahia [Goliad] with dispatches. (*San Antonio Express,* June 23, 1878)

E. Esparza

In after years I was told that six hundred of them had been killed by the one hundred and eighty-two Texians who died fighting at the Alamo. (Driggs and King: 230)

Becerra

Our loss in front of the Alamo was represented at two thousand killed, and more than three hundred wounded. (Beccera: 24)

Candelaria

There were just 177 men inside of the Alamo, and up to the time no one had been killed, though cannons had thundered against us, and several assaults had been made. (*San Antonio Light,* February 19, 1899)

Dickenson

The Mexicans numbered several thousands while there were only one hundred and eighty-two Texians. (Morphis: 175)

* * * *

. . . 182 Texians and 1,600 Mexicans were killed. (Maverick: 136)

---

107. Incorrect. Flank batteries existed on the south and east, which is probably why no *soldados* breached there.

FIG. 40   A MEXICAN WOMAN PLACES A CROSS ON THE CHEST OF A SLAIN DEFENDER

Almonte

On the part of the enemy the result was 250 killed, and 17 pieces of artillery—a flag, muskets and fire-arms taken. Our loss was 60 soldiers and 5 officers killed, and 198 soldiers and 25 officers were wounded—2 of the latter General officers. The Battalion of Toluca lost 98 men between wounded and killed. I was robbed by our soldiers. (SHQ 48:23)

de la Peña

According to documents found among these men and to subsequent information, the force within the Alamo consisted of 182 men; but according to the number counted by us it was 253. Doubtless the total did not exceed either of these two, and in any case the number is less than that referred to by the commander in chief in his *communique*, which contends that in the excavations and the trenches alone more than 600 bodies had been buried. What was the object of this misrepresentation? Some believe that it was done to give greater importance to the episode, others that it was done to excuse our losses and to make it less painful. Death united in one place both friends and enemies; within a few hours a funeral pyre rendered into ashes those men who moments before had been so brave that in a blind fury they had unselfishly offered their lives and had met their ends in combat. The greater part of our dead were buried by their comrades, but the enemy, who seems to have some respect for the dead, attributed the great pyre of dead to our hatred. I, for one, wishing to count the bodies for myself, arrived at the moment the flames were reddening, ready to consume them. (Perry:54-55)

Filisola

All of the enemy perished with only one old woman and a Negro slave left alive. The soldiers spared them out of compassion and because it was supposed that only by force had they been kept in such danger. Of the enemy dead there were 150 volunteers, 32 people of the Town of Gonzáles who under cover of darkness joined the group two days before the attack on the fort, and some twenty people and tradesmen of the city of Béxar itself. (Woolsey, 2:178)

* * * *

Thus, although the Alamo fell, this triumph cost the Mexican army more than seventy dead and three hundred wounded. . . . In the Capture a greater number of our men died than that of the Texians, which was only natural in view of the great advantages that they had with the trenches and the artillery with which they defended themselves. For that reason it was impossible to attack the trenches and silence the fire of the cannon without a great loss among the attackers who had no wall other than their own breasts. (Woolsey, 2:173-174)

Caro

Though the bravery and intrepidity of the troops was general, we shall always deplore the costly sacrifice of the 400 men who fell in the attack. Three hundred were left dead on the field and more than a hundred of the wounded died afterward as a result of the lack of proper medical attention and medical facilities in spite of the fact that their injuries were not serious. This is a well-known fact, as stated before, which made the fate of those who were instantly killed or mortally wounded enviable to those who lingered in pain and suffering without the proper comfort or relief. The enemy died to a man and its loss may be said to have been 183 men, the sum total of their force. Six women who were captured were set at liberty. (Castañeda: 105-106)

Santa Anna

. . . The Alamo was taken, this victory that was so much and so justly celebrated at the time, costing us seventy dead and about three hundred wounded, a loss that was later judged to be avoidable and charged, after the disaster of San Jacinto, to my incompetence and precipitation. I do not know of a way in which any fortification, defended by artillery, can be carried by assault without the personal losses of the attacking party being greater than those of the enemy, against whose walls and fortifications the brave assailants can present only their bare breasts. It is easy enough, from a desk in a peaceful office, to pile up charges against a general out on the field, but this cannot prove anything more than the praiseworthy desire of making war less disastrous. But its nature being such, a general has no power over its immutable laws. Let us weep at the tomb of the brave Mexicans who died at the Alamo defending the honor and the rights of their country. They won a lasting claim to fame and the country can never forget their heroic names. (Castañeda: 14-15)

* * * *

We suffered more than a thousand dead or wounded, but when the battle was over, not a single man in the Alamo was left alive. At the battle's end, the fort was a terrible sight to behold; it would have moved less sensitive men than myself. (Crawford: 51)

* * * *

Sir: Victory belongs to the army which at this very moment, 8 o'clock a.m. achieved a complete and glorious triumph that will render its memory imperishable.

As I had stated in my report to Your Excellency of the taking of this city, on the 27th of last month, I awaited the arrival of the First Brigade of Infantry to commence active operations against the Fortress of the Alamo. However, the whole Brigade having been delayed beyond my expectation, I ordered that three of its battalions, viz: the Engineers—Aldama and Toluca should force their march to join me. These troops, together with the Battalions of Matamoros, Jiménez, and San Luis Potosí, brought the force at might disposal, recruits excluded, up to 1400 Infantry. This force, divided into four columns of attack and a reserve, commenced the attack at 5 o'clock a.m. They met with a stubborn resistance, the combat lasting more than an hour and a half, and the reserve having to be brought into action.

The scene offered by this engagement was extraordinary. The men fought individually, vying with each other in heroism. Twenty-one pieces of artillery used by the enemy with the most perfect accuracy, the brisk fire of the musketry which illuminated the interior of the fortress and its walls and ditches, could not check our dauntless soldiers, who are entitled to the consideration of the Supreme Government and to the gratitude of the nation.

The fortress is now in our power, with artillery stores, etc. More than 600 corpses of foreigners were buried in the ditches and entrenchments, and a good many who had escaped the bayonet of the infantry, fell in the vicinity under the sabres of the cavalry. I can assure your excellency that few are those who bore to their associates the tidings of their disaster.

Among the corpses are those of Bowie and Travis who styled themselves colonels, and also that of Crockett, and several leading men, who had entered the fortress with dispatches from the Convention. We lost about 70 men killed and 300 wounded, among whom are 25 officers. The cause for which they fell renders their loss less painful as it is the duty of the Mexican soldier to die for the defense of the rights of the nation; and all of us were ready for any sacrifice to promote the fond object; nor will we, hereafter, suffer any foreigners, whatever their origin may be, to insult our country and to pollute its soils. I shall, in due time, send to Your Excellency a circumstantial report of this glorious triumph. Now I have only the time to congratulate the nation and the President ad interim, to whom I request you to submit this report. The bearer takes with him one of the flags of the enemy's Battalions, captured today. The inspection of it will show plainly the true intentions of the treacherous colonists, and of their abettors, who came from parts of the United States of the North. God and Liberty! (Chariton: 324-325)

Nuñez

When the Americans were all dragged out and counted there were 180 including officers and men. Upon the other hand this four day's siege and capture of the Alamo cost the Mexican nation at least a thousand men, including killed and wounded, a large majority of this number being killed. Our officers, after the battle was over, were of the opinion that if the Americans had not made holes in the roof themselves, the Alamo could not have been taken by assault. It would either have had to have been starved out or demolished by heavy artillery. (*SHQ*, July 1990: 83)

Ruiz

Santa Anna's loss was estimated at 1600 men. These were the flower of his army. The men burnt numbered one hundred and eighty two. I was an eyewitness. . . . (*Texas Almanac*, 1860:56-57)

Mexican Soldier

257 corpses without counting those who fell in the previous thirteen days. (*El Mosquito Mexicano:* April 5, 1836)

Navarro

Two hundred fifty seven of their men were killed; I have seen and counted their bodies. But I cannot be glad because we lost eleven officers with nineteen wounded, including the valiant Duque and Gonzáles; and two hundred forty-seven of our troops were wounded and one hundred ten killed. It can be truly said that with another such victory as this we'll go to the devil.

After the capture of the Alamo, I proposed to the commandant General, Don Martin Perfecto de Cós, that the valiant officers and soldiers who died in the assault be buried in the cemetery of the chapel of the said fort, that the names of each be inscribed on a copper tablet made from one of the cannons captured to be placed on a column at the base of which these eight lines might be written:

The bodies that lie here at rest
Were those of men whose souls elate
Are now in Heaven to be blest
For deeds that time cannot abate.
They put their manhood to the test,
And fearlessly they met their fate;
Not fearful and, a patriot's fall
Leads to the highest life of all.

My suggestion was not approved and I believe that it was not the fault of General Cós, consequently, I wished to write down the said verses here not so much for the purpose of passing myself off as a poet as to render due their tribute in the only manner in my powers to the illustrious, gallant, and untimely victims. The dead, it appears, were not the only "untimely victims." There are no hospitals, medicines, or doctors; and the condition of the wounded is such as to cause pity. They have no mattresses on which to lie or blankets with which to cover themselves, in spite of the fact that on entering Béxar, we took from the enemy the remnants of three or four stores and that one has been set up and called the government store, where everything is sold at a high price and for cash. (Navarro: 150-151)[108]

108. The casualty figures must be used to determine the accurate strength of the garrison. In general the numbers range from 180 something to 200 something. The difference comes from the bodies in the Alamo proper and a possible late Texian reinforcement. The compound contained the 182 (+/-) that *Alcalde* Ruiz counted. What he failed to examine and where the difference lies is the fifty to sixty Texians in the vicinity of the *alameda* who were dispatched by the cavalry. When the compound amount by Ruiz and those dead at the *alameda* are added together, the amount resembles the number the majority of the Mexican sources give.

Where did all these Texians come from? In Williamson's letter of the 3d, he told Travis that several hundred colonists from different sources were en route to the Alamo. Is it possible that following Travis' last known correspondence on March 3 another batch of Texians entered the mission? Could this have been what Mrs. Dickenson was referring to when Crockett entered the fort with three other men? Or could the Texian numbers have been reported wrong all along; instead of the gallant 180 was it instead the brave 250? Travis' numbers do not always jibe. On the 3d he reports his strength as 146 when it was at least 185. Is it possible, then, that on the night of the 4th or 5th, while the Mexicans were positioning, a large body of colonists made it inside the compound?

Endnotes to Illustrations

FIG. 1   MEXICAN VANGUARD AT THE MEDINA

1. Jose Enrique de la Peña, *With Santa Anna in Texas: A Personal Narrative of the Revolution.* Translated and edited by Carmen Perry. (College Station: Texas A&M University Press, 1975), p. 57.

2. Claudio Linati, *Costumes Civils, Militaires et Religieux de Mexique*, Brussels, 1828, plate 27, "Officier de Dragons"; and Carlo de Paris, oil sketch for the (now lost) painting, "The Battle of Tampico," reproduced in *The Spanish West*, Time-Life's The Old West Series (New York: Time-Life Books, 1976), p. 111.

3. Mrs. Angelino Nieto, Mrs. John Nicholas Brown, and Joseph C. Hefter, *The Mexican Soldier, 1837–1847*, Editions, Mexico, 1958. Plate VIII, Fig. a shows a brigadier general of 1840 in this style cloak.

4. See contemporary print of Spanish cavalry capturing Father Hidalgo, *Texas and the War With Mexico* (New York: American Heritage, 1961), p. 27.

5. See painting of Holy Week celebration, Mexicans parading a number of army implements of uncertain vintage, including a mounted figure with this type of halbred-lance (*American Heritage*, April 1969), p. 24.

6. *Alamo Images: Changing Perceptions of a Texas Experience*, by Susan Prendergast Schoelwer (Dallas: De Golyer Library and Southern Methodist University Press, 1985), p. 64. This is not meant to suggest that the low-crowned hats were not also worn at this time.

FIG. 2   RAISING OF THE TWO-STAR TRICOLOR IN MILITARY PLAZA

1. Visual documentation of the flag can be found in José Juan Sánchez-Navarro's "Vista" of the Alamo, reproduced in *La Guerra de Tejas; Memorias de un Soldado*, ed. Carlos Sánchez-Navarro (Mexico City, 1938). It is shown, explicitly, flying over the Alamo church's southwestern corner.

FIG. 3   THE BLOOD-RED BANNER

1. Ruth R. Olivera, and Liliane Crete, *Life in Mexico Under Santa Anna, 1822–1855* (Norman and London: University of Oklahoma Press, 1991), p. 201.

2. See photograph of a guidon carried by a Mexican guer-rilla lancer, p. 198, in David Nevin, and the editors of Time-Life Books, *The Mexican War,* the Old West Series (Alexandria, Virginia: Time-Life Books, 1978).

FIG. 4   THE FLAG OF TRUCE

1. Reproduced in color in *The Mexican War* (Alexandria, Virginia: Time-Life Books, The Old West Series, 1978), p. 53.

2. *William Bollaert's Texas*, edited by W. Eugene Hollon (Chicago: The Newberry Library) and (Norman and London: University of Oklahoma Press, paperback edition of 1989), facing p. 232; also, *San Antonio: A Historical and Pictorial Guide*, by Charles Ramsdell (Austin: University of Texas Press, 1959), p. 85.

FIG. 5   THE ESPARZA FAMILY ENTERS THE ALAMO

1. See the painting by Lee, reproduced on page 449 in Schoelwer, Susan Prendergast, "The Artist's Alamo: A Reappraisal of Pictorial Evidence, 1836–1850," *Southwestern Historical Quarterly*, Vol. XCI, No. 4, April 1988.

FIG. 7   REPLY OF THE EIGHTEEN-POUNDER

1. Phone conversation with Thomas Ricks Lindley, June 26, 1996.

2. "Alamo Artillery: Number, Type, Caliber and Concussion," by Thomas Ricks Lindley, *The Alamo Journal*, Issue 82, July 1992, p. 7.

3. See eighteenth-century chart for iron gun dimensions, *Round Shot and Rammers*, by Harold L. Peterson (New York: Bonanza Books, 1969), p. 42.

4. In the advertisement reporting his escape, Joe was described as being "25 years old, about five feet six or seven inches in height, very black, and of good countenance." *Texas Telegraph and Register*, May 27, 1837.

5. The pattern here was derived from a mid-1830s sketch by George Catlin of a Cherokee. *A Pictorial History of the American Indian*, by Oliver LaFarge (New York: Crown Publishers, Inc., 1956), p. 42.

FIG. 8   THE BOMBARDMENT OF THE ALAMO

1. *The New Orleans Bee* of May 11, 1836, reported that "a brass howitzer" was captured by Houston's men at San Jacinto.

2. Sánchez-Navarro, #21 in the key to his "Vista y Plano del Fuerte del Alamo," *La Guerra de Tejas; Memorias de un Soldado,* ed. Carlos Sánchez-Navarro (Mexico City, 1938).

3. This crumbled section is suggested by a Seth Eastman sketch of three stone houses in this vicinity, drawn in 1848, by then repaired with vertical timbers in Tejano fashion. See p. 31, Schoelwer, *Alamo Images.*

Our drawing also shows the foundation remains of the stone arches that once, in mission days, fronted the houses of the Indian converts, forming shaded porticoes along the tree-line irrigation ditch.

4. The roofless rear section of the church included walls actually higher than any other point in the fort.

FIG. 9   THE ATTACK FROM LA VILLITA

1. See theoretical profile of lunette and trench, "South Gate and Its Defenses," *Alamo Lore and Myth Organization,* Vol. 3, Issue 4, December 1981, p. 3.

2. Anne A. Fox, *Archaeological Investigations in Alamo Plaza, San Antonio, Bexar County, Texas, 1988 and 1989,* Center for Archaeological Research, The University of Texas at San Antonio, Archaeological Survey Report No. 205, p. 23, fig. b.

3. *Ibid.,* p. 24, fig. a.

FIG. 10   SANTA ANNA'S CONCUBINE

1. *Hispanic Texas, A Historical Guide,* ed. by Helen Simons and Cathryn A. Hoyt (Austin: University of Texas Press, 1992), p. 63; also *William Bollaert's Texas,* ed. by Eugene Hollon (Norman and London: University of Oklahoma Press, 1989), p. 217.

FIG. 12   THE NORTHER OF FEBRUARY 26

1. Regarding the coat, Crockett wrote: "I have tried [it], and would risk my powder under it for forty days and nights." *Davy Crockett's Own Story As Written by himself,* Citadel Press, New York, 1955, p. 189. Whether he brought the garment to Texas is not yet known; however, Col. James Walker Fannin was wearing an overcoat of India rubber when he was executed at Goliad. Jerry J. Gaddy, *Texas in Revolt: Contemporary Newspaper Account of the Texas Revolution* (Fort Collins, Colorado: The Old Army Press, 1973), p. 72.

FIG. 14   THE BURNING OF THE *JACALES,* FEBRUARY 26

1. Joseph H. Labadie, ed., *La Villita Earthworks: A Preliminary Report of Investigations of Mexican Siege Works at the Battle of the Alamo.* Center for Archaeological Research, The University of Texas at San Antonio, Archaeological Survey Report, No. 159, 1986, pp. 50, 51, 53.

2. *Ibid.,* pp. 73-100. The ditch itself, as excavated, was only about thirty-one feet long, the short part of the L and eleven feet. In width it was but six or seven feet—hardly sufficient cover for a battalion.

3. See Gentilz painting, for instance, in Time-Life books, eds., *The Spanish West* (New York: Time-Life Books, 1976), pp. 84-85.

FIG. 17   TEXIAN WEAPONS AND AMMUNITION

1. Frank W. Johnson, *A History of Texas and Texans,* Vol. I (Chicago and New York: The American Historical Society, 1914), p. 351. It is not insignificant that Travis requested "ten kegs of rifle powder" in his letter of March 3.

2. See color reproduction on cover of *Southwestern Historical Quarterly,* Vol. XCI, No. 3, January 1988.

3. Henry J. Kauffman, "Jacob Dickert, Lancaster Gunsmith," in *Guns and Other Arms,* ed. by William Guthman (New York: Mayflower Books, Inc., 1979), p. 88.

4. The Daughters of the Republic of Texas, *The Alamo Long Barrack Museum* (Dallas, Texas: Taylor Publishing Co., 1986), p. 30.

5. Randal B. Gilbert, "Arms for Revolution and the Republic," *Military History of Texas and the Southwest,* no. 9, 1971, p. 192.

6. James W. Pohl, and Stephen L. Hardin, "The Military History of the Texas Revolution: An Overview," *Southwestern Historical Quarterly,* Vol. LXXXIX, No. 3, January 1986, p. 282.

7. Michael J. Koury, *Arms For Texas* (Fort Collins, Colorado: The Old Army Press, 1973), pp. 11-19.

8. Stephen L. Hardin, *The Texas Rangers* (London: Osprey Publishing Ltd., 1991), p. 4.

9. David Nevin, and the Editors of Time-Life Books, *The Texans,* The Old West Series (New York: Time-Life Books, 1975).

10. Norm Flayderman, *Flayderman's Guide to Antique American Firearms . . . and Their Values* (Northbrook, Illinois: DBI Books, Inc., 1994), p. 289.

11. Herman Ehrenberg, "A Campaign in Texas," Littel's Living Age, VIII, February 28, 1846, p. 421.

12. Gaede, Frederick C., "U.S. Infantry Accouterments: Model of 1828," *Military Collector and Historian: The Journal of the Company of Military Historians,* Vol. XXXVII, No. 3, Fall 1985, pp. 99-101.

13. See reproduction in Jack Jackson, *Los Tejanos* (Stamford, Connecticut: Fantagraphics Books, Inc., 1982), p. 128.

14. Robert Abels, *Classic Bowie Knives* (New York: Robert Abels, Inc., 1967), p. 13.

15. *Ibid.,* p. 17.

16. *The Alamo Long Barrack Museum,* p. 8.

17. Carl P. Russell, *Firearms, Traps and Tools of the Mountain Men* (New York: Alfred A. Knopf, 1967), p. 222.

18. *Ibid.,* p. 263.

19. Harold L. Peterson, *Round Shot and Rammers* (New York: Bonanza Books, 1969), p. 45. For notes on the gunade, consult Thomas Ricks Lindley, "Alamo Artillery: Number, Type, Caliber and Concussion," *The Alamo Journal,* No. 82, July 1992, p. 6.

FIG. 18   MEXICAN WEAPONS AND AMMUNITION

1. The Linati prints of soldiers of Mexico's 1826 army seem to suggest that a decade before the fall of the Alamo Spanish or French muskets were the rule in the infantry.

2. Sidney B. Brinckerhoff and Pierce A. Chamberlain, *Spanish Military Weapons in Colonial America, 1700–1821* (New York: Stackpole Books), pp. 41-42.

3. Nieto, Brown, and Hefter, *The Mexican Soldier, 1837-1847,* Mexico, 1958, p. 53.

4. M. L. Brown, *Firearms in Colonial America: The Impact on History and Technology, 1492-1792* (Washington City: Smithsonian Institution Press, 1980), p. 176.

5. Philip Haythorthwaite and Richard Hook, *British Cavalryman, 1792-1815,* Osprey Warrior Series. London, 1994, pl. F. fig. 21.

6. Nieto, Brown, and Hefter, *Ibid.,* pl. XV, fig. 9.

7. R. R. Brown was captured by a lasso during the ambush of Dr. Grant's party on March 2, 1836. See Stephen L. Hardin, *Texian Iliad* (Austin: University of Texas Press, 1994), p. 159.

8. William Guthman, ed., *Guns and Other Arms* (New York: Mayflower Books), p. 177, fig. 1B.

9. Terence Wise and Richard Hook, *Artillery Equipments of the Napoleonic Wars*, Osprey Men-At-Arms Series, London, 1979, pp. 18-20.

FIG. 19 ADVANCING THE SAP

1. According to Almonte. Navarro says that Lieutenant Colonel Ampudia directed the work.

2. Sap rollers were still being used as late as the American Civil War. See daguerreotype of 1863 depicting one used by Federal troops, in *The Photographic History of the Civil War*, Francis Trevelyan Miller, Editor-in-Chief (New York: Thomas Yoseloff, Inc., reprint of 1957), Vol. 5, p. 209. Mantlets—wooden shields rolled on wheels—often served the same purpose.

FIG. 23 THE ADVANCE OF MORALES' COLUMN

1. De la Peña, p. 46.

2. *Ibid.*

3. His coat has two bullion-fringed gold epaulettes, with a bright red silk sash around his waist, under his sword belt. Morales' actual coat, captured at San Jacinto, can be seen in David Nevin, and the Editors of Time-Life Books, *The Mexican War* (Alexandria, Virginia: Time-Life Books, 1978), p. 53.

FIG. 24 CÓS ATTACKS THE WEST WALL

1. Probably Sánchez-Navarro.

2. *Richmond Enquirer*, April 1, 1836.

FIG. 25 DECIMATION OF THE TOLUCA CHASSEURS

1. The Toluca grenadier company had been detached to serve with the reserve column.

2. de la Peña, p. 47. Considering the understrength condition of the Mexican field force, "half the company" might have numbered but fifteen to twenty men.

FIG. 28 THE FIRING FROM THE BARRACKS ROOF

1. R. M. Potter, "The Fall of the Alamo," as printed in Frank W. Johnson, *A History of Texas and Texans* (Chicago and New York: American Historical Society, 1914), p. 414.

FIG. 30 ATTACK ON THE HOSPITAL PATIENTS

1. Three contemporary documents verify this: the plat and key to the compound attributed to Green B. Jameson, and Sanchez-Navarro's two plans and keys to the fort.

2. Anne A. Fox, Feris A. Bass, Jr., and Thomas R. Hester, *The Archaeology and History of Alamo Plaza*, Center for Archaeological Research, The University of Texas at San Antonio, Archaeological Survey Report, No. 16, 1976, p. 7. In earlier mission days the second floor housed the cells of the Franciscan monks.

3. Letter of Samuel Maverick to Governor O. B. Colquitt, San Antonio, Texas, February 2, 1912. Copy provided by Craig Covner.

4. Pascal Wilkins, "Illness At the Alamo," *The Alamo Journal*, Issue #85, February 1993, p. 12.

5. José Enrique de la Peña, *With Santa Anna In Texas: A Personal Narrative of the Revolution*, translated and edited by Carmen Perry (College Station, Texas: Texas A&M University Press, 1975), p. 63.

FIG. 31 TAKING THE SOUTHWEST CORNER

1. See Jake Ivey, "Southwest and Northwest Wall Gun Emplacements," *Alamo Lore and Myth Organization* newsletter, Vol. 3, No. 3, September 1981, pp. 1-4.

FIG. 32 ROMERO'S COLUMN BREAKS INTO THE HORSE CORRAL

1. *New Orleans Bee*, January 4, 1836.

FIG. 36 INTERCEPTING THE FUGITIVES

1. Sesma's report has his horsemen "15 steps," or "pasos," from the fort. A Spanish "paso," or pace, is 1.52 yards; therefore, 15 paces puts the cavalry 22.8 yards—68.4 feet—from the walls. See table of measurement, *Webster's New International Dictionary of the English Language*, 1953, p. 1523.

2. In 1835, English actor Tyrone Power sketched a scene of "border gallants" arriving from their plantations at a Natchez, Mississippi, theater dressed in this fashion (their blanket coats white or grass-green in color). See his sketch in *The American Stage*, by Oral Sumner Coad and Edwin Mins, Jr., The Yale Pageant of America series, vol. 14, p. 164; 1973 reprint of the 1929 original.

3. See example of 1835 manufacture, *Classic Bowie Knives*, by Robert Abels (New York: Robert Abels Inc., 1967), p. 19, no. 11.

4. Nieto, Brown, Hefter, *The Mexican Soldier*, p. 58.

FIG. 37 SANTA ANNA ORDERS THE EXECUTIONS

1. Obviously the main gate through the low barracks.

2. Ruiz's account as published in Frank W. Johnson, *A History of Texas and Texans* (Chicago and New York: American Historical Society, 1914), p. 409. Ruiz's correct location of the bodies of Travis and Bowie makes him a reliable source for confirming where Crockett's corpse was found.

FIG. 38 SANTA ANNA'S SPEECH

1. See reproduction in *The Spanish West*, by the editors of Time-Life Books, The Old West Series (New York: Time-Life Books, 1976), p. 111. Mexican senior officers were allowed to wear articles of civilian clothing, when not in line of duty. As El Presidente, Santa Anna's military dress code was naturally the most flexible of any.

2. See reproduction in *Texas and the War With Mexico*, by the Editors of American Heritage (New York: American Heritage Junior Library Edition, 1961), p. 75.

3. Jerry J. Gaddy, *Texas in Revolt: Contemporary Newspaper Account of the Texas Revolution* (Fort Collins, Colorado: The Old Army Press, 1973) , p. 55 (caption by J. C. Hefter for his illustrations).

Bibliography

The following abbreviations are used in sources throughout text:
DRT = Daughters of the Republic of Texas Library, Alamo
SHQ = Southwestern Historical Quarterly
TSL = Texas State Library, Archives Division

Almaraz, Felix D. *Tragic Cavalier: Governor Manuel Salcedo of Texas, 1808-1813*. Austin: University of Texas Press, 1971.

Almonte, Juan N. "Statistical Report on Texas." *Southwestern Historical Quarterly* 28, no. 3 (July 1944).

———. "The Private Journal of Nepomuceno Almonte, February 1-April 16, 1836." *Southwestern Historical Quarterly*, vol. 48, no. 1.

Alsbury, Juana. "Mrs. Alsbury's Recollections of the Alamo." An interview in the John S. Ford Papers, pp. 122-124. Center for American History, University of Texas.

Archivo Historico Militar Mexicano, Secretaria de la Defensa Nacional, Mexico City, Mexico. Expediente XI/481.3/1149; Expediente XI/481.3/1655.

Baker, Karle Wilson. "Trailing the New Orleans Greys." *Southwest Review*, vol. 22, no. 3 (April 1937).

Baugh, Virgil E. *Rendezvous at the Alamo: Highlights in the Lives of Bowie, Crockett, and Travis*. Lincoln: University of Nebraska Press, 1985.

Barker, Eugene C. "Finances of Texas Revolution." *Political Science Quarterly*, vol. 19, no. 4 (December 1904).

———. "Land Speculation as a Cause of the Texas Revolution." *Southwestern Historical Quarterly*, vol. 10, no. 1 (July 1906).

———. "The Texas Revolutionary Army." *Quarterly of the Texas State Historical Association*, vol. 9, no. 4 (April 1906).

Barr, Alwyn. *Texans in Revolt: The Battle for San Antonio, 1835*. Austin: University of Texas Press, 1991.

Becerra, Francisco. *A Mexican Sergeant's Recollections of the Alamo and San Jacinto*. Austin: Jenkins Publishing Company, 1980.

Binkley, William Campbell. *The Texas Revolution*. Baton Rouge: LSU Press, 1952.

———, editor. *Official Correspondence of the Texas Revolution, 1835-1836*. 2 vols. New York: D. Appleton Century Company, 1938.

Blake, R. B. "A Vindication of Rose and His Story." *The Shadow of History*, edited by Frank Dobie, Mody C. Boatright, and Harry H. Ransom. Austin: Texas Folk-lore Society, 1939.

Bonham, Milledge L., Jr. "James Butler Bonham: A Consistent Rebel." *Southwestern Historical Quarterly*, vol. 35, no. 2 (October 1931).

Borroel, Roger. *The Papers of Colonel José Enrique de la Peña, Selected Appendixes from his Diary, 1836-1839*. East Chicago, IN: La Villita Publications, 1997.

———. *The Concordance of Lieutenant Colonel José Enrique de la Peña's Diary and Appendixes—A Critical Analysis*. East Chicago, IN: La Villita Publications, 1997.

———. *After the Battle of the Alamo: Documents Published by General Juan José Andrade on The Evacuation of San Antonio de Béjar, Texas, May 1836*. East Chicago, IN: La Villita Publications, 1997.

Bradfield, Jane. *RX Take One Cannon; The Gonzàlez Come and Take It Cannon of October, 1835*. Shiner, Texas: Patrick J. Wagner Research and Publishing Co., 1981.

Brierley, Ned F., trans. *The Journal of Sergeant Santiago Rabia*. Austin: Texian Army Investigations, 1997.

Brogan, Evelyn. *James: A Hero of the Alamo*. San Antonio: Theodore Kunzman, 1922.

Buquor, María de Jesús. Account in *San Antonio Light*, July 19, 1907.

Burke, Jackson. "The Secret of the Alamo." *Men's Illustrated*: August 1956.

Burke, James Wakefield. *David Crockett: Man Behind the Myth*. Austin: Eakin Press, 1984.

Caballero, Rome Flores. *Counterrevolution: The Role of the Spaniards in the Independence of Mexico, 1804-38*. Lincoln: University of Nebraska Press, 1974.

Callcott, Wilfrid Hardy. *Church and State in Mexico, 1822-1857*. Durham, NC: Duke University Press, 1926.

———. *Santa Anna: The Story of an Enigma Who Once Was Mexico*. Hamden, CT: Archon Books, 1964.

Candelaria, Andrea Castañòn de Villanueva. Account in *Dallas Morning News*, March 9, 1930.

Candelaria, Andrea Castañón de Villanueva. Account in *San Antonio Express*, March 6, 1892, and February 19, 1899.

Castañeda, Carlos Eduardo. *The Mexican Side of the Texan Revolution by the Chief Mexican Participants*. Austin: Graphic Ideas Incorporated, 1970.

Chabot, Frederick Charles. *The Alamo: Altar of Texas Liberty*. San Antonio: Naylor Printing Company, 1931.

———. *The Alamo: Mission, Fortress and Shrine*. San Antonio: The Leake Company, 1935.

Chariton, Wallace O. *100 Days in Texas: The Alamo Letters*. Plano, Texas: Wordware Publishing, Inc., 1989.

Chemerka, William R. *Alamo Almanac & Book of Lists*. Austin: Eakin Press, 1997.

Colletti, Sarah. "Found: Alamo Traitor's Grave." *The Shreveport Times*, May 25, 1975.

Connelly, Thomas Lawrence. "Did David Crockett Surrender at the Alamo?" *Journal of Southern History*, vol. 26, no. 3, (August 1960).

The Constitution of the Republic of Mexico, and of the State of Coahuila & Texas. New York: Ludwig & Tolefree, 1832.

Costelos, Michael P. "The Mexican Press of 1836 and the Battle of the Alamo." *Southwestern Historical Quarterly*, vol. 91, no. 4 (April 1988).

Coy, Trinidad. Account in *San Antonio Light*, November 26, 1911.

Crawford, Ann Fears. *The Eagle: The Autobiography of Santa Anna*. Austin: State House Press, 1988.

Crawford, Ann Fears, and Crystal Sasse Ragsdale. *Women in Texas: Their Lives, Their Experiences, Their Accomplishments*. Burnet, TX: Eakin Press, 1982.

Crimmins, M. L. "American Powder's Part in Winning Texas Independence." *Southwestern Historical Quarterly*, vol. 52, no. 1 (July 1948).

Crisp, Jim E. "Back to Basics: Conspiracies, Common Sense, and Occam's Razor." *Alamo Journal*, no. 100 (March 1996).

———. "Truth, Confusion, and the de la Peña Controversy: A Final Reply." *Alamo Journal*.

———. "Davy in Freeze-Frame: Methodology or Madness." *Alamo Journal*, no. 98 (October 1995).

———. "Trashing Dolson: The Perils of Tendentious Interpretation." *Alamo Journal*, no. 99 (December 1995).

Crockett, David. *An Account of Colonel Crockett's Tour to the North and Down East, Etc.* Philadelphia: E. L. Carey and A. Hart, 1835.

———. *Col. Crockett's Exploits and Adventures in Texas.* Philadelphia: T.K. and P.G. Collins, 1836.

———. *A Narrative of the Life of David Crockett of the State of Tennessee, Written by Himself.* Lincoln: University of Nebraska Press, 1987.

Crutchfield, Jim, ed. *Davy Crockett's Almanacks, 1835-1843: The Nashville Imprints, Union City.* Union City, TN: Pioneer Press, 1986.

Cruz, Gilberto Rafael, and James Arthur Irby, eds. *Texas Bibliography: A Manual on History Research Materials.* Austin: Eakin Press, 1982.

Curilla, Richard. "The Degüello." *Alamo Lore and Myth Organization*, vol. 3, no. 3 (September 1981).

Curtis, Gregory. "Forgery Texas Style." *Texas Monthly* (March 1989).

———. "Seer and Scholar." *Texas Monthly* (December 1993).

Daughters of the Republic of Texas. *Muster Rolls of the Texas Revolution.* Austin, 1963.

Davis, William C. *Three Roads to the Alamo: The Lives and Fortunes of David Crockett, James Bowie, and William Barret Travis.* New York: Harper Collins, 1998.

Day, James M. *The Texas Almanac, 1857-1873.* Waco: Texian Press, 1967.

De Leòn, Arnoldo. *The Mexican Image in Nineteenth-Century Texas.* Boston: American Press, 1982.

———. "Tejanos and the Texas War for Independence: Historiography's Judgment." *New Mexico Historical Review*, vol. 61 (April 1986).

———. *They Called Them Greasers: Anglo Attitudes Towards Mexicans in Texas, 1821-1900.* Austin: University of Texas Press, 1983.

De Shields, James T. *Tall Men with Long Rifles: The Glamorous Story of the Texas Revolution As Told by Captain Creed Taylor.* San Antonio: Naylor Printing Company, 1935.

Díaz, Juan. Account in *San Antonio Light*, September 1, 1907.

Díaz, Pablo. Account in *San Antonio Express*, July 1, 1906.

———. Account in *San Antonio Light*, October 31, 1909, and March 26, 1911.

Dickenson, Susannah. "Statement of Mrs. S. A. Hannig, wife of Almeron Dickenson." Adjutant General's Miscellaneous Papers, Archives Division, Texas State Library, Austin.

———. "Testimony of Mrs. Hannig touching the Alamo Massacre. September 23, 1876." Archives Division, Texas State Library, Austin.

———. Account in *San Antonio Express*, April 28, 1881.

———. Account in *San Antonio Express*, February 24, 1929.

Dobie, J. Frank. "Rose and His Story of the Alamo." *The Shadow of History.* Austin: Texas Folk-lore Society, 1939.

"Document Reveals Possible Survivor of Alamo Massacre." *Victoria Advocate*, July 18, 1985.

Douglas, C. L. *James Bowie: The Life of a Bravo.* Dallas: Banks Upshaw and Company, 1944.

Driggs, Howard R., and Sarah S. King. *Rise of the Lone Star: A Story of Texas Told by its Pioneers.* New York: Frederick A. Stokes Company, 1936.

Ehrenberg, Herman. *With Milam and Fannin: Adventures of a German Boy in the Texas Revolution.* Dallas: Tardy Publishing Company, 1935.

Elfer, Maurice. *Madam Candelaria: Unsung Heroine of the Alamo.* Houston: Rein Company, 1933.

Esparza, Enrique. "Story of the Massacre of Heroes of the Alamo." *San Antonio Express*, March 7, 1905.

———. "Alamo's Only Survivor." Interview by Charles Merritt Barnes. *San Antonio Express*, May 12 and 19, 1907.

———. Account in *San Antonio Light*, November 10, 1901.

———. DRT Library at the Alamo, San Antonio Clipping Files, Historic Sites: The Alamo. Cobblestone Series, by Dorothy Crawford.

Fehrenbach, T. R. *Lone Star: A History of Texas and Texans.* New York: American Legacy Press, 1983.

Ferris, Sylvia Van Voast, and Eleanor Sellers Hoppe. *Scalpels and Sabers: Nineteenth Century Medicine in Texas.* Austin: Eakin Press, 1985.

Filisola, General Vicente. 1885-87. *The History of the War in Texas.* Translated by Wallace Woolsey. 2 vols. Austin: Eakin Press, 1987.

Foote, Henry S. *Texas and Texans.* 2 vols. Philadelphia: Thomas, Couperthwaite and Co., 1841.

Ford, John S. Papers. Archives Division, Texas State Library, Austin.

Fox, Anne A., Feris A. Bass, Jr., and Thomas R. Hester. *The Archaeology and History of Alamo Plaza.* San Antonio: Center for Archaeological Research, University of Texas, 1976.

———. *Archaeological Investigations in Alamo Plaza.* San Antonio: Center for Archaeological Research, University of Texas, 1992.

Gaddy, Jerry J. *Texas in Revolt: Contemporary Newspaper Accounts of the Texas Revolution.* Fort Collins, CO: Old Army Press, 1983.

Garver, Lois. "Benjamin Milam." *Southwestern Historical Quarterly*, vol. 38, nos. 2 and 3 (1934).

Gibson, Charles, ed. *The Black Legend: Anti-Spanish Attitudes in the Old World and the New.* New York: Alfred A. Knopf, 1971.

Gilbert, Randal B. "Arms for Revolution and the Republic." *Military History of Texas and the Southwest,* vol. 13, no. 1.

Gray, William F. *From Virginia to Texas, 1835.* Houston: The Fletcher Young Publishing Company, 1965.

Green, Michael Robert. "El Soldado Mexicano, 1832-1836." *Military History of Texas and the Southwest,* vol. 13, no. 1.

Green, William. "Remembering the Alamo." *American Heritage,* vol. 37, no. 4.

Groneman, Bill. *Alamo Defenders: A Genealogy: The People and their Words.* Austin: Eakin Press, 1990.

———. "Crockett's Last Stand." *Alamo Lore and Myth Organization,* vol. 4, no. 4 (December 1982).

———. *Eyewitness to the Alamo.* Plano, Texas: Republic of Texas Press, 1996.

Hamill, Hugh M., Jr., ed. *Dictatorship in Spanish America.* New York: Alfred A. Knopf, 1966.

———. *The Hidalgo Revolt: Prelude to Mexican Independence.* Gainesville: University of Florida Press, 1966.

Hardin, Stephen L. *Texian Iliad: A Military History of the Texas Revolution.* Austin: University of Texas Press, 1994.

Harris, Helen Willits. "Almonte's Inspection Tour of Texas in 1834." *Southwestern Historical Quarterly,* vol. 41, no. 3.

Haythornthwaite, Phillip. *The Alamo and the War of Texan Independence, 1835-1836.* London: Osprey, 1986.

Heale, M. J. "The Role of the Frontier in Jacksonian Politics: David Crockett and the Myth of the Self-Made Man." *The Western Historical Quarterly,* vol. 4, no. 4.

Henson, Margaret Swett. *Anglo-American Women in Texas, 1820-1850.* Boston: American Press, 1982.

———. *Juan Davis Bradburn: A Reappraisal of the Mexican Commander of Anahuac.* College Station: Texas A&M University Press, 1982.

Holman, David. *Buckskin and Homespun: Frontier Texas Clothing, 1820-1870.* Austin: Wind River Press, 1979.

Humphreys, R. A., and John Lynch. *The Origins of the Latin American Revolutions, 1808-1826.* New York: Alfred A. Knopf, 1965.

Ivey, James E. "Construction Methods Used at the Alamo." *Alamo Lore and Myth Organization,* vol. 4, no. 2 (June 1982).

———. "The Problem of the Two Guerreros." *Alamo Lore and Myth Organization,* vol. 4, no. 1.

———. "South Gate and its Defenses." *Alamo Lore and Myth Organization,* vol. 3, no. 4 (December 1981).

———. "Southwest and Northwest Wall Gun Emplacements." *Alamo Lore and Myth Organization,* vol. 3, no. 3 (September 1981).

Jackson, Jack. *Los Tejanos.* Stanford, CT: Fantagraphics Books, Inc. 1982.

Jackson, Ron. *Alamo Legacy: Alamo Descendants Remember the Alamo.* Austin: Eakin Press, 1997.

———. "In the Alamo's Shadow." *True West,* vol. 45, no. 2 (February 1998):14-18.

Jenkins, John H. *Basic Texas Books: An Annotated Bibliography of Selected Works for a Research Library.* Austin: Texas State Historical Association, 1983.

———, ed. *The Papers of the Texas Revolution, 1835-1836.* 10 vols. Austin: Presidial Press, 1973.

Joe. Account in *New Orleans Commercial Bulletin,* April 11, 1836.

———. Account in "Fall of San Antonio and its One Hundred and Eighty-Seven Gallant Defenders." *Columbia (Tennessee) Observer,* April 14, 1836.

———. Account in *National Intelligencer,* April 30, 1836.

———. Account in "Letter from Texas." *Frankfort (Kentucky) Commonwealth,* May 25, 1836.

"Juan Diaz, Venerable San Antonian . . . Witnessed the Attack on the Alamo." *San Antonio Express,* 1907.

Kiev, Ari. *Curanderismo: Mexican-American Folk Psychiatry.* New York: Free Press, 1968.

Kilgore, Dan. *How Did Davy Die?* College Station: Texas A&M University Press, 1978.

King, Richard. *Susanna Dickenson, Messenger of the Alamo.* Austin: Shoal Creek Publishers, 1976.

Koury, Michael J. *Arms for Texas: A Study of the Weapons of the Republic of Texas.* Fort Collins, CO: Old Army Press, 1973.

———. "Cannon for Texas: Artillery in the Revolution and the Republic." *Military History of Texas and the Southwest,* vol. 10, no. 2 (1972).

Labadie, Joseph H., comp. *La Villita Earthworks: A Preliminary Report of Investigations of Mexican Siege Works at the Battle of the Alamo.* San Antonio: Center for Archaeological Research, University of Texas, 1986.

Lack, Paul D. *The Texas Revolutionary Experience: A Political and Social History, 1835-1836.* College Station: Texas A&M University Press, 1992.

Laflin, John. "Highly Suspect." *Texas Monthly,* March 1988.

Leclerc, Frederick. *Texas and its Revolution.* Houston: Anson Jones Press, 1950.

Lindley, Thomas Ricks. "Alamo Artillery: Number, Type, Caliber and Concussion." *The Alamo Journal,* no. 82, July 1992.

———. "James Butler Bonham: October 17, 1835- March 6, 1836." *The Alamo Journal,* no. 62 (August 1988).

———. "Killing Crockett, It's all in the Execution." *Alamo Journal,* no. 96 (May 1995).

———. "Killing Crockett: Lindley's Opinion." *Alamo Journal,* no. 98 (October 1995).

———. "Killing Crockett (part III): Theory Paraded as Fact." *Alamo Journal,* no. 97 (July 1995).

Linenthal, Edward Tabor. "A Reservoir of Spiritual Power: Patriotic Faith at the Alamo in the Twentieth Century." *Southwestern Historical Quarterly,* vol. 91, no. 4 (April 1988).

Linn, John J. *Reminiscences of Fifty Years in Texas.* New York: D&J Saddler & Company, 1883.

Lofaro, Michael A. *Davy Crockett: The Man, The Legend, The Legacy, 1786-1986.* Knoxville: University of Tennessee Press, 1985.

Long, Jeff. *Duel of Eagles: The Mexican and U.S. Fight for the Alamo.* New York: William Morrow and Company, 1990.

Lopez, Antonio. *Santa Anna: Revolution and Republic.* Dallas: American Guild Press, 1957.

Loranca, Sergeant Manuel. "Santa Anna's Last Effort, the Alamo and San Jacinto: Narrative of a Mexican Sergeant who belonged to Santa Anna's Army." *San Antonio Express,* June 23, 1878.

Lord, Walter. *A Time to Stand.* New York: Pocket Books, 1963.

Lozano, Ruben Rendon. *Viva Tejas: The Story of the Tejanos, The Mexican Born Patriots of the Texas Revolution.* San Antonio: Alamo Press, 1985.

Lundstom, John B. "Assault at Dawn: The Mexican Army at

the Alamo." *The Magazine of Military History*, no. 1, Summer 1973.

Lundy, Benjamin. *The War in Texas*. Upper Saddle River, NJ: Gregg Press, 1970.

Mahan, Dennis Hart. *A Complete Treatise on Field Fortification*. New York: Greenwood Press, 1968.

Manual of Instruction for the Organization and Operations of the Army in War and Peace. Fort Sam Houston Museum.

Matovina, Timothy. *The Alamo Remembered: Tejano Accounts and Perspectives*. Austin: University of Texas Press, 1995.

Maverick, Mary A. *Memoirs of Mary A. Maverick*. Edited by Rena Maverick Green. San Antonio: Alamo Printing Company, 1921.

McDonald, Archie P. *Travis*. Austin: Jenkins Publishing Company, 1976.

McDonald, David, and Kevin R. Young. *Siege of the Alamo: A Mexican Army Journal, February 23–March 10, 1836*. Privately published, 1987.

McGraw, A. Joachim, John W. Clark, and Elizabeth A. Robbins, eds. *A Texas Legacy: The Old San Antonio Road and the Caminos Reales, A Tricentennial History, 1691–1991*. Austin: Texas State Department of Public Transportation, 1991.

Menchaca, Antonio. *Memoirs of Antonio Menchaca*. San Antonio: Yanaguana Society, 1936.

Military Collector & Historian, vol. XLVIII, no. 1.

Milsaps, Isaac. *Letter from the Alamo*. DRT Library at the Alamo.

Mixon, Ruby. "William Barret Travis: His Life and Letters." Master's thesis, University of Texas, 1930.

Moorehead, Max L. *The Presidio: Bastion of the Spanish Borderlands*. Norman: University of Oklahoma Press, 1975.

Morphis, J. M. *History of Texas*. New York: United States Publishing Company, 1875.

Muir, Andrew Forest. "Tories In Texas, 1836." *Military History of Texas and the Southwest*, vol. 4, no. 2.

Myers, John Meyers. *The Alamo*. New York: E. P. Dutton and Company, 1973.

Nelson, George. *The Alamo: An Illustrated History*. Dry Frio Canyon, Texas: Aldine Press, 1998.

Nevin, David. *The Texans*. New York: Time-Life Books, 1975.

Newell, Chester. *History of the Revolution in Texas*. New York: Arno Press, 1973.

Nieto, Angelina, Mrs. John Brown, and Joseph Hefter. *El Soldado Mexicano, 1837-1847*. Mexico: Privately published, 1958.

Nofi, Albert A. *The Alamo and the Texas War for Independence, September 30, 1835-April 21, 1836*. Conshohocken, PA: Combined Books, Inc., 1992.

Nosworthy, Brent. *With Musket Cannon and Sword: Battle Tactics of Napoleon and His Enemies*. New York: Sarpedon, 1996.

Nuñez, Fèlix. "Fall of the Alamo." *The Fort Worth Gazette*, July 12, 1889.

———. Stephen L. Hardin. "The Fèlix Nuñez Account and the Siege of the Alamo: A Critical Appraisal." *Southwestern Historical Quarterly*, July 1990.

Perry, Carmen, editor. José Enrique de la Peña, *With Santa Anna in Texas: A Personal Narrative of the Revolution*. College Station: Texas A&M University Press, 1975.

Peterson, Harold B. *The Book of the Continental Soldier*. Harrisburg, PA: Stackpole Company, 1968.

Pohl, James W., and Stephen L. Hardin. "The Military History of the Texas Revolution: An Overview." *Southwestern Historical Quarterly*, vol. 89, no. 3.

Potter, Reuben M. *The Fall of the Alamo: A Reminiscence of the Revolution of Texas*. Edited by Charles Grosvenor. Hillsdale, NJ: Otterden Press, 1977.

Pourade, Richard F. *The Sign of the Eagle: A View of Mexico, 1830-1855*. San Diego: Copley Press, 1970.

Presley, James. "Santa Anna in Texas: A Mexican Viewpoint." *Southwestern Historical Quarterly*, vol. 62, no. 4.

Procter, Ben H. *The Battle of the Alamo*. Austin: Texas State Historical Association, 1986.

Pruett, Jakie L., and Everett B. Cole, Sr. *Goliad Massacre: A Tragedy of the Texas Revolution*. Austin: Eakin Press, 1985.

Ragsdale, Crystal Sasse. *The Women and Children of the Alamo*. Austin: State House Press, 1994.

Reglamento para el Ejercicio y Maniobras de la Infanteria. Mexico City, Mexico, 1829.

Roberts, Edith Rydell, ed. *The Mexican War Logbook & Letters of Capt. Jeffersen Peak*. Richardson, TX: The Descendants of Mexican War Veterans, 1996.

Rodriguez, Josè Maria. *Rodriguez Memoirs of Early Texas*. San Antonio: Standard Printing Company, 1961.

Rosenthal, Phillip, and Bill Groneman. *Roll Call at the Alamo*. Fort Collins: Old Army Press, 1985.

Ross, John F., ed. *Readings on the Alamo*. New York: Vantage Press, 1987.

Sanchez Lamego, Miguel A. "The Battle of Zacatecas." *Texana*, vol. 7, no. 3 (1969).

———. *The Siege and Taking of the Alamo*. Santa Fe: Blue Feather Press, 1968.

———. *Sitio y Toma del Alamo*. Mexico: 1968.

———. *Apuntes Para la Historia del Arma de Ingenieros en Mexico: Historia del Battalion de Zapadores*. Mexico: Secretaria de la Defensa Nacional, Taller Autografico, 1943.

Sánchez Navarro, Josè Juan. *La Guerra de Tejas: Memorias de un Soldado*. Edited by Carlos Sànchez Navarro. Mexico City: Editorial Polis, 1938.

———. "A Mexican View of the Texan War: Memoirs of a Veteran of the Two Battles of the Alamo." *The Library Chronicle*, vol. 4, no. 2.

Santos, Richard G. *Santa Anna's Campaign Against Texas, 1835-1836*. Salisbury, NC: Documentary Publications, 1968.

Schoelwer, Susan Prendergast, with Tom W. Glaser. *Alamo Images: Changing Perceptions of a Texas Experience*. Dallas: DeGolyer Library and SMU Mexican Press, 1985.

Schwarz, Ted. *Forgotten Battlefield of the First Texas Revolution: The Battle of the Medina, August 18, 1813*. Austin: Eakin Press, 1985.

Seguìn, Juan N. *Personal Memoirs of John N. Sequin, From the Year 1834 to the Retreat of General Woll from the City of San Antonio 1842*. San Antonio: Ledger Book and Job Office, 1858.

Shackford, James Atkins. *David Crockett: The Man and the Legend*. Chapel Hill: University of North Carolina Press, 1986.

Sibley, Marilyn McAdams. "The Burial Place of the Alamo Heroes." *Southwestern Historical Quarterly*, vol. 10, no. 2 (October 1966).

Smithwick, Noah. *Recollections of Old Texas Days*. Austin: University of Texas Press, 1984.

Sutherland, John. *The Fall of the Alamo*. San Antonio: Naylor Press, 1936.

Teer, L. P. "Was There a Coward at the Alamo?" *Frontier Times,* vol. 39, no. 6 (October/November 1965).

Teja, Jesús F. de la. *A Revolution Remembered: The Memoirs and Selected Correspondence of Juan N. Seguìn.* Austin: State House Press, 1991.

———. "Bèxar: Profile of a Tejano Community, 1820-1832." *Southwestern Historical Quarterly,* vol. 139, no. 1 (July 1985).

Timmons, Walter H. *The Anglo-American Advance Into Texas, 1810-1830.* Boston: American Press, 1981.

Tinkle, Lon. *Thirteen Days to Glory.* College Station: Texas A&M University Press, 1985.

Travis, William Barret. *Diary of William Barret Travis: August 30, 1833-June 26, 1834.* Edited by Robert E. Davis. Waco: Texian Press, 1966.

Trotter, Robert T. *Curanderismo, Mexican-American Folk Healing.* Athens: University of Georgia Press, 1981.

Turner, Martha Anne. *William Barret Travis: His Sword and Pen.* Waco: Texian Press, 1972.

Unknown Mexican officer. 1836. "Texas." *Frankfort (Kentucky) Commonwealth,* July 27, 1836.

Urizza, Capt. Fernando. "Urizza's Account of the Alamo Massacre," *Texas Almanac,* 1859.

Vargas, Juan. Account in *San Antonio Light,* April 3, 1910.

Vàsquez, Josefina Zoraida. "The Texas Question in Mexican Politics, 1836-1845." *Southwestern Historical Quarterly,* vol. 139, no. 3 (January 1986).

Velasques de Leon, Juan L. "Traduccion de una Carta de R.M. Williamson al Cabecilla Barret Travis." *El Nacional,* suplemento al numero 79, March 21, 1836.

Von Schmidt, Eric. "The Alamo Remembered—From a Painter's Point of View." *Smithsonian,* vol. 16, no. 12 (March 1986).

Wagner, Patrick J. "Come and Take it Comes Home." *Alamo Lore and Myth Organization,* vol. 4, no. 1 (March 1982).

Walraven, Bill and Marjorie. *The Magnificent Barbarians: Little Told Tales of the Texas Revolution.* Austin: Eakin Press, 1993.

Wantland, Clyde. *The Five San Antonio Missions: Where the Texas Longhorn Started.* San Antonio: Privately published, 1962.

Williams, Amelia. "A Critical Study of the Siege of the Alamo and of the Personnel of its Defenders." *Southwestern Historical Quarterly,* vol. 36, no. 3 and vol. 37, no. 4.

———. "Notes on Alamo Survivors." *Southwestern Historical Quarterly,* vol. 49, no. 4.

Wise, Terence. *Artillery Equipments of the Napoleonic Wars.* London: Osprey, 1979.

Woolsey, Wallace, trans. *Memoirs for the History of the War in Texas.* Vols. I and II. Austin: Eakin Press, 1987.

Yorba, Eulalia. Account in *San Antonio Express,* April 12, 1896.

Young, Kevin R. *Texas Forgotten Heroes.* Goliad, TX: Goliad County Historical Commission, 1986.

Zuber, William Physik. *My Eighty Years in Texas.* Edited by Janis Boyle Mayfield. Austin: University of Texas Press, 1971.

Index